PACIFIC MISSIONARY GEORGE BROWN 1835–1917

Wesleyan Methodist Church

Margaret Reeson

Australian
National
University

E PRESS

Published by ANU E Press
The Australian National University
Canberra ACT 0200, Australia
Email: anuepress@anu.edu.au
This title is also available online at http://epress.anu.edu.au

National Library of Australia Cataloguing-in-Publication entry

Author: Reeson, Margaret, 1938-

Title: Pacific missionary George Brown 1835-1917 : Wesleyan Methodist Church /
            Margaret Reeson.

ISBN: 9781921862977 (pbk.) 9781921862984 (ebook)

Notes: Includes bibliographical references.

Subjects: Brown, George, 1835-1917.
            Wesleyan Methodist Church--Missions--Oceania--History.
            Missionaries--England--Biography.
            Missionaries--Oceania--Biography.
            Oceania--History.
            Oceania--Description and travel.

Dewey Number: 266.7195092

Cover design and layout by ANU E Press

Cover image: 'George Brown with Gemu and Wongi, Roviana, Solomon Islands 1905',
by H.P.M.Berry, in *George Brown D.D. Pioneer Missionary and Explorer: an Autobiography*,
London: Hodder and Stoughton 1908.

Printed by Griffin Press

This edition © 2013 ANU E Press

PACIFIC MISSIONARY GEORGE BROWN 1835–1917

Wesleyan Methodist Church

Margaret Reeson

Contents

Illustrations

Maps

Abbreviations

ABM   Australian Board of Missions
CMS   Church Missionary Society
LMS   London Missionary Society
MOM   Methodist Overseas Missions
WMMS   Wesleyan Methodist Missionary Society

For my family

Acknowledgements

The help and advice of many people, in many places over many years, has been needed in order to weave this particular account of the lives of George and Lydia Brown from scattered threads. I am grateful for the box of documents relating to the Brown family which came to me from New Zealand, collected during the 1980s by George and Nancy Carter; that was the beginning. It has been a joy to meet and spend time with two great-grandchildren of the Browns, Nancy Joyce in Sydney and Julian Brown visiting from Canada, who shared family memories, photographs and personal archives.

My great appreciation goes to those who introduced me to the places where the Browns lived; Mary Lowes in Barnard Castle, UK, Don and Bev Cullingford and Mr and Mrs Fred Gilbert in Raglan, New Zealand.

Conversations and correspondence about the project with people with specialist knowledge of the Pacific region has been invaluable; I am grateful for the generous advice of John Garrett, Hank Nelson, Andrew Thornley, Geoff Cummins, Morven Sidal and Fred and Marcia Baker. Ulrich and Ursula Fellmann provided lovely hospitality in Aachen, Germany and material about his grandparents Heinrich and Johanna Fellmann. Heather Sweet, Helma Neumann and Carina Moeller graciously helped with translation from German documents. Ron Reeson, John Mavor, Val Bock and Helen Lehman read the manuscript in its raw and over-long form and gave helpful wisdom. Eric Mobbs provided invaluable computer advice. I am sad that several of the kind friends who have helped me have not lived to see the finished work.

A number of institutions have been very helpful, through their staff. My great appreciation to the Mitchell Library, Sydney and the National Library of Australia, Canberra, where many documents relating to Brown are held; to Christine Gordon, Daryl Lightfoot and Moira Bryant through the Uniting Church in Australia Archives; to Patricia Egan of the Australian Museum, Sydney; to Peter Matthews and Isao Hayashi of the National Museum of Ethnology, Osaka, Japan. Carolyn Brewer of The Australian National University has given careful guidance toward a more professional result as copy editor, and the help of Duncan Beard at ANU E Press is also appreciated.

My beloved family has borne my long engagement with George and Lydia Brown with patience, grace, encouragement and some teasing about its endless nature. To Ruth and Glen Powell, Jenni and Colin Hudson, David Reeson, Colette Neumann, Barry and Merle Higman and all the grandchildren, thank you. And of course to my husband Ron Reeson, who has supported me in every way, travelled with me and made this work possible though his gift of a lifetime of love.

Prologue

The sun has set. The colours of the ocean have dimmed from blue and jade glitter to a silky gleam by faint moonlight. Two stand at the ship's rail. Below them a whale boat nudges the side of the vessel, loaded high with boxes and crates, everything they own. He has said all along that they don't need it all. She has clung to her things, her last link with home.

Nothing is familiar. The voices of the men in the whaleboat below speak a language they do not understand. They do not recognise the perfume that drifts from the land, of wild lime and vanilla. They have never seen the place that will become home and have only just met the man who will be their colleague. They barely know each other, this groom and his bride, and after three months of marriage are still learning to read the other.

The ship's captain has warned them. He is not willing to go any nearer to the island for fear of the reef and the rocky coast and as soon as they have climbed down into the whale boat he intends to set sail and be gone. Perhaps, for a wild moment, the girl thinks, I can't do this – this small ship is not comfortable but it could carry me home. It is only for a moment. She is not really afraid. With her upbringing, if any girl can do this, she believes that she can.

In the distance against a dark smudge of land there is a pinprick of lamplight. Another woman is waiting for them, longing for company, ready with food and a welcome. They have been told that it will take hours of rowing to reach her. The young husband is eager, excited to be so close to their destination. He clambers quickly down the ladder and drops into the whaleboat among the dark shapes of their cargo and the shadowy figures of the team of rowers. There is scarcely room for them to sit but he turns and reaches up to his bride who is edging backwards down the ladder, hampered by her long skirts.

She jumps down into his arms. In the darkness, it is hard to tell which of them is supporting the other.

1. 'The farthest place from England'

North Island, New Zealand
1860

The young Englishman arrived unheralded. He had an urgent question. In the wintry dawn the family watched him gliding across the beaten copper waters of the wide Whaingaroa Harbour in a Māori canoe. He walked up the slope to the mission house, unkempt, shaking river sand from his clothes and speckled with insect bites. The watching family was not offended, even if a little startled. Any traveller from Auckland, they knew, would have been on the track for most of a week, sleeping in the open, paddling in canoes on harbour and rivers, and tramping through rain-soaked bush and fern. The young man had reached the northern shore of the river after dark, nearly in sight of his destination. Unable to find a friendly Māori who would supply a canoe so late, he had half-buried himself in river sand to try to escape the hungry insects and waited for daylight.

He had come, young George Brown said, to ask for the hand of Miss Sarah Lydia Wallis in marriage. If she accepted him, it would mean leaving her missionary family in New Zealand for a missionary life in Samoa. His ship was due to sail soon so he needed her answer—and a wedding—almost immediately. It was July 1860.

If Lydia Wallis hesitated, it would have been understandable. If she said 'yes' then her future would be a mirror of her parents' past. But Lydia was a healthy, happy young woman of twenty-one, active, intelligent and practical, from a family widely known and respected in colonial New Zealand despite their isolation. She would always say that she knew, or at least hoped, that he was the man for her.

* * *

It was not surprising that Lydia Wallis was invited to become a missionary wife. More surprising was that this young man, George Brown, was her suitor. That they ever met at all was remarkable. He was born in the north of England, in a town on a river near the ruins of an ancient fortified castle. She was born in the north of New Zealand, at a lonely mission on a river near a fortified and populated Māori settlement. Still more unlikely was the thought that this young Brown should ever choose to become a missionary.

The two young people first met at the home of mutual friends when a group was holidaying on the west coast out of Auckland, where the rhythm of waves surged in from the Tasman Sea. Lydia Wallis and her older sister Elizabeth visited their parents' close friends and colleagues, Thomas and Sarah Buddle and met Mrs Buddle's nephew, George Brown, who had arrived from England in 1855. Lydia Wallis was seventeen or eighteen at the time, and young Brown's first impression was of 'that little Lyd Wallis that used to be prim and demure.'[1] At first glance, Brown may not have seemed particularly prepossessing himself. He was about twenty-years old, not very tall, quite slight, clean-shaven with gingery hair over his ears, quiet and polite even though a keen observer might have seen a lively gleam in his eye. The nephew came from the Buddles' home town of Barnard Castle in the north of England and, it was whispered, he had run away from home as a youth. Five years ago, his aunt explained, he had abandoned an apprenticeship without his father's or his employer's permission and run away to sea, restlessly travelling with naval transports in the Mediterranean and to Canada. Now he had turned up in New Zealand.

This young man must have seemed quite sophisticated to Lydia Wallis. She had lived her life on an isolated mission station and as a schoolgirl in a colonial town of 7,000 souls. He had travelled around the world. Auckland, so grand in Lydia's eyes, was described by a contemporary observer as 'like a small seaside town, but not so substantially built, nor does it convey the same idea of comfort or wealth.'[2] Her life seemed confined and mostly domestic. He had known adventures. Her world was centred on a mission and founded on Christian faith. If on arrival in New Zealand he had any religious convictions this was more out of respect for his aunt and uncle than something he owned for himself. Even so, Lydia was aware of the newcomer. They would meet rarely but news and gossip travelled.

The rebellious runaway had found harbour with the colonial community in Auckland. The Buddle family with his nine young cousins welcomed him into their home at Onehunga each weekend and he found work in Auckland town. Onehunga was a small port township on Manukau Harbour on the western side of the narrow isthmus that divided the western coast of the North Island from the eastern coast. He was being absorbed into the community of young men in the town, many of them linked with the churches. The small colonial community of the late 1850s included a number of gifted people; wide interests embraced politics, relationships with the Māori community, education and business affairs, churches and missions as well as experience in the Pacific Island regions of Tonga, Samoa and Fiji. They might be isolated and perhaps insular, but never

---

1   George Brown, letter to Lizzie Buddle, 1872, Brown, Letter Book, 1871–76, ML A1686-2 CY 2767.
2   John Gutch, *Martyr of the Islands: The Life and Death of John Coleridge Patteson*, London, Auckland, Sydney: Hodder and Stoughton, 1971.

dull. In this circle of society, the people with most influence on young Brown were those of the Christian faith. In the warm Buddle household, he wrote later, 'Every week I experienced the power of sermons which were never spoken.'[3] His five years in New Zealand had shaped the young man in ways that he might not have predicted.

Early in 1860 Lydia's father, the Rev. James Wallis reported to his family that George Brown had applied to the Auckland gathering of Methodist ministers, asking to become a minister himself and to serve as a missionary. There had been hesitation among the brethren. A good enough young man, certainly, and there were no problems with his preaching but, they said, 'He is such a meek, mild, young lady-like person that we are sure he has no spirit whatever that would make a missionary. He is utterly devoid of any self-assertion, and we, therefore, do not think he is fit for mission work.' One or two spoke for him, believing that there was more to this young man than met the eye. They took the vote and by a very small majority George Brown was accepted for missionary service.[4] The church rule was that he must now 'find a wife'. Whether or not he had ever given her any real cause to expect it, when the time came he had no doubts. He would tell a biographer that 'there was nobody else but Lydia Wallis, the bright, comely, capable girl.'[5] Lydia's intuition had been right.

Two young people now faced a moment of decision. There was much that they still needed to discover about the other. There were questions about the future that they could not answer. There would be time for that. For now, Lydia Wallis placed her hand in the hand of George Brown and agreed to share his future.

* * *

George Brown was born on 7 December 1835 in the town of Barnard Castle, County Durham, in the northeast of England, son of George Brown and his wife Elizabeth, formerly Miss Elizabeth Dixon. The town and district carried memories of generations of those who had gone before; ancient Celts, Roman armies, a succession of invaders and newcomers, lords and serfs, the violent and the oppressed, farmers and factory owners. By the time of the birth of George Brown, the twelfth-century castle on the River Tees had been in ruins for several hundred years. Nineteenth-century industries clustered below the broken castle walls along the banks of the Tees, with the crowded housing of the workers, and a tight web of narrow cobbled streets lay against the steep hillside. Past eras were hinted at through street names—Butter Cross, Horse Market and

---

3 George Brown, *George Brown, Pioneer Missionary and Explorer: An Autobiography*, London: Hodder and Stoughton, 1908, p. 17.

4 Brown, *Pioneer, Missionary and Explorer*, pp. 18–19.

5 C. Brunsdon Fletcher, *The Black Knight of the Pacific*, Australasian Publishing Co. Pty. Ltd, Sydney, 1944, p. 51.

Galgate that once led to the gallows on the hill—and solid buildings of grey stone, some showing the craft of masons and others the irregular patterns of dry-stone walls. Beyond the town lay the jade, emerald and sage green of the undulating hills of Teesdale and the North Pennines, the forests and the ordered fields and hay meadows of centuries of rural cultivation, with a scattering of limestone farm houses and barns.

The young George Brown had no memories of his mother, other than a moment when, as a little boy of nearly five, he was lifted to kiss her cold dead cheek. His father, George Brown senior, was the central figure in his life as a child and youth. The older George Brown had arrived in Barnard Castle as an orphaned youth, relying on his own efforts to make a living; and through the years had earned rare respect in the region. A man of many interests, he had risen to the role of solicitor from humble beginnings. He was widely read, fascinated by science, and a skilled amateur botanist and geologist. He collected and lectured on the wildflowers of the region and taught his young son the names of rare flora surviving from the ice age. The older Brown also edited a local newspaper, supported the Mechanics' Institute offering education to workers and the organisation working to bring railway to their region, as well as being a devout and active Christian in his church and community. His son loved and respected him, and no doubt inherited his energy, enthusiasm and broad-ranging interest in many different disciplines.

His mother's parents, William and Hannah Dixon, had died before he was born. His mother's grave was near theirs in the old churchyard behind St Mary's Church, with memorials to uncles and siblings he could not remember.[6] A few Dixon relatives remained in the district, but around the time of his mother's death at the age of twenty-nine, her older sister Emma had migrated to Canada with her family and the other sister, Sarah, had migrated to the unimaginably distant New Zealand as the bride of missionary Thomas Buddle. Rare letters were the only link.

* * *

Three years after George Brown was born in northern England, Sarah Lydia Wallis was born on 3 December 1838 at Tangiteroria, a remote missionary post on the banks of the Kaipara River on the North Island of New Zealand. In the dense forests, coastlines and waterways of that southern land, legends were told of the ancestors who had come many generations earlier, courageous voyagers venturing over invisible ocean paths from other islands across the wide Pacific to establish a Māori society of tribal chiefs, their communities, artists and slaves. Others had followed more recently; sealers, whalers, traders, tentative settlers,

---

6   Letter from Harry Watson, Barnard Castle, Co. Durham to George Carter, 20 March 1986. Visit to Barnard Castle, and churchyard of St Mary's Church.

land speculators, timber men cutting the fine kauri timber, and missionaries. At that time the people of that region lived beyond the sphere of British or any other colonial power, beyond the rule of law, although many of the settlers and missionaries had sent a plea for intervention to the authorities in Great Britain.

At the time of Lydia's birth, her parents, the Reverend James and Mrs Mary Ann Wallis, were young, lonely and struggling to make sense of what seemed to them a serious error of judgment on the part of their Mission superiors. They had been Londoners themselves before travelling as newly-weds to the ends of the earth as Wesleyan Methodist missionaries to the Māori of New Zealand. But now London seemed very far away. Those who sat in church offices in London streets, deciding what was best for those of their mission staff in other parts of the world, seemed to be blinded by the impossible curve of the earth, unable to see what was beyond their limited horizon. The new baby Sarah Lydia, their third child, arrived just after the fourth anniversary of their arrival in New Zealand. Their frustration was justified; since first entering the Hokianga River on the north-west coast on 1 December 1834, they had worked in three locations and now were being instructed from afar to move yet again.

It had begun well. A number of Māori tribes in the north might have welcomed them, but internal tensions between new and established missionaries had sent Wallis and his friend John Whiteley away from Mangungu to attempt new work further south. They began work at Whaingaroa and Kawhia, on two rivers that cut into the western coastline of the North Island, south of Auckland, They needed courage. It was tough pioneering work, in dense forest 'not easily nor often traveled by the foot of men and never by beast', as Wallis wrote, among a warlike and suspicious people.[7] Despite the extreme challenges, they were beginning to make progress. Then, to their acute disappointment, their mission officials in London instructed them to leave the region to the Church Missionary Society (CMS). The distant directors of the CMS claimed that they had intended to work in the area where Wallis and Whiteley had begun, and had funding for this. Wallis and Whiteley were to leave immediately.

Obedient but angry, James and Mary Ann Wallis, with their first baby Elizabeth, left Whaingaroa River and everything they had worked to establish over the previous year or so. On 1 June 1836 James wrote in his journal:

> Left Whaingaroa this morning with a heart overwhelmed with sorrow and not without some doubts relative to the propriety of the steps we are taking…. When I looked at the chapel, the schoolroom, the dwelling

---

7   James Wallis, letter to Committee of Wesleyan Methodist Missionary Society, London, 19 February 1845, in Letters to Mission Secretaries, 1809–1895, Wesleyan Methodist Missionary Society (WMMS), London, written between 15 December 1834 and 10 May 1854. Typescript. Original held at Auckland Institute and Museum, MS # 320, 'Letters and Papers concerning Rev. James Wallis.'

house, the garden, the field, and the station generally I felt desirous to remain in possession of them: but my leaving these are only a light trial compared to the tearing myself away from the weeping natives to whom I had had the honour of presenting the gospel of Christ.[8]

Frustrated and disappointed, the young couple attempted to begin again in a clearing hewn from dense forest, near a centre of Māori population at Tangiteroria on the Kaipara River. Their new neighbours were not interested in anything they might want to offer them and certainly did not welcome them. In a world of violence, slavery, sorcery and treachery, James Wallis struggled. His letters home were filled with memories of the work they had left behind, and after a year in the new location, James wrote bitterly that all the signs suggested that 'the Lord has nothing for us to do here.'[9] The whole country was racked with lawlessness; warring tribal groups, unscrupulous whites grabbing land and anarchy in some white settlements. Wallis was grieved to hear that the CMS had still not taken any action at Whaingaroa, the mission he had been forced to abandon.

The turning point came in October 1838, only weeks before the birth of their third child, Sarah Lydia. The Wallis family learned that, in the light of pleas from Māori chiefs from Whaingaroa and the inaction of the CMS, James Wallis and his family could return to the work that had never been far from their hearts. Infant Sarah Lydia Wallis would have no memory of her birthplace yet may have inherited some of the renewed optimism, hope and joy of her parents at that time. A visiting senior missionary, the respected Reverend Nathaniel Turner, baptised baby Sarah Lydia on 21 February 1839. Within days they had sailed, and by 4 March arrived back on the Whaingaroa River. Home again; it would be home for the next twenty-five years.[10]

Even in the initial euphoria of returning, things were not simple. The large Māori population, though welcoming, had moved from the northern to the southern side of the river; their original house was not habitable and the land did not belong to the mission. They would have to begin again. Many years later, James Wallis wrote, 'No settlement being near where the vessel anchored, our goods were landed on the beach where they had to remain some days. Meanwhile we secured shelter by setting up a four post kauri bedstead which we roofed with boards and blankets and which answered the double purpose of drawing room and bedroom.'[11]

---

8   Wallis, Journal entry, 1 June 1836, in Letters to Mission Secretaries, 1809–1895.

9   Wallis, Journal entry 23 July 1837, quoted in letter to WMMS Committee, London, 4 August 1837.

10   Rev. James Wallis, Letters to Mission Secretaries, 1809–1895, Wesleyan Methodist Missionary Society, London, written between 15 December 1834 and 10 May 1854. Original held at Auckland Institute and Museum, MS # 320, 'Letters and Papers concerning Rev. James Wallis.'

11   Wallis, Narrative written for grandson Rev. T.J. Wallis, p. 6.

Clutching her children around her under the flimsy roof of blankets, Mary Ann Wallis cared for small four-year-old Elizabeth, two-year-old William and three-month-old baby Sarah Lydia on the bedstead until the Māori erected an open-sided building of local material to provide temporary accommodation at one end and a church at the other. As the weather cooled into autumn, with cold winds and then rain, decisions were made to follow the people to the southern side of the wide river, to purchase land on a pleasant rise overlooking the water called Nihinihi and to build a weatherboard house there.[12]

Despite the practical difficulties, they were full of hope. Small Sarah Lydia was too young to be aware of some of the events of her early childhood. The Māori population nearby was beginning to consider the Christian message. Her father was working hard and was often away, leaving his wife and young children alone. Wallis added his signature to the Treaty of Waitangi in 1840 as a witness to the mark of a local chief, the Reverend Thomas Buddle and his bride Sarah arrived from the town of Barnard Castle in County Durham, England in 1840 to work beside Wallis; they would become life-long friends. Relations between the Wesleyan Methodists and the CMS caused Lydia's parents much anxiety during the 1840s, with endless debates over baptism, ordination, schisms and lay participation. The sound of the Māori language and the presence of Māori people in their home was natural, the swirling intricacies of facial and body tattoos as familiar as the faces of their parents.

At intervals, significant guests came to stay in the mission house on the river. Governor Hobson and Captain Best arrived in 1842, with the hope of purchasing Māori land for the Crown, for the use of settlers. Already large tracts of land had been obtained in other parts of the island, often amid controversy. James Wallis was not impressed and quoted a Māori leader, 'When you see an island you think you would like, you go and kill the people there and take their land. Where are the people of Port Jackson? They are lost, you white people have destroyed them ... perhaps we shall be lost too. These thoughts tell me not to sell my land.'[13]

Lydia Wallis was a five-year old when the new mission Superintendent, the Reverend Walter Lawry, arrived at their home exhausted; he had made the journey in the winter of 1844 and was appalled at the demands made on his scattered and isolated people— 'such violent and wasting travels,' he wrote.[14] In the same year the artist George French Angas appeared at the mission house. With his party, twenty-two-year old Angas had travelled through 'a succession of flooded fernland, swamps and dripping forests ... through the intricate

---

12   Ibid.
13   Wallis, Letter to Wesleyan Methodist Missionary Society, London, July 1842.
14   E.W. Hames, *Walter Lawry and the Wesleyan Mission in the South Seas*, Auckland: Wesley Historical Society, 1967, p. 31.

mazes of which we wound our way over slippery roots, ankle deep in mud.' He described the magnificent vistas until they saw from a hilltop 'the many-branched harbour winding amongst the hills,' the cloud-topped Mount Karioi and the ocean beyond. James Wallis was away, but 'his wife received us most kindly, surrounded by a group of half a dozen fine rosy-cheeked children who bore testimony in their health and happy countenances, to the salubrity of the New Zealand climate.'[15] Wallis was beginning to record changes in their environment since their first arrival; tribal wars were fewer, there were fewer murders, slaves were being set free and there was less infanticide.[16] Though still a remote and dangerous place, the atmosphere seemed to be lightening.

To a young girl growing up on a slope overlooking the harbour, the world of childhood would have seemed the only world possible. Lydia and her eight siblings all survived the ills of childhood. They had many Māori playmates and spoke the language fluently. It was a busy household linked with the activities of the Māori community, the church and school, set in a place of great scenic beauty. She would have watched the Māori women creating beautiful cloaks of feather, fur and fibre. She would have visited young friends in their homes, stooping to enter through the low doorway and squatting by the smoky fire in the ring of stones on the earthen floor while rain fell on the thatched roof. The elegant curves of carved house posts and lintels of the Māori meeting house echoed the lines of curling fern. Staring eyes and protruding tongues, carved into the design, were frightening, but familiar. The long sweep of canoe and paddle, slicing the water below their house, the glow of greenstone ornament and delicacy of fine feather were all part of the known landscape. There would have been times when her mother called her urgently—'Come away! Come away now'—from sights and sounds that could have led to childhood nightmares, and times when she and her brothers and sisters were kept within the family home but always with Māori companions and house servants. Years later Lydia would tell a friend, 'I lived among the Maoris [sic] as long as I can remember.'[17]

* * *

On the far side of the world, the boy George Brown was attending school in Barnard Castle. In later years he was dismissive of the quality of his own education in a small private school. Even so, his education had equipped him with a fluent writing style, a wide vocabulary, flawless spelling and competence with figures. From his father he inherited an active curiosity about science in all its forms and a love for books and self-education. When George Brown was ten-years old, his father remarried. The boy did not take kindly to the firm

---

15   George French Angas, quoted in C.W. Vennell and Susan Williams, *Raglan County: Hills and Sea 1876–1976*, Auckland: Wilson & Horton, 1976, pp. 50–51.
16   Wallis, Letter to Wesleyan Methodist Missionary Society, London, 19 February 1845.
17   Fletcher, *The Black Knight of the Pacific*, p. 65.

discipline of his new stepmother, Mrs Jane Brown. Home became an uneasy place, with a strong-willed and rebellious lad, a father who was often absorbed in his many enterprises and a woman of strong character who was attempting to be 'mother' to a boy who resented her presence. It was no easier when a son and then daughters were born to the older Brown and his new wife. As the boy became a youth, he did not make life easy for his stepmother, who declared that he seemed to be heading for the gallows.

The gallows or an early grave due to disease or misadventure were certainly possibilities. As he grew older, he often seemed to skirt perilously close to disaster. As a bright thirteen-year-old, he was sent to work for the Barnard Castle physician, Dr. Isaac Cust, with a view to a possible medical career. He learned some things of practical use during that time, but almost managed to blow up himself and the good doctor, with a misguided chemical experiment. It was decided that he had no special gifts for the medical profession.[18]

It was while he was working for Dr. Cust that he had another brush with death. Barnard Castle had attracted an increasing number of industries during the nineteenth century, and the river was polluted from the slaughter house, tanning works and guano warehouse. Town drainage was inadequate and conditions were ripe for disease. In common with most of the rest of world of the time, the connection between contaminated water and cholera had not been made. Cholera struck Barnard Castle in 1849. Nearly half of the town's population of over 4,000 people became ill and many died. Among the survivors was George Brown who later recalled 'a very narrow escape from death.'[19] His father became very active with other citizens in forming a local Board of Health which moved rapidly to provide sewerage and clean water to their town.

* * *

On the banks of the pristine Whaingaroa River, Lydia and the other Wallis children may have been content with the only life they knew. Their parents however were very anxious indeed about the future of their children. They were not Māori, so had no place in the Māori system, nor had they any opportunity to become productive members of European society. James Wallis had raised the question of education for their children with the Mission leadership in London on a number of occasions but with no response. The Wesleyan Methodist missionaries were increasingly distressed. On their behalf, James Wallis wrote to London. He believed that his children should be 'taken away from native scenes and native society or they will be in danger of being ruined. In this part

---

18   Brown, *Pioneer, Missionary and Explorer*, p. 7.
19   Ibid.

of the country there is no English society, no not a soul, and all my brethren in the District can testify that I have tried every means within my reach to get my children educated, but in vain.'[20]

He and his wife were neglecting some of their missionary duties while they tried to educate their children themselves, and would continue to do so 'unless it can be made to appear that we ought to instruct the heathen though our children are allowed to grow up in ignorance and error.' He concluded 'if your Missionaries' children are not taken care of, the sooner you recall your missionaries from New Zealand the better.'[21]

It was a clear warning. The mission superintendent, the Reverend Walter Lawry, took action. Wesleyan College and Seminary was established in Auckland in 1849 with the parents of students becoming shareholders.[22] Lawry requested the appointment of 'a thoroughly good school master for the children of my hardworking brethren' and the Reverend Joseph H. Fletcher and his wife Kate were sent. A large building was built on eight and a half acres in Upper Queen Street, Auckland, looking down from a hilltop across the harbour with its traffic of trading canoes, whalers, coastal vessels and brigs sailing for Sydney or San Francisco. At first the school accepted only boys but the parents insisted that their daughters must also have an opportunity. Despite the misgivings of some shareholders, the new school decided to be a rare institution for the period, accepting both boys and girls as students and boarders. When students arrived to begin school in January 1850, travelling from missionary households in Pacific islands regions or from rural New Zealand, eleven-year-old Sarah Lydia Wallis joined siblings Elizabeth, William and Thomas at the new school.[23] The school would report proudly at the end of 1851 that 'we furnish almost the only high-aiming Educational agency in the entire Island. This must be regarded, at least, as a memorable experiment to supply Education to the middle classes under the auspices of unsectarian Christianity.'[24]

The school Principal, Joseph Fletcher wrote at the end of the first year that the school was indeed greatly needed. Some of the children from the more distant islands could barely speak English and 'it was surprising that the children had imbibed so little poison from the impure Pagan atmosphere which had surrounded them from their birth—the result of an amount of parental vigilance and fidelity which it is not easy to appreciate sufficiently.'[25]

---

20   Wallis, Letter to Wesleyan Methodist Missionary Society, London, 15 October 1847.
21   Ibid.
22   Hames, *Walter Lawry and the Wesleyan Mission in the South Seas*, pp. 33–36.
23   Cash Book 1849–1856, Wesleyan College and Seminary, Auckland.
24   Wesleyan College and Seminary Annual Report, 1851.
25   Rev. Joseph Fletcher to Rev. Dr. Beecham, letter from Wesleyan College and Seminary, Auckland, NZ, 27 December 1850.

While he observed that children from the families in New Zealand were often very healthy and strong, however 'the frequent absences of the father, the abundant occupations of both parents, and the want of Society in many of the Bush Stations, were all unfavourable to mental discipline and systematic instruction or indeed to any successful attempt to qualify young people for active and useful life.'[26]

Just before the students scattered to their remote homes for summer holidays in December 1852, at the end of Lydia's second year at the school, the annual examination was held before an audience of public and parents. They were grateful for evidence of 'a sound and liberal education based on Christian principles' being offered in their young colony. Around the classrooms, students displayed specimens of their work—writing, drawing, needlework—and girls nervously performed on the piano for admiring parents. The oral examination was exciting as the boys and girls were questioned on mental arithmetic, astronomy, physiology, the classics, general knowledge and the rest. Lydia Wallis had just turned fourteen and was among the girls, including her special friends, the daughters of the Buddle, Whiteley and Buller families, who were commended. The audience was delighted that the girls had participated well in the general questioning. An observer wrote that this 'gave ample assurance that they also had received in full proportion the able and zealous care which had evidently marked the entire course of tuition in the College.'[27]

Sarah Lydia Wallis was given a small bound autograph book sometime late in 1853. The entries shed light on the people who inhabited her world. On the opening page a family friend wrote:

> To Miss S.L.Wallis:
>
> Soft blows the breeze of early Spring
> and so does youthful life begin;…
> Live, dearest girl, live while you may;
> You should enjoy life's fleeting day.

The little book, with pages of religious verse and biblical quotations, captured the signatures of school friends and teacher Mary Fletcher, missionary friends of her parents, residents of Auckland and travellers from distant England and Australia.[28] Hinting at the multi-lingual world where Lydia Wallis lived, entries were given in Māori, Tongan, Fijian, French and 'Kaffir' as well as in English.

* * *

---

26 Ibid.
27 'Wesleyan College and Seminary,' in the *New-Zealander*, December 1852.
28 Autograph Book (entries from 1853–1880) kept by Lydia Brown, is in the keeping of Lydia Brown's great-granddaughter Nancy Joyce, Artarmon, Sydney. Among the signatures are those of William Boyce and Robert Young, commissioners sent by the British Methodist Conference to enquire into Wesleyan Methodist affairs in the Antipodes in 1853.

In 1851, while Lydia Wallis was still a school girl in New Zealand, fifteen-year-old George Brown left his home in Barnard Castle. Perhaps he had just had another confrontation with his stepmother. Much as he loved his father, he seems to have had few regrets as he left his home town. He was not happy at home and the town itself, despite its setting in a beautiful region, was grey, rather grim and unhealthy and described by a contemporary observer as a sink of vice and profligacy. He turned his back on it all, travelling north-east along the ridge with a panorama across the green hills of the Pennines etched with dry-stone walls. On past the bulk of Raby Castle, through the ancient city of Durham, along roads winding north-east through farmland until at last he reached the home of his Uncle Forster. His uncle lived in the town of Sunderland on the River Wear where it enters the North Sea. The wide grey expanse of water, glimpsed through winter fog, was his first sight of the sea, with tantalising hints of the unknown worlds beyond the mist. Uncle Forster lived in a tall, narrow terrace house and found his nephew work with a local wholesale chemist.[29] It would be several years before Brown returned to Barnard Castle, and then only briefly. The youth who turned away from his birth place did not know that, though it would remain a mythical Home, it would never truly be 'home' again.

The boy was restless. It was not long before he abandoned any attempt to learn the business with the chemist in Sunderland and moved on to the port town of Hartlepool further down the coast. The lively quayside bustle of sailors and shopkeepers, ships' chandlers, sword smiths, sail makers and smugglers enchanted him. Although he was now apprenticed to a draper in Hartlepool, he was far more interested in the sight of tall sailing ships entering the harbour. The draper soon discovered that young Brown was useful and very willing as a courier of smuggled goods to and from foreign ships. Although he still had a lot to learn about ships, he began the risky business of carrying parcels of English fabric to foreign ships in the middle of the night, and bringing back cigars, tobacco and other dutiable goods. He was almost caught once. As the rowing boat he was in came toward the mooring, he saw a Customs officer watching from the quay. Very aware that he had several hundred contraband cigars packed around his body under his clothes, the youth tried to look innocent. Keeping himself and his aromatic cargo downwind of the officer, he climbed on to the stone-paved quay brazenly talking of the latest news until he was safely away.[30]

The temptation of a life at sea instead of behind a shop counter became too much. George Brown decided to run away to sea. It was not a wise plan, as it meant breaking his apprenticeship agreement and could lead to prison if caught. Even so, pretending that he was going home for Christmas 1851, he travelled north to Newcastle and took a steerage passage on a ship for London, just after

---

29   Mr. Forster lived at 3 Park Terrace, Toward Road, Sunderland. He was evidently a man of substance.
30   Fletcher, *The Black Knight of the Pacific*, pp. 29–30.

his sixteenth birthday. It did not begin well. The ship ran into a violent winter storm; the wreckage of six other ships, lost with all hands, tossed around them as they struggled to safety. Arriving in London without friends, funds or experience, he tried to find employment with ships anchored in the Thames. An incompetent attempt at being a ship's cook was a failure and he found himself lurking in dockland streets trying to dodge men sent by his father's solicitors to bring him home. When they caught up with him, his choices were few but the runaway managed to persuade a reluctant father to give permission for him to become a sailor. Uncle Forster, evidently a forgiving man, arranged for him to become a crew-member on a troop-ship, a large East Indiaman the *Santipore*, under the command of a friend of his, ferrying regiments between British locations. His first experiences at sea in winter were difficult. High aloft on the topsail yard he struggled with stiffly frozen sails in a gale on their way to Cork. Then they sailed into the warmer Mediterranean—Corfu, Malta and Gibraltar— and then across the Atlantic, to Quebec. The work was hard and exhausting but he learned much about sailing ships. He also observed the machinery of the British Empire and its influence on the international stage as British troops were located in strategic places and a great navy gathered near Malta.

An accident on the day the troops disembarked in Quebec from the *Santipore* altered, in an instant, the direction of the young sailor's life. While he was on an errand to an upper deck, a ladder was dislodged and the boy found himself plunging down toward the depths of the hold. Crashing across the 'tween-deck hatch, he escaped death but broke his leg badly. The ship sailed without him, to be lost with all hands on their next voyage. He found himself, aged about seventeen, in the large Marine Hospital in Quebec, a stranger in a strange land and was touched by the regular visits to the ward of an old Roman Catholic priest, who showed him kindness even though Brown was a Protestant. On recovery, he set out to explore Canada, passing through Montreal and travelling as a deckhand on a cargo steamer which carried him up the St Lawrence, through the system of canals and across the breadth of Lake Ontario and Lake Erie. His aim was to find his dead mother's older sister, Aunt Emma, who lived with her family in the then small community of New London in Ontario. At last he found his relatives and was welcomed to their home and community.

* * *

Icy winter in Canada and warm summer in New Zealand. At the end of 1853 George Brown was working for a general store in New London, where local farmers and store keepers were taking advantage of the firm snow to transport goods to the farms in a region where there were few made roads. On the far side of the world in early summer Lydia and her sister Elizabeth Wallis left the College and Auckland behind. The journey home was an adventure, in a time before roads for coach or wagon, or railway. After crossing Manukau Harbour to its southern shore, the Wallis and Whiteley boys and girls walked with their fathers and a number of Māori carriers until they reached the river system that formed a watery highway. Launching their canoes, they paddled south between high banks, shaded by kauri and rimu, bush tangled in supplejack, cabbage tree palms and the vivid scarlet blossom of the summer-flowering pohutukawa. Through the heat of the day on the river they chatted and read, and looked for things to eat in their boxes. As the sun set each evening they made camp, lit fires and prepared a meal. Under the stars of a southern summer sky, they sang and prayed their evening prayers, and slept on the rustle of fern spread with blankets. Some days they left the river to walk along narrow tracks through bush or high fern fronds, until they reached another stretch of river. For most of a week they travelled on, cooled by rain, burnt by sun, torn by prickles, tripped by tree roots, slowed by swamp.[31] By the time Lydia and the others came at last across the final barrier of Whaingaroa Harbour to the mission house on the slope at Nihinihi, and were embraced by their mother and the little brothers and sisters, she knew that any future visit to Auckland would demand the same journey unless a ship came. At fifteen, she was to stay home to help her missionary parents and care for the younger children.

Lydia and her sister Elizabeth must have been influenced by the way their parents went about their work. There was respect for the people of the place, although the missionaries retained their sense of being a superior race. There was compassion, kindness, spiritual depth and concern for the well-being of the community. Lydia was very familiar with everything that was raw, discouraging, frustrating, frightening and challenging about the life of a pioneer missionary. And she had seen with her own eyes that people could change. She knew that a community with traditions of fear and revenge could be transformed into a people of hope and peace, though not easily, not without cost, and not without the times when they returned to their traditions. James Wallis believed that a missionary to another culture 'must have become acquainted with their customs and manners, not from books merely, but from observation. He must understand their modes of thinking and reasoning…. Ignorance in these matters has often made wise men look ridiculous, and not infrequently exposed them to danger.'[32]

He was committed to learning the language of the people and using it, writing at the beginning of his missionary career 'the missionary's object cannot be accomplished until he is able to converse with the people in their own tongue.'[33]

---

31   Rev. Joseph H. Fletcher, quoted in Robert Young, *The Southern World: Journal of a Deputation from the Wesleyan Conference to Australia and Polynesia, including Notices of a Visit to the Goldfields,* London: Mason, 1854, pp. 177–78.
32   Wallis to Wesleyan Methodist Missionary Society Committee, London, 21 December 1850.
33   Wallis, letter to Wesleyan Methodist Missionary Society, 27 January 1835.

Many years later, having become fluent, he wrote 'I have had much reason to admire the Maori tongue, it being in some respects more definite and expressive than the English.'[34]

The Wallis family, although isolated, ('ours is the only house in the place and we are the only English' he wrote in 1852) was self-sufficient, growing their own vegetables, grinding their own grain, keeping sheep, goats, pigs, cows and poultry and only relying on store goods for luxuries like tea and sugar. Mrs Wallis had learned to manage with what she had and taught her daughters to do the same. Mary Ann Wallis came to be known as 'Mother' among the Māori people. When the Wallis family moved at last from Whaingaroa to Auckland in 1863 after twenty-four years, the people lamented; 'O Mother.... We weep for you because you are absent from our homes,' and to James Wallis, 'Farewell, the man through whom peace flourished in the land ... you it was who increased the desire for peace.'[35]

* * *

Late in 1854, by a slow and circuitous route, George Brown began a journey that would finally bring him to a new life direction and to Lydia Wallis. Despite the kindness of his relatives in New London, Ontario and promotion in the general store, he was still restless. An inconclusive romance that led to bad feelings with a co-worker led to a serious quarrel. Harsh words, quick fists, threats with a knife followed and later an accident with a gun that could have been fatal. A pugnacious but sobered Brown realised that he ought to move on soon; he had come close to being charged with murder.[36] Home, England, his father, the beauty of the Pennines and the sound of the local accent of Durham became more and more attractive. Letters from his father had kept him in touch with affairs in Barnard Castle and now George was homesick after three years of travel. Travelling back to Quebec, he found a place as an ordinary seaman on a ship carrying cargo across the Atlantic to Bristol, working with a particularly rough crew. Almost back in England, the ship came close to running aground on cliffs on treacherous Lundy Island in the approach to the Bristol Channel, due to a sleepy watchman—yet another escape from an untimely death for the runaway Brown.

When at last he arrived home in Barnard Castle, he found that home was no longer truly home. The stone houses climbing the steep hill from the river past the hexagonal Market Cross, the ruins of the castle keep on the rocky cliff, the cattle market on Galgate, the churches and chapels of the town, all these were familiar. Some things were changing; among his father's many civic interests

---

34 Wallis, Narrative written for grandson the Rev. T.J. Wallis.
35 Ibid.
36 Brown, *Pioneer, Missionary and Explorer*, pp. 13–14.

was the new clean water supply in the town and the laying of some miles of sewer pipes (despite some public opposition to the 'interference' of the Board of Health), as well as great excitement over the progress toward establishing the Darlington and Stockton Railway Company to bring rail transport to Barnard Castle. In St Mary's churchyard there were new graves. A year after he had gone to sea, his half-brother Frederick had died, aged five; and Dr. Cust had died, too. A memorial stone now stood at the spot where 143 victims of the 1849 cholera epidemic lay buried: 'In the midst of life we are in death.' At home he discovered the difficulty of settling back into old patterns and relationships after several years away. He was now a young man but his relationship with his stepmother was still brittle. His younger half-sisters, Anna and Emma, were pleased to have him home, but he had grown away from them. Even though his father offered to arrange work for him, in his own office or elsewhere, the younger Brown was unwilling to stay. To his father's disappointment he was determined to travel again—to Central Africa, China, anywhere. Years later he would write that although he could not at the time give any reason for his stubborn pursuit of passage away from his original home, he now believed that God was 'leading me by a hand which I did not see. I decided to go to New Zealand, I think simply because it was the farthest place from England.'[37] George Brown left Barnard Castle for the second time. He sailed from Gravesend on the Thames on 28 March 1855 with the *Duke of Portland*; this time, at the insistence of his father, as a steerage passenger on an emigrant ship rather than as crew. This voyage was to take him to the far side of the world, to other seas and other stars.

* * *

Under the southern stars, in 1855 the Wesleyan Methodists of New Zealand, Fiji, Tonga and the colonies of Australia became an independent Conference linked with British Methodism, an important step for Wallis and his friends. More settlers arrived in the district where once the Wallis family had been the only migrants and the new village was named Raglan. In January 1855 a young man, the tutor William Fletcher from the Wesleyan College in Auckland, came courting twenty-year-old Elizabeth Wallis. Fletcher intended to offer himself as a Wesleyan minister and potential missionary to Fiji. Elizabeth Wallis was in love and would have gone anywhere with William. By the end of that year Fletcher had been accepted as a minister by the Wesleyans. Fletcher wrote in Lydia's autograph book: 'To SLW ... may you be a centre whence shall be ever radiating holy and happy influences,' and Elizabeth squeezed her own entry on to the same page. Elizabeth Wallis and William Fletcher were married at Raglan in 1857, with Lydia Wallis as bridesmaid, and went to Fiji as missionaries that year.

---

37 Brown, *Pioneer, Missionary and Explorer*, p. 16.

George Brown arrived in the colonial town of Auckland, New Zealand on 5 July 1855. On board ship during the long voyage he met the Anglican Bishop Selwyn and his younger colleague the Reverend J.C. Patteson (later Bishop Patteson of Melanesia). Although he was impressed by the character of Patteson and attended his Bible classes on board ship, he later wrote that 'I cannot remember receiving any great spiritual benefit at that time.'[38] Brown's first step on arrival was to ask directions to the Buddle household at Onehunga. His aunt Sarah Buddle and her husband the Reverend Thomas Buddle were his only contacts in New Zealand; they had migrated from Barnard Castle in 1840 when he was only a little boy but now they opened their home to him. The 'friendless lad', as he saw himself, had once more found a family in a foreign land. Sarah and Thomas Buddle's influence on him was profound. He began to

> feel that there was something wanting in my life and, under God, I attribute my conversion to the good impressions I received there. I was not preached to except by the powerful influence of Christly lives. Day by day I realised more and more that there were higher things than I had dreamed of, that the life I had lived was very far from that which I ought to live.[39]

The close circle of colleagues and friends of his uncle was rich in character and many made a deep impression on Brown. Joseph H. Fletcher, school Principal, led a study group for young men each week. At the Methodist Church in High Street, Auckland and through the Young Men's Christian Association he found friends. Young George Brown continued to reassess his life and question the way he had been living it. Over a period he experienced the 'throbbings of a new life, new thoughts, new desires, and a new purpose in life.'[40] John Whiteley led church services where George Brown brought to a climax his growing desire to follow Jesus Christ, and invited him to become a lay preacher.[41] Isaac Harding encouraged him to consider the Christian ministry as a vocation. R.B. Lyth, missionary doctor in Fiji for sixteen years, challenged Brown with the needs of Fiji, urging him to consider missionary work, and this thought caught like a burr in his mind. Thomas Buddle introduced him to the complexities of relationships between Māori tribes and Māori and white settlers, taking him to witness some key events; the 'fire in the fern' would flare into violence over the next decade and more.

* * *

---

38 Brown, *Pioneer, Missionary and Explorer*, p. 16.
39 Ibid., p. 17.
40 Ibid., p. 18.
41 E.W. Hames, *Out of the Common Way: The European Church in the Colonial Era 1840–1913*, Auckland: Wesley Historical Society of New Zealand, 1972, p. 9.

The young woman from the river in the New Zealand bush and the young man from northern England via Canada did not meet often. It was often enough. Lydia spent four months in Auckland in 1859, and although George Brown's name is not among the autographs collected during that time in her little book, they must have met often in the small world of that colonial town. Perhaps she was too shy to ask him to sign her book. By September 1859 Lydia was home in Raglan. A few months later she was a witness at the wedding of her older brother William and his bride.[42] For herself, she could only wait.

It was mid-winter, late July 1860, and George Brown had come. He had come with his question and now Sarah Lydia Wallis had promised to be his wife. The wedding would need to be almost immediate as George was under instructions to be ready to sail for Sydney, then on to Samoa in five weeks time. In the few days of preparation, the family made urgent appeals for a marriage license and borrowed a wedding ring. Lydia gathered her things to begin a life far from home among a warrior people in an unknown land with a man she barely knew. She now found courage to offer him her autograph book. His entry, carefully signed 'Mission House, Raglan, 26 July 1860' was a curious choice of words for a young man wanting to encourage his chosen bride. His message ran for three pages of breathless prose and verse. For a man whose prose was usually lucid, this note edged towards incoherence. He used the imagery of the effort of planting a crop and the joys of a hoped-for harvest. His little sermon spoke of

> many a long weary day of toil has to be endured … we who are commissioned to sow the seeds of great and glorious truths … the promise-keeping God … shall we doubt His power and love? Oh, no … Though the day may be full of toil and sorrow … yet the day will come when they who have gone forth weeping bearing precious seed shall doubtless come again with rejoicing.[43]

No word of romance, no mention of love, just the honest statement of a man who knew that they would be sharing tough challenges, but believed that his 'promise-keeping God' had a good purpose for them both. On the same day her father James Wallis added his own words, with the conviction of experience. The first sentence was firmly underlined twice:

'I will never leave thee'. In every circumstance of difficulty, in every situation of danger, in every season of sorrow, and in the vale of death, the Christian may be guided and defended, supported and comforted by the divine assurance 'I will never leave thee'.[44]

---

42 William Wallis married Harriet Hamlin at Raglan in January 1860.
43 Lydia Brown's Autograph Book.
44 Ibid.

Lydia Wallis and George Brown were married at the Mission House, Raglan, just eight days after he arrived to ask his question, on 2 August 1860. Her father the Reverend James Wallis performed the marriage ceremony and when completing the formal documents identified Lydia's occupation as 'missionary' instead of the more common 'spinster'. Whether he meant that she was already working as a missionary with her family at Raglan, or that he knew she would work beside her missionary husband in the future, it was an acknowledgement of her place as a fellow worker.[45]

Within days it was time to go. At the last minute, her mother added her blessing to the autograph book: 'The Lord bless thee and keep thee; the Lord make his face shine upon thee, and be gracious unto thee; the Lord lift up his countenance upon thee, and give thee peace.'[46] On a cold morning the whole family crossed the harbour in canoes with all the cargo. Then with many embraces and prayers and tears they saw Lydia ride away on horseback, with a second horse loaded with many bundles, parcels and boxes, her husband of four days, her younger brother and two Māori lads. None of them could guess how long it would be before they would meet again.

It was in no way a classic honeymoon but George Brown declared later that it was 'the best journey I have ever made ... I was happy all the time.'[47] Lydia the bride was as experienced at such journeys as her bridegroom. Together in the new intimacy of marriage, they began their winter trek with light hearts, making fun of the hazards as they followed narrow bush tracks along the sea coast. In Brown's later record he described long walks through dense bush, skirting swamps, tripping over hidden tree roots in mud 'almost up to our knees,' struggling with an unwilling horse as they tried to swim it across the harbour at Waikato Heads. All the baggage, much of which Brown 'often fervently wished had been sunk in the harbour before we started,' then had to be carried by one horse while Lydia walked. For six cold nights they camped out and on the last night on the west coast they were caught in wind and heavy, driving rain that 'blew down our little shelter tent, and drenched us most pitilessly, long before daylight.' They were offered kindness by Māori people along the way. The final stage of the journey took them across the waters of Manukau Harbour, west of the isthmus, and to the welcoming arms of the Buddle family. Years earlier Thomas Buddle had written to the mission leaders in London of his prayers for

---

45   George Carter, 'An introduction to the South Pacific activity of Wesleyan Methodism,' in *Wesley's South Seas Heritage: South Pacific Regional Conference*, Auckland: World Methodist Historical Society, 1987, pp. 25–26.
46   Numbers 6: 24–26, King James Bible.
47   George Brown, *Pioneer, Missionary and Explorer*, p. 18.

the boys and girls in the Wesleyan school: 'If the Lord but pour his Spirit upon us … we shall not have to look to England for a constant supply of missionaries for the Islands of the Pacific.'[48] His prayers were being answered.

Bride and groom had almost no time to themselves in the final weeks in Auckland with shopping, farewell meals, church services and special farewell presentations.[49] There were times spent with the Buddle family around the fire at home at Onehunga, laughing with the young cousins and learning of the latest tensions among the Māori. Just six weeks after George Brown appeared to ask Lydia Wallis to marry him, they sailed from Auckland, New Zealand, on 4 September 1860 on the 700-ton steam ship the *Prince Alfred*, bound for Sydney to join the mission ship, the *John Wesley*. As the steep green suede and corduroy of the familiar hills receded, and the tearful faces of beloved friends faded, Lydia may well have been alarmed at what she had done. She was now Mrs Brown, linked to a man who was still almost a stranger. They had already had time for their first misunderstandings and arguments. Her husband would remind her years later of the 'bright happy girl' he married, 'though you did think that I was tired of you after three weeks of married life.'[50] Since their wedding they had rarely been entirely alone, their tentative relationship always tempered by the presence of others. Even now, they were part of a shipboard crowd. At sea, George relished the return to the open ocean while Lydia struggled with seasickness as the vessel ran into storms. He was delightedly travelling on again, leaving a place that had always been temporary. She was leaving her home and beloved family behind. Her own parents had left their home in England and had never returned. She had to ask herself, will I ever see my home and family again?

It was early springtime in Sydney as they passed through the great sandstone cliffs of Sydney Heads, a foreign landscape to them both, another palette of colours. They were expected, and the Methodists of Sydney town gathered them up in welcome. It had been a wretchedly long wet winter, they were told, with floods and storms. Even in the centre of the city the muddy roads were almost impassable. Everyone was glad for warmer breezes and sun shining on the pink and white of fruit blossom. In the streets near the harbour new sandstone and granite buildings were rising among private houses. Local talk was of the discovery of gold in New South Wales at Kiandra and Lambing Flat, of Garibaldi in Italy, of the recent departure from Melbourne amid great fanfare of an inland expedition with Mr Burke and Mr Wills—and the fighting in New Zealand. The local newspapers were full of news of the Māori King movement

---

48   Thomas Buddle, letter to Wesleyan Methodist Missionary Society, London, 9 October 1851.
49   Among other gifts, Brown was presented with a large Bible, signed by thirty young men from the Young Men's Christian Association.
50   Brown to Lydia Brown, 3 September 1908, Brown Letter Books, 1902–1909, ML A1686-7 CY 2810.

and Thomas Buddle was quoted extensively.[51] If Lydia admired the 'Spring novelties' on sale at the store of David Jones & Co, she knew that silks and gloves and striped Swiss cambric were not going to be any use where she was going. They were invited to the homes of church members and made some new friends who encouraged them with their prayers. George was invited to preach at the churches at Balmain and Paddington and did his best to speak about a future which was still not clear to him.

Figure 1. George and Lydia Brown, wedding portrait, Sydney 1860.

Source: Brown family album per favour of Miss Nancy Joyce.

One day in Sydney they sat, solemn and still, while a photographer captured their image. Twenty-one-year old Lydia gazed directly at the camera with George Brown beside her. Her hands lay calmly in the lap of her fashionable wide crinoline skirts while he was perhaps a little tense. It was a record of that moment in between, in the space between the known and the unknown, the youthful past and whatever was to lie ahead. There would be many other photographs but they would never look so young again.

Ten days after they arrived in Sydney, George Brown was ordained to the Christian ministry in the family of Methodism on 19 September 1860 at the Wesleyan Methodist Chapel in York Street, Sydney. They were surrounded by

---

51 *Sydney Morning Herald*, issues from 14 August to 25 September 1860.

new Christian friends. Two of the clergy who laid hands on Brown in blessing would be important to him in later years in their roles as General Secretary of the Wesleyan Methodist Missionary Society; both the Reverend John Eggleston and the Reverend Stephen Rabone would, in their turn, be his link with the wider church.[52]

A week later, on board the sailing ship the *John Wesley*, now listed with the honorific of Reverend and Mrs Brown among the handful of passengers, they passed again through the Heads and headed out to sea under sail with a course set for Tonga and then north for Samoa.

---

52   Brown, *Pioneer, Missionary and Explorer*, p. 24.

2. 'Alone yet not alone'

Samoa
1860–1864

The twelve Samoan oarsmen were singing and the small light across the water began to draw closer. The ship *John Wesley* was gone. The overloaded whaleboat strained towards the shore with George and Lydia Brown, cramped, uncomfortable and excited, staring across the dark waters to the island of Manono. It was 30 October 1860. The sun had set hours earlier and now they were nearly home.

Their new colleagues Martin and Sarah Anne Dyson were delighted to welcome them. For many months they had waited in vain for a promised co-worker. The four of them talked late into the night and discovered an immediate promise of real friendship. Martin and Sarah Dyson, originally from Yorkshire, were only a few years older than George and Lydia; Martin Dyson had just passed his thirtieth birthday and Sarah was expecting a child soon. As well as the practical matters of Brown's future appointment, however, Dyson raised a disturbing question. Whether or not they had heard hints of this, they now learned that there was debate over their presence in Samoa. Ought the Wesleyan Methodist Missionary Society (WMMS) be working in Samoa at all? Another Protestant mission in Samoa, the London Missionary Society (LMS), believed that their presence was provocative and unnecessary. Dyson told Brown that an LMS man had told him 'The frown of God is upon your mission in Samoa.'[1] Although the WMMS Secretary in Sydney had assured Dyson that 'You have a delightful and honourable sphere of labour,' Dyson's reaction was: 'Very true, if it were not already occupied by other labourers…. The Church of Christ is one. Shall we edify it in these beautiful isles by dividing the people who profess to belong to it?'[2] Brown and Dyson now asked themselves: had their church made a mistake in sending them to Samoa?

Whether or not it was a mistake, George and Lydia Brown had arrived and soon began to explore their new tropical home. The small island of Manono lay between the major island of Upolu to the east and the volcanic mountains of the island of Savai'i to the west. Rows of small and large canoes were pulled up clear of the beach shingle and fishing nets hung to dry. Unfamiliar trees—breadfruit, pandanus nut—shaded several small graves spread with white pebbles near the

---

1   Martin Dyson, Papers, Journal, 1858–1865, 14 June 1860, ML A 2579 CY 269.
2   Ibid., 9 July 1859.

mission house with its neatly trimmed lawn. The church building of split bamboo was large enough to seat three hundred people. On their first Sunday they were intrigued by the curious range of garments chosen by the congregation, and troubled by the comparative closeness of the neighbouring chapel of the LMS.

George and Lydia Brown did most things together in those early months. Lydia was young, fit and active, happy to join her husband on walks and canoe trips. Brown, in his new journal, described climbing together to the rim of an extinct volcano on a nearby island and attempting to talk to the local people in fragments of language. He noted: 'Blazing hot day but we enjoyed our walk very much.'[3] Both George and Lydia were determined to learn the local language, as Lydia had spoken the Māori language from childhood. They began lessons under the guidance of Martin Dyson and with the help of Samoan speakers. George made a habit of waiting by the road until a Samoan came along who was willing to talk, then experimenting, mimicking words and phrases, prepared to make mistakes for the sake of adding words to his vocabulary. Lydia is more likely to have learned her language among the women. Dyson set Brown to working on passages of Scripture in Samoan translation and noted in his diary that 'Mr. Brown gets the language quicker than I did—his memory is younger, stronger and better cultivated than mine was in the commencement of my mission life.'[4] Within the first months of their time in Samoa, Dyson wrote to a colleague in England that Brown and 'his excellent wife' had stayed with them 'while they got a little of the language. They both of them succeeded very well with it.'[5] He also noted that Brown had preached his first sermon in Samoan, from a text prepared by himself and corrected by Dyson, just fifty-four days after his arrival in the country. Brown crowed in his own journal 'Bro. D. said that I did very well indeed and he was quite astonished.'[6] He realised that it was a rare gift and wrote just before Christmas 1860, 'I feel that God has greatly blessed me and assisted me in acquiring the language of the people. O may this talent thus given be employed in His service.'[7]

Martin and Sarah Anne Dyson were very happy to have their company. Dyson wrote of his 'exceeding great joy' in the answer to his prayers for a colleague and relished their conversations, although he worried that their conversation had included worldly subjects and feared that they may not all have been edifying. Brown appeared to have had no qualms, and if he did, he did not record them. On George Brown's twenty-fifth birthday, 7 December 1860, Sarah Dyson went into labour and gave birth to a son. They were very thankful

---

3 George Brown, Journal, 27 November 1860, ML A1686-8-9 CY 225; Dyson, Papers, Journal, 1858–1865, 27 November 1860.

4 Dyson Papers, Journal, 1858–1865, 16 December 1860.

5 Dyson, letter to Rev. John Thomas, 1861, London: Methodist Archives.

6 Brown, Journal, 5 December 1860.

7 Ibid., 23 December 1860.

to have Lydia Brown with them, as, whether or not she was an experienced midwife at that time, she was able to offer practical help. Sarah was very ill for weeks following the birth with a breast abscess and mastitis. They treated her with doses of purgatives, rhubarb, antimonial powder and opium but, to their distress, she did not improve. Dyson noted that it was a 'great comfort to have Mrs Brown in the house to take household cares off my hands.'[8] On the evening of 25 December, Lydia Brown herself became ill, though she quickly recovered. No one mentioned that it was Christmas. By the end of December, Dyson was desperate with worry. His beloved wife was dying and the new baby screaming with hunger. Just when they were losing hope, a LMS man with medical skills arrived to help them. Sarah recovered at last and the baby lived. George and Lydia Brown had been in Samoa for less than three months. It was clear that life on an isolated tropical island had many hazards, and that pregnancy, childbirth, maternal health and the well-being of children were neither simple nor safe.

Map 1. Western Samoa.

Source: Drawn by Margaret Reeson.

During January, George and Lydia Brown travelled across to the larger island of Upolu and visited established LMS communities at Apia, Fasitaotai and Malua for the first time. They saw signs of unbroken influence in the area for over thirty years, with training school, extensive translation program, printing press and growing number of Samoan and overseas staff to serve many congregations. In contrast, the Wesleyan enterprise may have seemed inadequately resourced and with much to learn.

On 21 January 1861, the Browns left Manono with Martin Dyson and crossed the passage for their future home on the island of Savai'i. George had visited the mission site at Satupa'itea during December and their cargo had already been delivered. As they neared the beach that day, George Brown's 'feelings were of

---

8   Dyson Papers, Journal, 1858–1865, 13 December 1860.

a very mixed character but I bless God for the faith which enables me to trust in him.'[9] The next day, Dyson left them 'and we are alone, as regards European society, alone yet not alone.'[10]

By this time they had learned more of the background of their new home. They were not starting pioneer work on a blank page. Their village region of Satupa'itea had been a leading community and headquarters of the Wesleyan movement in Samoa before any European missionaries had arrived in that land. The early influences had been through Tongan visitors, related to the Samoans through language, race and family ties, who brought with them rudimentary forms of Christian teaching in the wake of a strong move to the Christian faith, the *lotu*, among the Wesleyan Tongans in the 1820s. When the LMS brought Tahitian missionaries to Samoa in 1830, political alliances and rivalries between regions intersected with the new message of Christianity brought by two groups, *lotu* Tonga and *lotu* Tahiti. The people of Satupa'itea aligned themselves with *lotu* Tonga, the Wesleyans.[11] The Reverend Peter Turner arrived at Satupa'itea in 1835 to a tumultuous welcome and began visiting, teaching, preaching and translating Scriptures and hymns, with striking results. Unfortunately, tribal rivalry rode alongside religious rivalries. From London, the two missionary organisations decided that it was not right for both groups to continue to work in the same island group. To his profound disappointment, the Wesleyan missionary was ordered to withdraw from Samoa. He left, very reluctantly, in May 1839. Nonetheless, some of the Samoan Wesleyans were not willing to give up their identity and those around Satupa'itea persisted in following what they believed were Wesleyan practices.[12] As King George Tupou of Tonga declared in 1843, 'The friends in England are not able to change the minds of the people of Samoa or Tonga, as to what religion they shall be of.'[13] Samoans with family associations with Tonga were reluctant to be absorbed into the LMS. Sadly, some of the handful of Tongan Wesleyan workers who remained had lost their way, spiritually and morally. LMS staff members were offended when the WMMS in Australasia, recently independent of the British Wesleyan Missionary Society, were persuaded to re-establish the Wesleyan mission in Samoa in 1857, rather than let the remnant of Wesleyans finally accept the leadership of the LMS.

At Satupa'itea, their new home, the work had been re-established in 1859 with the appointment of the Native Assistant Minister, the Tongan leader Barnabas 'Ahongalu. 'Ahongalu, a widely respected man, had first come to Samoa in the days of Peter Turner and continued through most of the years since that time to

---

9   Brown, Journal, 21 January 1861.
10   Ibid., 22 January 1861.
11   A. Harold Wood, *Overseas Missions of the Australian Methodist Church Vol.1 Tonga and Samoa*, Melbourne: Aldersgate Press, 1975, p. 267.
12   Ibid., pp. 270–82.
13   Ibid., p. 285.

serve in Samoa with the remnant Wesleyans. Most Samoan Wesleyans viewed him as the father of their church. He had acquired a large block of land at Satupa'itea on the western shore of the bay, built houses and a church with local materials and gathered fifteen young men and their families into a mission community. The fertile land rich with fruit and nut trees was close to a large village population. Dyson was very impressed with his work and said he was 'worthy of commendation'. 'Ahongalu would become a wise friend and trusted mentor for Brown.

Although Lydia Brown had grown up in a household where her mother managed an efficient establishment in an isolated place, this was the first home of which she was mistress. Her family home at Raglan had been established for years, with livestock, food gardens and grain. At Satupa'itea the little bamboo and thatch house let wind and rain seep through, and until they found some woven mats, the floors were of earth. An LMS missionary wrote to them: 'Take care of your health—I would not sleep in that house of yours on this Island for a £1 a night.'[14] George began to make plans to strengthen the walls and to build, if possible, a more substantial house of stone. In the meantime, Lydia was responsible for providing them with food, water, heating, light, clothing and basic hygiene—a daunting task.

Life was often an adventure for the young couple in their first year together. Everything in Samoa, at this time, was novel and interesting, and Brown filled pages of his journal with observations of the detail of their surroundings. There was the rhythm of preparation and preaching, a new class for young men, evening prayers after their meal, the beginning of work on a stone house. He reported his early nervous attempts to provide medical help to local villagers, with limited skill and the limited medications of his day.[15] He would have preferred to spend more time on language learning. Although he was preaching now from a written text, he was frustrated. 'Oh, that the time will soon come when I shall be able to speak freely to these people in their own tongue. I cannot bear to read when my heart is full.'[16]

He recorded tales of exploring the district with Lydia and Barnabas ('Ahongalu); arriving home soaked and muddy through tropical rain one day 'we consoled ourselves with the idea that although it was bad then it would be pleasant to remember afterwards.'[17] Another time they left by boat two hours before daybreak and travelled along the iron-bound coast of scoria rock, fascinated by the explosions of water from blowholes among the rocks. Unlike introspective

---

14   Brown, Journal, quoting George Pratt, 30 February 1861.
15   The medical supplies in the Samoa mission medical inventory in 1860 included Epsom salts, flowers of sulphur, ipecacuanha, opium, spirit of ammonia, extract of hemlock, castor oil and powdered ginger.
16   Brown, Journal, 10 March 1861.
17   Ibid., 21 February 1861.

Dyson, who used his journal to ponder his spiritual state, Brown's journal was the record of a practical man, filled with events, people, plans, observations, frustrations, illnesses and notes on matters that he thought might need a formal record—a Minute—in the future. As time went on he was less likely to comment on his spiritual life although he kept a disciplined record of the scripture from which he preached. As all Wesleyan missionaries were required to keep a journal with the expectation that selections could be used in mission publications, there was a degree of self consciousness in Brown's writing.

George and Lydia Brown welcomed their friends Martin and Sarah Dyson to Satupa'itea in May. After three months apart they all 'felt pleasure in again speaking in our own tongue.'[18] Brown, Dyson and 'Ahongalu left together before dawn on 7 May 1861, with two whale boats and crews, to begin Brown's first journey around the island of Savai'i to visit the villages affiliated with the Wesleyans. The women were left as company for each other while they were away. As the men travelled west through rough seas along the southern coast, Brown discovered that his friend was not as good a sailor as he was. Brown was exhilarated and observed that it was a 'grand and awful sight to witness the turmoil of those troubled waters.'[19] After ten hours of rowing, and sailing when the wind was right, they reached the western village of Gagaemalae and the pattern of visits began. At each place they made pastoral visits to Wesleyan teachers, inspected the simple village schools, questioned candidates for baptism and gathered the people for meetings where Brown and Dyson took turns in preaching. Villagers queued for help with medical problems and brought their annual offerings, mostly in the form of coconut oil, for the work of the mission. Over the next weeks they continued their journey, sometimes by boat, risking a wreck on the reef as they approached land, sometimes on foot along muddy tracks. In village after village they were welcomed by the local teacher and often given generous offerings of food. As they walked, they began a habit of planting young coconuts on land where chapels had been built; Brown noted that although he had first suggested it as a simple reminder of his first visit, they decided that perhaps it would prove 'a hold on the land and might secure it to us'.[20] There were some nights as they worked their way around the coast when they were still in the boat in heavy seas and rain until almost dawn and they both grew very weary. Dyson was not well, but kept going. There was little choice.

Despite the fact that the LMS and the WMMS had identified particular villages as being their territory, the Samoans had minds of their own. Although two or three hundred people might come to hear the visiting preachers out of

18   Ibid., 26 April 1861.
19   Ibid., 7 May 1861.
20   Ibid., 11 May 1861.

curiosity, Brown described several villages, on that first journey, as being 'very heathenish'. From his perspective, the traditional marks of long uncut hair, body tattooing and participation in the Night Dance 'proclaimed in unmistakeable language of the spiritual darkness within.'[21] Many were simply not interested in Christian teaching. And yet he also saw things that gave him hope for change. One evening, sitting with a crowd of Samoans in the shelter of the roof of the large village *fale*, as they listened to speeches about Christian themes, he

> thought that there was no need for Cloister Cell or vast Cathedral to excite deep and solemn thoughts, no one, I fancy could look upon that assemblage and after allowing his mind to dwell for a few moments upon the many diabolical scenes that have taken place under that roof—and then contrast the fact of their being met together to worship God in the same place … without his heart filled with thanksgiving to God.[22]

In another village on a moonlit Sunday evening he was moved to hear his mission boat crew near the beach 'breaking the stillness of the lovely tropical Sabbath evening by their hymns of joy concerning the "new Kingdom".' He recognised the leader as one who had previously been the leader in the 'obscene songs of the Night Dance…. I'm sure I never saw the Southern Cross appear more beautiful … this lovely constellation seems to be a sweet remembrance of Calvary and him who died for me.'[23]

Some of the schools were very basic, described as 'only average', but others gave them some encouragement. At one village school the students presented themselves mostly dressed in white and Martin Dyson 'was so elated … that in his speech he said they reminded him of Angels—can't go as far as that—hope to find Heaven tenanted by fairer Sisters than they,' wrote Brown.[24] At intervals, the missionaries had interviews with young men who hoped to become Native Assistant Missionaries. At that stage there was no serious effort at training by the Wesleyans. He wrote, 'When shall we have a training school is a subject of frequent conversation. When?'[25] The novelty of the daily first aid call in each village soon wore off and Brown muttered in his journal, 'what wearying work…. If the people would exercise as much faith in the Doctrines we preach as they do in the medicine we administer we should soon have an incipient Millennium in Samoa.'[26] He became increasingly short with anyone whom he considered was

---

21 Ibid., 3 May 1861.
22 Ibid., 15 May 1861.
23 Ibid., 26 May 1861.
24 Ibid., 14 May 1861.
25 Ibid., 18 May 1861.
26 Ibid., 20 May 1861.

wasting his time over medical help; for one client, given to sleeping in church, he prescribed a cathartic and 'in addition a course of castigation with a good thick stick.'[27] As he admitted, he was out of his depth.

> I knew very little of the Principles and still less of the Practice of Physic when I came here and though I have endeavoured by reading and patient study to meet the exigencies of the case yet still I feel that unless assisted from above I am very very incompetent.[28]

Three weeks after leaving Satupa'itea on their journey of some 150 miles around the island, they came in range of more of the chapels and stations of LMS on the north eastern coast of the island. They were given hospitality by LMS men Pratt and Bird as they travelled. Here was an odd and awkward division. On the one hand, missionaries from similar backgrounds, though different missionary organisations, offered each other mutual kindness and hospitality as fellow strangers in a foreign land. On the other hand, each group was uneasy about the presence of the other.

Brown and Dyson arrived back at Satupa'itea very wearily on 11 June 1861. Brown wrote that night that they were

> heartily glad to greet once more those who make home dear indeed— found that the same kind Father who had watched over and protected us had also extended the same blessings to those so dear unto us and we found abundant reason for thankfulness.[29]

When they had privacy Lydia would have shared with him her own news; by that time she would have had clear signs that she had conceived. The pattern was set. From now on for the rest of their lives, George and Lydia Brown would spend much of their time in separate places. He was the pilgrim. She was the home base to which he always returned.

Only days after that first journey around Savai'i, Brown was away again to travel around Upolu. On Upolu he found fewer Wesleyans and stronger LMS and Catholic mission work. Brown recognised that for some Samoans their affiliation with any denomination or mission was often linked with clan affiliations. He considered that for many 'it is a matter of supreme indifference who they pretend to serve.'[30] In a climate of inter-church competition on that 1861 visit, a priest, Father Louis Elloy, accused Brown and Dyson of making statements about the Catholic Church which greatly offended him and challenged them to a public debate. At Lufilufi, seat of one of the most influential 'talking chiefs' and before

---

27   Ibid., 28 Feb 1862.
28   Brown to Eggleston, Wesleyan Methodist Missionary Society, 16 April 1862, in George Brown, Letters, 1862–78, ML MOM 102.
29   Brown, Journal, 11 June 1861.
30   Ibid., 3 July 1861.

a large audience of Samoans who respected oratory, Catholic and Wesleyan men debated for three hours, all in Samoan language. Later Brown wrote a long and detailed description of the event but pondered, 'Was it wise to accept the challenge and what impression was left on the minds of the Natives?'[31] Perhaps to his own surprise, he was impressed by the young priest who 'behaved in the most courteous and gentlemanly manner and seems to be a very intelligent and well-read man—we both wished that his talents were consecrated to a better cause.'[32]

For nearly a year George and Lydia had waited in vain for any news from New Zealand, Sydney or England. One night, 'just after we had finished family prayers a tap was heard at the door and oh joy oh joy a parcel from Manono and a large bundle of letters and so our long waiting was at an end.' It was 29 July 1861. The bundle of thirty four letters contained mail from George's family in England, Lydia's family and friends in New Zealand and church correspondence from Sydney. 'Such a treat as I have seldom enjoyed,' George wrote. 'We read until with aching heads we were obliged to go to bed but it was hours before we could get to sleep from excitement.'[33] By the time George and Lydia celebrated their first wedding anniversary on 2 August 1861 he could write 'Both my dear Wife and I feel that we have great cause to record our gratitude to God for his great goodness to us during the past year.'[34]

It was inevitable that George Brown and Martin Dyson would clash from time to time, despite their friendship. More than once Brown recorded 'misunderstandings' between the two strong-minded men. In a letter to Dyson offering an apology, Brown wrote that he thought it 'best to express my views and have done with them than keep them and sulk over them…. I abhor the very thought of coldness between us.'[35] They both agreed that it had been a mistake for the Wesleyan work in Samoa to have been revived in 1857, but while Dyson believed that they ought to withdraw again, Brown considered that they ought to continue in support of those who identified themselves as Wesleyans. Dyson was so frustrated that he began to talk about leaving. This concerned Brown. Following a difficult meeting of the District Committee he wrote a letter to the General Secretary of the WMMS, the Reverend John Eggleston, and made a copy in his journal 'in case I should ever want the exact words.' He wrote,

> Bro D[yson] makes a very chivalrous offer to lead a Mission to Papua, many thanks for the offer but I tell him that Manono is his place and

---

31 Ibid., 11 July 1861.
32 Ibid., 10–11 July 1861. Fr. Elloy became Bishop Elloy from 1864–1878. See John Garrett, *To Live Among the Stars: Christian Origins in Oceania*, Geneva: WCC Publication, Geneva, 1982, pp. 131–35.
33 Brown, Journal, 29 July 1861.
34 Ibid., 29 July, 2 August 1861.
35 Ibid., 6 Oct 1861.

there he will remain—he knows Samoan and he does not know Papuan
... however I am not afraid of his going. I should not like to see him
attempt it for his own sake as well as my own he has not strength for it
but he has been reading Dr Coke's life and I suppose has got a little fire
from reading the life of that devoted man.[36]

This letter, written on 24 August 1861, is the first of many references by Brown
to 'Papua', a place almost unknown by the rest of the world apart from the tales
told by adventurous sea captains.

The shine of excited first impressions had faded by the time Brown set off for
his second and later journeys around Savai'i. The responsibility was his and
it was often dispiriting work. He missed Lydia, who went to stay with other
missionary households while he travelled. He faced storms and dangerous
surf, heat and exhaustion and often rejection. After a day of rain, trudging
between five villages to preach, Brown wondered about the legendary giants
of former missionaries; their fabled feats of endurance would be 'impossible
to the dwarves of the present day,'[37] he decided. He was not well, suffering
from severe headaches and a painful swollen leg. Once settled at home again,
he studied his medical books; 'my leg very painful—hope I am not going to be
disabled here so soon. This attack presents all the appearance of Elephantiasis.'[38]
Christmas 1861, like the previous Christmas which had passed without mention,
was very quiet. For some years, a celebration of Christmas Day was deemed too
Catholic a festival for Protestants so Brown wrote disconsolately, 'December 25.
I wish all our friends a merrier Christmas than I am spending, my leg is painful
and as the powers that be have ordained that no notice shall be taken of Xmas
day—no services held—why, we would not know that it was Xmas except the
Almanack reminded us.'[39] The service of Watchnight at midnight on New Year's
Eve, commended by John Wesley to his people, was a substitute and the chapel
was filled with perfumed garlands as they dedicated themselves to God for the
New Year.

Lydia was looking ripe for childbirth and by the middle of January George sent
Barnabas to fetch Sarah Dyson. George Brown had delivered at least one Samoan
infant but this was his own wife and their first child and they were far from
medical help. Lydia Brown gave birth to a baby girl in the early hours of the
morning of 21 January 1862 after what Brown described as 'a very easy labour'.
To their alarm the placenta did not come away as expected and they endured
five hours of mounting fear before it finally was expelled. They were both very

---

36   Ibid., 24 August 1861.
37   Ibid., 17 November 1861.
38   Ibid., 24 December 1861.
39   Ibid., 25 December 1861.

grateful to Sarah Dyson for her help. The baby girl was named Mary Elizabeth to honour her mother and his, and was baptised at Manono by Martin Dyson in March.[40]

So the motifs for the long life and work of George and Lydia Brown were all there, or hinted at, in their first year in Samoa. Isolation and illness with the hazards of childbirth, conflict between missions and tribes, the rigours of island travel and the resistance of island communities to change, kindness and misunderstandings between colleagues; it was all there. And that was just the first year.

Lydia Brown was faced with a difficult choice—to travel together with her husband or to stay at home. She wanted to be part of the excitement of discovery. She did not want to be scared, sunburned and seasick. She wanted to be with her husband. She wanted to sleep in her own bed. She did not want to be alone at home. She wanted to go. She wanted to stay home. An early attempt to take her baby on a journey was not a complete success; delayed by a storm, Brown complained that he 'could not stir at all—a wife and child I find are not so easily disposed of—had I been alone I could easily have gone on.'[41] Lydia was not deterred and she continued to travel with him on day trips. Of one experience Brown wrote, 'Wife and Child and I went to Tufu in Barnabas' boat—entrance rather rough but we got in safely after all—L. was very frightened but not hurt.'[42]

Their dream of having a third missionary in Samoa to work with the Wesleyan Methodists seemed to be short-lived. A new colleague came, and left again within a year due in part to the illness of his wife. Brown tended to be unsympathetic, suggesting that the woman's symptoms were probably due to hysteria. His own wife was not often ill, and was stoic about it when she was. All the references to Lydia Brown in her husband's letters and journals suggest a participant, not an onlooker. Lydia travelled long distances to support other isolated missionary women through childbirth. She taught a class of women to read and work with figures and was frequently hostess for passing travellers. In addition, Brown asked his wife to attend to correspondence; 'I have been obliged to give most of that work to Mrs B,' he told General Secretary Egglestone.[43] Her many personal letters to family and friends, although now lost, are listed in Brown's Letter Book.

---

40   Ibid., 21 January 1862. The story of Mary Elizabeth Brown has been told in Margaret Reeson, *A Singular Woman*, Adelaide: Openbook Publishers, 1999.
41   Brown, Journal, 19 March 1862.
42   Ibid., 12 April 1862.
43   Ibid., 27 July 1862.

Lydia would have been aware that George was finding travel more of a burden. The tone of his journal had changed by May 1862. No longer were there long lyrical passages about the beauty of the scenery. He was away from his family, tired and often ill. Even for a keen sailor, the storms, inhospitable rocks and reefs of the coastline made travel both stressful and exhausting. At each village community he worked for long hours on church tasks as well as medical work; 'I gave up at dark wearied and depressed,' he wrote.[44] Brown's journal was now studded with words of discouragement and disappointment—'very unwell ... cast down,' 'incompetence of some of our Teachers,' the 'ignorance' and lack of any training of some of the preachers. At home at Satupa'itea he felt guilty over the very slow progress on building a better house for Lydia. By May 1863 the new stone house was still not ready and their temporary 'shanty' was a shelter for rodents. Brown complained that he was 'sick and tired of this—no room—no privacy—books and goods all spoilt by the damp and dew and our own health suffering from it.'[45] Even though she knew the journey would be hot, uncomfortable, possibly dangerous and would last for at least five weeks, Lydia Brown decided to take her toddler Lizzie and join her husband on his next journey around Savai'i.

They left home together on 26 May 1863, spending the first six hours in an open whale boat on a hot windless day. The rhythm of classes, meetings, collections of gifts, baptisms, first aid and preaching in each village was all familiar to Brown. For Lydia, every place was new. The teachers and people in each place offered kind hospitality. She sat with the women, chatted, played with Lizzie and bore with the minute scrutiny to which the women subjected her, touching her skin and clothing, curious about this young woman who was a very long way from home. Her child made a natural point of contact between the local women and herself, and she was able to sit with them on the floor of village chapels for church services while little Lizzie staggered happily from welcoming lap to lap. While George Brown met with class leaders Lydia accepted the task of dispensing medicine.[46]

They travelled on. Lydia was happier on foot, walking between villages past gardens of taro, banana and leafy greens. Together they met villagers, heard complaints, inspected little schools and extended their language skills. Most days, however, she had to brave the ocean beyond the reef. One day, leaving the village of Samata, they saw their own boats waiting for them beyond the reef. Brown wrote later,

> The opening was very rough indeed and looked very bad. Mrs B was very much frightened indeed and for some time we gave up the idea

---

44   Ibid., 20 May 1862.
45   Brown to Eggleston, 27 July 1863.
46   Brown, Journal, 9 June 1863.

of trying but at length we determined to trust the people of the place. We sat in a large Native Boat high and dry on the beach and every man stood by the side of the boat with his paddle in his hand. At length the Steersman who had been watching the breakers cried out 'Away with her, Quick, Quick' and instantly every man seized the boat and dragged her into the sea and the next instant we were dashing through the surf the crew yelling and shouting like madmen. We were out in a very short time just mounting over an immense billow that rolled a few yards further and then dashed his waters in wild confusion on the place we had just passed. Our Crew stopped rowing and all indulged themselves in a most unearthly yell of triumph.[47]

A few hours later they were off the village of Neiafu caught between dangerous surf breaking over the reef and an approaching black storm. 'We gave the boat up to the charge of the people of the place and committed ourselves to God—then watching a chance we followed an immense wave on to the reef.' In the turmoil of surf, a wave crashed over them, half-filling the boat, but at least they were over the reef or 'our fine Boat would have been broken up into matchwood and we left to do the best we could…. We were kindly received by the people and soon had a few dry clothes on.'[48] It may have been a great adventure for Brown. Lydia, clutching her child, sunburned, soaked to the skin and still shaking, may well have wondered what had possessed her to come on this journey. She still had more than three weeks of travel before her.

They went on. There was more of the same; new villages, unfamiliar places to sleep, and a weary, fractious and insect-bitten child to settle. By the time they reached the LMS mission station at Matautu and the kindness of missionary Pratt and his family 'My wife and Lizzie seemed very glad indeed to exchange the *faa-Samoa* for civilized usages again.'[49] When at last they reached home again, Lydia was becoming aware that some of her discomfort during their journey had been morning sickness.

The Brown family finally moved into their new house at Satupa'itea on 13 August 1863. It was large and stone-built, lime-washed with steep thatched roof, glass windows and wide verandahs. No doubt Lydia was grateful for the space and comfort. She would make shorter journeys in the following months but next time her husband set out for a journey right around Savai'i, Lydia did not travel with him.

* * *

---

47   Ibid., 5 June 1863.
48   Ibid.
49   Ibid., 13 June 1863.

As the new year of 1864 began, George Brown was not satisfied with his own spiritual life. He wrote 'I want to have a more earnest vigorous piety that my sermons and prayers may burn their way into all hearts.' He felt that he should spend more time at his desk in biblical study, translation and writing.[50] Brown was still on probation as a new minister. He had been offered no formal theological education prior to being sent to Samoa. Now he needed to prepare for a ministerial examination on the basis of study of a reading list of theological and other books.[51] There was limited time for reflection or for study, however. It was a period of high energy and high expectations. He was still debating with Dyson over the presence of their mission in Samoa.[52] He was deeply concerned about the practice of 'many of the Church Members here in mixing up and taking part in the Heathen Customs that are now being revived again.'[53] The old ways of the past were so closely enmeshed in their lives that it seemed almost impossible to disentangle the ways of tradition from the practices and beliefs of Christianity and the veneer of Christian faith was very thin in places.

Lydia Brown may have felt that there was no convenient time for her to give birth. Her husband was absorbed with his new project of opening a Wesleyan Training Seminary for Samoan teachers on a new site not far from the mission house at Satupa'itea. When Lydia began to experience the signs of the onset of labour, George was busy with preparations for the ceremonial opening of the seminary with the first sixteen students. On 17 March 1864, the Training Seminary was opened with speeches, gifts and feasting. Martin Dyson believed that they could not have made a better beginning: 'much praise is justly due to the assiduity and perseverance of Brother Brown. Our shrewd and devoted Native Assistant Missionary [Barnabas 'Ahongalu] opened the way and he, Brother Brown, made it.'[54] At the end of a long and exciting day Brown recorded that 'my dear wife began to feel a little unwell.'[55] This was understatement; the infant was presenting in a dangerous breech position, feet first. To their great relief, a daughter, Amy Eadith, was born safely not long after midnight on 18 March 1864 and after the bloodstained sheets had been removed and Lydia made clean and comfortable, George, Sarah and Martin gathered around the bed to thank God.[56] The danger to Lydia was not over. Within days she was very ill. Acting on what he thought to be good practice, Brown gave her repeated doses of laudanum, a tincture of opium, until she complained of extreme giddiness; he had given her an overdose. Although she recovered, neither of them could avoid the knowledge that childbirth and its aftermath was always life-threatening.

---

50   Ibid., 1 January 1863.
51   Ibid., 21 February 1864.
52   Ibid., 25 January 1864.
53   Ibid., 19 June 1864.
54   Dyson Papers, Journal, 1858–1865, 17 March 1864.
55   Brown, Journal, 17 March 1864.
56   Ibid., 18 March 1864.

As the year 1864 went on, George and Lydia Brown and their two little girls were often ill. When they heard news of the deaths of four young LMS mission staff, a shaken Brown wrote, 'Oh what solemn lessons and warnings God is giving us.'[57]

Before the end of the year 1864, George Brown was formally received as a minister of the Wesleyan Methodist Church in Australasia, having completed all obligations of study and service. At the same meeting Martin Dyson gave his resignation from the Samoan Mission with a request to be transferred elsewhere. Brown was very disappointed. He would now have to take on the responsibilities of being Chairman of a difficult District. He was still not thirty-years old.

---

57   Ibid., 24 August 1864.

3. 'With aching hearts…'

Samoa
1865–1868

Hurricane winds and storms of controversy shook the early months of 1865. Writing in his journal after the annual Watch Night service, George Brown reflected that he was 'more determined to live nearer to God than I have yet done. I felt very conscious of many shortcomings during the past year … I want to advance in piety and holiness of life and also in wisdom.'[1] It may have been just a pious note, but he was going to need holiness and wisdom.

Although Martin Dyson had applied for a transfer away from Samoa, he was still there and having an influence. Brown was disturbed to learn that Dyson had attempted to negotiate with London Missionary Society (LMS) leaders about possible areas of influence and had received a blistering response from the LMS; 'a most serious attack on his [Dyson's] character.' They accused Dyson of 'proselytizing aggression,' 'taking advantage of petty native quarrels and cases of discipline' to draw disaffected LMS members into the Wesleyan fold, and of buying land and building chapels 'and holding out the prospect of European missionaries' in competition with their Society. They considered his residence in Samoa 'a hindrance to the peace and harmony of our Mission.'[2] Brown sympathised with Dyson but worried that his friend sometimes took action without consultation. The shackles of trying not to offend the 'other Society' chafed against the longing for freedom to take initiatives and establish new work. Wisdom was indeed needed.

A great storm was coming. The atmosphere was often heavy with humidity. Steam rose from the earth as the sun followed violent rain. This time, their people told them, there was going to be a cyclone. As the winds rose, Brown and a local trader secured the windows and school boys prepared protection for the thatch on the roof of their strong stone house. With their children, servants and some neighbours, George and Lydia Brown gathered in the dining room of their house listening to the crash of falling trees and the howl of the wind as it tore at the thatch. 'The tide outside our house was driven into our front gate,' Brown recorded. 'No one dreamt of sleeping as we were quite uncertain how it would end.'[3] As the eye of the cyclone passed and the wheeling wind

---

1   George Brown, Journal, 1860–71, 1 January 1865, ML A1686-8-9 CY 225.
2   Ibid., 3 January 1865.
3   Ibid., 27 January 1865.

shifted direction, some Samoans risked trying to add to the layers of coconut palm fronds weighing down the thatch in the darkness and pouring rain. 'They succeeded partly and then we all lay down on the floor and between dozing and starting up at some heavier blast than usual the night passed away.'[4]

It was three days before the winds eased. The mission grounds were littered with uprooted trees and torn branches, the tossed and shredded wreckage of the storm. Coconut palms looked like tattered furled umbrellas. Some food gardens had been destroyed. To their great relief, the new house constructed with such amateur and laborious toil had withstood the storm and they were safe.

It was not an easy start to the year. Brown was working hard but was often discouraged. There were some signs of hope but many things made him anxious. Some members and leaders were losing interest and 'falling away'. He felt disappointed in his own preaching and noted that 'I might as well be preaching to the Posts as to many of that congregation.'[5] The people were quite prepared to change religious allegiance; when he asked a Samoan why he had left the Methodist church to become a Catholic, he was told that it was 'because you threw us away and we despaired of you coming back again.'[6] Dyson was hoping to leave Samoa for another region and his mind was already turning elsewhere. A promised new staff member had not yet come. Letters from the General Secretary in Sydney demonstrated that he did not understand their context in Samoa, and only served to irritate. Brown was often ill, little Lizzie and Amy were both ill with whooping cough—and Lydia was pregnant again. Just before Brown left for his mid-year journey around Savai'i, they learned that Dyson had been appointed to Tonga. He would soon be gone.

George Brown was on the final day of his journey around the coast, on 17 July 1865, when a lad arrived with an urgent letter from Barnabas 'Ahongalu. 'Satupa'itea and Tufu are fighting and a man is killed,' he wrote, 'the Devil is awake at last.'[7] Brown and another Tongan teacher left immediately to hurry on foot over the last fourteen miles back to Satupa'itea. Darkness fell and they pushed on along a rocky beach by the light of flaring torches. At a large village they found a family mourning over the body of a young man who had just been killed. The men of the village had already gone to seek revenge. By the time he encountered Barnabas and his party he learned that a temporary truce had been struck and the bodies of the dead had been returned to their people. Late that night Brown reached home. He was relieved that Lydia and the children were away with Sarah Dyson while he was travelling, but the deserted house seemed very comfortless. Next morning after an exhausted sleep Brown sewed

---

4   Ibid., 28 January 1865.
5   Ibid., 15 March 1865, 16 July 1865.
6   Ibid., 30 June 1865.
7   Ibid., 17 July 1865.

and dressed some terrible axe wounds then went to sit with others to attempt peacemaking. He noted later that 'we did all we could to get them to make peace but in vain.' They did agree to a temporary cease-fire.[8]

The uneasy stand-off between antagonists held for the next two months. Lydia Brown and the children came home and Brown tried to go on with his work but he knew that the fragile truce could not last forever. At midnight on 11 September 1865 he heard that an attack was about to begin. With teachers and students from the training school, he waited through the night by fires. At dawn they sat together blocking the narrow path at the boundary between the villages in their role as 'holders back' or peacemakers, waiting for the fighters to arrive. Brown found it difficult to recognise the antagonists when they came prancing down the path, seeing

> great stalwart fellows almost entirely naked, brandishing their Guns, Spears and Clubs leaping and shouting right up to the place where we were sitting. They were all shining with oil and had their hair dressed with bright scarlet flowers and their brows bound with frontlets made of the bright inner shell of the Nautilus which glistened amongst their dark hair.[9]

Unwilling to trample the peacemakers for fear of ill fortune, the warriors leaped and shouted, 'Why do you stop us?' Threats were met with speeches, and still more speeches as the peacemakers sat for hours in the hot sun refusing to move. Just when it seemed that peace was possible, at sunset there was news that outlying groups had clashed. Two men from Satupa'itea were dead. That night he wrote, 'All talking was at once given up and it was soon felt that any attempt at mediation just then would be quite useless.' People of neutral groups were sent to retrieve the mutilated bodies and the Browns were very shocked when they returned bearing two bloodied heads. They knew those faces; the dead men had helped to build their house. That night they went to sleep with the sound of distant wailing in their ears.[10] Even though there was a formal gathering of chiefs and people at the end of September to declare that the fighting was at an end, this would not be forgotten. Memories of loss and plans for revenge were to linger on, hidden but poisonous.

* * *

As Lydia Brown's third pregnancy progressed, her husband wrote to his father that he was worried that the baby would come when their house was

---

8   Ibid., 17–18 July 1865.
9   Ibid., 11 September 1865. In *George Brown: Pioneer-Missionary and Explorer: An Autobiography* (London: Hodder and Stoughton, 1908), Brown retells this story, from his journal, but dates it as happening on 11 September 1866. The original journal entry is 11 September 1865.
10   Brown, Journal, 11 September 1865.

overcrowded with guests, the much hoped-for new missionaries—or when they were entirely alone.[11] Five weeks after the deadly fight in their community, the mission ship the *John Wesley* was sighted at last. They had been waiting for many months. Brown and Dyson took a crew out to meet her while Lydia and Sarah excitedly prepared a welcoming meal. A great gathering of Samoans, at their most charming, crowded to greet the visitors as they came on shore. One of the newcomers recorded his impression, of 'the large stone Mission House which stood about one hundred yards back from the landing place, looking so cool and pleasant among the surrounding trees, and with its door wide open, inviting us to rest.'[12]

George and Lydia Brown were delighted to discover that not one but two new missionary couples had arrived; Frank and Nellie Firth and John Austin and Jane, his bride of one month. Austin would later write of the 'hospitable care of Mrs Brown' and describe how they all gathered in the dining room and sat down to 'what seemed to us the most sumptuous repast we had ever had—a large dish of roast pigeons, with plenty of native vegetables, followed by some kind of pudding, I forget what. While Mrs. Brown was lamenting that she had nothing better to set before us, we were rejoicing over the splendid dinner.'[13]

It was a day of high delight for everyone. It was as if the troubles of the previous month had never happened. Villagers came with songs and flowers, gifts of food, *tapa* cloth and fine mats. Although the newcomers had been warned on their way through Tonga that the mission work in Samoa was in a low state, their first impressions were all positive. Brown wrote, 'We had so many blessings that day … I could have cried with joy and had hard work to keep quiet.'[14] That night they had four mission families under their roof.

To the deep regret of the Browns, Martin and Sarah Dyson left them with the *John Wesley* on 2 November 1865, on their way to Tonga. Frank and Nellie Firth were to take the place of Dysons at Manono but it was soon clear that the Austins would need to stay with the Browns for some time. Their arrival had been a pleasant surprise and so there was neither an appointment nor a house ready for them. Brown knew that this appointment would need to be considered with great care. John and Jane Austin could begin learning the language at Satupa'itea and Jane, fresh from Sydney, could begin to feel more at home

11   Brown to George Brown Sr., 15 August 1865, in Brown, Letters, 1862–78, ML MOM 102. George Brown senior in Barnard Castle continued to support his distant son with his letters, and among other things, had reported that he had been called to the Bar in the Middle Temple, a significant achievement for a largely self-educated man.

12   John Austin, *Missionary Enterprise and Home Service: A Story of Mission Life in Samoa and Circuit Work in New South Wales* (illustrated), Sydney: J.A. Packer, 1922, p. 83.

13   Austin, *Missionary Enterprise and Home Service*, p. 83.

14   Brown, Journal, 16 October 1865.

among friendly but curious Samoans before moving to a more isolated place. Lydia wondered how the nervous Jane would respond to tribal warfare or the sight of bodiless heads.

Two weeks after the Dyson family left them Lydia rose early. The signs of labour had begun. Her husband recorded in his journal that she 'was able to set the Breakfasts but did not stay at the Table. Just as breakfast finished all was over and we were rejoicing over the speed and safe birth of our third little girl.... The Lord is very good to us.'[15] This time Lydia did not suffer some of the problems of previous deliveries and new baby, Monica, was also well.

At the beginning of 1866, Brown had just turned thirty and found himself Chairman of a large and demanding district fraught with problems. His close friend had gone. He experienced attacks of elephantiasis which made long walks painful. Sea travel was often dangerous. Having new staff was a mixed blessing. In their rivalry for prestige and power, a number of the Samoan chiefs were competing over the privilege of having a resident missionary and threatening to take their people to another mission if they did not get their way. As Brown and Austin circled the island of Savai'i in January 1866, chiefs in each area argued over the appointment of Austin. One moonless night during their journey, John Austin went outside in an unfamiliar village and almost plunged over a precipice into the sea far below; Brown, who was wearying of the arguments, noted that 'a step or two further and the question of his appointment would have been decided forever.'[16] The decision was finally made to settle the Austins at Gagaemalae, thirty miles to the west of Satupa'itea in an area of substantial population with affiliation with the Wesleyans.

It was a hard year. Although the news did not reach them for three months, they learned that a tsunami had caused serious damage on the Tongan island of Tongatapu and the mission ship *John Wesley* had been carried on to a reef by the tidal waves. It was now a wreck. Martin Dyson and three other Wesleyan missionaries had been on board at the time, but had been rescued. Now the mission ship, their lifeline between the rest of the world and their lonely place, was gone. Each day the physical demands and the emotional pressure took a toll on Brown's energy; working among people with a very tentative grasp of Christian faith and strong connection to traditional belief and custom was a challenge. Lydia Brown's life had become an endless round of providing meals for guests and managing her own three little girls. Even after the Firths and the Austins had gone to their appointments, they kept returning to Satupa'itea for extended periods because of illness, loneliness and waiting for childbirth. Lydia helped both Nellie Firth and Jane Austin with the births of their babies that year.

---

15   Ibid., 16–17 November 1865.
16   Ibid., 5 January 1866.

After nine months of almost constant houseguests, Brown wrote to his uncle, 'We are getting pretty tired of it now.'[17] Whenever she could, Lydia travelled with George to the nearer villages, with her children and cheerful parties of servants, school boys and teachers, on foot or by mission boat. Perhaps some of these outings were a form of escape from an overcrowded house. In the middle of 1866, just before leaving for another long journey, Brown recorded a prayer in his journal.

> I have again dedicated myself to His service this morning … I feel more than ever determined to preach Christ and desire to make this the great object of our visit. O for a Baptism of Fire. O for more personal holiness. May God bless and keep my dear wife and our precious little ones.[18]

It was a struggle. The entries in his journal became fewer and briefer. He was too unwell and too tired to be bothered.

* * *

While the Wesleyan missionaries in Samoa met for their District Meeting in October 1866, in Sydney a sub-committee was investigating a disturbing letter that had come to them from the LMS in Samoa. Brown, Firth, Austin and Barnabas 'Ahongalu had a good and harmonious meeting unaware of the criticism that was being levelled against them. The Reverend A.W. Murray had written on behalf of the London Missionary Society in Samoa that 'The greatest hindrance to our work' was not heathenism, tribal wars nor the work of Catholic priests 'but Wesleyan intrusion.'[19] The debate was still unresolved: should the Wesleyans ever have returned to Samoa? The committee in Sydney concluded that the original withdrawal had been the result of a misunderstanding, and that the return was justified because of the pleas from Samoan people who had remained faithful to the Wesleyan cause. In a letter copied to Wesleyan leaders in the Australian colonies and New Zealand, the Wesleyan Committee apologised for giving offence to fellow Christians but stated: 'We are unanimously of the opinion that under no circumstances will the Wesleyan Church be again induced to voluntarily discontinue its Missionary operations in Samoa.'[20] Unfortunately, the rhetoric was not matched by practical support. That year their mission ship had been lost, colonial interest in missions was limited and Samoa held a much lower priority in their plans than Fiji or Tonga. Their forceful letter would only serve to antagonise the people of the LMS.

* * *

---

17   Brown to Rev. Thomas Buddle, 11 July 1866, in Brown, Letters, 1862–78.
18   Brown, Journal, 1 June 1866.
19   A.W. Murray, letter of 20 August 1866, quoted in Minutes of Wesleyan Methodist Missions Committee, 22 October 1866, ML MOM1 CY Reel 354.
20   Wesleyan Methodist Missions Committee, New South Wales, Minutes, 22 October 1866.

The pattern of journeys continued in 1867, although now Brown could limit himself to the eastern and north-eastern districts of Savai'i. Barnabas took the main responsibility for the training of young men in their Seminary, but Brown took his share in teaching, as well as the weekly round of mission work. He was often ill and weary and discouraged. The pattern of frequent houseguests continued as did local quarrels and rumours of quarrels among Samoan communities. At the beginning of the year he had written, 'I am not methodical enough and so waste much precious time and have very little to shew at the end of the year. Lydia and I had a long talk about it and we have determined by God's help to be more methodical and regular in all our engagements.'[21]

Far from being more methodical, however, his daily discipline of keeping his journal slipped away and was soon reduced to a bald list of preaching places. He was worried about both his new mission colleagues. Mrs. Firth had seen one child die and was quite often ill herself, and Mrs. Austin was finding the isolation and demands of life in Samoa very stressful. In periods of particular difficulty the Austins would retreat to the Browns' home at Satupa'itea and by July 1867, were back there again. Austin was suffering from boils and Jane Austin had a newborn infant. Lydia Brown had taken delivery of a sewing machine early in the year to help her clothe her family, but may have had limited time to use it.

* * *

In the clusters of villages in the district where the Wesleyan Methodist mission was established at Satupa'itea, although there were several chapels linked with both the LMS and the Wesleyan Methodist Missionary Society (WMMS), the more significant alliances and loyalties were with clan and community. Each person knew where they belonged in rank, in family and in village community. They understood the alliances. There was a long and bloody history of inter-tribal battles, revenge begetting revenge, a death for a death, memories stained with mutilations, murders and beheadings. The mission community knew that, one day, old memories would transform into new violence.

There were hints that fresh trouble might be on the prowl just before George Brown left to visit the northern coast of the island in August 1867. A revenge killing in the area, followed soon after by another death, made some of his young men nervous about leaving home as boat crew, but Brown decided to travel anyway. He was just beginning to feel some encouragement; in one area he observed cooperation between LMS and WMMS people and wrote 'they prove most distinctly that *they* at all events do not regard our mission here as a "hindrance" to the cause of Christ.'[22] But then he received urgent messages from Austin and 'Ahongalu urging him to return home as quickly as he could. The

---

21   Brown, Journal, 7 January 1866.
22   Ibid., 5 August 1867.

fighting men of neighbouring Palauli had warned that they planned to attack the large community of Satupa'itea within days. Abandoning his program Brown hurried back overland and by canoe. He found the people very disturbed and ready to defend themselves. That night he wrote that they 'commenced at once to prepare their double canoe. We are anxious.'[23]

They had reason to be anxious. For a week, despite great tension between the two opposing alliances of Satupa'itea and Palauli, there was no action. Brown attempted to carry on his normal work. They all knew that sooner or later someone would take the first step into battle. The mission household through that period included George and Lydia, six months pregnant, their three small daughters, Lizzie, Amy and Monica, Jane Austin with her two infant daughters, Jane's niece who had come to help her and, for some of the time, John Austin. Brown did his best to dissuade the Palauli people from fighting and when the threatened deadline for the Palauli attack came and went he hoped that the threat had passed. His Satupa'itea neighbours assured him that their enemies were simply waiting for more allies to join them. In all the small chapels church members were gathering at dawn to pray for peace. A week passed in anxious waiting, but the lull could not last.

Rumours and action, advancing and stepping back, threats and false assurances of peace, fervent prayers and violent killings, wars of words and wars of weapons; the next weeks were confused and grim. Working with local teachers, Brown attempted to use a Samoan cultural style of mediation in time of war, offering gifts of a fine mat and a Bible. These offerings were rejected and countered with the insult of symbols of firewood and stones, hinting at a killing and cooking of enemies. They all went away angry. By evening, one group 'had laid waste all the plantations of Satupa'itea. The Nuts and Breadfruit trees were nearly all cut down and the flourishing plantations of last week were all destroyed. It will take years and years to repair the damage.'[24]

That night at the prayer meeting he was grieved to hear the desperate petitions of the local people, outnumbered, surrounded on every side by their enemies. Other leaders tried to mediate, and Brown, with pastoral responsibility for church members in all the warring communities, travelled among them though a landscape of damage and waste. He knew it was no use. By now many women and children, with the old and the ill, had come to the Mission House for refuge, crowding into the outside buildings near the main house while their men waited for an attack.

On the morning of 30 August 1867, Brown made another attempt to find a compromise between the men of Palauli and the men of Satupa'itea, even

---

23   Ibid., 9–11 August 1867.
24   Ibid., 23 August 1867.

though it was clear that a battle was imminent. As he wrote, 'I had just stated my proposition to the Rulers of Palauli and they were considering it when we were all startled by a gun fired 20 or 30 yards behind us.... We almost held our breath until it was answered by another and then we knew at once that all mediation was at an end.'[25]

The combatants immediately left the scene and Brown found himself trapped between two groups of warriors. Stumbling through thick bush, confused, temporarily lost and with the sound of nearby gunfire in his ears, Brown finally emerged on to a beach and made his way home, shaken but safe. The grounds around his house and the outbuildings were now full of fleeing women, children and the aged. Wounded men were carried onto the mission grounds, each new arrival causing a wave of dismay. Knots of people, mainly women, gathered in outbuildings and on the house verandahs to pray together. 'Poor creatures, they wept sore and we wept with them.' Passing one of the groups, Brown heard 'one of our best leaders praying most fervently, and I longed to go and join them for God was there, but I had work to do.'[26] The battle raged all that day. By evening an outlying village was on fire, while the sound of drum beats reverberated against the noise of gunfire. Well after dark the sound of gunfire eased and, outnumbered, the men of Satupa'itea reluctantly decided that the only way to avoid more loss of life was to retreat. Under cover of darkness and with the protection of the double canoe 'which still kept blazing away at anything that moved,' they launched all their canoes, taking on board the wounded, the elderly men and boys, leaving the women and children in the mission house. 'After this we had a little peace and the poor heartbroken creatures that filled our rooms laid down to try and get a little rest. It was little use however.... It was a dreadful night and we eagerly welcomed the first signs of daylight.'[27] The sun rose on an empty beach and the sight of the double canoe in the distance under sail for Safotulafai with all the others.

Daylight revealed the full horror. Twenty men were dead and many more wounded. Through the day, with the help of men from the Training Institution, some teachers and some women, they went to retrieve the remains of the dead, heads and bodies, fallen in

> a dense Bush full of vines and creepers and so stony it was almost impossible to walk over it. It was a ghastly sight to come across the poor fellows lying in that gloomy bush headless and mutilated. Poor fellows, we had lived amongst them for almost seven years and many of them were most intimate with us. And yet there they were.[28]

---

25   Ibid., 30 August 1867.
26   Ibid.
27   Ibid.
28   Ibid., 31 August 1867.

That night he recorded their names and places in his journal. They had been men of prayer, men driven to fight against their wishes by loyalty to their clan. Brown was angry at the waste of life and destruction of livelihood. Next morning he preached to a heartbroken congregation and in the afternoon went with teachers to search again for the dead and 'brought in two heads and one body.'[29]

John Austin arrived from Gaegamalae to the sight of a village house on fire and the sound of rumours that the enemies planned to come back to burn the town and kill the women and children. Brown and Austin met warriors on their way to inflict more damage and, to their relief, saw them turn back. There was not much left to destroy. Enemies had been carrying away anything of value and torching any houses that remained. Brown sent Austin to Apia to report the fighting. A few days later, with Lydia, Jane Austin and her niece, Brown noted that 'in the evening we all took a walk down through the Village. We had better have stayed at home as we came back with aching hearts when we saw the desolation and destruction caused by this sad war.'[30]

When John Austin returned to Satupa'itea he brought new staff, the Reverend John Osborne and his wife, as well as 'a very seasonable supply of flour etc as we were getting very short.'[31] Osborne would later describe the 'hearty welcome from the Chairman and his thorough missionary wife,' although he observed that, understandably, 'Brother Brown was quite cast down.'[32] Lydia Brown had been facing her own challenges. During those difficult days she was managing a frightened houseguest with two very young children, and three young children of her own with a fourth kicking under her apron. All her outbuildings—kitchen, wash-house, store—were filled with frightened refugees making it almost impossible to move and work there. There were wounded men bleeding on the floor, grieving women to comfort, prayer meetings on the verandahs, a reckless husband off being a hero. Her sewing machine was silent. The last of the flour was full of weevils and the local food gardens had been shredded. She is rarely mentioned in the record, but she lived this experience beside her husband.

In the aftermath of such a time of violence and upheaval, what should they do now? The people of the four villages in the immediate vicinity of the Mission House had fled and now lived as refugees in distant villages. The stone Mission House, which had survived, stood alone with no friendly population around

29 Ibid., 1 September 1867.
30 Ibid., 5 September 1867.
31 Ibid., 9 September 1867.
32 Osborne, Letter, in *Wesleyan Missionary Notices relating to the Missions under the Direction of the Australasian Wesleyan Methodist Conference*, November 1867.

it. No one knew when they would return home. Normal mission work was not possible. Brown may have been tempted by letters from his father assuring him that he would find a welcome and a church in England.

After many months of a house crowded with guests, at last their colleagues began to depart, each going to their appointments. On 16 November 1867, with the minimum of fuss, Lydia gave birth to a fourth daughter, Claudia. Their colleagues had gone. The Samoan people were scattered. Their stone house at Satupa'itea was almost deserted. The day came when the decision was made. They would have to move away.

4. 'A great waste of men and money'

Samoa
1868–1874

The workmen came to George Brown, spades in hand. They had struck rock, they said, and were giving up their attempt to dig a well for fresh water. It was one more frustration to add to months of trouble. The community was ripped to shreds over tribal warfare, the fine mission property at Satupa'itea had been abandoned, and there was continuing tension between missionary societies. He had been separated from his family for months while he built a new house for them at another location, Saleaula in the north-east of the island of Savai'i. They were often ill. To add to his troubles, Brown learned that a large group of Samoans had recently defected from the Wesleyan Methodist mission and joined the London Missionary Society (LMS). In his journal he lamented:

> It quite upset me and I was very nearly ill from its effect. I cannot imagine how people can act thus. Such an act of black ingratitude I never expected to find in Samoa.... I cannot imagine why they have turned over. I do indeed wish that the way were made plain for us to leave Samoa. It seems a great waste of men and money to keep us here. I wish I could go to Fiji or New Guinea anywhere out of this.[1]

And now the workers had struck rock and he couldn't even provide a decent well for his half-finished house. The dry rocky hole taunted him, but, as he told the Mission Secretary, he did not like to be beaten. His men would keep digging in new places until fresh water was found.

With her four little girls, Lydia Brown joined her husband in a new but unfinished house at Saleaula early in June 1868. Only weeks later a passing ship brought news that shocked Brown. His father had died in Barnard Castle on 12 March 1868.

> I could scarcely understand it. I have had so many trials lately which I thought were heavy enough but all as nothing compared with this. I feel very sad.... My Father was a good man. Thank God I can say this now ... I have often wished to go to England and see my Father there.[2]

---

1   George Brown, Journal, 20 May 1868, ML A1686-8-9 CY 225.
2   Ibid., 23 June 1868.

His father had earned great respect in his community and some eight hundred mourners followed his funeral procession through the steep cobbled streets of the English town. Months later his son, who had defied the father and run away from home, read his father's final letter: 'It was full of love to us and my heart was wrung.'[3]

* * *

Debate was lively when the District Meeting gathered in September 1868. It was one of the rare periods when four British Methodist missionaries were in Samoa at the same time, working beside several Tongan Native Assistant Ministers. They were not of one mind on whether the time had come to abandon their work in Samoa and leave the way clear for the LMS. Finally, with some reluctance, it was agreed that Brown, with two Tongan Native Assistant Ministers, Barnabas 'Ahongalu and Tevita Kata, should attend the Australasian Wesleyan Methodist General Conference in Sydney in January 1869 where church policy would be formed. 'I wish to have the Samoan question settled once and for ever,' Brown told them.[4]

Two months later George Brown and his family sailed with the replacement mission ship *John Wesley*. After eight years in the insular world of Samoa with the many burdens of responsibility, Brown looked forward to the stimulation of visiting larger communities and hearing other voices. His journal, which for months had been mere fragments of notes about the mundane and the frustrating, now recorded his delight in the business of sailing, and his time with friends Martin Dyson, Barnabas 'Ahongalu and other new contacts. As they travelled south, they called first at Tonga where he left Lydia and the four little girls with her brother, the Reverend James W. Wallis and his wife Jeannie, and saw King George Taufa'ahau Tupou I. They sailed on to Fiji where he observed colonial life. He reported that 'we had an opportunity of seeing that famous personage [Chief Cakobau]. He was much more free than King George of Tonga but I think George is very much his superior in everything becoming a King.'[5] In Samoa there was no single clear leader but a continual jostling for position and power with no resolution in sight.

On 19 January 1869 the *Wesley* sailed in through the sandstone cliffs of Sydney Heads. Last time George Brown had been in Sydney he was young, unknown, newly ordained and without island experience. Now he returned as Chairman of the Samoa District and anticipated taking part in debates. Among the men who had travelled from all the British colonies of the region was his beloved uncle Thomas Buddle from New Zealand, with news of the extended family. In

3   Ibid., 26 June 1868.
4   Ibid., 28 September 1868.
5   Ibid., 6 September 1869.

Samoa, their church meetings were comparatively small. In Sydney, seventy men gathered in the Centenary Chapel in York Street for the General Conference of the Australasian Wesleyan Methodist Church, with ladies in the gallery and journalists with pencils poised. For so long he had felt cut off from the support of his fellows, believing that 'in seasons of trial and deprivation the missionary was forgotten and that the interest in missions and missionaries almost extinct.'[6]

His first chance to tell his story was at the public Missionary Meeting, along with others who told of Fiji, Tonga, New Zealand and work among the Chinese in Melbourne. Although he could not have imagined the future, George Brown used this opportunity to present two themes that were to be continuing motifs through his life: the importance of the ministry of island people in the region and the need for the Church to continue to move into new areas of ministry. With the imposing Barnabas 'Ahongalu and Tevita Kata on the platform beside him, Brown could see that these men were not only exotic in the eyes of the audience but impressive. He assured the audience that there were many other men of similar calibre and that 'the great hope of the missionary was in their agency ... the time would come when, in order to extend the operation of this and other agencies, those islands would have to be given up to native teachers.'[7]

He spoke with great respect for the work in Samoa of the LMS, their 'great and glorious work', and the excellence of their translation of scripture into the Samoan language. He went on, referring to LMS plans to pioneer new work in New Guinea, 'They taught us a lesson too. There are islands to which he and others longed to go—to Papua, and all the adjacent islands, and *they would gladly receive the order*.'[8] Although, he admitted, religion and social stability was in a low state in Samoa, even so he believed that many faithful Samoan Christians would be found among those who gathered around the throne of God.

If Brown had hoped that the meeting would see the virtue of withdrawing from Samoa in order to pioneer new work, those hopes were dashed when Barnabas stood to speak. Barnabas, a natural and confident orator, spoke in Samoan with George Brown translating. 'Although our languages are different, yet we have one scheme pointed out to get to heaven,' he said. In parable form Barnabas told the story of how he had gone with the Reverend Peter Turner as pioneer Wesleyan missionaries from Tonga to Samoa in 1835, planting a new garden for God. For over thirty years he had laboured in that plantation even though their mission had been withdrawn. He had returned to try to restore the garden, now overgrown and full of weeds, to health: 'We are trying hard to overthrow the Devil in those lands,' he said.[9] Listening to the cheers as Barnabas sat down,

6 *Sydney Morning Herald*, 26 January 1869.
7 Ibid.
8 Ibid.
9 Ibid.

Brown knew that the audience had heard the passion of Barnabas to continue Methodist ministry in Samoa and had been deaf to his own plea for new pioneer work in other regions. Immediately, the next speaker began at great length to urge the audience to new heights of energy and faith, to understand that the needs of the Pacific Islands were the responsibility of the churches of Australasia. His speech was greeted with loud and impassioned cheering.[10]

It was no surprise, then, when a few days later the subject of whether the WMMS should withdraw from Samoa was debated, that the final decision was 'that the Mission of this Society in Samoa ought to be sustained in full efficiency.' A letter was to be sent to the LMS Secretary in Australia informing him of the decision and 'stating that it is under the necessity of declining any further communication with the LMS on this subject.'[11] A deputation of senior church officials would travel to Samoa when Brown returned to ensure that their decision was unambiguous. Whether Brown was relieved or frustrated by this answer, he had been given a clear direction. The tension caused by the collision of two Societies in Samoa was not to be relieved.[12]

Through that summer, George Brown stayed in Sydney speaking in churches about Samoa. As the weather cooled into autumn, the mission ship returned. At the end of April, Brown sailed from New South Wales, in company with Dyson and other mission staff including the Reverend Shirley Baker and his family returning to Tonga. George and Lydia Brown were joyfully re-united in Tonga and with their children sailed back to Samoa and their new house on Savai'i. They were both refreshed and in better health. They would need to be.

* * *

Samoa was not a simple or comfortable island paradise. The endless elbowing and shoving between representatives of territorial and traditional interests was becoming more insistent. Interleaved with the layers of tradition and local prestige were the interests of foreigners seeking to invest in island land and trade. Brown recalled the stories his father-in-law Wallis told of the way Māori people had lost land to foreigners in earlier decades, and was worried. Shifting alliances among those who identified with a particular church were often more political or traditional than religious or theological in basis. Samoan communities were at odds with traditional enemies, religious communities in rivalry with each other, new traders and settlers jostling for space with traditional landowners. By the end of 1869 Brown's colleague Austin wrote that Samoa was 'in a state

---

10 Ibid.
11 Minutes of General Missions Committee of Australasian Conference of Wesleyan Methodist Church, 1865–1898, 28 January 1869, ML MOM 1-4 CY 354.
12 *Sydney Morning Herald*, 26 January 1869.

of unrest from one end to the other.'[13] And despite the encouraging visit of the church officials from Sydney, the Wesleyan mission was still on shaky ground; two of the four British missionaries had gone and a third was anxious to leave. They were grateful when Lydia's brother James W. Wallis joined them in Samoa, but James soon decided that it was a mistake for the Wesleyans to be in Samoa. By the time George Brown reported the birth of his fifth child, a son George Frederick, in March 1870, his sparse journal was a record of illnesses, hard travels, and 'the War'. Once again, childbirth had been hazardous for Lydia and when she began to haemorrhage George had been afraid that she would die; far from skilled help, he used every remedy he knew. Both Lydia and baby Fred lived but they knew that there was no room for complacency.

The continual conflict between Samoan groups during that period led to a grim loss of life and destruction of villages and subsistence food crops. In an attempt to persuade the Samoan communities with whom they had strong connections to make peace with their enemies, the missionaries of the LMS and the WMMS along with men working in consular affairs and trade entered into an alliance in August 1870. On the island of Upolu the deputation of white men supported by Samoan teachers, students and Church members approached the assembled Chiefs and Rulers to plead for peace. George Brown was asked to act as their spokesman: 'No one else was disposed to accept the work and so I had to consent though quite unprepared,' he wrote. Doing their best to follow formal Samoan protocol, the deputation presented to the Chiefs, 'our united request for them to make peace. We got no very decided answer but the general opinion was that a good impression was created.'[14]

There followed a time of intense negotiation and attempts at diplomacy and, on 25 August 1870, Brown wrote in his journal that they had met and 'agreed to make peace very much to our satisfaction.'[15] The peace, however, was to be short-lived. It would be said that the interference of meddling white men could never resolve the deep divisions that existed. The strife would continue for at least another three years. Public strife was mirrored by the smaller conflicts within the churches, where temporary periods of calm were brief.

On Palm Sunday, 2 April 1871, Lydia Brown was taken ill in chapel. Their five children were all suffering from whooping cough and needed a lot of care, broken sleep and anxiety adding to Lydia's own health problems. For a week she suffered what was described as enteritis and by Easter Day, her children were brought to her bedside to say goodbye. Brown told a friend, 'we almost despaired of a favourable outcome.... It was a most anxious and trying time for me but

---

13   J.S. Austin, *Missionary Enterprise and Home Service: A Story of Mission Life in Samoa and Circuit Work in New South Wales* (illustrated), Sydney: J.A. Packer, 1922, p. 150.

14   Brown, Journal, 18 August 1870.

15   Ibid., 25 August 1870.

God was with us.'[16] Lydia lived, but anxiety remained. George and Lydia Brown had been in Samoa now for nearly eleven years. Lydia had had no break from the demanding work and life in the tropics. Both George and Lydia experienced frequent ill-health; Brown was frequently semi-crippled with a swollen leg and eye infections troubled his vision. They were concerned over the education of their children as their older daughters approached adolescence; Lydia had been teaching them with the help of Jeannie Wallis, wife of J.W. Wallis, and both girls were gifted. Unfortunately, there seemed to be little chance that the Brown family could leave Samoa. Both the Austin and Wallis households intended to leave Samoa. Brown confided to new Mission Secretary Stephen Rabone that, if both men left Samoa, he would be forced to stay on, despite their health problems and the need for their children to attend school. 'The only plan I can see at present is for me to send Mrs B. and the children up to New Zealand and stay down here a while myself.'[17]

* * *

Many years later, when George Brown gathered his memories and documents to be shaped into the story of a long life, he chose to limit the material he selected to represent fourteen years in the islands of Samoa. In a single chapter he described Samoan landscape, language, customs, cyclones, local warfare, the hazards of island travel and some key events. There were few personal references. In a single paragraph he wrote a summary of the long-running difficulties between the LMS and the WMMS. 'I do not think it necessary to enter here into details of the dispute (now, I believe, amicably settled).'[18] There was a passing reference, unexplained, to 'times of depression we had when we seemed to be labouring in vain,'[19] but the impression is given that the Samoan period was not of sufficient interest to warrant much attention in the long volume.[20] Brown's journal was neglected during much of the period from 1870 until he finally left Samoa in 1874. However, many letters were written and have survived. These records suggest that much material was deliberately left out of the formal autobiography, not because it was dull but because much of the period was frustrating, painful and deeply discouraging.[21]

No mission region was without its problems. In Fiji some mission staff attracted criticism for buying land and property for private use, against mission policy. In Tonga there was dissension among the missionaries which led to some

---

16   Ibid., 2–10 April 1871; Brown letter to S. Rabone, 14 April 1871, in Brown, Letter Book, 1871–76, ML A1686-2 CY2767.
17   Brown to Rabone, 14 April 1871.
18   George Brown, *George Brown: Pioneer-Missionary and Explorer: An Autobiography*, London: Hodder and Stoughton, 1908, p. 29.
19   Brown, *George Brown: Pioneer, Missionary and Explorer*, p. 35.
20   In a manuscript of 536 pages, only thirty pages were given to the period 1860–1874 in Samoa.
21   George Brown, Letter Book, 1871–76, ML A1686-2 CY 2767.

making charges against the moral character of Shirley W. Baker to which he made counter-charges of libel. Brown told a friend that Baker was 'too smooth-tongued for me and so he never stood *very* high in my opinion.'[22] In Samoa, Wesleyan Methodist Mission colleagues were at odds over whether or not they should remain in that country, and in a troubling twist, Brown's chief antagonist was his own brother-in-law, James Wallis. Brown was persuaded that, if the General Conference had made a decision to remain, then it was his duty to continue his work there. Wallis disagreed. Over the next years, Brown wrote one letter after another to Wallis. In May 1871 Brown wrote:

> You are a Methodist preacher and promised honestly and solemnly to obey the Australasian Conference and to labour where ever they choose to appoint you; they have decided over and over again on the strength of the evidence which was enough for them that they ought in justice to our people here to resume our Mission here and with that and with your own consent they have appointed you here. Perhaps they are wrong, you at all events think they are but that doesn't at all affect the matter, so long as they rule, you as a Christian man pledged to them are bound to obey.[23]

If Wallis was unhappy in Samoa, Brown argued, he should seek a change of Districts and bring his opinions through the usual channel for change, the Conference. However, he should remember that:

> letter upon letter has been written, protest, resolutions etc have been showered upon them and still they profess their decided opinion that they are pledged to Samoa and mean to remain. I went to Sydney to satisfy myself and did so; 'twas no silent vote that was given in Conference ... they had had the whole affair up over and over again and at one time had given two days to it and nothing could be clearer ... simple justice and a sense of duty and right compel us to advocate a certain course which we feel to be painful both to ourselves and others.[24]

Brown concluded that Samoan communities would form alliances—and break them—for their own reasons and not because of decisions made in London, Auckland or Sydney. He asked the question, 'By what law Independent, human or divine are they to be denied the right to choose their own Pastors?'[25] To another missionary he wrote,

---

22 Brown to Frank Firth, 5 May 1871.
23 Brown to James W. Wallis, 10 May 1871.
24 Ibid.
25 Brown to Frank Firth, 20 July 1871.

Let the way be clear, let it appear to be His will for us to go, to give up our Mission here, and I am ready at once to do so. I have nothing to reproach myself with nor should I feel grieved or ashamed if the whole affair was to collapse the day I left.... You know well that I have ever regretted the necessity which I firmly believe to exist for our Mission here but I do not and cannot see how a breach of trust (if it was one) can justify another one now ... our LMS Brethren and we ourselves are and have been reaping what was sown in past years.[26]

It was an awkward situation. Brown and Wallis were tied together as brothers-in-law, with mutual love and respect for Lydia and Jeannie as well as ties with the extended Wallis family in New Zealand. James Wallis was concerned for his sister Lydia who was exhausted, often ill and by late 1871 was expecting a sixth baby. He tactlessly told his brother-in-law that he considered that Brown would murder his sister and commit suicide himself if the Brown family did not take leave soon. George Brown was offended. To Wallis he wrote, 'You call it Murder and Suicide to stay, neither of which I wish to commit,'[27] but he complained to others that the only reason he was not free to take leave was because his brother-in-law was neither willing nor competent to be left in charge in Samoa. While Brown admitted that he needed to 'guard against a tendency to pugnacity' he still cared about Wallis, but was becoming increasingly irritated with him.[28]

* * *

In between violent bouts of letter writing, Brown was continuing his regular work. There were the long journeys around Savai'i, the visits to villages and congregations, the teaching and class meetings, preaching, district meetings, medical work and dealing with small conflicts. Their home was usually open to their Samoan neighbours. Samoan people worked beside Lydia in the house, played with their children and joined them for daily family prayer. The Browns frequently spoke Samoan, or a mix of Samoan and English, in their home. They were both sincere in cultivating 'those relations with the Natives in [their] own family or outside which are generally thought necessary to a Missionary's success and influence.'[29] George and Lydia had lived in Samoa for so long that it was a familiar home with their plentiful food gardens, cows, chickens, pigs and three horses. Brown told his sister Anna in far Lincolnshire, 'We like Samoa and on the whole are perhaps as comfortable here as we should be elsewhere ... more independent here.... Our time is fully occupied.'[30]

---

26 Brown to J. Osborne, 10 July 1871, from Saleaula.
27 Brown to James W. Wallis, 10 May 1871.
28 Ibid.
29 Ibid.
30 Brown to his sister, Mrs Anna Caukwell and Rev. Henry Caukwell, 13 November 1971.

Brown was developing what would become a life-long interest in local tropical flora and fauna, as well as language, ethnology and culture—beginning collections in several fields of endeavour. Brown was also a keen observer of the political movements of the region. Colonial powers were jockeying for power in locations across the Pacific that were perceived to be strategic or had commercial value. There were already German and American traders in the islands and Brown believed that soon Samoa would become either a German or an American colony. By December 1871 he would observe that 'speculators are buying up land in every direction and we can be sure that it will not be allowed to remain idle.'[31] Land sales in the next few years were to reach such proportions, and involve such complexities of individual or communal ownership, that the time would come when land claims would amount to two and a half times the total land mass of the islands of Samoa.[32] Continued unrest between Samoan clans meant that they had no shared strength to resist colonial incursions; Brown described them as a rope of sand.

* * *

Piles of paper and buckets of ink flowed from Brown's desk as he kept up a lively correspondence with colleagues in Sydney, Auckland, London, Apia, Fiji and Tonga. Brown had opinions on everything.[33] With long periods between writing a letter and receiving a response, dreams were not tempered by other wisdoms; misunderstandings grew and mild arguments developed muscles. At times he was forced to apologise for immoderate language in a letter, and he told a correspondent, 'A good rule for many of us is never to touch a pen until 48 hours after any exciting letter.'[34] At such a distance from the theological niceties of the British Church, he was sometimes at odds with the accepted doctrines of the day, describing his own views as 'heterodox'. 'I have no faith myself in extreme views and not much in very sudden conversions,' he told a friend. He did not believe that he would be at home in the Anglican system, which would not suit 'any intellectual man of an ardent and impulsive temperament.'[35] He preferred the model of the Wesleyan Methodists. He strongly affirmed the work of the Bible Society as they provided scriptures for many language groups. 'This will make them Christians,' he wrote, 'I don't care a fig to make them into Methodists, they will adopt that if it suits them best.'[36] While on one hand he was very antagonistic toward the Catholic Church, he also insisted that 'I am no

---

31   Brown to S. Rabone, 18 December 1871.
32   I.C. Campbell, *Worlds Apart: A History of the Pacific Islands*, Christchurch: Canterbury University Press, 2003 [1989], pp. 114–15.
33   For correspondence in the period 1871–1874, see Brown, Letter Book, 1871–76.
34   Brown to J. Osborne, 10 July 1871.
35   Brown to W. Fletcher, 20 July 1871.
36   Brown to J.W. Wallis, 10 May 1871.

bigot and never try to keep up and perpetuate miserable sectarian distinctions. I am not generally considered narrow minded in other matters, my danger has been thought to consist in an opposite tendency.'[37]

Two themes played in counterpoint for Brown over the period between 1871 and 1874. The bright strand was his growing vision for moving into new fields with the gospel. A darker strand was the exhausting debate over the presence of the Wesleyan Methodists in Samoa. An LMS missionary hurt him by suggesting that the LMS had the 'feast' of good Christians in Samoa and the Methodists only had the 'leavings' that no one else wanted. More painful still was the sharp division of opinion with his brother-in-law Wallis. Brown complained to General Secretary Stephen Rabone that Wallis 'really talks and acts more like one with a shingle short than anything else.'[38] Wallis was threatening to send a long letter of complaint against Brown to Conference, which was, Brown declared, 'full of old stale matter and a lot of gross misrepresentation.'[39] In one of many letters exchanged between them, Brown told Wallis that he and Austin would defend themselves, but urged his brother-in-law to reconsider sending this material into the very public gaze of Conference. 'If you send this paper up it will certainly cause a great deal of unpleasantness if not something worse … [it] must end in pain for us all, both here and at home.'[40] Over many months the debate continued, with vacillation from Wallis about whether or not to send his document.[41] Rumours and gossip spread among the LMS community. Wallis demanded a transfer to another district then changed his mind at the last minute. Relationships with members of the LMS continued to be frayed around the edges, even though there were times when the Brown home was crowded with friendly LMS house guests at the same time as some of their leaders were criticising their host. To add to the discomfort of a difficult relationship, Brown carried the daily pain of a grossly swollen leg as well as continual concern about the welfare and education of his children. It was not a happy time.

* * *

News of a murder shook George Brown. Anglican Bishop John Coleridge Patteson, who had impressed him so much when he sailed with him from England to New Zealand in 1855, had been murdered on 20 Sept 1871 while visiting in the area of Santa Cruz in the eastern Solomon Islands. It was said that the killing was related to 'blackbirding' village men for plantation labour forces. Perhaps this

---

37   Brown to J. Osborne, 10 July 1871.
38   Brown to S. Rabone, 24 June 1872.
39   Brown to F. Firth, 10 November 1871.
40   Brown to J.W. Wallis, 7 November 1871.
41   Brown to Rabone, 24 August 1871, 20 September 1871.

news jolted Brown out of any lethargy caused by local disappointments and frustration. Time was limited. Who knew how long any missionary had to bring some change? There was no time to waste.

Brown had been thinking about other mission possibilities for a long time, almost as long as he had been living in Samoa. In 1862, in a light-hearted note about his work load to then Mission Secretary Eggleston, he suggested that he might slow down when he was older, 'that is if you don't send me away to Papua or some such place.'[42] The following year, on hearing Martin Dyson talk of distant Papua, Brown assured Eggleston that Dyson could not be spared from Samoa but 'if you want to send, let some of us young ones go.' He added, 'It is a great field and there must be plenty of room for all. May God hasten the time where those poor Papuans also shall be won for Christ.'[43] In his journal at a time of particular conflict with the LMS in 1868 he had complained 'It seems a great waste of men and money to keep us here. I wish I could go to Fiji or New Guinea anywhere out of this.'[44] He was very outspoken when he heard that some Methodist benefactors in Sydney had sent generous funds for missions in Europe; this was not right, he declared, 'so long as India, China, New Guinea, New Caledonia and hundreds of other places have not the Gospel. I would never give one sixpence for those Missions.'[45] He told his brother-in-law William Fletcher, 'I wish we could make an attack on New Guinea, there's room enough there for all. I will go any time if only they will raise the wind.'[46] Now, in 1871, Brown learned that the LMS had at last taken the first step in a plan that had been mooted for many years; they were planning to begin new mission work in New Guinea.

* * *

Early in November 1871 Brown began a marathon of letter writing with letters for family, colleagues and the Mission Board. As he wrote letter after letter his new idea took clearer shape. He had heard that the Board was considering selling the *John Wesley*. Don't sell the mission ship, he urged, but use it in a different way. 'I am going to propose to the Committee *not* to sell the Wesley,' he told Wallis, 'but let her take up New Guinea doing our work and also that of the LMS for the present.'[47] To Austin he wrote,

> No single Society can hope to take up that immense Island, FAR larger than Great Britain. Let us have a District marked out and let us begin with Native Teachers. Let also the *Wesley* do the LMS work at the same

---

42   Brown to J. Eggleston, 21 November 1862.
43   Ibid., 27 July 1863.
44   Brown, Journal, 20 May 1868.
45   Brown to J.W. Wallis, 7 November 1871.
46   Brown to W. Fletcher, 20 July 1871.
47   Brown to J.W. Wallis, 7 November 1871.

time ... there would be no clashing in future.... We could get Teachers from Fiji, Tonga and Samoa and one Missionary could go every year with one of the LMS.[48]

To colleagues in Fiji he explained his idea that instead of 'the old plan of crowding expensive Missionaries into a field' they should work more with trained islander agents. 'I wish we could plant ten or twelve of your Fiji Institution men under the charge of some good Native Minister on Papua, they would soon make themselves felt.'[49]

By the time he wrote his formal proposal to Secretary Rabone, the principles had been formed. He proposed a new work, in a region negotiated with the LMS where there would be no risk of future competition, staffed by trained islanders rather than Europeans and supported by regular communication, supervision and supplies by the mission ship. It was a model for pioneer work very like that of the LMS.

> I oppose the sale of our vessel with all my might, and propose that she be employed more exclusively as a mission vessel in opening out new fields.... I propose that we have a part of New Guinea marked out for us, and that we at once begin there with a band of native teachers placed under one or two of our native missionaries ... visited every year by the *Wesley* with a deputation, and as soon as possible, having a few European missionaries among them for general oversight and translation work ... we also could soon find plenty of good and pious men to carry out the plan.... We must excite an interest, and then the funds will rise.... If you begin a fund, I know one who will guarantee £5 for five years, and will go himself, if wanted.[50]

Perhaps, if he was honest, Brown knew that his grand vision was only in part a call from God for the sake of the populations who had never heard the Christian gospel. In the mail bag that carried his dream of a new mission enterprise were also letters of criticism and recrimination over local grievances. His vision for New Guinea also offered a way of escape from the bondage and limitations of Samoa.

When replies came from the Board in Sydney many months later, they learned that the Board saw their dispute as a storm in a teacup. They realised that the Board was not persuaded by the Wallis arguments that they should reconsider the Methodist presence in Samoa. The Board directed that they should talk

---

48   Brown to J. Austin, 7 November 1871.
49   Brown to J. Nettleton, Fiji, 10 November 1871.
50   Brown to S. Rabone, 14 November 1871, 18 December 1871.

directly to each other and work things out. Sadly, relations were soured still further. Brown's enthusiastic letter about beginning a new mission did not even rate a mention in the Board Minutes.[51]

Isolated and unhappy, Brown struggled on. Lydia was busy with their sixth baby, Geoffrey Patteson Brown, born 23 January 1872. With great grief, they had risked sending their two eldest daughters Lizzie and Amy away alone on a small sailing vessel to their grandparents in Auckland. Their relationship with James W. Wallis was still difficult. His good friend and colleague John Austin had left, taking his ailing wife away to the colonies, where she was to die. Far from giving permission for the Brown family to take leave, the Board directed the *John Wesley* to bypass Samoa entirely on its 1873 voyage, citing delays due to weather and needed repairs. Brown's ill health, aggravated by the physical strain of island travel and the emotional strain of frequent disappointments, dragged him down into depression. Samoan Christians did not always live up to their protestations of faith; the power of the traditional attitudes out-ranked the strength of the new religion. Warfare between Samoan tribal groups was always either actual or threatened during that time, and the political divisions were echoed by denominational divisions; one allegiance was linked to the other with shifting loyalties playing out in the social, political and religious spheres. Brown was worried about the way Samoan communities were selling their land to foreigners, and about the dim prospects for stable government in the region.[52]

Late in 1872, Brown was shocked to learn of the sudden death of his trusted mentor, Mission Secretary Stephen Rabone on 21 July 1872. Now, without their leader, the Mission Board was distracted by many other things. Questions in the letters from Wallis and Brown were not addressed until a year after they had been received, when new General Secretary for Missions, the Reverend Benjamin Chapman, took up the reins. The Board once again dismissed the Wallis proposal that the Methodists should withdraw from Samoa. The view from Samoa was very different. Brown felt that his hands were tied. Over the months the poison of suspicion and criticism had been infecting the body of missionaries, both the WMMS and the LMS. Two leaders of the LMS, George Turner and Henry Nisbet, were amassing a long list of grievances against the WMMS and Brown in particular. By the end of 1873 yet another long letter of accusations was on its way to the Board.[53]

George Brown knew that some of the LMS leaders were angry with him, but perhaps he had not imagined the bitter force of a letter that LMS leaders Dr.

51   Minutes of Wesleyan Methodist Missions Board, 1865–1898, 19 February 1872, 26 February 1872, ML MOM1-4 CY 354.
52   Brown to F. Firth, 12 January 1872.
53   Dr. George Turner and Rev. Henry Nisbet, letter from Apia, 16 December 1873, quoted in Minutes of Wesleyan Methodist Missions Board, 1865–1898, ML MOM 1-4 CY 354, 23 February 1874.

George Turner and the Reverend Henry Nisbet sent to the Wesleyan Methodist Board in Sydney in December 1873. The Board, when it met to debate the letter in February 1874, was faced with a diatribe. Turner and Nisbet wrote that although 'the most cordial sympathy and good will ought to exist between the agents of the two societies' this was not true in Samoa.

> The presence of Wesleyan Missionaries in Samoa is a serious breach of missionary confidence, and unwarrantable violation of deliberate and repeated engagements entered into between the Directors of the parent Societies in England, a sinful misappropriation of Mission funds and waste of Missionary strength and a continually felt hindrance to our work … some of their [WMMS] agents who have laboured or are now labouring in Samoa, and especially the Rev George Brown, have made it their custom to resort to acts which are in manifest violation of the sacred engagement and promises entered into between the agents of the Australasian Wesleyan Conference and the London Missionary Society.[54]

Turner and Nisbet went on with accusations that 'unseemly strife' between the agents of the LMS and the WMMS was causing 'perpetuation of sectarian distinctions'. Though, they conceded, George Brown claimed to forbid proselytising, his Samoan workers ignored this. His willingness to forgive, prematurely, those who had been disciplined by the LMS for engaging in tribal warfare had led to LMS leadership being 'prevented from the strict exercise of discipline by the fear of losing their people,' who threatened to leave in a body. Brown was accused of recently purchasing several plots of land 'where there are at present no Wesleyans' and that at least one was for a WMMS chapel. The letter concluded with a request that WMMS officials meet with LMS people in Samoa for a consultation on the problems, at which time they would provide proof 'of all the above assertions which we will be prepared to lay before the United Conference should you accede to our request.'[55]

The formal reply came from the deliberations of the New South Wales and Queensland Wesleyan Methodist Conference in February 1874. Conference replied that they were offended by the discourtesy of the original letter and declined the request for a consultation in Samoa. Such a consultation, they believed, would 'virtually resolve itself into a court of judgment on the character and conduct of the Chairman' Brown,[56] who was planning to leave Samoa in any case, and Conference requested that the LMS deal directly with the official leadership of the Wesleyan Methodist Conference. They repeated their 'unshaken confidence' in their agent George Brown and quoted the recent

---

54 Ibid.
55 Ibid.
56 Minutes of New South Wales and Queensland Conference of Wesleyan Methodist Church, February 1874, included in Minutes of Wesleyan Methodist Missions Board, 1865–1898.

resolution of the Samoa District Meeting, which mentioned their 'highest regard for his Christian character and its admiration of the earnest, conscientious and self-denying manner in which, during a period of 13 years he has devoted himself to the work of elevating and Christianising the Natives of Samoa.'[57]

They did not mention the latest letter from Brown, which set out his own defence against the accusations and suggested that the LMS people assumed 'that the Natives could be parcelled out into Pens like so many Sheep or Cattle without any regard for their own feelings and inclinations.'[58] The resolution concluded on a defiant note, stating that the WMMS 'asserts its perfect freedom to obey its convictions of duty and the indications of Providence.'[59]

Whatever others might be saying about him, George Brown was beginning to detach himself from life in Samoa. He and his family needed a holiday, whether or not those in authority over him were willing to entertain his vision for a new mission somewhere in the northern islands of New Guinea. Some suggested that he return to New Zealand or New South Wales, but the idea of a suburban congregation was now as alien to him as once the community of a Samoan village had been. He dreaded having his 'feelings rasped by any ignorant and miserly fellows at Quarterly Meetings ... I could never beg for my salary.' Nor was he eager to travel around as a missionary deputation, entertaining indifferent congregations with tales of exotic Samoa. 'I have no ambition to do the Dancing Bear business about the country,' he told Wallis Sr.[60] In a letter to his daughters in Auckland he encouraged them 'always to trust God not merely believe in him,'[61] but there were times when he found this hard to do. It was hard to settle to anything when, he hoped, the mission ship would soon arrive to take them away. The every-day supervision of a large District had to go on, but even that could be exhausting. In January 1874, Lydia went with him to spend time with new young missionaries, the Reverend James Mathieson and his wife, at Lufilufi on Upolu. Lydia was with him as they struggled to deliver Mrs Mathieson's first baby, an infant who almost died. Their later journey home was difficult; a capsized boat, which left their clothing soaked and Brown's bundle of correspondence damp and a blur of smudged ink, a night outdoors then a long walk through bush and more than five miles along the shore. Samoan companions tried to carry Lydia over 'a rather formidable bush road but she got down and walked nearly all the way at a stiff pace. There is no other missionary's wife who would dream of attempting to do it,' Brown told his father-in-law proudly.[62] As for himself, it just made him feel tired.

---

57   Ibid., quoting Minutes of Wesleyan Methodist Mission, Samoa District, 2 October 1873.
58   Brown to B. Chapman, 1 January 1874.
59   Minutes of New South Wales and Queensland Conference of Wesleyan Methodist Church, February 1874.
60   Brown to James Wallis Sr., 28 May 1873.
61   Brown to Mary Elizabeth and Amy Brown, 23 December 1873.
62   Brown to Wallis Sr., 23 January 1874.

The District Meeting had sent off the retirement Minute for him months earlier. His health was still not good and now they had to wait for the *John Wesley* to come to take them away. Their boxes were nearly all packed up for the journey. If they had known that the *John Wesley* was still delayed in Sydney waiting for repairs, and had still not left for the islands by the end of March 1874, they might not have bothered packing so soon. Brown continued to question visiting sea captains about possible locations for a new mission, telling Chapman, 'Tis no use we thinking of the Solomons. The Bishop goes there and it is best not to interfere. I think we ought to take up New Britain and New Ireland. They are large Islands and unoccupied.... I will gather up all the information I can to take up with me.'[63] If they had heard the enthusiastic debates in the distant Board room about new possibilities for work in Port Darwin, North Australia among the Chinese community—with a side glance toward the presence of many Aboriginal people in that region—and the request for missionaries from French officials in New Caledonia, they might have despaired of anything coming of Brown's dreams for New Guinea.[64] He was still under a cloud of uncertainty about how his church at home viewed his actions in Samoa and knew he would have to face an enquiry by the Board.

The only thing they could do was to wait.

---

63   Brown to B. Chapman, 27 January 1874.
64   Minutes of General Missions Committee of Australasian Conference of Wesleyan Methodist Church, 1865–1898, 23 February, 30 March, 7 May 1874, ML MOM 1-4 CY 354.

5. 'We are all in God's hands...'

Samoa, Australia, New Zealand, Fiji
1874–1875

The brand new journal was a sign. George Brown's old journal had declined into blank pages. For months he had thought that there was nothing worth recording. Now he was ready for a fresh start. The opening entries were bald and brief: '27 June 1874 Saturday *Wesley* arrived at Saleaula late in the evening.' '1 July Wed Left Samoa about 10 am.' Nothing more. At the time he was too busy, too emotionally exhausted and too focused on the future to record the tears, gifts and speeches of appreciation and farewell from their Samoan and missionary friends. The mission ship, months late, had come at last and that was enough. For eight weeks the Browns, together with James and Jeannie Wallis, travelled first to Rotuma, where they had a happy family reunion with Lydia's sister Lizzie and her husband William Fletcher, then to Fiji for mission meetings and finally through storms to Sydney. In harbour once more, George recognised that Lydia had not just been suffering from seasickness; she was pregnant with their seventh child.

The *John Wesley* came into Sydney Harbour on 24 August 1874. George Brown knew he must face the Mission Board alone. James Wallis, with health failing, had travelled on to New Zealand almost immediately. Would the Mission Board see him as a discomforting maverick or as a visionary leader? He came to them under a cloud to face the criticism of his brother-in-law, the accusations of the London Missionary Society (LMS) and possible censure for actions in Samoa. He was known to the Board mostly through his many long, agitated and demanding letters rather than as a friend. He was coming armed with a new scheme of action which he feared many of them would view with disapproval, or at best caution. Either he would be rebuked and disciplined, or he would be released from the limitations of Samoa to begin something new.

It was a strange meeting. Eighteen men, clergy and lay, met Brown on 9 September 1874 in the Methodist Book Depot in King Street. Brown was encouraged to see some old friends among the group, but he had reason to be apprehensive. They began with the discipline matter. The Wesleyan Methodists had been irritated with the attitude of the London Missionary Society leaders, Brown learned, ever since receiving the letter from them early in 1874, addressed to the Conference. The offending letter was re-read aloud, with their reply. They took strong exception to the language used, rejected the request for a meeting in

Samoa and determined to reserve their own judgment until they heard Brown's version of events. They were not inclined to promise either to withdraw or limit any future expansion.[1] George Brown gave his own explanation of his actions, giving specific examples and reasons in response to non-specific accusations. He pointed out that the LMS men had not given him a copy of their letter of complaint; if they had done so, he would have been able to answer them directly and honestly. This time he could speak persuasively, and not be limited to stating his case, as he had done many times, from the inky nib of a pen. By the time he had finished, and answered questions, the Mission Board recorded 'that this meeting is perfectly satisfied with the explanation given by Mr Brown.'[2] A formal response would be drafted, they told him, and sent to the LMS.[3] He need be anxious no more.

The fog had lifted at last. With great relief, he now painted a picture for the Board members. A new land. A new opportunity. A people who had never heard the name of Jesus. Indeed, a region that no Christian Church had ever even visited. A place where they would not be elbowing any other mission for space, or apologising for being there at all. He had been writing letters about it for so many years, but now he could let these men see the light in his eyes and hear the passion in his voice. Although he had never been to those strings of islands in the north, he had talked with sea captains who had sailed in those little-known waters; they spoke of mountainous coastlines and large populations, of tropical rain and active volcanoes, of the legendary sailors who had glimpsed the region over the past two hundred years—Tasman, Dampier, Carteret, Bougainville, D'Entrecasteaux, Hunter—and the handful of white traders who had attempted to live there, usually retreating in defeat. There were rumours of violence and cannibalism. But, he reminded his hearers, the same could have been said for Fiji forty years earlier, and only a few weeks earlier he had witnessed a generally Christianised Fiji. Best of all, he said, although the LMS had established new mission work on the south coast of the main island of New Guinea in 1872, they were a very long way from the region he was promoting. He displayed charts to illustrate this.[4] Would they permit at least an exploratory visit to the area in the north east known as New Britain and New Ireland?

---

1   Letter from Rev. Dr. Turner and Rev. Nesbit, London Missionary Society, Samoa to NSW and Queensland Conference of the Australasian Wesleyan Methodist Church, 1874, 16 December 1873; Letter from NSW and Queensland Conference of Wesleyan Methodist Church to London Missionary Society, Samoa per Dr. Turner and Rev. Nesbit, February 1874, p. 213, both in Minutes of General Missions Committee of Australasian Conference of Wesleyan Methodist Church, 1865–1898, ML MOM 1-4 CY 354.

2   Minutes of Wesleyan Methodist Missionary Society (WMMS) Board, 9 September 1874, ML MOM 1 CY 354.

3   Minutes of WMMS Board, 21 September 1874.

4   George Brown to J.W. Wallis, 12 September 1874, in George Brown, Letter Book, 1871–76, ML A1686-2 CY 2767.

How could they resist? After an initial assessment of their improved financial position, they made their decision. It was still a qualified agreement, and if he was serious about this plan he would need to do some significant fund-raising to support it, but they recorded that the Board

> regards with favour the proposal to send the Mission ship on her next voyage in March or April 1875 to visit the large Islands of New Ireland and New Britain with a view to the commencement of Missionary operations and if upon enquiry it should still appear that there are openings of importance and that the enterprise is practicable, it will give its sanction to the undertaking.[5]

The Mission Board was attracted to the proposed new field for mission not least because, in a climate of continued unease with the LMS, 'its inhabitants have never yet heard the glad tidings. We cannot, therefore, be charged with building upon other men's foundations.'[6] They approved Brown's proposal that a team of Fijian, Samoan and Tongan men be settled in that region and that a British missionary make regular visits.

That night, George Brown recorded in his Journal: 'I then introduced my plan for a New Mission and advocated it to the best of my ability. It was most favourably received and I have full permission to [agitate? advocate?] the affair. May God help us all.'[7]

* * *

After years of dreaming and frustration, Brown was now free to follow a new direction. Days after the turning point of the Board meeting, Lydia sailed for New Zealand with the younger children in the comfort of the *Hero*, a 1600-ton steam ship that plied between New Zealand and Australia. She would be reunited with her older daughters and her parents once more. Brown recorded, '15 Sept My dear wife and children left today 4.30 pm per *Hero*. I feel very desolate tonight without them but feel also that we are all in God's hands and that I am endeavouring to do his work.'[8] Two days later he sailed for Melbourne. The task of raising funds had begun.

---

5   Minutes of WMMS Board, 9 September 1874.
6   Benjamin Danks, *New Britain Mission: A Brief History*, Sydney: Australasian Wesleyan Missionary Society, Epworth Press, 1901, pp. 6–10.
7   George Brown, Journal, 9 September 1874, in George Brown, Journal, 1874–1876, ML A 1686-10-12 CY 2759.
8   Ibid., 15 September 1874.

Figure 2. George Brown 1875.

Source: Brown family album per favour Miss Nancy Joyce.

Figure 3. Lydia Brown 1875.

Source: Brown family album per favour Miss Nancy Joyce.

It was just as well that Lydia and her children were safely in the arms of her wider family in New Zealand. Lydia knew that, as deeply as he loved his family, George's mind was now focused on a new project, and she was glad for him. For the next four months George Brown was on the road, travelling, speaking, inspiring and then moving on to the next town, the next congregation, the next hosts and the next bed. Stories of Samoa were part of it, but now he was trying to persuade people in the colonies to support what was now called the New Mission, in a place he had never seen. The fundraising journey took Brown through the colony of Victoria in spring. The gold of wattle in bloom and signs of new wealth from the gold diggings fascinated the man from the tropics as he began in Ballarat, finding a responsive audience among the congregations of the city founded on gold mining. By train, by horse and buggy, by stage coach behind four horses, he traversed Victoria as summer warmed the countryside, speaking in churches in country towns and to large congregations in Melbourne churches and then on to Tasmania. With his growing connections with scientists in the fields of anthropology, botany and natural history, this gregarious man relished visits to museums, botanical gardens and the zoo, as well as cricket matches and picnics with friends. In December 1874, in Sydney the Mission Board decided, on the advice of sea captains, that the small cluster of the Duke of York Islands located between the larger islands of New Britain and New Ireland would be a relatively safe location from which to approach the 'warlike and savage' people of that region.[9] In Auckland, Lydia was in the eighth month of her pregnancy. Brown sailed from Melbourne for the South Island of New Zealand to begin another sequence of fund-raising meetings. He was still a long way from Auckland. Although he was impatient to reach his family, he managed to miss the train from Christchurch to the harbour at Lyttelton by one minute and 'I badgered the Station Master until he promised to let me go by luggage train.'[10] George Brown was finally united with his family on New Year's Day 1875.

* * *

Auckland did not feel like 'home', despite the presence of Lydia, his children and a wide circle of extended family and old friends. His mind was elsewhere. Although he managed to buy a small cottage in Hepburn Street, Ponsonby for his family during January, it needed renovations and was not ready to be occupied. While Lydia bore the heat of summer in her final weeks of pregnancy, George spoke at missionary meetings, persuading his New Zealand friends to support the New Mission. He also had long conversations with Captain Simpson and officers of the *Blanche,* poring over charts of the coastline of Blanche Bay. Lydia listened with alarm as they gave a very bad character to many of the people, although they assured the Browns that the people of the Duke of York Islands were friendly. Brown was single minded. The unborn child was perhaps a beloved distraction but he was focused on planning a great new enterprise.

Lydia's seventh baby, Mabel Wallis Brown, was born in the home of Lydia's parents, James and Mary Anne Wallis, at Grafton Road, Auckland on 23 January 1875, on little Geoffrey's third birthday. Her father George was there for the birth but was immediately impatient to be on his way. Six days after her birth he wrote, almost apologetically, to Chapman in Sydney explaining why on the 'earnest advice of the Brethren and friends here' he had decided not to sail for Sydney the next day but would wait another week and sail on *Hero,* hoping

9   Report brought from Captain Saunders of *Alacrity* in Minutes of WMMS Board, 3 December 1874.
10   Brown, Journal, 22 December 1874.

to arrive in Sydney by 13 February.[11] Perhaps he had shocked his Auckland friends by his disregard for his wife's needs. Yet he seemed to be torn between his family and the demands of the New Mission. He would not be the first or last person to wear the blinkers of preoccupation with a cause. Lydia was no doubt exhausted with a very new baby and six other children and experiencing the emotional and physical upheaval for a woman following childbirth. She knew that her husband was either fearless or more optimistic than realistic. George wrote, Lydia

> is still very weak and my departure just now would probably have a very dangerous effect on her. It is well known to her [from the captain and officers of the *Blanche*] that the New Britain natives are very fierce and though she has always said that if it is God's will that I go on with this work she will bear her share of the sacrifice and will not throw any obstacles in my way yet it is very evident that she is fretting about the matter and so all here advise my waiting a few days longer. I spoke to her last night about it and though she told me to do what I thought was my duty to God and to His work it was very plain that she felt it to be a great relief when I decided to stay. She is better this morning.[12]

Despite the fact that the house for his family was not yet ready, he found time to attend the New Zealand Wesleyan Conference that was meeting in Auckland, admitting to Chapman that he was writing his letter while sitting in the Conference. A steam launch for the new work was being donated and he was anxious to reach Sydney in order to organise it. He wrote, 'I should like very much to see my family quietly and comfortably settled before I leave as Mrs B. is quite unaccustomed to colonial life and feels some little anxiety about beginning housekeeping here and taking the sole charge of our children.'[13]

Lydia had no idea how long her husband would be away but knew it would be months. He was going into potentially dangerous situations. She had lost her trusted Samoan staff who had worked with her and helped with the children. She had also lost her ample kitchen garden with the chickens and cow, the familiar tropical diet and the place that had been home for fourteen years. Her parents and extended family were in Auckland, but once she left her parents' house, in many ways she would be alone.

George Brown left New Zealand again five weeks after arriving in Auckland and returned to Sydney to prepare for the New Mission. He assured Lydia that he expected to take a party of islander missionaries to New Britain, establish them

---

11 Brown to Chapman, 29 January 1875, in George Brown, Letter Book, 1871–76, ML A1686-2 CY 2767.
12 Brown to Chapman, 28 January 1875.
13 Ibid.

in suitable places, and then return with the *John Wesley*. By the time the Mission Board met on 22 February 1875 he was ready to share with them his latest plans and to be instructed by them.

* * *

For years Brown had been dreaming of new challenges, a New Mission. He had escaped at last from the narrow and crowded world of Samoa. Now he would have freedom to initiate, to plan, to try to communicate the message of Christ to people who had never heard it in any of its forms. Even the Board was giving him discretionary powers to modify their plan if necessary. Inevitably there were delays before he was free to leave. The new steam launch was not ready, supplies were not complete. The Board decided that the *Wesley* should carry arms; recent Anglican and LMS pioneer missions in the northern islands had done so, as the local people were said to be 'extremely savage'. A party of naturalists including Baron Anatole von Hügel requested permission to travel with the *John Wesley*. Brown was open to this, with his own scientific interests and links with the Australian Museum; that year there was much interest in New Guinea, with reports of exploration and debate about possible annexation of the region by a colonial power.

Not long before the *John Wesley* was due to sail for Fiji, Samoa and Tonga, to collect the planned pioneer band of island missionaries, news came that put the whole scheme in jeopardy. In Sydney they already knew that there was an epidemic of measles in Fiji, begun in January 1875. They had not realised how devastating the epidemic had been. In Fiji the death drums had been beating a rhythm of fear and tragedy; among the thousands of people who were estimated to have died within a few weeks were a great many Wesleyan church members, nine 'Native Ministers' and two hundred catechists. Men who had volunteered to be part of the pioneer group for the New Mission had died, or were too damaged in health to leave home. When the *Wesley* sailed from Sydney on 27 January 1875, they were under orders to bypass Fiji, only pausing to unload passengers and cargo at Levuka.

Brown was shocked when he arrived in Fiji. His whole scheme depended on having the help of men from the islands. Now he heard that, because of the measles infection in Fiji, Tonga was also applying strict quarantine to its borders to protect its people. The Fijian Methodist Church had lost a great many of their trained leaders.[14] Brown wrote disconsolately that a key minister who had intended to lead the pioneer group was now an invalid 'and we found it

---

14   A. Harold Wood, *Overseas Missions of the Australian Methodist Church, vol. 11, Fiji*, Melbourne: Aldersgate Press, 1978, p. 202.

difficult to get another in his place.'[15] If Fiji, which he knew had a fine system of training Fijian men for Christian ministry, could not help, Tonga was out of bounds and Samoa could afford few men, then the whole vision of beginning a New Mission based on the service of islander ministers and teachers would fail before it began.

At this point, George Brown chose to exercise the 'discretionary powers' the Board had permitted. Against instructions, he left the *Wesley* in harbour in Levuka. He met with the missionaries in Fiji and with their support told the Board, 'We fully considered the case and have decided to try and carry out our original plan.'[16] They could take fewer men, they would only take men who had already recovered from measles (the doctor had assured him that was safer) and they could take precautions against further risk of infection. 'On coming on board,' he wrote from Levuka, before any men had volunteered, 'they will be rubbed all over with Carbolic Acid and Oil and all old clothes destroyed.'[17] Confident that the man on the ground knew better than a distant Board, Brown set off through the islands to try out his new steam launch, named for his benefactor *Henry Reed,* in an attempt to recruit a new team. A faintly apologetic letter was sent to the Board justifying his actions. The Board noted the letter and, ominously, added to their Minutes, 'No action was taken.' Perhaps there was some vigorous debate about what should be done with a disobedient pioneer who took it on himself to 'deviate from instructions'.[18]

The journey through Fiji, unauthorised or not, confirmed for him many things about this new enterprise. He began in Levuka, with the beach community on the island of Ovalau, where some hundreds of whites lived. British authority had been established only months earlier in 1874 after the formal cession of Fiji; colonial law and order, he saw, could be applied to warring tribal groups. He visited the island of Viwa where his one-time mentor, Dr Richard Lyth, had served thirty years earlier in a time of great brutality and spiritual transformation; therefore transformation must be possible even in the most unpromising places. Then to visit Bau, a small island of great potency, where the power of chiefs and custom had terrified generations; now the killing stone where victims had been clubbed on their way to cannibal ovens had become a baptismal font. Brown knew that it was naïve to imagine that a Christianised and colonised Fiji was now free of problems. As the little steam launch made a noisy moonlight passage up the Rewa River, startling the villagers along the

---

15 Letter from George Brown from Levuka, Fiji, June 11, 1875, in George Brown, *Communications Respecting the Wesleyan New Mission to New Britain etc.*, Leaflet published Sydney, 20 July 1875, NLA JAFp BIBLIO F7493a. Men who had originally considered going with the pioneer group included the Reverend Ioeli Nau and Silas Naucukidi.

16 Ibid., Brown to Chapman, 21 May 1875, from Levuka, Fiji.

17 Ibid., Brown to Chapman, 21 May 1875, from Levuka, Fiji.

18 Minutes of WMMS Mission Board, 14 July 1875.

river banks with its fiery huffing and its siren, Brown was reminded of the murder of the Reverend Thomas Baker in that region six years earlier, as well as continued tension and violence between tribal groups, white landowners and the local people, the newly appointed British authorities and the planters and businessmen, and between planters and their migrant labour force. Yet the Fiji of 1875 was a very different place from the Fiji of 1835. The thought of being at the beginning of something new and raw, with the hope of witnessing a spiritual and social transformation, must have excited him. What he needed now was a team of workers.

At the mouth of the Rewa River, on the morning of 1 June 1875, George Brown met with a gathering of eleven missionaries—British and Tongan.[19] They had met at the Navuloa Theological Institution. Brown pleaded his cause. Unless a party of Fijian workers travelled with him to establish the New Mission, the whole vision would fade. If no Native Minister was available, could he appeal to the students at the Theological Institution? It was not an easy decision, given the newly fragile state of the Wesleyan Church in Fiji. Even so, these leaders made a critical decision. If suitable men and their families were willing and the colonial surgeon pronounced them fit, then Brown was authorised to form a team of Fijians to pioneer the New Mission. In the evening eighty-three Fijian theological students, many of them still recovering from measles, listened to Brown. Sitting in semi-darkness in the school hall, the light of a few small lamps casting deep shadows, the men heard Brown speak of the dream of going to a people who were known to be barbarous but had never heard the name of Christ. The people of those northern islands were cannibals, he told them, and beyond the rule of law. The climate was trying, diseases like malaria would threaten them and their families, the food would be unfamiliar, they would be alone and isolated from family and church support. It would undoubtedly be hard, and perhaps some might even die there, far from home. Were they willing to risk such a difficult challenge? 'The whole matter was placed before them in its blackest and darkest colours,' he would write later. 'Who is willing to volunteer?' he asked, but the Institution Principal Joseph Waterhouse interrupted him.[20] Waterhouse wisely urged the men to pause and consider, to talk with their wives, to listen first to God in quietness. Then they could give their answer.

The following day they met again. In later years the dramatic story of the Fijian students' response to the appeal for missionaries would be told and retold. At the time, Brown wrote simply, 'We had plenty of volunteers from the students;

19   This decision was signed by D.S. Wylie, Lorimer Fison, Arthur J. Webb, William Weir Lindsay, Joeli Bulu, Eroni Fotofili, Jemesa Havea, Tevita Nauhaamea, Meli Fifi, Joeli Nau and Joseph Waterhouse. Appendix 1, 1 June 1875, in Brown, *Communications Respecting the Wesleyan New Mission to New Britain*.
20   Brown to Chapman, 2 June 1875, in Brown, *Communications Respecting the Wesleyan New Mission to New Britain*, p. 5.

in fact they all volunteered.'[21] The impressive old missionary from Tonga, Joeli Bulu, with memories of his many hard years of struggle in wild and cannibal Fiji, rose to challenge the young men to imagine a day when the people of wild and cannibal New Britain also would be changed by the power of the gospel of Christ.[22] Nine men, six of them with wives and families, were chosen from the many and within days were on their way to Levuka ready to sail.

Their path was still not clear. On 12 June, Brown wrote 'We hoped to have sailed today but the action taken by the Government here has prevented us. We heard a slight rumour yesterday that they were going to throw some obstacles in our way.'[23] The 'slight rumour' was the understandable concern of the representatives of the newly established British Government in Fiji for the well-being of the Fijians; were they indeed volunteers and did they understand the hazards they faced? Brown was instructed to bring the mission party to the Council Chambers to meet Administrator E.L. Layard and Colonial Secretary John Thurston with the Executive in the Council Chambers.[24] Layard pointed out to Brown that as the Fijians were now British subjects it was his responsibility to ensure that they knew what they were doing. Brown then described the steps that had been taken, with his original instructions, the first group of men who had volunteered and the impact of the measles epidemic:

> then of our coming here and not being able to collect these men, and so having to make a second call for volunteers. I told them that in response to that call the whole of the students of Navuloa volunteered, that we had selected nine of the number who were now present, and finished by assuring them that no one had spoken to the teachers on the subject.[25]

Mr Layard spoke through an interpreter to the Fijians. They were British subjects, he explained, and could not be compelled to go and 'that he was responsible for their safety; that if any of them went away now and got killed and eaten the Government here would be blamed by the Home Government.' Layard then repeated that the people in New Britain were 'great cannibals and very fierce,' that the islands were unhealthy with great risk of disease, food was

---

21 Ibid.

22 Wood, *Overseas Missions of the Australian Methodist Church, vol. 11, Fiji*, pp. 65, 148–49.

23 Brown to Chapman, 12 June 1875, from Levuka, Fiji, in Brown, *Communications Respecting the Wesleyan New Mission to New Britain*, p. 6.

24 Present at the meeting were: 'His Honour the Administrator, E.L. Layard, Messers Thurston (Colonial Secretary), Horton, Bentley, Frazer, Ratu Mele, Ratu Tevita, Scott (interpreter), Secretary of Council, George Brown and nine teachers,' Appendix 3, in Brown, *Communications Respecting the Wesleyan New Mission to New Britain*.

25 Brown to Chapman, 12 June 1875, from Levuka, Fiji, in Brown, *Communications Respecting the Wesleyan New Mission to New Britain*, p. 6.

scarce, and they would be left alone without protection for months. If they still wanted to go, however, he would 'wish them God speed.'[26] One of the Fijians, Aminio Baledrokadroka, replied and Brown described the scene, as Aminio

> with deep feeling said that they were not surprised at what they had just been told, that it was not a new thing to them, as they had heard it all before from the missionaries before they volunteered for the service. He said, 'We have fully considered this matter in our hearts; no one has pressed us in any way. We have given ourselves up to do this work, and if we die, we die and if we live we live.'[27]

Layard and Thurston persisted. They did not want to hinder but to protect, they explained. To satisfy everyone, a statement in Fijian language was prepared to which the group agreed, then all signed an English translation. The statement read,

> We the undersigned Wesleyan teachers, do solemnly and truly declare that we were fully and carefully informed by the promoters of the mission to New Britain, New Ireland, etc., of the dangers which may be incurred to life and limb ... and we declare that fully knowing all this, we make an election to proceed on this mission of our own free will, not compelled thereto by orders or authority of any, but simply desirous of spreading the knowledge of the gospel of Christ among the heathen inhabitants of those islands.[28]

When Brown concluded his long communication with his home Board, he did not know how prophetic his next statement would be. He gave the Government officials

> credit for sincerity in the matter. They have instructions from home to look after and protect the Fijians; and may believe that we also are going to sacrifice our men in some fanatical way. As they suppose if any Fijians are murdered in the islands to which we are taking them, there will be an enquiry into the matter as they are now British subjects, and they naturally desire to be in a position to prove that all due precautions were taken by them to protect the interests of the people whom they are appointed to govern.

He added honestly, 'Most of the whites here have a most unreasonable prejudice against the mission.'[29]

---

26 Ibid.
27 Ibid.
28 Appendix 3, Department of Native Affairs, Nasova, June 12, 1875, in Brown, *Communications Respecting the Wesleyan New Mission to New Britain.*
29 Brown, 14 June 1875, in Brown, *Communications Respecting the Wesleyan New Mission to New Britain.*

Even though permission had been granted, they were still not yet free to go. There was official paper work to be completed, customs to be cleared, duty to be paid on their cargo—'duty calculated on every pound of pepper or package of bath bricks … it was really sickening.'[30] To make matters worse, the Fijian recruits, who Brown believed were a fine lot of men, were being subjected to taunts by their countrymen:

> Every day as any of our teachers pass along the beach some friend of missions will laugh at them and try to frighten them. 'Are you one of the fellows going to the New Lands?' 'Yes.' 'Oh, Oh! What a fool, you'll be killed and eaten most certainly, etc. etc.' It is really wonderful that some of them don't get fainthearted about it.[31]

The naturalist von Hügel had decided not to travel on with the *John Wesley* after all. Brown was not greatly disappointed at this news. He wrote, in that context, 'I always had some doubts about the propriety of men landing with arms and firing away before we might be able to inspire the people with confidence in us.'[32] As a final act before sailing, Brown presented his long record of the meeting with Layard and the Executive to the British officials to confirm that the record was correct. Brown concluded:

> The whole thing was a grand triumph for us, and yet the Government was not placed in the position of a defeated party, but was rather considered by us a helper. This takes away all feelings of soreness which is a good thing.… I had a really kind letter from Mr Thurston this evening wishing us God speed, and assuring us of the deep interest they will feel in our voyage.[33]

The last-minute yams were loaded, the final pieces of cargo received, the steam launch secured back in its place on deck, the travellers embarked. Early on 15 June 1875, the missionary party sailed in the *John Wesley* for Samoa and on towards the islands in the north.

---

30   Ibid.
31   Ibid., 12 June 1875.
32   Ibid., 21 May 1875.
33   Ibid., 14 June 1875 from Nausova.

6. 'I see no reason to die of fear'

New Britain, New Ireland, Duke of York Islands
June 1875–August 1876

There was now time to think. Brown had agreed that he would escort a party of island teachers to the New Mission, settle them there, and leave with the ship. This had seemed perfectly reasonable from the perspective of Sydney. Now he was beginning to have his doubts. As the mission ship *John Wesley* began to trace the familiar arc from Fiji to Samoa, there was one delay after another. In Samoa to recruit more helpers, Brown revisited places and people he had thought only a year earlier that he had left forever. Sitting in his old study at Saleaula, looking across the lagoon, he wrote to Lydia: 'It did not seem natural to come here and find no good little wife and merry youngsters to welcome me.'[1] They sailed on to the island of Rotuma to collect Lydia's sister Lizzie and her husband, the Reverend William Fletcher, who were leaving Rotuma after eighteen years of missionary service.

Weeks were passing and they had still not reached their destination. Brown had warned the island teachers of all the hazards; disease, hunger, loneliness, violence, helplessness in their isolation from home. His respect for the families was growing. These good men and their wives were willing to face all the risks. How could he abandon them and sail away for home almost immediately? As they left Rotuma behind, Brown wrote in his journal,

> Instead of steering for Fiji as we have been wont to do we are going almost due west. May God grant us His blessing day by day and guide us right in all things. I am quite expecting now to stay behind. I cannot possibly see how I can leave these poor fellows by themselves as we shall have such a short time to prepare the people to receive them.[2]

---

1   George Brown to Lydia Brown, 17 July 1875, from Saleaula, Savai'i, Samoa, in George Brown, Letter Book, 1871–76, ML A1686-2 CY 2767.
2   Brown, Journal, 31 July 1875, in George Brown, Journal, 1874–1876, ML A 1686-10-12 CY 2759.

Map 2. Region of New Guinea, New Britain, New Ireland, Bougainville, Solomon Islands.

Source: Drawn by Margaret Reeson.

As they sailed on into unfamiliar territory, Brown pored over nautical maps with the ship's captain, tracing the long necklace of islands spilling south from the great island of New Guinea. Explorers, traders and naval vessels passed through those waters but in the north there were no missionaries. The new maps tempted Brown to some ambitious imagining; if, he thought, a point near the Duke of York island group was taken as a centre, then a sweep of two hundred miles from that point would include many island populations—'an exceedingly compact and densely populated district. All these places are fields open ready to the hand that will first scatter the sower's seed.'[3] Passing through the region where the (Anglican) Melanesian Mission was working, he considered their mission strategy; they recruited young men from the islands, trained them on distant Norfolk Island then sent them back to their home areas as missionaries.[4] He noted,

> What a fine field they have here and yet how little seems to have been done. Their system I am certain is a bad one and yet placed as they are

3   *Christian Advocate*, May 1875.
4   John Garrett, *To Live Among the Stars: Christian Origins in Oceania*, Geneva: World Council of Churches Publications, 1982, pp.182–85.

without native teachers from any old established Mission tis difficult to say what else they can do. Wouldn't it be best for the Mission to settle down permanently in some central place and work from there?'[5]

Two months after leaving Fiji they were at last in sight of their goal. On their final Sunday at sea, Brown was moved by the preaching of one of the Fijians who spoke on the words from St Paul's letter to the Romans, 'It has always been my ambition to preach the gospel where Christ was not known, so that I would not be building on someone else's foundation.'[6]

A week later, the *John Wesley* moved at last into St George's Channel, with the bulk of New Britain in the distance on their left, New Ireland on the right and the cluster of small islands named for the Duke of York in between. On Sunday, 15 August 1875, they sailed up the channel and, along with the trader Captain Alex Ferguson's barque, *Sydney*, they anchored in Port Hunter, Duke of York Island. Missionaries, collectors and crew stared at the people of the place and the people of the place crowded on to the deck and stared back.

They were not the first to visit these islands. Traders, explorers, naval ships and now scientists and collectors had been coming for some years. Local men had travelled with traders to Sydney and other ports, and come back with tales of strange and wondrous worlds as well as fragments of English language. To their surprise, this latest party of white people refused to trade with them, even though they brought fresh vegetables, fruit, pigs and chickens. The attempted explanation about being unwilling to trade on the Sabbath lost something in translation, leaving the hopeful sellers bemused. The most powerful chief of that part of the island, To Pulu, came on board, confident in his place and power among these interlopers. He, with other local chiefs, saw advantages in recruiting newcomers for his own prestige, the value of their trade goods and to strengthen his authority in the region.

At first glance, George Brown found the people who had come on board 'not at all prepossessing'.[7] Apart from an occasional string of beads, and a rattle of shells worn by the chief, they were all naked with hair and bodies daubed with white lime or ochre clay. Mouths were stained bright orange-red from chewing betel nut and lime. Many carried their fighting tomahawks or spears. Lydia's sister, Lizzie Fletcher, was present on the ship and watched their visitors from a discreet distance. Lizzie would no doubt report her observations to Lydia; what did she think?

---

5   'San Christobel in sight,' Brown, Journal, 6 August 1875.

6   Romans 15:20–21, in Brown, Journal, 8 August 1875.

7   Brown, Journal, 15 August 1875.

That afternoon, the two groups gathered on deck. Local people of the Duke of York Islands watched curiously as a mysterious ritual unfolded. Strange sounds not recognised as music, unexplained bowing of heads and obscure gestures, a strange language; they watched and wondered. The shipboard community of fifty-five souls—Fijian, Samoan,[8] Rotuman, German, Scot, Irish and English and a single local man, their interpreter Teem[9]—thanked God that they had arrived safely and prayed for success for their mission. They were confident in the rightness of their cause. After the sun set in a blaze of brightness over the water, Brown walked the deck in the warm evening. Across the water, hidden in darkness and the dense coastal bush, were the people of the place. Now the missionary team must commit themselves to the next step. Brown thought of his family at home, his health, even his orders from the Mission Board, but decided that when the ship left, he would stay behind.[10]

In the morning, in company with his brother-in-law, William Fletcher, Brown landed on the island. There was no time to lose. Within weeks, the mission ship would leave and they needed to find a suitable site for a mission and build bush houses to shelter the team as a matter of urgency. Brown would write to a cousin, 'I am as careful of my life as anyone can be but I see no reason to die of fear. Mr Fletcher and I went on shore and walked all around the Island and did not see the slightest cause for more than ordinary caution.'[11]

Local ownership of land was a complex matter. When they negotiated for a site on a headland near the village of Kinawanua, overlooking Port Hunter, they needed to deal with three local chiefs, including To Pulu.[12] Building began immediately. Fijian and Samoan teachers and the ship's crew levelled ground, cut bush timber, gathered and bundled leaves for thatch. The whole party would share one single structure for sleeping and stores.

In the first week, the *John Wesley* sailed further up the channel and anchored in Blanche Bay, New Britain. Villagers in nearly a hundred canoes crowded around the ship, excitedly bringing produce and pigs for sale. The crew, thoroughly unnerved and thinking of cannibalism, demanded that the captain supply them with arms but he refused. In the flurry and ambiguity of trade, bartering for curios, confrontation, unfamiliar island politics and snatches of unfamiliar languages, Brown and Fletcher tried to make sense of what they were seeing. Over the next days, they landed in several locations on New Britain, including Matupit Island and Nodup, using the steam launch to travel to places beyond

---

8   Aminio Baledrokadroka, Misieli Loli, Setaleti Logova, Livai Volavola, Elimotama Ravono, Peni Caumia, Peni Luvu, Mijieli Vakaloloma, Pauliasi Bunoa, Timoci.

9   Brown to Benjamin Chapman, August 1875, written at sea off Guadalcanal, Solomon Islands.

10   George Brown, *George Brown: Pioneer-Missionary and Explorer: An Autobiography*, London: Hodder and Stoughton, 1908, p. 89.

11   Brown to cousin Lizzie (Buddle) Arthur, in Auckland, 7 September 1875.

12   Brown, *George Brown: Pioneer-Missionary and Explorer*, p. 90.

the range of the ship. The convolutions of local alliances and enmities, trust and mistrust, were still a mystery to the visitors, but the sight of many women and children reassured Brown that they were in no danger. On one of these visits a fight broke out among the people with much brandishing of weapons. Brown's party was temporarily separated from the steam launch and were thankful when they escaped unscathed, though some saw it as proof that it was unsafe to stay in the region. Brown offended some of his group by suggesting that they ought to wear petticoats, not trousers,[13] but they thought he was unwilling to face reality.

* * *

The *John Wesley* sailed on 6 September 1875. Only one of the naturalists, young Cockerell, was prepared to stay. One of them was willing to sell his photographic equipment to Brown; this made possible a substantial photographic record in the years to come. At the last minute, an old sailor called Jack Holmes volunteered to stay with Brown to help with the steam launch. Brown sent some last minute letters to his relatives in Auckland with a plea, 'You must all try and comfort Lydia as well as you can. I feel so thankful that she is near you.'[14] As the *John Wesley* moved slowly out to sea, the group on shore knew that they were stranded in those islands for many months. That night they all found a place to sleep, crowded together in the newly built thatched house in among the boxes and bundles. Old Jack, they found, had managed to abstract a collection of very useful items from the ship without the captain's knowledge; Brown turned a blind eye in gratitude. He slung his hammock from poles suspended over the cargo and tucked his treasured photos of Lydia and the children into the woven fibre of the wall beside him. He tried to imagine his distant family. 'My darling wife,' he later wrote, 'I have your picture hung up just by my side and I often look at it my dear, and that of the dear children and long to be with you.'[15] But he was not. He told a cousin, Lizzie Arthur,

> Long and anxiously did I consider the claims of my dear wife and little ones and my own health but the matter was simply this. If I returned in the *Wesley* the expedition would be a failure, if I remained it would in all probability be a great success. How could I hesitate in such a case? I feel it to be a great sacrifice and feel it still, but one who is not ready to deny himself has certainly not learned the lesson of self sacrifice which the life of our Lord teaches us.... I should have been miserable and unhappy for the rest of my life if I had proved craven or cowardly in such a case as this.... Pray for us Lizzie, but don't be afraid.[16]

---

13 Brown to cousin Lizzie (Buddle) Arthur, in Auckland, 7 September 1875.
14 Brown to cousin, Tom Buddle, in Auckland, 6 Sept 1875. Tom and his wife lived in Hepburn Street near Lydia.
15 Brown to Lydia Brown, in Auckland, 8 September 1875.
16 Brown to cousin Lizzie (Buddle) Arthur, in Auckland, 7 September 1875.

Figure 4. Brown children 1875: Amy, Monica, Geoffrey, Lizzie, Fred and Claudia Brown.

Source: Brown family album per favour Miss Nancy Joyce.

His decision was not based on heroics or an inflated sense of his own importance. He believed that the New Mission was more likely to succeed if they had an experienced leader. The islander teachers were almost all students rather than experienced men. None of them spoke the local language. They were likely to become ill and he had medication and some modest medical skill. As a British citizen he had some contacts and resources that the Pacific Islander families did not. Together, their mission had some chance of success. Without his participation, the challenges would probably be overwhelming.

Days later, the friendly trader Alex Ferguson also left the area. In some last-minute letters home, Brown suggested that perhaps he might return to the colonies early in 1876. Maybe. Now their last link with the rest of the world was gone.

* * *

'Not very well again today.' 'I do so wish I was well and strong.... I feel much depressed sometimes.' 'Still far from well all day.... Oh! How I feel the want of my dear wife when I am so unwell. I feel such a longing today to have her near me. Still I feel that I am doing what is right, and God is with us.'[17] A debilitating complaint that had been troubling George Brown since Fiji continued to drag him down and there was a regular refrain about illness, depression and medication in his journal. He was lonely and often homesick. Old Jack and young Cockerell couldn't abide each other. The Fijian and Samoan teachers were willing and helpful but often struck down with malaria.[18] The local chiefs were manipulative, trying to manoeuvre the newcomers to their own purposes. The complexities of local political alliances and understandings of the supernatural and natural world were impenetrable. Although he was gathering words and phrases of the language of the Duke of Yorks, its structure was a complete mystery to him and he was realising that every district had its own language. Human bones tipped the spears he purchased by barter, human skulls were revered in chiefly houses and the odour of decay hung around a nearby tree where the corpse of a respected leader was suspended. Evidence of violent death and cannibalism were always part of their new world. The climate was very hot and humid, sapping energy and leaving most new residents slow and exhausted. Under the weight of all these things, it is not surprising that Brown felt weary, unwell and depressed.

Determined to fight against everything that conspired to defeat him, Brown turned to his work at a furious pace. Unless he made arrangements to locate his Fijian and Samoan people with chiefs and village groups who were prepared to accept them, he would not be free to leave the island group for home, even if an opportunity presented itself. He set himself a gruelling program of travel. Using the steam launch and the whale boat, he made repeated forays to meet the leading people of the region. He was determined to introduce himself and the Pacific Island men, and attempt to gain the confidence of local leaders. In each place he tried to gauge whether or not the people would welcome a teacher. He

17   Brown Journal, 20 August, 11 September, 15 September 1875.
18   Ibid., 26 November 1875.

was assured by each community that while they themselves were benign, other groups meant him and his companions harm. Despite the sight of many people crowding around their boats as they explored the coastline, Brown suspected that the people enjoyed the drama of displaying their strength to rare visitors, and the presence of children among them was a good omen. Of one visit he wrote,

> We were a little uneasy at seeing so many Natives assembled all heavily armed and with spare bundles of spears.... I certainly did not like their appearance but we kept walking quietly on right into the midst of the crowd and I began to barter with them.... I believe that our fears were quite groundless as far as to any intention of the Natives to injure us ... the normal state of society here seems to be one of constant warfare.[19]

On another occasion he wrote,

> I have long since ceased to believe them when they tell these tales about places they themselves do not visit.... They are at war with almost every other District farther inland and on either side of them. What a blessing it will be ... when the reception of the religion of Jesus will cause the wars to cease and will teach them all to live together in peace and to love each other.[20]

They were not quite as alone as they had imagined. During October the German businessman Captain Hernsheim passed through on his way from Hong Kong to Sydney in his brigantine *Coeran*, and offered Brown a passage back to Sydney. Brown was tempted but declined. In letters home he explained,

> You must believe me fully when I tell you that I do not consider it [his illness] at all serious or I would leave by the *Coeran* ... tis much better now.... I hope to see you all before many months are over as I have fully made up my mind to station the Teachers as soon as ever I can now so as to be ready for any good chance [to leave].[21]

Sheer stubbornness pushed George Brown on in the months that followed, and he was rarely at home. He had promoted this cause vigorously in Australia and New Zealand and now would do everything possible to avoid the disappointment of failure before the work was fairly begun. Not all his activities were directly religious. He worked to build relationships with the principal men in the area, explored coastlines, bought local approval through trade and barter, collected artefacts and specimens for museums, tried ineffectually to keep the steam launch functional and attempted to collect words of the local languages. As he became

---

19 Ibid., 27 October 1875.
20 Brown, Letter Book, 28 October 1875.
21 Brown to Lydia Brown, 25 October 1875.

known in the region, some village leaders accepted the offer of a teacher to live among them. Fijians and Samoans began to move to strategic locations away from Port Hunter. With their families, men risked being separated, sometimes by several days travel, from their original settlement, and went to live on other small islands in the Duke of York island group and in villages on New Britain and New Ireland.[22] Brown continued to travel to visit them for encouragement and support, bringing quinine and other medication when they were ill. The first of their party died at the end of November, and they all knew that he would not be the last to die far from home.

Scrambling through the dense thickets of entangling jungle, finding his way along pathways leading to places he had never seen, Brown must have wondered when things would become clearer. He was entangled in a web of suspicion, and dire warnings against enemies. Should he believe them? He tended to assume that most new groups would become his friends in the end. It was his belief that the principal men were jealously guarding their own authority by warning against all others. In his journal he noted that 'King Dick [To Pulu] told Mr Blohm the other day that we are a most intractable set of white men! Other white men (he said) did what they told them, and only went to places where they told them to go, but we go anywhere and everywhere. Poor Dick, he doesn't like it.'[23]

In his more reflective moments he wondered whether it was wise to interfere in local matters. When was a risk too great? When a local chief attacked and almost killed the favourite of his seven wives, Brown and the Fijian teacher Beni Luvu gave the stricken woman refuge in the bush mission house at Port Hunter. The furious chief demanded that Brown and his colleagues give the woman up, so that he could kill her and give her body to his allies for a feast. Vulnerable and fearing that the angry man would torch the dry thatched roof over their heads, Brown attempted to bargain for her freedom with a good steel axe. To their great relief, the axe was finally accepted and the crisis was averted. In later years he 'often wondered whether we were wise in the action we took.... If we had been killed we should no doubt have been blamed for our folly ... the question still remains, apart from success or failure: was it right to interfere and take the risk? And I certainly believe that it was.'[24]

In the week of his fortieth birthday, George Brown was a long way from his birthplace in Barnard Castle in northern England, a long way from Samoa and a long way from his wife and seven children in New Zealand. He was travelling

---

22   Brown, *George Brown: Pioneer-Missionary and Explorer*, p. 176. Aminio Baledrokadroka was appointed to Molot, Misieli Loli to Urakukuru, Setaleti Logova to Utuan, Ratu Livai Volavola to Nodup, Elimotama Ravono to Kabanut, Penisimani Caumea to Matupit, Peni Luvu to 'Bulilalai's village', Pauliasi Bunoa to Kalil, Mijieli Vakalolo to Waira.

23   Brown, Journal, 17 January 1876, quoted in Brown, *George Brown: Pioneer-Missionary and Explorer*, p. 143.

24   Brown, *George Brown: Pioneer-Missionary and Explorer*, pp.188–92.

north along the western coast of New Ireland, beyond the usual range of traders and collectors. In a village he tried to talk with the local chief about his purpose in coming but found him very distracted. 'I scolded him for his inattention,' he wrote in his journal that night.[25] One of his young travelling companions, Kaplen, seemed very uneasy. That evening, weary from travel and with aching head, Brown gathered words of the local language from a group of men in the house before a restless sleep. It wasn't until they were well away the next day that Kaplen explained his agitation. While walking in the village he had come across a hut behind the chief's house where a woman was baking a human leg and thigh on hot stones; the chief had murdered his victim the previous day. He did not mention this to Brown at the time because, he said, 'I knew he was such a fool that he would try and get it (the thigh and leg) away from them. Then they would be angry and would probably kill him, and if so, I knew they would kill me also.'[26] With the whaleboat, they continued north. On a beach they encountered a large armed crowd, 'the wildest lot I have yet seen and I was glad to get well away,' but Brown believed that even these men meant them no harm.[27]

On Sunday 5 December 1875 the first service of Christian worship was conducted at Kalil on New Ireland, observed by a group of curious people. The watchers, armed with tomahawks and spears with shafts of human bone, listened bemused to the mysteries of the preaching and praying, though Brown thought that 'we managed to make them understand very well.'[28] They had agreed to receive a Fijian teacher. By the end of the week of hard travel, Brown was unwell, weary and sunburned; 'I want to do all I can whilst we are here, but this Body of mine rebels occasionally,' he noted.[29] Even so, despite everything, he was feeling very positive. In his journal he recorded, 'No mission could have had a more promising beginning than ours has had in all these islands.'[30]

Somewhere between that first service at Kalil on New Ireland and a night spent with his crew rowing slowly back to Port Hunter, Brown passed his fortieth birthday. The day would come when the events of that week, and all the other weeks of that period of first contact and exploration, would have been told and retold, embellished, dramatised and turned into legends. The day would come when *Boys Own Magazine* would publish his story to entertain their young readers.[31] At the time, with the sting of sweat and dried salt spray crusting on his body, skin peeling off his sunburned nose, skinny frame chafing against

25 Brown, Journal, 30 November 1875.
26 Ibid., 1 December 1875; Brown, *George Brown: Pioneer-Missionary and Explorer*, p. 134.
27 Ibid.
28 Ibid., 5 December 1875; Brown, *George Brown: Pioneer-Missionary and Explorer*, p. 135.
29 Ibid., 3 December 1875.
30 Ibid.
31 *Boys Own Magazine*, 6 November 1913; Letter from Alfred Cooper in UK to Brown asking for a photograph to accompany an article about Brown for *Boys Own Magazine*.

whaleboat timbers and bamboo beds, digestion playing up and every muscle aching, he was not in the mood for heroics. He did, however, feel hope. He wrote in his journal, 'The reception of the religion of Jesus will soon produce peace and order where now all is discord and confusion.'[32]

* * *

The mission ship *John Wesley* did not come. Months passed with no sign of a familiar sail, even though it had been promised early in 1876. Far away, his family was living without him in the cottage in Hepburn Street, Ponsonby, but the distance between them seemed impossible. Six months after leaving Fiji, a trader brought him his only letters from Lydia—and then nothing. The faces of his family, frozen in time in the small card photographs near his hammock, must be changing as they matured; but he was not there to see. Nor would they be able to imagine the sights and sounds that filled his world; the rattling of spears, the rows of human jawbones hanging from house rafters, the glimmer of the tiny fire they had built after almost drowning from a capsized canoe. He was often ill, frequently feeling weak, depressed and suffering fearsome headaches. The best remedy, he decided, was 'more work and plenty of travelling'.[33] As the months passed, the sense of both homesickness and alienation from home grew.

Running through the frenetic activity of Brown's days was a unifying thread. Some might say that he was in those islands to escape the tensions of Samoa, prepare for a colonial enterprise, collect rare artefacts, or to relish the excitement of exploration and first contact in a little-known world. Though there was a truth in all of those, he was clear about his essential purpose. What drove him on was his belief that God valued all humankind and wanted those who had never heard this message to discover that their Creator loved them. He believed that God had called him to this work. Nevertheless, it was far easier to nail together a little bush church building than communicate great themes in an unknown language. Brown would sit for hours in a village with an interpreter, local leaders and people, talking and listening, back and forth, testing the communication with questions. It seemed to him that long conversations with a chief by moonlight would be repeated, discussed and debated long after he left, and were of more value than any attempt at a sermon. His themes were the love of God for all people without favouritism; Jesus Christ, Son of God, who came 'to save sinners ... to make us fit to go and dwell with God, where God is, in heaven' and practical instructions for living that would benefit them; 'build better houses, wear clothes, live peaceably with all men and stop this continual fighting.'[34] He did not focus his preaching and teaching on the wickedness

---

32 Brown, *George Brown: Pioneer-Missionary and Explorer*, p. 136.
33 Brown, *George Brown: Pioneer-Missionary and Explorer*, p. 220.
34 Brown, Journal, 23 July 1876; Brown, *George Brown: Pioneer-Missionary and Explorer*, p. 206.

of the people and their need to repent but rather on the love of God and the transformation that was possible for a society that lived in continual fear, suspicion and brutality. A Scripture that encouraged him was from St Paul's second letter to the Corinthians, 'If any man be in Christ, he is a new creature,'[35] and he dreamed of the day when the people of these northern islands would be changed.

In the meantime, the barrier of language was still defeating him. There was more than one language in the region and he soon realised that, even if he managed to learn one language or dialect, there would be another beyond the next range or river. He knew that he was deluding himself about how much the people understood of his message about one called Jesus Christ and wondered 'how long it would be before these people rightly understand what we are trying to teach them.'[36] Even if he could speak fluently, there would still be mystery, meanings concealed, secrets kept. Were the people of these islands simply buying the rights to the new and foreign rituals, just in case they were efficacious? There were periods of deep discouragement and yet he clung to the vision that one day these people too would be among those of every tribe and nation and language who would worship God together, and as St Peter had foretold, 'Sing the praises of Him who loved and redeemed them, and called them out of darkness into his marvellous light.'[37]

There were occasional gleams of hope. Meeting with his dear friends the teachers and their families in April 1876, two of the men reported some good news. A village group that had been feuding with another for a long time, and had intended to fight that day, asked the two to take a peace-offering to their enemies with a message: 'It is to make the road good between our villages.... Let us embrace the *lotu* [Christian message] and live in peace.' The enemy villagers had responded with their own peace-offering and the message 'our mind is also to *lotu,* and to live in peace.'[38] Buoyed up with hope, Brown wrote, 'I have been homesick today but I feel glad that I am privileged to take part in this great work.... I feel so conscious of doing so little, and yet having such good results, and I feel certain that our success is simply God's answer to the prayers of his people who plead with him for us.'[39]

One year after he had first landed in the Duke of York Islands, the *John Wesley* finally anchored again in Port Hunter on 10 August 1876. Mission Board and mission ship had been distracted by events in other parts of the Pacific, with

35 Brown, *George Brown: Pioneer-Missionary and Explorer*, p. 195; see 2 Corinthians 5:17, King James Bible.
36 Brown, *George Brown: Pioneer-Missionary and Explorer*, p. 155.
37 Ibid., pp. 205–06; see Revelation 7:9–10; 1 Peter 2:9–10, King James Bible.
38 Brown, Journal, 23 April 1876, in George Brown, Journal, 1874–1876, ML A 1686 CY 2759; Brown, *George Brown: Pioneer-Missionary and Explorer*, p. 196.
39 Ibid.

significant problems in Fiji and Tonga, and the needs of the New Mission had slipped out of sight for a time. Now the ship brought a pastoral visitor, the Reverend Eroni Fotofili, to meet the Fijian and Samoan teachers, bringing a new team of Fijian missionaries to strengthen the work. It was nearly time for George Brown to leave. Before he sailed he was able to make arrangements for appointments for all the new workers, provide supplies and make some final visits to more remote areas with the help of the mission ship. He had made contact with many groups of people in many locations. He had survived illness, danger at sea and physical threats. Sometimes foolish, often foolhardy, he had brushed off perceived danger with a refrain of 'they never meant any harm'.[40] Often exhausted, frequently depressed or unwell, regularly angry or frustrated, he was patient in some things but short-tempered in others. Homesick, but rarely, he realised, really lonely. It had been a very tough year.

On 31 August 1876, George Brown sailed from Port Hunter with the *John Wesley*. He was on his way home.

---

40   Brown, *George Brown: Pioneer-Missionary and Explorer*, p. 145.

7. 'If God had called me to that work Lydia dared not hinder'

Sydney, Auckland, Fiji, Samoa, New Britain, Duke of York Islands
1876—1878

For forty days at sea George Brown allowed himself a rare time of rest. Landing in Sydney on 10 October 1876, he knew once more the sense of disconnection and alienation as he entered the remembered environment of tall stone buildings, horse-drawn carriages, a railway and fashionably dressed crowds. The Mission Board welcomed Brown, and the visiting Tongan minister, the Reverend Eroni Fotofili. They assured him that they had not forgotten the New Mission, although there had been other demands on their attention. Secretary Benjamin Chapman recorded their 'high appreciation of the services of Mr Brown and prays that he may long live to extend our mission work in this part of the world.'[1] Sadly, Fotofili died suddenly days later.

Lydia Brown must have known before he finally arrived back in Auckland on 30 October 1876 that her husband would not be ready to settle down to a comfortable life in a New Zealand congregation. For years he had been reluctant to face middle-class church life. After sixteen years of marriage she knew where his heart lay. Their reunion as a whole family was joyful. Lydia and their children had been lovingly cared for in his extended absence by their Auckland family. It was wonderful to be together again, but his family quickly discovered that it would not be for long.

Almost as soon as the first flurry of greetings and welcomes were over, the cargo unloaded, and the first astonishing tales told, George wanted to put a proposal to Lydia. The Mission Board in Sydney, he said, had asked him whether he was willing to go back to New Britain. He had not given them an answer. First he needed to talk to her. Should he go back? Would she go with him? What about their children? Lydia knew her man well. The man who had come home to her after almost two years away was alight with excitement. True, he was bone-thin, and his red hair and beard had more grey in it. He assured her that he was

---

1 Wesleyan Methodist Missionary Society (WMMS) Board Minutes, 12 October 1876 in Wesleyan Methodist Missionary Society Correspondence and Papers, vol. 1, ML CY 1365. Present: President of Conference, J.B. Waterhouse; in chair, General Secretary Benjamin Chapman; Revs Gaud, Hurst, J. Watkin, W. Fletcher, Tait, Martin; and Messrs Dawson, Barker, Reeve, Henson, Read, Crawshaw, Dowsett and Dr Moffit.

much better in health but admitted to recurring malaria. Yet this was a very different man from the hurt and frustrated person who had dragged himself through the final months in Samoa. Then he had been battling over lines of sectarian demarcation, or arguing over the precise wording of critical letters. He had written at that time, 'I feel these things too much, in fact they make me either very combative or very nervous ... my blood boils.'[2] Now, everything was different. He was relishing the natural hazards of pioneering something new and independent.

When George described the scene many years later, he wrote,

> There was never the slightest doubt in my mind as to what the decision would be. My wife, as all our friends know, is a woman of few words, and she simply said: 'I can never be a hindrance to you in your work. If it is God's will that you return to New Britain I am sure that it is also His will that I should go with you. God will take care of our children.'[3]

At the time, however, in a letter to a friend he described it somewhat differently. Brown had set everything before Lydia, the challenges and the work, and how he believed that his experience, as well as his knowledge of the languages of the mission team,

> seemed to show that it was my duty to go but that I could only decide after hearing her decision. We agreed to leave it for a day and she laid the matter before God in prayer. I am thankful to say that grace was given to her and she told me the next day that if God had called me to that work she dared not hinder but would willingly bear her part of the burden and go with me to help as best she could.... The painful part is of course leaving our little ones.[4]

Within days of arriving in Auckland, Brown had sent a message to the Mission Board in Sydney to say that both he and Mrs Brown were prepared to return to the New Mission. Five of their children would remain in Auckland. The Board was grateful and recorded in their Minutes their high appreciation of the pioneer Brown, noting 'the Christian heroism and devotedness possessed by him, and not less by Mrs Brown as is proved by their offer.'[5] Someone would later cross out the hand written words 'not less'. The Secretary was correct the first time.

* * *

2   George Brown to Mathieson, 31 December 1873, George Brown, Letter Book, 1871–76, ML A1686-2 CY 2767.

3   George Brown, *George Brown: Pioneer-Missionary and Explorer: An Autobiography*, London: Hodder and Stoughton, 1908, p. 222.

4   Brown to William Fletcher, November 1876.

5   WMMS Board Minutes, 15 November 1876.

Their holiday together as family was very brief. There was a rush of invitations to visit friends and family, meetings to attend and a family visit to Thames on the Coromandel Peninsula. The most immediate challenge was to make arrangements for their children. Years before, George had written to his father-in-law that 'Lydia does not at all relish the idea of parting with her chickens,'[6] and that was only for a brief holiday. George Brown had barely seen his older daughters Lizzie and Amy in three years or Monica, Claudia, Fred, Geoffrey and Mabel in two years. Although he loved them all dearly he was accustomed to living apart from them. It was not so easy for Lydia. Some family members were appalled that she would consider going with him. They were grateful to a benefactor who offered to pay for their daughters' education in Auckland while the parents were in the New Mission.

Having made the decision, Brown insisted on leaving Auckland early in January in order to be in time to attend the Wesleyan Methodist Conference of NSW and Queensland in Sydney. There was much interest in news of the New Mission though he knew that few had much understanding. Following the Conference, Brown accepted many invitations in several of the colonies to speak about the New Mission. The first impressions and early experiences were already beginning to be shaped into stories to leave audiences open mouthed. His hearers were astonished, shocked or amused by the images that his words conjured up. They came to him, after his addresses, to murmur admiring words about how very brave he must be, and the dreadful savagery of the island people. He had always felt reluctant to do 'the Dancing Bear business about the country,'[7] performing missionary tricks for audiences in the colonies in order to raise funds and interest. So he would listen politely to those who tried to understand. It encouraged his ego to be elevated to a high pedestal, but even so he could not wait to get away and return to his work.

Lydia Brown joined her husband in Sydney, bereft of five of her children with only five year old Geoffrey and two year old Mabel at her side. Most things were ready for them to sail; an entire prefabricated timber house was loaded on the *John Wesley*, with stores for their community. Just before they sailed, a rumour arrived in Sydney that 'war had broken out' in the region of the New Mission and George Brown was more anxious than ever to return to his work. On 18 May 1877, the ship sailed through the Heads at Sydney Harbour, out into the open sea. For one of the few times in their married life, George and Lydia Brown spent much of the next three months in each other's company, as the mission ship made a frustratingly slow passage through the mission regions. Fiji was almost a holiday with social events and visits with friends; a journalist enthused 'He [Brown] won golden opinions from all sorts of men during his short stay among

---

6   Brown to Rev. James Wallis Sr., 17 November 1870, in George Brown, Letters, 1862–78, ML MOM 102.
7   Brown to Rev. James Wallis, Sr., 28 May 1873.

us, and one of our newspapers published a sub-leader filled with high eulogy of his valuable work in the cause of Science.'[8] Samoa was a disappointment in some ways. Although they were able to meet some old friends, bad weather meant that they were not able to visit their old home on Savai'i, with Satupa'itea tantalisingly visible but unattainable in the distance. George risked a boat ride to visit his friend John Austin at Saleaula. Lydia could only watch from the ship's deck and remember her home there, and the beloved Samoan friends who had wept when they left three years earlier and who were now almost, but not quite, near enough to hug. While he was on shore at Saleaula, Brown saw a letter sent by one of the Samoan teachers in the New Mission, to Austin, his former mentor. Seteleti had written in February 1877 and his letter clarified the rumours about murders in the northern islands. He had written,

> It is still very difficult for these people to understand the Word of the Lord. True, they have great love to us, especially the chiefs of the land; but the great difficulty is, their hearts are still very dark, except a few who are beginning to receive the light, and learn about Jesus; but there are a great many who say 'There is no God'.... War is still going on, and these are dreadful people for eating each other—they are continually doing it.... We have all been very sick ... the people are continually doing wicked things.... We go [to preach] with crying because we don't know whether we shall live or die; but we go with great love to them because of their darkness ... there are signs of improvement, especially in the place where Mr Brown lived.[9]

This was the first real news that Brown had received and, though it was mixed, there were at least signs of hope. The further north they sailed, the further they were from their children in Auckland. If it took the *John Wesley* so long to travel the sea route between mission regions, it would never be possible to reach the children in an emergency. Lydia believed that she could adjust to living in a new and strange island society, but it was separation from her children that took courage.

Three months after leaving Sydney, after a detour back to Fiji and a stop in Rotuma, the *John Wesley* came in sight of New Ireland and then at last Port Hunter on 21 August 1877, just two years after Brown's first arrival. George Brown had been absent for a year and was eager for news. Five of the party he had left behind had died; a teacher, two of the wives and two children. Others had been ill. Neighbouring traders had had serious troubles, with a murder, a poisoning and conflict with the local people. Although the original party had

---

8   Mansel Hall, columnist in Fiji, quoted in the *Weekly Advocate* (early October 1877).
9   Seteleti Logova, in Duke of York Islands, to John Austin, 1877, quoted in Brown, Journal, June 1877, ML A1686-13, 14, 15 CY 2762.

stayed at their posts and were doing well, most of the Pacific Island teachers who arrived in 1876 had failed to go to their appointments, choosing to stay clustered in the comparative safety of Kinawanua. Brown was very disappointed and irritated by this.[10] He felt the need to rebuke the teachers for what he believed was simple laziness and also because some of them were carrying guns to guard their women when they went fishing, 'when there was no occasion at all for them.'[11] He did not seem to recognise that his Fijian and Samoan colleagues may have had cause for a degree of nervousness.

Figure 5. Original Mission house, Kinawanua, Duke of York Islands.

Source: George Brown photograph collection: Australian Museum V6406.

Lydia Brown, at a time of life when many women have established their homes, now moved into the house built from bush materials that had sheltered her husband and his companions in their first year, while they waited for the new prefabricated building to be constructed. The bush house was already dilapidated, inhabited by mice, lizards and assorted insects and with a few leaks through the thatch. It was filled with their stores, leaving very little space for living, even though all the cooking was done over a fire beyond the house. Nearby was the house of To Pulu, a house darkened by violent memories and

10   Brown, *George Brown: Pioneer-Missionary and Explorer*, pp. 224–26.
11   George Brown, Journal, 1877–Dec 1879, 8 October 1877.

superstition.[12] Outside that house was a dead branch on which were lined up seven skulls of men that To Pulu had killed and eaten. Lydia may have thought wistfully of the comforts of Samoa, but even there she had waited for years for the promise of new houses to materialise. She had managed housekeeping then and no doubt she could do it again. A small village of local houses had sprung up around the original mission hut to accommodate the growing number of Pacific Island families where her children were welcomed. Lydia was grateful that George had recruited two Samoan couples who had worked for her in Samoa to help her with her work. The *John Wesley* sailed, carrying letters to their older children, and their contact with the rest of the world was gone once more.

Figure 6. To Pulu and wives, Kinawanua 1880.

Source: George Brown photograph collection: Australian Museum V 6419.

Things were changing, little by little. Trading companies were becoming better established and the local people were attracted to steel axes and colourful cloth. The building and gardening methods of the Fijians and Samoans were sometimes copied. More scientists and collectors were arriving so that Brown had competition for the artefacts he collected. Adventurers from around the

---

12   Benjamin Danks, *In Wild New Britain: The Story of Benjamin Danks, Pioneer Missionary*, from his diary, ed. Wallace Deane, Sydney: Angus and Robertson, 1933, p. 70.

world called in. Most interesting of the changes, from Brown's perspective, was the increasing mobility of the people of the region. People who had dared not travel far from home for fear of attack by enemies, and had always carried a spear and an axe, now could be seen unarmed and taking tentative steps away from their own places. Late in 1877, when the new mission house was being built, a chief and his party came to Kinawanua

> to have a look at our house. This is the first time they have ever been to this village, though they live within three miles of us. The old chief told me that he had never set foot in it before today, and they all said that it was only through Christianity that they had been able to come. As it was, they were all well armed and only came in force, and with much fear and trembling.[13]

On New Ireland, people were telling Brown that 'before the *Lotu* came to them they were always at war, but now they are almost forgetting how to fight. Tis indeed the same blessed Gospel of Peace still.'[14] Though this was overstating the matter, there were fragile signs that the fear-fuelled isolation that had created so many different dialects and languages in so narrow a region was easing. Outsiders had encouraged local chiefs to travel with them into unfamiliar places to meet face to face those whom they had long feared from a distance, and the fear was slowly diminishing. There were also signs that even attitudes to cannibalism were undergoing a change, although that was more ambiguous. A man, who admitted to eating human flesh while Brown was away in 1877, said that he was taking the opportunity while Brown was away as he might not get another chance. 'He said, "Mr Brown is away so we may eat this one. When he comes back he would scold me and I should not be able to eat it".'[15] Others chose their moment when they did, or did not, eat human flesh.

Over the months, their new house was taking shape. It was a slow process, as predicted, as Brown frequently asked the builder McGrath to leave his work to travel with him on journeys to distant areas. The half-built house had a fine view from a broad verandah across the St George's Channel with the long island of New Ireland beyond. They began a garden and Brown wrote, 'I have planted lots of oranges and guavas and custard apples—all new fruit here. Some other fellow will eat the fruit of them. It's always been my lot to build houses for others to live in and to plant trees for others to eat the fruit.'[16]

---

13 Brown, *George Brown: Pioneer-Missionary and Explorer*, p. 229, Brown, Journal, 22 November 1877.

14 Brown to Chapman, Sydney, 30 October 1877, published in *Wesleyan Missionary Notices relating to the Missions Under the Direction of the Australasian Wesleyan Methodist Conference*, 1 July 1878, p. 174; Brown, *George Brown: Pioneer-Missionary and Explorer*, p. 229.

15 Brown, Journal, 7 October 1877.

16 Brown to his cousin Miss Australia (Tralie) Buddle, Auckland, 9 November 1877, in George Brown, Letter Book, 1876–1880, ML A1686-3 CY 2772.

Lydia Brown needed to be self-sufficient as George was often away for days at a time with several Fijian teachers and the steam launch. She knew that their welcome in the villages was still uncertain and none of them was skilled with managing the steam launch. On one occasion storms delayed their return from New Ireland, and a journey that should have taken four or five days kept them away for ten. Brown admitted to the General Secretary, 'Mrs Brown had been very anxious about us as we were much longer away than we expected, and the wind had been very strong at Duke of York, so she was glad enough to hear the steamer's whistle just at daybreak and see her puffing round the South Head into the port.'[17]

It was not only her frequently distracted and absent husband that made Lydia anxious. Five of her children were very far away and they had had no news of them since leaving Sydney. Brown wrote to his cousin Tom Buddle, 'We often think about the children and wonder how they are all getting on. Poor Lydia I fancy sometimes feels a little anxious about them but we know that they are in good hands.'[18] That was not all. She had been in good health for most of the time since they arrived but by November she was sure that she was pregnant again.

* * *

Now that their leader had returned, the whole team had renewed energy. Island missionaries who had been reluctant to go to their appointments moved to their new places. There were men located in twenty-three sites in the Duke of York group, New Britain and New Ireland with a total of thirty-four 'preaching places'. They had begun one little school and a Sabbath school, still in embryonic form. At a staff General Meeting in October they decided together that their immediate priorities were to begin schools, make pastoral visits to each community, erect buildings, translate hymns and scripture passages, and to maintain regular meetings of staff for prayer and consultations in each district. There were even a few local people who had indicated that they were seriously interested in this new way of thinking.[19] Brown was moved to tears when two of these men joined the missionary group for their regular prayer meeting for the first time. They were invited to pray, and a Duke of York man, Peni Lelei, after a nervous start, astonished him by offering a simple, beautiful prayer to God.[20] Brown was not always satisfied with the work of the Fijian and Samoan teachers, but believed that it was always useful to place them in strategic locations. He

17   Brown to Benjamin Chapman, Sydney, 30 October 1877.
18   Brown to Tom Buddle, Auckland, 12 November 1877.
19   Mission Returns for New Britain District for 1877, sent to B. Chapman, 20 December 1877.
20   Brown to Mrs Reed, Tasmania, 1 November 1877, in George Brown, Letter Book, 1876–1880, ML A1686-3 CY 2772.

dreamed of more men and their families coming to extend the work and wrote to Chapman, 'About the supply of Teachers, I can say little, except that I could locate at once ten or twenty more than I have.'[21]

Not long before Christmas in 1877, the Brown family moved into their fine new house even though it was not finished. Lydia had lived on a building site before and it was better than the temporary bush building. On Christmas Day, Brown preached on the message of the angels: 'Glory to God in the highest, and on earth peace, good will toward men.' They invited the British adventurers from the ketch *Star of the East*, Wilfred Powell, Granville Wood and George Turner, to share their Christmas dinner, where they remembered 'Christmas at home and in the Colonies.'[22] Brown set off on New Year's Day 1878 in the steam launch in company with the party from the *Star of the East* and other companions, to make further exploration along the southern coast of New Britain. The new year of 1878 was full of promise. Or so they thought.

As he had done in Samoa, George Brown asked his wife Lydia to help with correspondence. She copied out his journal entries to send to New Zealand and to the Mission Secretary Benjamin Chapman.[23] He was too busy to do it himself. There was page after page of description of the journey of exploration along the southern coast of New Britain. With his companions they had seen unfamiliar bays and rivers, observed and collected vegetation and fauna, were stoned, yelled at and subjected to some obscene gestures by unfriendly groups on the beach as they tried to approach—and Brown had decided that this new region would make a fine location for mission teachers. He had been ill and confined to a bunk on the ketch, with malaria and then with elephantiasis, which left one leg grossly swollen for some time. Still unwell, he had travelled to visit sick and dying teachers.

Tremors shook the earth at Kinawanua late in January and great drifts of floating pumice came down the St George's Channel below their house. A volcano had erupted on the edge of Blanche Bay, New Britain, some twenty miles away. Two weeks after the initial eruption, Brown set out to see this remarkable volcanic phenomenon and to confirm that the teachers and their families on New Britain were safe. By the time Brown and his party were in sight of New Britain they could see the column of dark smoke and flame, hear the rumble of intermittent explosions of ash and pumice stone and breathe the smoky atmosphere that blanketed the coastline.[24] Neatly copying the many pages of notes her husband

---

21 *Wesleyan Missionary Notices relating to the Missions under the Direction of the Australasian Wesleyan Methodist Conference*, 1 July 1878, pp. 176–77.

22 Brown, Journal, 25 December 1877.

23 Brown to Rev. Thomas Buddle, 24 February 1878, in in George Brown, Letter Book, 1876–1880, ML A1686-3 CY 2772.

24 He made the journey with Wood, Turner, McGrath, Howard, three Fijian teachers, Peni Lelei and they were later joined by trader Hicks from Matupit.

had made, Lydia Brown may have wondered whether his actions had been in the interests of science, or over-excitement and stupidity. He had written of pulling in close to an island newly thrust from the harbour floor and with the trader William Hicks jumping out into shallow water that was still very hot and walking on 'masses of pumice and hard igneous rocks, fissured in every direction with deep cracks, through many of which smoke and steam still issued violently.'[25] They went on to explore the area around the main eruption, to witness the devastation of the gardens and fruit trees, the floating dead fish, and the thick grey layer of ash weighing down the blighted vegetation. They were shocked to see the extent of the damage.[26] Even nature was unstable and unpredictable.

A volcanic eruption in January; a devastated landscape in February; an epidemic of illnesses in March. One after another the Pacific Island teachers, their wives and children, as well as the German and British traders, scientists and explorers, fell ill, many with malaria. Many sick traders gathered at the home of the German trader, Blohm, not far from Kinawanua; Blohm worked for Hernsheim's trading company. Blohm's Samoan wife was the first to die. From that time on through the month, George and Lydia Brown offered care, nursing and hospitality to many people. Brown frequently was called to visit those who were sick on nearby islands. He believed that 'many owe their lives to the fact that my stock of quinine and other medicines was a large one.'[27] Although not well himself, he made many trips by boat and sometimes sat with patients through the night. In his journal he wrote, 'Still more sickness. It is really enough to frighten us all. Everyone seems to be ill or just recovering.... The season seems to be a most unhealthy one.'[28] To their grief, some of their own Samoan people died. The Browns took Blohm into their own home where Lydia helped to care for him as well as their own people.

Lydia Brown and his children were rarely mentioned in his journal. Yet in personal letters to family members and friends he wrote lovingly and with appreciation of the role of Lydia. Describing the long period of ill health for their community he wrote, 'My good wife is almost the only one who escaped, though, when all our servants and most of the teachers were ill, she had rather more to do than she ought to have had.'[29] Writing to their children in New Zealand, George said, 'Mama keeps so well and hearty, she has never had the

25   Brown, Journal, 16 February 1878.
26   Brown, Journal, 16 February 1878; *Wesleyan Missionary Notices relating to the Missions under the Direction of the Australasian Wesleyan Methodist Conference*, 1 July 1878; Brown, *George Brown: Pioneer-Missionary and Explorer*, pp. 237–46.
27   Brown to Chapman, 25 January 1878.
28   Brown, Journal, 26 March 1878.
29   Brown to Chapman, 24 June 1878.

fever at all. Everyone seems to like her. She is a great comfort to me. It is so different coming home now from a long journey to what it used to be in the old times when I was here alone—it is home now, it wasn't then.'[30]

Lydia was now heavily pregnant in a steamy tropical climate and was probably very weary indeed. She went to support a trader's wife in childbirth, cared for her sick husband, and was responsible for young Geoffrey's education and little Mabel's wellbeing; Geoffrey preferred to play and although an intelligent lad was a reluctant scholar. There were often extra guests at her table. The explorer Wilfred Powell recorded some glimpses of Lydia during that period: 'a missionary's wife I have the pleasure of knowing…. We found Mr Brown at home [in the temporary bush house], who, with his good wife, made us welcome to a meal of somewhat native fare, though there was that which we had not tasted since leaving Australia, a good loaf of bread.'[31]

Even while her pregnancy was progressing, Lydia seemed to escape from the general illness and her husband declared, 'Lydia has enjoyed splendid good health all through. I don't know what I should have done without her.'[32] By the time the season of illness began to wane he was very weary indeed. They would take a short holiday, he decided. He would take Lydia and the children for a week or two away on New Britain. They would stay with one of the Fijian households, perhaps with the family of Sailasa Naucukidi or with Ratu Livai Volavola.

But now it was April 1878. A voice at a window, speaking out of the darkness, made such a plan impossible.

---

30   Brown to his children in Auckland, 8 September 1878.
31   Wilfred Powell, *Wanderings in a Wild Country: Or Three Years Amongst the Cannibals of New Britain*, London: Sampson Low, Marston, Searle, and Rivington, 1883, pp. 35, 45.
32   Brown to Rev. Thomas Buddle, 2 July 1878.

8. 'A great sinking of heart'

New Britain, Duke of York Islands 1878

There would be no holiday. The evening before they planned to set out, Brown was spending time at home skinning birds to be preserved for museums. He heard a tap on the window. From the darkness a voice said, 'I have just heard that the New Britain natives have murdered Sailasa and some teachers.'[1] As Brown later noted in his journal,

> We have heard hundreds of tales like these before and have paid but little attention to them; but this time I felt a great sinking of heart as soon as I heard it, and felt assured that there was some truth in it, knowing as I did that Sailasa and some of the teachers had planned a journey inland. When we held our Quarterly Meeting some few weeks ago, Sailasa told me that he had been up inland, and was very kindly received by the natives, and that they all wished him to go again.... He asked me for a few beads, &c, to give the chiefs, and I gave them to him telling him that I was going over soon to New Britain, and would also go inland further up the coast and hoped to get some fine openings for the *lotu* also.[2]

Brown's fears were justified. The next day Fijian chief Teacher Ratu Livai arrived from New Britain bringing confirmation.[3] The Reverend Sailasa Naucukidi from Fiji, mission teachers Peni Luvu and Livai Naboro, with Timoti, a Fijian youth who had come as a workman for Sailasa, were all dead and their bodies had been distributed to neighbouring groups for cannibal feasts. Their wives and little children were still in their homes and at great risk. Ratu Livai told how eight teachers had agreed together to approach the inland communities, four starting from the southern coast of the peninsula and four from the north. Ratu Livai and his companions had moved from the south, but being warned of a possible plot against them had retreated. The others had gone on, unknowingly, to their deaths on 6 April 1878. A local chief Taleli was said to have directed the attack.[4]

In company with some mission teachers and some white neighbours, Brown set off for New Britain. Brown was shocked by the loss and deeply grieved by the

---

1 George Brown to Chapman, 26 June 1878, George Brown, Letter Book, ML A 1686 CY 2772.
2 Ibid.
3 George Brown, Journal, 1877–Dec 1879, 9 April 1878, ML A1686-13, 14, 15 CY 2762.
4 Ibid., 10 April 1878.

death of his close comrade Peni Luvu, who had been among the pioneer party. When they reached Sailasa's house at Kabakada they were greeted by Sailasa's weeping widow, Merejieni, and the other women who wailed in their grief, demanding that their dead husbands explain why they had abandoned them. As Brown wrote in his journal, 'Twas little use trying to speak any trite words of comfort and we could only sit silent with them as sharers of their sorrow.'[5]

As Brown wrote, the descriptions of the murders and rumours that there were plans to murder the women and children 'made my blood boil'. He watched the Fijian and Samoan teachers and observed by 'their significant sullen silence that their feelings were so deeply moved that they were no longer masters of their passions.'[6] With the heartrending cries of the women and the whimpering of the frightened children filling the house, Brown sat on a bed with his head in his hands trying to block his ears to the sounds of chaos and anguish. He knew that he was given to acting swiftly and on impulse. Now was not the time for that. He tried desperately to think clearly and to pray for help.[7] Even as he tried to think what to do, with the turmoil pounding in his mind, blood and gut, he heard that

> the Teachers were planning an expedition to Taleli's village that night and were determined to go without telling me of it for fear I would prevent it. The Fijians and Samoans had consulted together and were prepared to go and two of our party Mr Turner and Mr McGrath had agreed to accompany them. This action brought matters to a crisis and I was compelled to decide what course I would pursue.[8]

The Fijians and Samoans were from warrior peoples, powerful men whose fathers and grandfathers had wielded mighty clubs of war. They had been outraged at the murders of their friends. Brown knew that his own action or inaction would have a part in whatever happened next and he must make a choice. At some point he decided 'to take the matter into my own hands.'[9] Within days of the murders he began to keep a detailed record of events in his journal.

Just how he should act was not immediately clear. Most urgent was to take the widows and children to a place of safety. Taleli was already sending messages taunting the traders and missionaries; he was not afraid of any foreign man-of-war, he could dodge the bullets of any musket, the wives of Brown and the teachers should expect the unspeakable, he planned to eat more victims and

---

5   Ibid., 11 April 1878.
6   Ibid.
7   Brown to Rev. Thomas Buddle, 2 July 1878.
8   Brown, Journal, 11 April 1878.
9   Ibid.

'had said that he was especially anxious to get me.'[10] According to Wilfred Powell, Taleli informed Brown 'that the taro was cooking with which to eat *him*.'[11] Traders and other whites were nervous and armed. Fijian and Samoan missionaries were angry and ready to act independently. Local clan alliances and loyalties were difficult to assess; who might support any retribution against Taleli and his allies? Why had the murders happened at all, when the teachers had believed that they were welcome? Brown came to the conclusion that they were not killed because of cannibal greed, or because they were Christian missionaries, but 'because they were foreigners'[12] and so trespassing in places where they were ignorant of the codes and boundaries of local authority, ownership and trade. They had moved across the invisible lines of local power and paid the price for it.

But what should he do and who would be affected by any decision he made? There was his own family with Lydia six months pregnant, the Fijian and Samoan teachers, the white men in the region and the wider community with its complex networks of chiefs and followers, clan groups with long histories of connection or animosity. The mission teachers were already preparing to act because they believed that their mission was at risk and life would no longer be safe if the murderers went unpunished. Brown considered forbidding them, but feared that they would then 'lose all hope and interest in their work and our work would only result in failure.'[13] The traders, many of them younger than Brown and an independent crowd living in a frontier world beyond the rule of colonial law, were determined to mount a punitive raid whether Brown joined them or not. Most troubling was the question of how the local tribes would view his action or inaction, for these were the people he was trying to influence. Would direct action against Taleli and his people cost him the trust of the people and turn them against the Islander Teachers? Or would inaction make them despise him for weakness? Either way, the whole missionary enterprise was at risk of failure.

Brown considered his options. When missionaries had been murdered in the Pacific region, as they had in the past decade, there had been retribution. In some cases the responsibility had been in the hands of an island Paramount Chief or King. In others, colonial authorities had sent in troops. In New Britain there was neither a Paramount Chief nor colonial troops within range. He could wait for the visit of a passing man-of-war but was dubious as to whether a

---

10   Wilfred Powell, *Wanderings in a Wild Country or Three Years Amongst the Cannibals of New Britain*, London: Sampson Low, Marston, Searle, and Rivington, 1883, p. 123; Brown, Journal, 11 April 1878.
11   Powell, *Wanderings in a Wild Country*, p. 123.
12   Brown statement, published in the *Weekly Advocate*, 21 September 1878.
13   Brown, Journal, 11 April 1878.

ship's captain would be willing to interfere. It seemed to Brown unwise for their vulnerable community to be seen to depend on outside help for their protection. He noted,

> When a Ship of War is seen after any such crimes the perpetrators are at once on their guard and take to the hills where it is almost impossible to follow them, a few shells are fired and some houses burnt and this in the majority of instances is all that the most determined Captain can effect even if his instructions allow him to do so much.[14]

Should he wait to inform the Commissioner Sir Arthur Gordon in Fiji, and place the matter within the jurisdiction of the Western Pacific High Commission? It would be at least three months or more before any message could reach Fiji and perhaps several months more before a High Commission ship's company would reach the islands. A lot could happen while they waited. They might all be dead, he thought.[15] Should he retreat with his family? Should he withdraw the Fijian and Samoan families? But where was safe? In any case, the difficulties of moving so many people quickly were insurmountable: the little steam launch was unserviceable, the ketch *Star of the East* was beached and under repairs, the trader *Johan Caesar* was too small, the *John Wesley* was not due for months—which left the mission whale boat. With a widely scattered community of outsiders including some twenty-six island missionary families, as well as about twenty white and mixed-race traders, collectors and missionaries, an evacuation was neither possible nor advisable. Should they simply behave as if nothing had happened, and carry on with their work? It was probably the course of action his Mission Board would expect.

The man who struggled with these questions was in a very vulnerable place. After three months of illness across the community, too many funerals and many sleepless nights, combined with the hard physical demands of constant travel, he was exhausted. In his private journal he admitted that 'often I have been on the very verge of despair ... I have often felt faint and weary under the burden but God has helped me.'[16] Isolated, depressed, physically run down, mired in grief, rage and a sense of impotence in the face of horrifying circumstances, objective decision making was almost impossible. He knew that he had built something of a reputation as a pioneer among the people of the Mission Board and the wider community of the Wesleyan Methodist Church, and that reputation would be seriously tarnished if people thought of him as the missionary who shot the

---

14   Ibid.
15   Powell, *Wanderings in a Wild Country*, p. 147. In remote New Britain, Brown was not aware that Gordon had only just received his commission in London early in 1878, and that the Commission was designed to deal with crimes by British subjects, or against native populations, but not criminal conduct by local people of the Pacific region.
16   Brown, Journal, 27 May 1878.

people of the place. Was this the end of the New Mission? If they evacuated, or were killed, or retreated to a single fortress somewhere, not daring to move out among the people, would the dream he had nurtured, and promoted, and worked for over so many years simply wither and die? Was this the end?

* * *

In the darkness, Lydia Brown woke from an uneasy sleep to the sound of voices and movement. It was three o'clock in the morning on Palm Sunday, 14 April 1878, and George had just arrived back at Port Hunter with the whale boat, the crews, the teachers and a load of exhausted and distressed women with their pitiful belongings. The widows and their little ones were settled and comforted and then George and Lydia Brown were able to tell each other the stories of the four days of his absence. News of the murders had reached the Duke of York group and there had been an evident change in the attitudes of some of the villagers to the recently-come traders and missionaries. There was insolence instead of friendliness, rude demands for goods instead of the usual trading, with barely veiled threats.[17] Lydia's friend, the wife of teacher Aminio Baledrokadroka, had been threatened at spear point, and with most of the men of their community away on New Britain, those who remained at Kinawanua felt very vulnerable. Rumours were already reaching them that a chief on New Ireland had kidnapped the wife, or was it the daughter, of one of the teachers in his area, and threatened the life of the teacher.

That Sunday morning at Kinawanua the congregation was tense and grieving. George Brown preached from Isaiah 55:8, 'For my thoughts are not your thoughts, neither are your ways my ways, saith the LORD. For as the heavens are higher than the earth, so are my ways higher than your ways, and my thoughts than your thoughts.' Perhaps he reflected on the mystery of the mind of God and the ways of God that he did not understand at all. All day his mind kept returning to the terrible end of Sailasa, Peni and the others.

He could hardly have preached from the final verses of Isaiah 55, which read 'For ye shall go out with joy, and *be led forth with peace.*' That afternoon there was a gathering of the teachers, scientists and traders with Brown to decide on their action. According to Powell, adventurer-scientist of the *Star of the East*, 'Mr Brown was the last person [connected with the occurrence] to allow that severe measures were necessary, and the most unwilling to do so.'[18] He went on,

> A council was held, at which it was determined that if we wished to save our lives we must either fight, and fight well, or withdraw altogether

---

17   Powell, *Wanderings in a Wild Country*, p. 124. 'Meanwhile in Mr Brown's absence the Duke of York natives became excessively insolent to Mrs Brown, and came demanding beads, red cloth, &c., from her.'
18   Ibid., p. 117.

from these islands at once. As this latter plan was impossible, the former was the only alternative, and Mr Brown at last was obliged unwillingly to admit that it must be so. I at once lent all my available muskets and ammunition to arm the teachers, as did some of the traders.[19]

Brown's journal, formerly a document where he recorded explorations, adventures and signs of hope, was now almost a confessional. As the days of April passed he recorded the reasoning behind his decision. He knew already that his decision would be questioned by mentors and friends in far places, and he would need to attempt to justify himself. He wrote of that time of painful decision making.

To say that I felt deeply the responsibility of my position is to say but little. I actually [crossed out] literally groaned under the weight of it and earnestly longed for some brother Missionary to share it with me. During these past few months whilst nearly every one around has been struck down with Fever I have felt much my solitary position but it never came upon me with such force as now. I felt that I alone was answerable for it and that if we failed or if any more of the Teachers were killed on me alone would rest the blame. I knew that I had no precedent to guide me and that many good people whose opinions I respect and whose esteem I value wd condemn my action as judged from their stand point. I considered also that I should probably be accused of trying to force Christianity by war on the people and that I must be quite prepared for some not very complimentary remarks on 'fighting Missionaries'.... All these things were fully considered and the conviction was forced upon me that we must endeavour to punish the murderers if only for the protection of our own lives. After arriving at this decision we determined to do it as speedily and effectually as possible always bearing in mind that we must so act that our conduct would bear any judicial investigation which might take place.[20]

It was all there. Isolation, lack of precedent, probably incurring the condemnation of people who had respected and even honoured him, expecting to be criticised and caricatured; he guessed, rightly, what to expect. It was almost a year since he had had contact with any fellow missionaries, no letters or conversations, not even a robust argument, and now he lived in a world of easy violence. Whatever action he chose to take he knew that 'I alone was answerable for it and that if we failed, or if any more of the teachers were killed, on me alone would rest the blame.' It was a terrifying thought.

---

19 Ibid., p. 125.
20 Brown, Journal, 17 April 1878.

Photo. by Dr. Brown.

Rev. Levi Volovola.   Rev. Dr. Brown.   Rev. Aminio Bale.

THREE NEW BRITAIN VETERANS.

Figure 7. Ratu Livai Volavola, George Brown, Aminio Baledrokadroka in Fiji in 1905. These men had shared with Brown the experiences of Easter 1878.

Source: The *Missionary Review: Methodist Church of Australasia*, April 1906.

Reluctant he may have been, but even while George Brown had been with the traders on New Britain in the days when he first visited the endangered women and children, he had chosen to arm himself. In the short term at least, there was no sign of peace. He had acquired lead for bullets from the captain of the *Johan Caesar* and at Kabakada he had 'bought a very fine Snider from Mr. Southwell for £4.'[21] Up until that point his armoury had been limited, with an old and dangerously unsafe musket left by a sea captain, and his fowling pieces, smooth bore weapons which fired buckshot and were used for shooting birds for the pot and as a collector. To purchase what appears to have been an expensive military breech-loading Snider-Enfield rifle was to mean serious business. He spent the next day 'running Bullets, cleaning musket, making cartridges and otherwise preparing for our journey.'[22] From their store he collected a roll of white calico to tear into strips for identification 'to bind around the head of every friendly native to prevent their being shot by any of our party.'[23] Having decided to participate in a retaliatory raid, his preparations were deliberate and thorough. 'My plan,' he would write later, 'was to attack at once from both sides of the promontory whilst the event was quite recent and before the Natives expected us to take any action. They thought only of punishment when a big ship came.'[24] Their aim was to push through 'to surprise the Natives in the very town where the Teachers were killed and where they never dreamt that a Whiteman or a Teacher would dare to go again.'[25]

It was a very strange Easter. Across the world, Christians were remembering the death and resurrection of Christ during Holy Week with solemn rituals on Good Friday and joyful celebration on Easter Day, 21 April 1878. Missionary Brown's journal made no mention of Easter. In a downpour of tropical rain and steamy heat, on the sacred days of Holy Week, men set out from Port Hunter, Duke of York Islands on 16 April heading for New Britain. Armed traders, missionaries and scientists divided their forces, one group to climb and march from the shores of Blanche Bay on the south of the peninsula, the other to stand guard in two whale boats on the northern side of the peninsula, to prevent the escape of fleeing people and to wait for the first group to join them. It would be a week of bloodshed, treachery, brutality, danger, looting and violence. By Good Friday, a number of villagers were dead or wounded, small children separated from parents in the panic, village houses and canoes reduced to smoking rubble, coconut palms and banana trees hacked down. On Easter Day, in the aftermath

---

21   Ibid., 12 April 1878.
22   Ibid., 15 April 1878.
23   Ibid., 17 April 1878.
24   Ibid., 11 April 1878 continuation. Commentary on events of April 1878, written on blank page marked 2 January 1877.
25   Brown Journal, 11 April 1878. The account begins as an entry on 11 April, and continues on previously blank pages in his Journal for 1877, at 1, 2 and 3 January.

of a violent week, the raiding parties met and held a church service at Matupit Island, off New Britain, and Brown prayed a prayer of thanksgiving that none of the people in their parties had been killed or injured.[26] They stayed at Matupit all that day, considering what they should do next. Although 'many of us thought that quite enough had been done' they decided that, although the villages of many people who had been involved in the murders and cannibalism had been burned, the place where the Fijians had died had so far escaped unscathed. They would put it to the torch and take more lives on Tuesday. Messages were sent out to village leaders demanding compensation in the form of traditional *diwara* shell-money, and charred bones believed to be those of Sailasa and Timote were returned to them.[27]

After dark on Wednesday 24 April 1878, Lydia Brown heard a chilling sound carrying across the water. A boat was approaching in the waning moonlight and the sound was one she associated with violent death and cannibalism. To her profound relief, she soon heard her husband's voice. He and his companions were safely home.

> We got to Port Hunter about 8 pm, the Natives yelling and shouting their songs of triumph all the time when we were nearly home. Their old shout when they had got a body to eat but they had none with them wherewith to regale their friends. Twas strange to hear their old cannibal cry under such circumstances and so deprived of its old meaning, Uē āh Uē āh Uē āh and then a loud prolonged cry, half song half shout.[28]

They had fought and survived. Village leaders in a number of places on New Britain had brought shell-money compensation for the original murders and the associated cannibalism. The careful re-building of relationships with the people who had been attacked had begun.

The question remained. What would the rest of the world make of their actions?

---

26 Powell, *Wanderings in a Wild Country*, p. 140.
27 Brown, Journal, 21 April 1878.
28 Ibid., 24 April 1878.

9. 'I shall not be surprised to hear that many condemn'

Sydney, New Britain, Duke of York Islands 1878

There was another problem now. George Brown was going to have to explain himself and his actions, and attempt to justify himself to his Mission authorities and the public in the colonies. Soon after he arrived home he began to record what had happened in his journal. 'I felt deeply the great responsibility I was assuming and I think it right now to state the position in which I was placed and the reasons which induced me to decide as I did.'[1] He marshalled his reasons. The teachers were planning to go anyway on the grounds that life was no longer safe, 'nor was mission work practicable if these murderers were not punished.'[2] The whites in the area said that they were no longer safe unless something was done. They had attempted to claim traditional compensation according to local custom before the attack, but had been refused. 'I felt that punishment was necessary not so much to revenge the deaths of the Native Minister and Teachers as to protect the lives of those who were left.'[3]

* * *

What had happened during those days of violence? It would be debated and argued over long after Easter 1878. Who had done what? Who had witnessed what? Who was to blame, if blame was appropriate? How many had died? Could a missionary ever be justified in participating in such a raid, much less being an active leader in it? Two participants, George Brown and Wilfred Powell, kept detailed written records and much oral evidence was collected later from the Fijian and Samoan teachers and other eyewitnesses. The details varied and the numbers of supposed dead or wounded were very fluid but there was no escaping that it had been a damaging and brutal week for a great many people both as actors and victims. Brown himself had been armed and with the party in whale boats off the coast under threat from many canoes. His account of his own actions was ambiguous until he described efforts at peacemaking when a party approached him, days later, wishing to 'pay for peace'.

---

1   George Brown, Journal, 1877–December 1879, April 1878, ML A1686-13, 14, 15 CY 2762.
2   Brown, Journal, continued from 11 April 1878, written on page marked 1 January 1877.
3   Brown, Journal, 11 April 1878.

I told them we fought now because our lives were in danger and not merely to revenge the Teachers. They acknowledged the truth of all I said, and said Tis true, tis true we began it not you. I accepted their offering, gave them a little present in return and told them we would make a formal peace according to their own customs in a few days.[4]

After George Brown returned home to Kinawanua on Wednesday 24 April, he wrote, 'I decided to do no more at present. We have taught the Natives a lesson they will not soon forget. They have lost as nearly as we can tell 90 or 100 killed and wounded besides their loss of houses and shell money.'[5] He was home. He was alive and safe, and so were his men. But in the euphoria of coming home alive from battle, Brown knew he would have to explain himself.

Even the large pages of Brown's 1878 journal were not enough to record the whole tragic affair and he was forced to continue the record on unused pages in his 1877 journal, marking the correct date as he went. It was inevitable that he would need to answer questions one day. He wrote with a degree of frankness about his feelings and actions. Even so, he did not choose to record whether or not he had inflicted injury on anyone. He had been present and armed as two whaleboat parties had scattered the men in forty canoes; he was skilled with a shotgun against birds but did not make clear whether he was equally adept with a military rifle. In her final weeks of pregnancy, Lydia Brown transcribed thirteen pages of the journal to be sent to Mission Secretary Benjamin Chapman. Knowing that this document was likely to be published in the church magazine and elsewhere, they added appropriate explanatory notes to the original text with the more dramatic incidents of danger, courage, cruelty, treachery and ultimate reconciliation. However, before the long letter to Chapman was completed, all references to a rifle, bullets, particular dead bodies or personal belligerence had mysteriously disappeared. Writing in self-justification on 13 May 1878, a month after the events of what would become known as 'the Blanche Bay affair', he wrote,

I have now made peace with the greater number of the towns with which we fought or rather which we punished ... I am certain that our Mission here stands better with the Natives than it did before and that we are in a better position to do them good. They respect us now as they never did before and as they all acknowledge the justice of our cause in punishing the perpetrators of the murders they bear us no ill will.... This lesson will not soon be forgotten by the tribes here. It was short

---

4   Ibid., 22 April 1878.
5   Ibid., 24 April 1878. Although Brown wrote that the people had 'lost as nearly as we can tell 90 or 100 killed and wounded,' it would later be assumed that 100 had been killed. This number was always uncertain. Evidence taken at the Inquiry by Captian Purvis on 21 September 1879 mentioned that between two and ten dead bodies were seen by each eye witness, ML A1686 CY 1365.

sharp and decisive and so it had its due effect on them. They say 'twas an earthquake not a fight'. I honestly believe that the plan I adopted was the best and was in fact the only one which could have saved the Mission and many of our lives. Tis true that many lives have been lost but the present and future good of thousands will far outbalance that.... This has been no unprovoked shooting of natives nor was it anything like an attempt to force a way into their country by force of arms.... [O]urs was an honourably conducted war to save our own lives and to prevent a recurrence of any such barbarities. There is not a native in the group who does not acknowledge that we did right and that no other resource was left to us.[6]

Even so, no amount of justification could help him escape from the shadow that now darkened his world.

* * *

It was evidence of their isolation. No ships had visited the area for months and the first opportunity to send mail was when the little trading ship *Johan Caesar* left for Fiji on 14 July 1878, three months after the murders and punitive expedition. Among the many letters that it carried to family, friends and the Mission Board was a letter from Brown to High Commissioner Sir Arthur Gordon and his colleague Sir John Gorrie in Fiji. 'It is my painful duty to inform you,' he began his succinct two pages of description of recent events. 'A large number of huts were burnt and a number of natives were killed in the Districts where the murders were committed ... everything is quite quiet now.'[7] On a happier note, George was able to report to the New Zealand family the safe birth of a son, Wallis, on 3 July. 'Lyd has done nobly this time no fuss and bother but in a nice quiet business-like manner she presented me with a fine lump of a boy and only indulged in a quiet cackle of satisfaction herself over the affair.'[8]

The months following the violence of April were difficult. Many of the teachers and other foreigners were ill with malaria and Brown's usual remedy of quinine with a dose of raw egg and brandy did not always work. Some of his valued teachers died. Brown was deeply discouraged and if he was actively engaged in general mission work apart from regular preaching appointments, it was rarely recorded. The goals set for the mission in November 1877—language learning and translation, schools, pastoral visiting—were not being met, except for the erection of some small church buildings. The island teachers were taking responsibility for preparing the few possible converts for baptism. The spiritual

---

6 Brown, Journal, 13 May 1878, partly recorded on page marked 13 January 1877.
7 Brown to Sir Arthur Gordon, Governor of Fiji and High Commissioner for Western Polynesia, 5 July 1878, George Brown Letter Book ML CY 2772.
8 Brown to Tralie Buddle, 11 July 1878 in George Brown, Letter Book, 1878–80, ML A1686-3 CY 2772.

transformation he had hoped to see among the local people was not evident. There were changes, certainly, and some chiefs were now inviting teachers and traders to their area, but this seemed to be motivated more by a desire for prestige and potential wealth to flow from the outsiders than from a desire to hear about the white man's god. Crowds of people would come for the first few mission services, out of curiosity, but then lose interest. People who had appeared to welcome the teachers had been persuaded, quite easily, to kill and eat them. The observer Wilfred Powell would write later, 'The mission had been there three years at the time of my visit, and I cannot speak very favourably of the progress it has made, though it was from no want of zeal on the part of the missionaries themselves, but from lack of sympathy in the natives.... I do not think there are ten *real* converts amongst the Duke of York natives.'[9]

Brown's own spirit was in a dark place. His journal was full of travel with the traders, his own health, collecting artefacts, hunting and fishing, irritation with his teachers and complaints about the brawling traders but with rare clues to his inner life. One journal entry read, 'The last six months have been most distressing ones to me and often I have been on the very verge of despair. Almost everyone has been ill and the care of all has been thrown on me alone. I have often felt faint and weary under the burden but God has helped me.'[10]

There was one thing that he could claim. Brown's repeated journeys to New Britain to negotiate with the clan groups and their leaders were producing results. Building on his knowledge of appropriate cultural models for peacemaking in Samoa, he had discovered and used the local system of compensation with the giving and receiving of gifts, demonstrating the symbols and rituals of peacemaking. Brown believed that he had been able to bind up the wounds of the dreadful days of battle and violence and restore the relationship to a place of friendship.[11] However, while the people of New Britain might have been prepared to live in peace, he was not sure that the Mission Board in Sydney or supporters in the colonies or England would be so forgiving. Although in private letters he was frank, boasting that 'I love the natives well and did them the kindest action I could do them by teaching that roast missionary is too expensive a dish for them to indulge in,'[12] he still feared that 'some of the goody goody folk will be very much shocked.'[13] To his cousin Tom Buddle he confided that he planned that he and his family would stay with the New Mission for the

9   Wilfred Powell, *Wanderings in a Wild Country or Three Years Amongst the Cannibals of New Britain*, London: Sampson Low, Marston, Searle and Rivington, 1883, pp. 45–46.
10   Brown, Journal, 27 May 1878.
11   Ibid., 13 May 1878.
12   Brown to Rev. Lorimer Fison, 6 July 1878.
13   Brown to Rev. Frederick Langham, Fiji, 5 July 1878.

full three years he had set himself, 'that is if our late action does not displease the powers that be. If it does I shall clear out with good conscience. If we have many such seasons as the last one this is not a billet many would covet.'[14]

Soon the letters he had sent with the ship *Johan Caesar* would reach Sydney. Would the Mission Board be shocked? Could he be called to face the church Committee of Discipline, or worse, the colonial judicial system? Although Brown assured a friend that he was 'quite content to defend our actions anywhere and before any tribunal,'[15] his bravado masked a deeper anxiety about his own future and the future of the new Mission.

* * *

On Friday 13 September 1878, two months after leaving New Britain and five months after the deaths of the Fijians, the *Johan Caesar* limped into Sydney Harbour, leaky and battered. The next day, George Brown's letters reached Benjamin Chapman and the *Sydney Morning Herald* published the first startling summary of events in remote New Britain. Members of the Mission Board read in their morning newspaper that three island missionaries had been attacked, killed and eaten and that an expedition of reprisal had gone out, leaving at least fifty people dead and property destroyed.

The Mission Board met urgently on Monday at the church office at 227 Pitt Street. Twenty-two men gathered in great dismay. If they had hoped that the newspaper account was wild exaggeration, Benjamin Chapman quickly disabused them of that hope. He presented them with Brown's very long letter, with a document signed by six white residents who had taken part in the raid. The Board members listened as Brown's words were read aloud. Their much-esteemed missionary had written, 'I have to tell you that this sad affair brought us into collision with the natives, and though that has resulted in good, I would rather not have had the tale to tell.'[16] The story unfolded in painful detail; whether it was called punishment, revenge or teaching a severe lesson, it sounded very rough justice indeed. The letter from the six white residents was an affirmation of Brown's action. They wrote, 'But for your prompt action in the matter, the lives neither of traders nor missionaries would have been safe in any part of these groups.... [We] express our conviction that your action is fully justified.'[17] The mission carpenter James McGrath had come with the *Johan Caesar* and was interviewed by an increasingly anxious Board.

---

14 Brown to Tom Buddle Jr., Auckland, 11 July 1878.
15 Brown to Consul Weber, Apia, Samoa, 6 July 1878.
16 Brown to Chapman 26 June 1878. The first thirteen pages were copied from the journal in the handwriting of Lydia Brown.
17 Letter from white residents, Port Hunter, Duke of York Islands, 23 May 1878, published in full in the *Sydney Morning Herald*, 23 September 1878.

Sitting among the Board members was a young man who listened with acute attention. This was not an academic exercise for him. As the troubling debate swirled around him, recently ordained missionary the Reverend Benjamin Danks pictured his bride Emma, waiting in Sydney to sail with him to their missionary appointment. The mission ship *John Wesley* was in Sydney Harbour, loaded with their cargo and the materials for their new house. They were due to sail the next day to join George and Lydia Brown in the New Mission.[18] He and Emma, newly married, were committed to going to the New Mission and they did not want to withdraw. Emma was the daughter of missionary John Watsford and had been raised on the legends of cannibal Fiji in the past.

The Board struggled for hours. Did Brown deserve severe censure, perhaps even withdrawal? How much information should be released to church members and the general public? What should be done about the new missionary Danks, ready to sail immediately for Fiji and then on to the New Mission? Everything had looked so promising but was now in jeopardy. The Board at last formed some careful statements 'which might possibly cover the considerable diversity of opinion as to the wisdom of the course which Mr Brown adopted.'[19] After summarising the information they had received, the Minutes of their meeting recorded that

> This meeting expresses its deepest sympathy with the Revd George Brown in the very perplexing, painful and dangerous position in which he was placed; but at the same time it deeply regrets that no other course seemed to him to be open, which would ensure the safety of himself and of the large number of persons belonging to the mission party of whom he was regarded as the protector.[20]

They decided to release all the information they had received for publication, and that Ben and Emma Danks should travel to the New Mission as planned. However, they instructed that the Danks' new house must be built as close as possible to the Brown's house at Kinawanua.

* * *

The day after the emergency meeting of the Mission Board and before the detailed news of the disaster in the New Mission was released Benjamin and Emma Danks sailed with the *John Wesley* on 17 September 1878. Emma's brother, James J.

---

18   Present at the meeting of the Missions Board on 16 September 1878 were clergy B. Chapman, G. Hurst, J. Watkin, W. Fletcher, F. Firth. W. Kelynack, G. Martin, C. Stead, F. Tait, J. Clifton, B. Danks; and laymen J. Barker, Miller, G. Read, Innes, Crawshaw, J. Hardy, Henson, Haigh, Dowsett, Reeve and Wearne, in Minutes of the Wesleyan Methodist Missionary Society, 16 September 1878, in Wesleyan Missionary Society Correspondence and Papers, ML CY 1365.
19   *Weekly Advocate*, 28 September 1878.
20   Minutes of General Missions Committee of Australasian Conference of Wesleyan Methodist Church, 1865–1898, 16 September 1878, ML MOM 1-4 CY 1365.

Watsford, went with them for a sea voyage after illness. Danks was not aware that his future senior minister Brown had told Chapman that he would prefer to have no new colleague unless that man felt that it was 'a privilege to come and cannot thank God from his heart for the opportunity of living and working, and of suffering, and perhaps dying here.'[21] They landed first in Fiji, hoping to recruit more Fijian workers for the New Mission but wondering whether news of the murders would discourage them. It was one thing to be told you *might* be killed by cannibals. It was another to learn that men you knew had indeed been killed and eaten. However, they found that the men who had volunteered to go were still determined to keep their promise. When one was offered the chance to withdraw from the mission party, he answered that his 'mind was made up that I go,' and his wife, when asked, said 'I am the outrigger of the canoe and when the canoe goes, I go.'[22]

* * *

As the new recruits sailed north, George and Lydia Brown were wondering about the way the news of the deaths and the raid would be received in the colonies. Months earlier, Brown had written with foresight to Chapman,

> There will, no doubt, be a difference of opinion about my conduct in connection with the punishment of the murderers—for that I am quite prepared—and I shall not be surprised to hear that many condemn the course we felt compelled to adopt. To them I can only give the reasons that influenced us, but I cannot make them feel their force as we felt them. The responsibility of our acts rests in a great measure upon me, and that responsibility I am quite willing to take.[23]

His prophecy was correct. As soon as the details of the events in New Britain were made public, a storm broke. In church papers and the general press everyone had an opinion. Those who supported Brown suggested that the circumstances were without precedent and that he had been forced to act to protect the lives of others; he deserved sympathy not blame, they said. Even those who wanted to defend Brown were guarded in their words, however, speaking of regret that he could not have found some other course of action. At the very least, they declared, the matter should have been reported to the High Commissioner for the Western Pacific, Sir Arthur Gordon, and left for him to take appropriate action. Why didn't Brown withdraw his people from danger, or gather in a defensive position at Port Hunter? Within the church community there was a war of words unleashed with sharp letters being published over many months, some critical of Brown and some attempting to defend him, until

---

21   Brown to Chapman, 24 June 1878.
22   James J. Watsford, Journal of a trip to New Britain 1878–1879, 10 October 1878, ML MOM 127.
23   Brown to Chapman, 24 June 1878, published in the *Weekly Advocate*, 21 September 1878.

the church paper declined to publish more correspondence on the matter. A number of journalists in the colonial newspapers from Sydney and Melbourne to Auckland and Fiji were savage in their condemnation and mockery of the missionary enterprise. Brown, wrote one, had 'befouled his character as a Christian minister.'[24] The Mission Board had 'had dust thrown in its eyes.'[25] Another was scathing of 'missionaries on the war path ... bearers of glad tidings who take care to have their muskets with them ... Christian arguments in the shape of bullets ... if Wesleyan Christianity obtains a foothold in New Britain it will have been by the means introduced by Mohammed—the sword in one hand, the book in the other—baptism or butchery the only alternatives of the people.'[26]

News of the troubles in New Britain travelled around the world. A report that reached England via the United States demonstrated the somewhat slippery grasp those in the northern hemisphere had of the geography of the Pacific; it was said that 'Five Wesleyan Missionaries are alleged to have been killed and eaten *by the Maoris* [sic] *in New Zealand.*'[27] In London, the Aborigines Protection Society brought their concerns about the distant missionary George Brown to Sir Michael Hicks-Beach, Secretary of State for the Colonies at Whitehall, requesting a judicial enquiry. They were assured that when Sir Arthur Gordon returned to Fiji later in the year he was instructed to 'hold as full and complete an investigation as circumstances will admit.'[28] Brown had predicted the concern of the Aborigines Protection Society; unrepentant, he suggested that those 'who remain snug and comfortable in their own safe and quiet homes and who think the poor natives are always right and are always ill-treated and oppressed by whites will condemn my action in this matter and be dreadfully shocked.'[29]

* * *

Brown was still isolated from the rest of the world and remained 'anxious to hear what you stay at home folk think of us.'[30] It was with some relief that they welcomed the unexpected visit of two British men-of-war to the area early in August. The captains of both the *Beagle* and the *Sandfly* had been unaware of the incidents of April but each undertook to enquire into the issue and provide an independent report for the colonial authorities. It is unlikely that villagers felt free to complain against the actions of outsiders to outsiders, especially as

---

24 *Fiji Argus*, 22 November, 29 November, 6 December 1878, quoted in the *Weekly Advocate*, 3 May 1879; letter to Editor, 'The Fiji Argus and the Rev. George Brown'.
25 Ibid.
26 *Melbourne Age*, 27 September 1878.
27 *Weekly Advocate*, 14 December 1878.
28 *Weekly Advocate*, 26 July 1879, quoting reports from the London *Times* of letters of 26 December 1878 (Aborigines Protection Society) and 27 May 1879 (Secretary of State for the Colonies).
29 Brown to Rev. James Wallis Sr., 2 July 1878.
30 Ibid., 9 September 1878.

Brown was also present on the ship. Nonetheless, reports were written which Brown believed were not unfavourable 'either as regards my judgement or my humanity'.[31] Despite the tension of waiting for long-delayed news from home, with his own illness and the death from disease of more of his teachers, Brown tried to go on with his work. He accepted an invitation by Captain Horne of the *Sandfly* to join them on a visit to the north coast of New Ireland in September. Unfortunately, their return was delayed. Lydia Brown was very alarmed to hear rumours that her husband had been murdered. When he did not return at the expected time, and day followed day without news, she became more and more terrified that the rumour could be true. She was alone, isolated and responsible for her children Geoffrey, Mabel and baby Wallis, while she prayed daily for her five other children; she had had no word of them for over a year. To her intense relief, the *Sandfly* came back at last, with Brown weary but unscathed. Brown brushed off the danger and complained that the villagers had 'most industriously circulated the report that I was killed by the natives at Topaia.'[32] The rumour could so easily have been true.

Figure 8. Lydia Brown and women at Kabakada, New Britain 1880.

Source: George Brown photograph collection: Australian Museum V6397.

---

31 Brown to Lizzie (Buddle) Arthur, New Zealand, 9 September 1878.
32 Brown, Journal, 22 September 1878.

The ship *Dancing Wave*, direct from Sydney, arrived in November. Here at last were the letters and newspapers they had long hoped to see. There were letters from their family, and the good news that Benjamin and Emma Danks were on their way to join them. Significantly, the bundle of newspapers made clear the attitude of the people in the colonies to the Blanche Bay affair. In his journal on 13 November Brown wrote, 'Most of them disapprove. Well I must just leave it for the present.... Whatever they think or say now I have a clear conscience about it.' Clear conscience or not, he added 'Not at all well today.'[33] He was angry to see the false accusation that the island teachers normally moved among village communities carrying weapons—the 'baptism or butchery' slur. The thing that hurt the most, however, was reading letters from those he loved and respected who spoke of their grief and regret that he could not have found some other way to respond to the murders. His good reputation was at serious risk.

Figure 9. Teachers and catechists of mission, Kabakada, New Britain 1880.

Source: George Brown photograph collection: Australian Museum V 6396.

In a curious way, at the same time as he was being severely criticised by distant peers, George Brown was beginning to see signs that the New Mission was making progress. Fewer people carried arms, women and children were more likely to move without protection, and sorcery seemed less common. People were attending church services in greater numbers and three men were almost ready for baptism. Brown reflected, 'Two years ago they laughed at us and the

---

33   Brown, Journal, 13 November 1878.

lotu and often wanted to know what we would pay them if they came to hear us preach.'[34] After long and patient negotiation, Brown had made his peace with the chief Taleli and his people and he believed that now reconciliation had been achieved with all the clan groups who had been part of the violence of April. As a sign of a more stable community, while one of the visiting ships was in harbour, the local villages presented a display of wealth with a canoe carried up the beach loaded with shell money and chief To Pulu standing aloft in it. Brown set up his photographic equipment and captured four images as 'the *dukduks* and all the people came on with weapons poised and keeping regular time to the drums until they all mixed in a mob in regular hurly burly.'[35]

* * *

Five days later, on 1 December 1878, in the middle of the night a ship entered the channel. It was the *John Wesley* at last. Waiting on board in the dark were Benjamin and Emma Danks. Their honeymoon holiday was over and now, although they assured each other that they were not afraid, they knew that they faced a new and very strange world. Across the water drifted the sounds of a village on the shore; the beat of drums, shouts, singing. They had been warned that there had been violence only months earlier, and it was hard to know what to expect. Ben was moved by the courage of his bride. A canoe came alongside and three men clambered on board. The new teachers watched while their wives gathered nervously around Emma Danks, astonished. In the lantern light they saw three naked men with a white streak painted down their chests and abdomens, greased hair, faces painted with black pigment or lime, mouths and teeth orange-red. Danks noted that 'the sight was not exhilarating.'[36] The new arrivals were relieved when George Brown came on board and met for the first time a couple who would become dear friends and colleagues for the rest of their lives. They rowed through the warm darkness to the landing place several miles distant. Danks would always remember the moment of arrival.

> The mission house was then situated on a jutting point of land, about one hundred and fifty feet high, which formed the northern head of Port Hunter. The path leading up to it was just a rough bush track. Mr Brown led Mrs Danks up this steep road while Mr Watsford and I stumbled after them. The jungle smelt damp and the way was pitch black. We reached the summit, and passing along the path in front of the house saw Mrs Brown standing in the doorway holding a lamp in her hand. As we stepped on to the verandah she gave us the heartiest of welcomes....

---

34 Ibid., 20 November 1878.
35 Ibid., 26 November 1878.
36 Benjamin Danks, *In Wild New Britain: The Story of Benjamin Danks, Pioneer Missionary*, from his diary, ed. Wallace Deane, Sydney: Angus and Robertson, 1933, p. 15.

As she took my dear one in her arms and kissed her, I experienced a feeling of relief and content, which helped me much in the succeeding days. Mrs Danks went to her like a daughter to a mother.[37]

It seemed that the time had come for a new beginning.

---

37   Danks, *In Wild New Britain*, pp. 16–17.

10. 'A fearful mistake'

New Britain, Sydney, New Zealand, Tonga, Fiji 1879

There was no time to waste. Obstacles seemed to be evaporating at last. George Brown was relieved to find that the new missionary Benjamin Danks was practical, energetic, sensible and good company. After so many months of isolation, ships were arriving at Port Hunter in the weeks before Christmas, including German businessman Hernsheim's *Pacific* and the mission ship *John Wesley*. Contrary to the directions of the Mission Board, Brown was determined to locate the house for the new missionaries some forty miles away beyond the water, on New Britain. Although the two men made a token exploration of other possible sites on Duke of York Island and later on New Britain, where Danks admired the 'untamed, wildly beautiful and romantically tangled bush,' the younger man soon realised 'from Mr Brown's conversation that we should find only one, at Kabakada.'[1] By the time Danks wrote to the Mission Board asking them to rescind their direction that the two British households should be located together, the timber had already been delivered to the Kabakada site. Danks assured the Board that 'we quite agree with Mr Brown when he says that building a house on Duke of York would be wasting timber.'[2]

Their first Sunday together was a great day. The Browns invited their guest the Reverend J.J. Watsford to baptise their six-month-old son Wallis, 'a fine fat fellow—one of the very finest I have ever seen.'[3] Later that morning, George Brown

> had the pleasure of baptizing seven of our young men, five Duke of York and two from New Ireland.... These are the first fruits of our work here. They have all been under instruction.... Twas a thrilling service and we all felt very much encouraged. It was especially gratifying to me and I felt very grateful indeed to God for His grace and help.... From today dates the beginning of the Church in this Mission. God grant that many many more may be added to the number.[4]

---

1 Benjamin Danks, *In Wild New Britain: The Story of Benjamin Danks, Pioneer Missionary*, from his diary, ed. Wallace Deane, Sydney: Angus and Robertson, 1933, pp. 18–24.
2 Danks to Benjamin Chapman, 25 December 1878, published in the *Weekly Advocate*, April 1879.
3 George Brown to Elizabeth, Amy, Monica, Claudia and Frederick Brown, 16 December 1878 in Brown, George, Journal, 1877–Dec 1879, ML A1686-13, 14, 15 CY 2762.
4 Brown, Journal, 8 December 1878, George Brown, Journal, 1877–Dec 1879, ML A1686-13, 14, 15 CY 2762. The men baptised were: Peni Lelei, Paula Kaplen, Jiali Noa, Inoki To Bagbag, Loti Alik, Petero Topilike, Apisa Turane.

That same day the seven young men shared in the service of Holy Communion for the first time. It was important to the Browns to have Watsford visit them. They knew that when he returned to the colonies he would be able to describe what he had seen and assure the church at home that the mission was indeed making progress. Before he left them, Watsford led an evening service in English, preaching from Psalm 40, 'I waited patiently for the LORD; and he inclined unto me, and heard my cry. He brought me up also out of an horrible pit, out of the miry clay, and set my feet upon a rock.... And he hath put a new song in my mouth, even praise unto our God.'[5]

The German ship, the *Ariadne* under Captain Bartolomäus von Werner, arrived in the region on 10 December 1878. George Brown went on board the next day. Travelling with the *Ariadne* was the German Consul for Samoa and Tonga, Theodor Weber, known to Brown from his Samoan years. They brought news from Fiji. Chief Justice Sir John Gorrie intended to visit the region to investigate the case and could arrive within weeks. There were rumours, they said, that Brown was 'to be put on his trial for manslaughter, and that he would be punished at least with five years imprisonment, as the privilege of defending his life in such a manner could not be allowed to a missionary.'[6] Brown was encouraged when von Werner and Weber expressed sympathy with his position, suggesting that bloody confrontation was the only way to gain the respect of savages and save the lives of their German compatriots. Weber and von Werner offered to write formal letters of vindication which Brown could use in his defence in court.[7]

Years later, when writing his life story for a wide audience, the visit of the *Ariadne* and the provision of letters of support were framed in terms of a friendly and fruitful encounter. The reality was otherwise. Consul Weber had an agenda; he wanted to negotiate the acquisition of two harbours for the German Reich, at Mioko and Makada in the Duke of York Island group, as a strategic base from which village men could be recruited and sent to Samoa to work on plantations. Brown, as interpreter and a person known and trusted by the village leaders, was ideally placed to facilitate this. He was already acting as interpreter and advisor in a local court case between village leaders and the traders. So letters of affirmation of Brown's role in the punitive raid were written by Captain von Werner and Consul Theodor Weber on 14 December but withheld from Brown. In exchange for Brown's help in facilitating the 'purchase' of the coveted harbours, they said, and a promise that he would not challenge the labour traffic but promote it, they would give him the letters of support.[8]

---

5   Psalm 40:1–3, King James Bible.

6   Captain Von Werner to Imperial Admiralty, Berlin, from Duke of York Island, 12 December 1878. Translation quoted in George Brown, *George Brown: Pioneer-Missionary and Explorer: An Autobiography*, London: Hodder and Stoughton, 1908, pp. 280–82.

7   Brown, *George Brown: Pioneer-Missionary and Explorer*, pp. 279–82.

8   Jacob Anderhandt, *Eduard Hernsheim, die Südsee und viel Geld*, Biography, Münster: MV-Wissenschaft, 2012, pp. 262–69.

Brown objected. During his years in Samoa he had been outspoken about the problems for Samoan communities when their land was taken over by foreign ownership and now he saw it happening again. The removal of numbers of young men from their island communities to labour far from home was also fraught with difficulties, as he well knew. At first he bitterly resisted what amounted to blackmail. For days he argued against these demands, struggling for a different solution. In frustration, Weber threatened to send a cable to Berlin condemning the missionary's actions during the 'Six Day War', knowing that this information would reach London and thence the Western Pacific High Commission in Fiji. Only then did Brown capitulate. In exchange for the letters of support he reluctantly agreed to their demands, prepared a form of legal contract of sale for the harbours, albeit with some concessions, and negotiated this with the village chiefs. Some time later, Captain von Werner sent a confidential message to the chief of the Imperial Admiralty in Berlin; he was uneasy about the tactic they had used against Brown, fearing that it had not been honourable, but admitted that the temptation to exploit the situation had been too great.[9] Brown now had letters about his 'heroic deed' but at a significant cost. He was gagged and unable to speak out on perceived injustices to the people of the place. The seeds had been sown for future decades of distrust and cynicism about the intentions of the German Reich.

By Boxing Day 1878, the *Ariadne*, *Pacific* and *John Wesley* had all gone, taking guests, curios, correspondence and reports with them. Although he had offered to serve in the New Mission for three years, Brown knew that his term could be interrupted at any moment. The Wesleyan Methodist Conference would meet in February and might choose to recall him. Chief Justice John Gorrie might arrive from Fiji any day; it was known that Gorrie was committed to the values of the Aborigines Protection Society in England, and a critic declared that he was 'most dangerous, for he invariably takes the part of the Natives against the white settlers.'[10] That did not bode well for Brown. So Brown threw himself and his team into their work. In January, February and March 1879, Brown was constantly on the move, travelling between the communities where the teachers lived, introducing Danks to the region, organising carpenter McGrath to begin the new mission house, opening new bush church buildings, preaching and selecting sites for new stations. He met with influential chiefs Taleli and Bulilai, 'always unarmed', and after exchanges of gifts and further conversations came to the conclusion that 'we are very good friends now'.[11] If he was frequently ill and exhausted, he put it down to the heavy demands of his work.

---

9   Ibid., pp. 268–69. Von Werner's confidential letter to the Admiralty remained in secret Archives for decades, separated from other material about the South Seas.
10   Bridget Brereton, *Law, Justice and Empire: The Colonial Career of John Gorrie, 1829–1892*, Kingston, Jamaica: University of West Indies Press, 1997, p. 130.
11   Brown, Journal, 22 January 1879.

It was all very well for Brown to state confidently of the punitive raid, as he did in his journal in January, 'I do not hesitate to say that good and only good has resulted... Our action then saved the Mission and saved our lives.'[12] He knew that by the end of the month his friends and his critics would meet in Sydney for their annual Conference, and would make their own judgement.

In early February 1879, the men of the Wesleyan Methodist Conference of New South Wales and Queensland met in the Centenary Church in York Street, Sydney. It was time to debate the question of the Blanche Bay Affair. The Reverend Benjamin Chapman, as Mission General Secretary, presented the range of documentary evidence from the ships' captains, the German Consul and Brown himself. The general opinion of all these witnesses, he told the Conference, was that Brown was not censurable for the course he had taken. There were, of course, other opinions. The Reverend William Moore, a veteran of the mission in Fiji who had experienced danger from cannibals, contended that any missionary to a pioneer mission should have known that they might be called on to lay down their lives but certainly not to take life. Brown ought to have been a 'protector of the natives whom they went to instruct and civilize,'[13] Moore said and declared that Brown,

> in the extremity of great and terrible difficulty, had committed a fearful mistake, which would yet have a very baneful influence on the missionary work in New Britain.... The Conference should express its regret at the course Brother Brown had taken, otherwise it would be a blot on their missionary character.[14]

The debate was lively. Members of Conference were divided between those who shared Moore's anxiety about militant missionaries and those who, often from personal loyalty, supported their friend George and argued that his actions had been justifiable. Should they give Brown the opportunity to defend himself at the next Conference? Should they leave the matter in the hands of the Western Pacific High Commission but fail to demonstrate whether or not his own Church approved Brown's actions? Speeches became more and more emotional. Motions, counter motions and amendments were offered. An awkward compromise was reached. After expressing sympathy for Brown in a desperate situation, the conference decided,

> It fully appears to us, that in the judgement of the natives themselves, Mr Brown has administered justice without seeking revenge; and whilst

---

12   Brown, Journal, 8 January 1879.
13   William Moore, quoted in the *Weekly Advocate*, 15 February 1879.
14   Ibid.

we still cherish the utmost confidence in Mr Brown as our agent in New Britain, we at the same time now solemnly affirm that we can never sanction the use of military measures in our missionary enterprises.[15]

The name of George Brown remained, however, one that stirred strong feelings, of embarrassment, anxiety, affection, irritation and loyalty. Even among his strongest supporters there may still have been a suspicion that, much as they loved the man, he may have made a 'fearful mistake'.

* * *

Ominously, the journal entries that George Brown had recorded in the early months of 1879 listed a demanding program that would have tested the fittest person. Scattered among references to long, hot, exhausting journeys in open boats or tramps through tropical bush were also frequent references to illness, particularly malaria. Through March he was ill for most of the month, often bedridden. By the first anniversary of the murder of the Fijians in April he was able to preach again near his home, but admitted in a letter to Benjamin Chapman that he was anxious about a planned trip to New Ireland to open some new church buildings. 'At present I am not fit for much. I never was very stout, as you know, but now I am as thin and miserable as I can well be. I had the fever very often and a little too much exposure and anxiety.'[16]

Colonial opinion and colonial justice were on his mind. 'Chief Justice Gorrie hasn't showed up yet,' he told a cousin unrepentantly, 'and so I am still out of "quod" [prison]'... I ain't a bit sorry and if ever I am spared to stand before another audience in the Colonies or in England I shall not be slow to tell them so. I suppose I've ruined forever my chance of spouting at Exeter Hall. So be it.'[17] Because of Brown's illness, Ben and Emma Danks had not yet moved to their new house on New Britain. Despite his inexperience, Danks was doing most of the work.

It was a hard decision but at the end of April 1879, when the opportunity came to send George Brown back to Australia for medical help with the small steamer *Alice*, it was decided that he should go. Danks had been shocked to see his superintendent looking 'like a walking corpse'.[18] The *Alice* was too small to accommodate Lydia and the children on the risky journey across the Coral Sea to Cooktown in North Queensland and so with deep anxiety Lydia farewelled

---

15   *Weekly Advocate*, 15 February 1879.
16   Brown to Chapman, 7 April 1879 in Brown, Letter Book, 1876–1880, ML A1686-3 CY 2772.
17   Brown to Tralie Buddle, 14 April 1879. Exeter Hall on the Strand in London during much of the nineteenth century was the scene of many influential gatherings for those committed to the evangelical missionary enterprise and social action, through organisations such as the Temperance Association and the Anti-Slavery League.
18   Danks, *In Wild New Britain*, p. 35.

her man. Danks sent a letter to Chapman: 'Mr Brown is very ill; so ill, that I am very much concerned about the future … he is almost worn out with continued suffering.'[19] He did not add that at the last moment before climbing into the whale boat to go out to the *Alice* Brown confided, 'I have not told Mrs Brown but I doubt whether I shall return.'[20] Weighted with the burden of responsibility, the younger minister with only five months experience in the region then returned to what he called 'the house of weeping hearts.'[21] Lydia Brown, it seemed, already understood.

There was now a great silence and an empty place that her active man had once filled. There was no lack of work to be done or challenges every day, but he was not there to share it. Lydia Brown had no way of knowing whether George had survived the voyage to Cooktown or whether he had gone on to Sydney. The newlyweds sheltered in the mission house at Kinawanua with Lydia Brown and her children, and they all valued the support and care of the island teachers in their community. Lydia Brown, as the most experienced and senior among them at the age of forty, took responsibility for the many who were ill, with the medicine and skill available to her; their recent guest Watsford had described her special qualities as 'her quietness' and 'nursing'.[22] When there was trouble in the nearby villages, as when the new convert Peni Lelei was being pressured to take a life in revenge for the murder of a kinsman, Lydia did her best to mediate but missed her husband's confident approach.[23]

The long hot days passed and still there was no news. A strong earthquake rattled everything in the mission house in June. Danks and Lelei began a little school with twenty-six students, despite the objections of some chiefs. Danks was making some progress on analysing the local language. News came from New Britain that British Commodore Wilson was in the area to investigate the murders and aftermath, and was annoyed to find that Brown was away and that many of the original British participants in the raid had now left the region or were dead. So the days went by through June, July and August as they went on waiting.[24]

* * *

Beyond their horizon, the *Alice* steamed south to Cooktown. George Brown was given hospitality there and again in Brisbane, finally arriving in Sydney still very unwell on 31 May 1879. His friends gave him a warm welcome but he soon realised that debate over his actions in the 'Blanche Bay Affair' was still

---

19   Danks to Chapman, 30 April 1879, published in the *Weekly Advocate*, June 1879.
20   Danks, *In Wild New Britain*, p. 35.
21   Ibid.
22   James J. Watsford, Journal of a trip to New Britain, 1878–79, ML MOM 127, note on back page.
23   Danks, *In Wild New Britain*, p. 39.
24   Ibid., pp. 44–50.

raging. In the colonies including Fiji a fierce battle of words was being waged through correspondence in a number of newspapers. The continuing interest in the controversy was so great that, unwisely, George Brown was persuaded to speak in the Bourke Street Methodist Church about his experiences. His sense of obligation outdid his strength. To the great alarm of his friends, Brown collapsed during his speech. His friends, in tears, were sure he was dying and Brown himself admitted later that he thought so, too. Chapman immediately rebuked those asking Brown to visit their churches, adding, 'Would they kindly take the hint that Mr Brown is too unwell to engage in this kind of work ... he needs rest.'[25]

Brown was a very sick man. As his condition grew progressively worse even the best medical advice in Sydney was unable to help him. (The tropical diseases that troubled him were outside their experience.) Chapman and Brown's brother-in-law William Fletcher were given the task of telling Brown that he was dying. Brown thought of his children in New Zealand, and asked that they be brought to Sydney. No ship was due to leave Auckland for another ten days, so Brown announced, 'Well! All I can say is I do *not* feel inclined to die just now,' and Chapman responded 'Well, don't die!'[26] And so, although a very difficult and wilful patient, he did not die after all. To the alarm of his friends, he then decided that a sea voyage would do him good and that he would sail for Auckland to visit his children there. He was told that he would surely die at sea. When he embarked on the *Hero* in July, the captain observed that all that could be seen was a hat, a great coat, and a pair of boots. Even so, his health began to return and Brown was able to enjoy a few weeks with his five children in Auckland before returning to Sydney in August.[27] He was anxious to be free to go back to the New Mission and Lydia but knew that he had almost certainly not yet escaped facing a tribunal on his actions the previous year. The Secretary of State for the Colonies had instructed High Commissioner Gordon to 'hold as full and complete an investigation as circumstances will permit.'[28]

So September 1879 began. Two lives—the man George and the woman Lydia—continued. Apart, invisible and silent to each other, they were each counting the days and hours until they could be together again. In Sydney in springtime, George Brown's health was better than it had been and although the Board was worried about him, they decided that they should 'leave him unfettered to act upon his own judgement on his arrival at the Duke of York'; he was anxious to

---

25   *Weekly Advocate*, 7 June 1879; Brown, *George Brown: Pioneer-Missionary and Explorer*, pp. 299–301.
26   Brown, *George Brown: Pioneer-Missionary and Explorer*, p. 302.
27   Ibid., pp. 301–03.
28   *Weekly Advocate*, 26 July 1879, quotes article from the *Sydney Morning Herald*, 19 July 1879, copied from the London *Times*.

attempt some Bible translation and offered to return for one more year.[29] He now prepared to sail from Sydney with the intention of visiting Fiji to meet with the High Commissioner there before returning, he hoped, to the New Mission.[30] He knew that by presenting himself to the judiciary in Fiji he was stepping open-eyed into the lion's jaws, but he just wanted the thing to be over. It was now nearly five months since he had heard news of his family. In the northern islands, still not knowing whether her husband had lived or died, Lydia Brown waited.

In the week that George Brown sailed from Sydney with the *John Wesley*,[31] a report was being written for the British authorities in Fiji about the Blanche Bay Affair. British naval Commodore Wilson had delegated his authority to Captain Purvis of the ship *Danae* to investigate the events of April 1878. One finding was that the original estimate of numbers of those who had been killed during the raid had been greatly inflated; when pressed, the many eyewitnesses each admitted to having seen no more than between two and ten bodies at most, and so the stories of up to one hundred dead appeared to be apocryphal. In addition, the witnesses had explained that Brown had not acted alone but as part of a larger group, and was in fact separated from the party that had done most of the killing and most of the destruction of property. The captain of the *Danae* assured Lydia Brown that his formal report was not entirely damning. Captain Purvis had written that

> Rev. Brown could not fail to be present in order to give the full weight of his authority to proceedings; he however appears to have spent most of the time on the beach trying to bring the natives of some of the other districts to reason and was not personally in the places where most of the natives were killed ... [and] could hardly have acted otherwise than he did.[32]

Lydia Brown sent letters to George in the hope that he would receive them in Fiji, and was able to tell him that they were all well. At last there seemed some hope that the miserable matter might be laid to rest and that her husband could come home.

The weeks were passing and by now George Brown was at sea with the *John Wesley*. If he could have had his way, he would have set a course direct to Duke of York and Lydia, but the ship went first to Tonga. There he fretted, acting begrudgingly as note taker while a disciplinary committee from the Conference

---

29 Minutes of General Missions Committee of Australasian Conference of Wesleyan Methodist Church, 1865–1898, 8 September 1879, ML MOM 1-4 CY 354.
30 *Weekly Advocate*, 20 September 1879.
31 Brown, Journal, 18 September 1879.
32 Official report of investigation initiated by Commodore Crawford Wilson and carried out by Captain Purvis of *Danae*, 21 September 1879, ML A1686-18 CY 1365.

attempted to deal with problems surrounding an intransigent missionary, the Reverend Shirley Waldemar Baker. Baker was a contemporary of Brown; their paths had crossed in the past and would cross, painfully, in the future. Conference intended that Baker should be recalled but Baker, supported by the King of Tonga and many petitioners had no intention of budging. At the end of three frustrating weeks Brown may not have been impressed when Baker announced publicly that 'if he were young, and did not love to remain in Tonga, he would go to the new Mission.'[33] On 30 October, they sailed for Fiji; Brown noted in his journal that he was 'heartily glad to get away.'

* * *

At Kinawanua during October, while Brown was delayed in Tonga, the spectre of grave illness stalked through the mission community once more. First, seven-year-old Geoffrey Brown fell ill with malaria. The next day, little one year old Wallis, who had just begun to toddle and was the delight of the whole community, began to have convulsions. He seemed to recover a little, but then Emma Danks also collapsed with malaria, to be followed a few days later by Ben Danks. Two of the teachers were also gravely ill and brought to Kinawanua. Lydia Brown and her Samoan house servants had the care of a household of sweating, shivering, vomiting, hallucinating, pain-racked people. On the day that George Brown was setting out from Tonga for Fiji, Danks wrote a grief-stricken letter to Chapman.

> We have passed through no small trouble since my last by the *Danae*. Death has cast a shadow over our home and our hearts are sore.… What a mercy that Mrs Brown was not taken ill! In the midst of all this care, suddenly, on Sunday morning the 12th of October, Wallis died. I will not attempt to describe our house that morning; enough to say that we felt that no greater calamity could befall us, and everything seemed dark. We buried him on Monday morning,—a sad task for me and a heart-rending one for the lonely mother!… We have been expecting the *Wesley* for a long time … [and] have now given up all hope of seeing her before the end of November or beginning of December.[34]

Lydia Brown was exhausted. And every day, while she heard news of more illness, white lawlessness and tribal violence on every side, she watched from her cliff-top verandah for a sail on the curve of the sea, the sign that her husband was coming back to her.

* * *

---

33   *Weekly Advocate*, 13 December 1879.
34   Danks to Chapman, quoted in Brown, *George Brown: Pioneer-Missionary and Explorer*, pp. 336–37.

In Levuka, the colonial headquarters of the High Commission of the Western Pacific in Fiji, the *Danae* had just arrived with letters for Brown and the report for the High Commissioner. As far as Brown knew, his family was still well and safe. There was further delay while they waited for the two key figures of authority, Sir Arthur Gordon the High Commissioner, and Chief Justice Sir John Gorrie, to be available in Levuka. It quickly became clear that each man insisted that he had the authority to deal with the case against Brown and they were overheard quarrelling furiously over it.[35] The Chief Justice sent Brown a summons to appear at court on 13 November 1879 with the charge, 'You have this day been charged before this Court for that you in or about the month of April 1878 did kill and slay certain natives of the island of New Britain whose names are unknown against the peace of Our Lady Queen her Crown and Dignity. Regina v. Brown.'[36]

The High Commissioner, on the other hand, saw no ground on which to institute any criminal charges, and he could not recommend any such proceedings. He declared that 'although I by no means commit myself to unqualified approval of Mr Brown's action, I altogether disapprove of his being treated as a criminal.'[37]

The next few days were tense. Some of the missionaries in Fiji were almost sick with worry on behalf of their colleague though Brown himself seemed surprisingly calm. At one point Brown was called to Government House to meet Sir Arthur Gordon and his Secretary J.B. Thurston; in the light of all the evidence before him, Gordon suggested that the measures taken in New Britain may have been 'hasty and unnecessary but there is a vast difference between indiscretion and criminality … nothing which has come before me would lead me to impute to you any suspicion of crime.'[38] Even so, the court case was to proceed. Far away, on the day of the court case, Ben Danks and Lydia Brown thought they recognised the mission ship in the distance. They were mistaken.

Fearing that Brown would be jailed for manslaughter, his mission friends arranged for a barrister to appear in his defence. On the morning of the court case they were astonished to discover that the case had collapsed. It was still not clear whether Brown would have been found guilty of manslaughter but the Prosecutor Attorney-General Garrick had withdrawn from the case and Chief Justice Gorrie had bowed to the superior authority of Gordon. With a sense of anticlimax, Brown heard Gorrie explain that because of the time that had elapsed since they first heard of the events of April 1878, the opinion of the

---

35   Brown, Journal, 10 November 1879.
36   Brown, Wesleyan Methodist Missionary Society Correspondence and Papers, 1890–1895, ML A1686 CY 1365.
37   Quoted in context of Letter to Editor from Rev. B. Chapman, in the *Weekly Advocate*, 29 November 1879.
38   Extract from the Minutes of Proceedings before HM High Commissioner for the Western Pacific, 11 November 1879, signed by Thurston, quoted in Brown, Journal, 11 November 1879.

High Commissioner 'that yours is not such a case as ought to be so prosecuted' and because of the lack of a prosecutor, 'I therefore in these circumstances do not propose to proceed further with this matter, indeed there is in point of fact no prosecutor (The Attorney General was here asked if it was not so and he replied Yes) and you are accordingly free to depart.'[39]

It was not an unqualified acquittal. No court had declared Brown innocent and there might still be a further enquiry. George Brown realised that he had come frighteningly close to a prison sentence. He had visited a man in prison that day, a trader he had known in New Britain who was incarcerated for murder. He too might have been in such a cell. That night he noted in his journal,

> There is very little doubt I fear that Mr Gorrie is not at all pleased that I am not convicted. I was told before I landed in Levuka by those who know him well that he had prejudged the case and was determined to get a conviction…. He wishes to get himself a name and also to show to the world what a great blessing this High Commissioner's court is to suffering humanity of whom he, Mr Gorrie, is the gallant champion.[40]

The *John Wesley* attempted to sail the day after the Court, but with little wind was forced to anchor for the night in the lagoon opposite the house of John Gorrie. Brown admitted that he was 'not very comfortable' about this. The mission ship eventually escaped from Fijian waters on 15 November and set sail for the north with six new mission families from Fiji and Tonga. After weeks of light winds and calms, as they began to pass among the most south-easterly of the scattered Solomon Islands, the wind began to pick up. At last, Brown thought, there was a good chance of a quick run through to the Duke of York Islands, and home with Lydia and the children.

Then, on the night of Monday 8 December 1879, a storm began. The barometer dropped rapidly, the wind blew in fierce gusts and the storm grew from a gale into a fierce hurricane, worse than anything he had experienced. In the darkness, buffeting and violent noise, with all his fellow travellers, Brown wondered not only whether he would escape the rage of the Chief Justice but would he survive the night. The ship was suddenly caught in a great wind gust. Everything not firmly anchored went flying.In his cabin, Brown narrowly avoided being crushed by the harmonium that was dislodged from its cleats and crashed across the space, stoving in the opposite wall; it was one of the more bizarre near-death moments of Brown's life. As he wrote,

> The cargo and the ballast all shifted to leeward, and the poor *Wesley* was forced down under water, and lay stricken and trembling there whilst

---

39 Brown, Journal, 13 November 1879.
40 Ibid.

the water rushed aboard…. We all felt her gradually settling down, and I climbed up the companion stairs, preferring to struggle and die in the open air than in the cabin…. No one could stand or face the storm and we all thought and felt that the end was come. There was no crying or confusion then, but just a quiet nerve-strung waiting for the ship's final plunge and the instinctive struggle for life that would follow. Many a fervent prayer ascended to heaven and many a goodbye to our loved ones far away.[41]

But the captain had not given up yet. There was a shout for axes. Axes and tomahawks were passed to men who desperately and in grave danger hacked at the masts. With a mighty crash first the main mast and then the foremast splintered and were sent overboard. But now the wreckage of masts and spars was dragging along beside the ship, still entangled with ropes attached to the shattered stumps; a courageous Tongan teacher Wiliami risked his life in the roaring darkness on the half-submerged deck to sever the remaining ropes with his axe and release the ship. The ship, shorn of its masts, was still afloat. With the help of crew and island missionaries, the ballast and cargo that had shifted to the leeward side was moved back, the hold was checked for leaks, and then they all waited for a dawn none of them had expected to see. Brown reflected that their ship could have disappeared at sea and no one would ever have known what had happened to them.[42]

* * *

In the quietness of the tropical evening on the next day, Lydia Brown opened her old autograph book and began to copy another mourning poem into its pages. It seemed a lifetime since the first entries had been written when she was a schoolgirl in Auckland. Now she was a mature woman and her heart was breaking. There were times when she disappeared into the store room and locked the door so that she could weep in privacy. Her husband seemed to be lost to her, her children distant, ill or dead, her companions often ill, some of the teachers were idle and others dead, their white neighbours antagonistic because of Benjamin Danks' opposition to the labour traffic and the local villagers indifferent or warlike. If she had been in Auckland she might have followed custom and clothed herself in dull black. She did not need to strip the colour from her faded clothing. The light and colour was fading from her world. On the page facing her sad poem was George's handwriting. Days before their

---

41   Brown, Journal 8 December 1879, also published in the *Weekly Advocate*, 31 January 1880.
42   Ibid.

wedding nearly twenty years earlier he had written of the imagery of seedtime and harvest: 'They that sow in tears shall reap in joy.'[43] The tears were real enough. Now the mother copied many lines of another's verse.

Sighs are but bubbles on the sea/Of our unfathomed agony...
Could love have saved, thou hadst not died...[44]

She signed the last page 'Copied Kinawanua D. of Y. Island. SLB In memory of darling Wallis Dec 9th 1879. Died Oct 12th 1879 aged 1 year 3 months.'[45] It was almost impossible to imagine any joy-filled harvest.

* * *

At sea in the leaden light of 9 December, the survivors surveyed the damage to the mission ship *John Wesley*. The jagged split stump of the mainmast stood only about the height of two men, with the foremast stump even shorter. Shattered bits of timber, ripped sails, tangles of ropes, the new whaleboat gone with most of the livestock, everything was in ruins and they were drifting helplessly on an endless ocean with sharks circling. For several days Captain Mansell was not able to identify their position but finally calculated that they were drifting some one hundred miles south of San Cristobal, an island among the more southerly of the string of Solomon Islands. With difficulty the crew was able to lash a spare topmast to the stump of the foremast and they set about repairing sails. George Brown was cheered by their position. They were all alive and with some repairs and clever seamanship they should be able to take control of the ship again. They were now well on their way to the Duke of York Islands and New Britain. San Cristobal was the nearest land and he was sure that they would find shelter there with members of the Melanesian Mission as well as traders linked with his friend Captain Alex Ferguson. One of Ferguson's ships could surely carry him and the island teachers on to their destination, Brown believed. Even the seasonal wind pattern should be in their favour.

With little else to occupy him, Brown kept detailed notes in his journal. At first, even when they had rigged up temporary sails no wind filled them. They were going nowhere. He became more and more anxious and noted, 'Still the same dead calm, a calm glassy sea and the sun as hot and fiery as it can well be. I keep thinking of my poor wife and I feel half mad at this detention and yet we are so powerless.'[46]

---

43   Psalm 126:5, King James Bible.
44   D.M. Muir, *Casa Wappy*, quoted in Lydia Brown's Autograph Book, entries from 1853–1880. Held by great-granddaughter Miss Nancy Joyce, Artarmon, Sydney.
45   Lydia Brown's Autograph Book.
46   Brown, Journal, December 1879.

A week after the storm, Brown and Captain Mansell had angry words. It seemed to Brown that the captain was not attempting to reach San Cristobal but instead was moving south. As the days passed his suspicions were confirmed, even though the captain had denied it at first. He was attempting the run of some 1700 miles south across open sea back to Sydney, with a disabled vessel carrying inadequate masts and spars for the sail needed, rather than turn north for the shelter of the Solomon Islands. Frustrated and furious, Brown wrote 'I can only pray that my dear wife may be comforted.... My heart aches tonight as I think of my dear wife. I feel sure that few, if any, in the colonies will justify our running away so heartlessly as we are doing now.'[47] On Christmas Day George Brown wrote disconsolately, 'Tis a sorry Christmas this to me. I have been thinking so much of my loved ones at home all day.... I know that my dear wife and all those at D of Y are thinking and talking of us today and wondering where we are.'[48]

Brown's journal filled with page after page of complaint against the ship's captain and he spent his days either keeping a grim silence or quarrelling with the man over his treatment of the island missionaries. No amount of fulmination against Captain Mansell made any difference. Every day through January the ship sailed further and further south.

* * *

There was little festivity on Christmas Day at Kinawanua. A passing ship had passed on the news that Lydia's husband had been summoned to appear in court in Fiji on a charge of manslaughter but that the proceedings had been stopped. But that had been back in November. Where was he now? This Christmas no friendly mission ship waited in the channel. No gathering of officers and friends sat at their table. Some of the neighbours among the trading community were at odds with Benjamin Danks for his criticism of the labour trade; unlike Brown he was free to speak his mind. Another neighbour, naturalist Kleinschmidt, was saying that their mission had a very bad name in Australian communities and that Brown cared more for collecting specimens—and having his name given to them—'than he did for all the souls of the New Britain people put together.'[49] It was hard to feel any lightness of spirit at Christmas. Lydia found herself thinking about the grim sequel to the story of the birth of Christ when a vengeful King Herod ordered the massacre of little boys in a bid to rid himself of the threat of a future king. She reflected on the gospel record of 'lamentation,

---

47 Ibid.
48 Ibid., 25 December 1879.
49 Danks, *In Wild New Britain*, pp. 76–77.

and weeping, and great mourning, Rachel weeping for her children and would not be comforted.'[50] Days later she wrote in her book a poem that ended: 'The heart of Rachel, for her children crying, Will not be comforted.'[51]

'Daily expecting the arrival of the *John Wesley*,' Lydia wrote. It was 23 January 1880 and the shared birthdays of eight-year-old Geoffrey and five-year-old Mabel. That same day the mission ship *John Wesley* at last made harbour.[52] Far from being near Port Hunter, Duke of York Island, just south of the equator, the crippled vessel limped into Port Jackson, Sydney. Since the storm, they had been at sea for forty-seven days and had only made contact with one other ship in the final days off the New South Wales coast. It was no use Lydia watching the Channel. Her husband was about 1700 miles away.

There was astonishment and consternation among the people gathered for the annual Conference in Sydney when Brown and the island teachers appeared. At least they were safe, but now a friend had to tell him that one of his sons was dead; this news came via Samoa. Brown wrote, 'He didn't know which but Mr Fletcher told me later on that it was my dear darling Wallis. Oh, how much I feel for my dear wife in this her grief and sorrow.'[53]

It was a very uneasy return. As he told members of the Wesleyan Methodist Conference, he did not want to be there at all. The shock of hearing that his beloved baby son was dead increased his outrage against the captain of the mission ship; he attempted a formal complaint against Mansell but chose to drop it when others saw it as a personal grudge. Brown sensed ambivalence towards him among his colleagues at the Conference. While some supported him, it was clear that others believed that he, a guilty man, had only escaped prison on a technicality. Distracted by his efforts to find a way to return to his family, Brown gave little attention to the debates in Conference over the formal recall of S.W. Baker from his missionary work in Tonga; Baker was granted permission to 'rest' without ministerial appointment for a year in New Zealand, on condition that he did not return to Tonga during that time.[54] The business of Shirley Waldemar Baker had not yet been put to rest and would return to Brown's orbit over the next decade.

On 13 February 1880, Brown sailed from Sydney once more on the *Avoca*, a schooner heading for the Solomon Islands, and sixteen days later reached harbour in Marau Sound, San Cristobal. Now, to his great relief, Brown found his old friend Captain Alex Ferguson with his trading steamer *Ripple* also in

---

50   Matthew 2:18, King James Bible.
51   Longfellow, *Resignation*, Lydia Brown's Autograph Book.
52   Brown, Journal, 23 January 1880.
53   Brown, Journal, 23 January 1880; *Weekly Advocate* 20 Dec 1879.
54   A.H. Wood, *Overseas Missions of the Australian Methodist Church Vol. 1, Tonga and Samoa*, Melbourne: Aldersgate Press, 1975, p. 163.

Marau Sound, and Ferguson offered to take Brown on to join his family as soon as he completed the job of discharging the cargo for his traders. While he waited impatiently, Brown explored the area until the *Ripple* began its progress through the islands on 9 March heading toward the Duke of York island cluster and home.

* * *

His family at Kinawanua was in grievous trouble. The relationship between Danks and the traders was deteriorating still further. Villagers had lost interest in the Christian mission, being far more attracted by the local customs of the *dukduk*. Lydia was becoming more and more afraid that her husband would never return. There had been no news of him since word that he had left Fiji in the middle of November over three months earlier. The ship, and George, must surely be lost. And then, before her father had even reached Marau Sound in the schooner *Avoca*, little Mabel fell ill with malaria on 22 February. Within days, Emma and Ben Danks as well as teacher Sositeni and his wife Seini were all ill and needing Lydia's help. She struggled to nurse everyone and to ignore the aching of her own body and heart. Of them all, the most desperately ill was Mabel, who was losing weight rapidly and had an uncontrollable fever. As the others began to recover their strength, Mabel grew weaker. No love and care, no medicine made any difference. Two days after her father left Marau Sound to coast through the beauties of the Solomon Islands, his daughter died. It was just five months to the day since her little brother Wallis had died and on 12 March a new little grave was dug beside his. Lydia Brown, though a 'shadow of her former self,' according to Danks, bravely attended to everything that needed to be done for her child, but when the funeral was over at last allowed herself to break down and weep and weep for all that she had lost, with Emma helpless to comfort her.[55] In time, Lydia added a note to her book under the entry about 'daily expecting' the mission ship. That had been over six weeks ago and there was still no sign. Perhaps George would never return. Now she added 'Dear little Mabel was taken ill on Sunday Feb 22nd and after 18 days suffering peacefully died on Thursday March 11th 9-30 p.m. "The maid is not dead but sleepeth".'[56]

It was all too hard. The sight of Mabel's doll, Mabel's sunhat, the open medical book, the useless medicine bottle and spoon beside the empty bed was unbearable. When Ben suggested that he organize a crew for the whale boat and that the two women and young Geoffrey go with him to visit the teachers on New Britain, they were glad to get away. Abandoning the mission house with all its signs of loss, they left Kinawanua in the open whale boat under the small protection of umbrellas from fiery sun and torrential rain. Over the next days

---

55   Danks, *In Wild New Britain*, pp. 81–84.
56   Lydia Brown's Autograph Book, 11 March 1880, p. 113.

they moved from one teacher's house to the next until they reached the new but empty house at Kabakada. Lydia tried to go for walks but there was no relief from staring onlookers, nowhere to go to escape into her private agony.

Figure 10. Lydia Brown at the graves of her children, Kinawanua, Duke of York Islands 1880.

Source: George Brown photograph collection: Australian Museum V 6398.

On the day Lydia left Kinawanua, George Brown sailed with Captain Ferguson from Roviana on the island of New Georgia in the Solomon chain. Leaving behind the headhunters of Roviana, who had made it very clear that they would not welcome missionaries to their region, the *Ripple* sailed north. Brown could hardly contain his excitement and anticipation during the final six days of sailing north. At last he would see his Lydia and the children, and could comfort her on the loss of their little Wallis. On Sunday morning 21 March, they were off Duke of York Island and watched a canoe coming out from a village about five miles from Port Hunter. Brown recognized Mijieli, one of his teachers. Mijieli found the encounter deeply disturbing. At first he reassured Brown that all was well with the rest of his family. But knowing that the dreadful truth had to be told sooner or later, he admitted, 'I fear, Sir, I have not told you aright about the children. You must forgive me but I had not the heart to tell you…. I couldn't bear to be the first to tell you…. There's only Geoffrey alive.' 'What! Is my wife dead?' 'No, Sir, she lives but Mabel has gone and Geoffrey alone is left.'[57]

For so long Brown had pictured the moment of his return. In his imagination he had sailed within sight of the mission house on the hillside at Kinawanua above Port Hunter and there on the verandah of the house had been the figures of his longed-for Lydia and the children, waving an excited welcome. He had imagined Lydia running to prepare a celebration meal, whisking through the house to be sure all was ready for her husband-guest, running back to the verandah to watch his progress across the water in the whale boat. He had pictured his children, jumping and shouting his name. But there was no sign. No one waved from the verandah. They had all gone to New Britain, Mijieli told him, and the house was deserted.

It was some time before George Brown could bring himself to leave the ship. His friend Alex Ferguson finally persuaded him and walked the bitter path beside him as he approached the empty house. 'Twas very sad to come home and find all so very desolate. The two little graves were just by the wayside as I entered the grounds and twas some time before I could enter the empty house,' he told his brother-in-law William Fletcher.[58] The mortar was still damp around the stones that one of the teachers had laid over the bare earth of Mabel's resting place. So close. If only… if only….

'We walked up the hill to the house and for the first time I think I really felt faint-hearted and began to think that our troubles and disappointments were never going to end.'[59] In the silent house, faced with an abandoned doll, a little pink dress and the dregs of useless medicine, George Brown was speechless with grief and shock. At last Ferguson put his arm around him and drew him gently away. 'Come away out of this, old man. I'll get up steam again and we'll go and look for Mrs Brown.' Stumbling from the house and pausing again beside the graves of his children, Brown followed his friend back to the *Ripple*. That night they left Port Hunter and steamed up the Channel for New Britain.[60]

At dawn on Monday 22 March 1880, almost eleven months since she had last seen her husband, Ben Danks woke Lydia Brown with the news that a steamer had just come into view round Cape Stevens. It was not clear, in the distance, what vessel it was but any visiting ship was welcome. Then, to their amazement, they recognised a signal. It was Ferguson with *Ripple* and the signal suggested that Brown was on board. The whaleboat was dragged to the water's edge, a

57   Brown, *George Brown: Pioneer-Missionary and Explorer*, pp. 344–45.
58   Brown to William Fletcher, March 1880, in Brown, Letter Book, 1876–1880, ML A1686-3 CY 2772.
59   Ibid.
60   Brown, *George Brown: Pioneer-Missionary and Explorer*, pp. 345–47.

crew called and Lydia climbed into it with Ben and Emma, every sense straining toward the ship where she could see, closer with every thrust of the oars, the bearded figure of George Brown. Her husband, unbelievably, lived.

Later, writing to Benjamin Chapman, Brown described watching the Kabakada mission house verandah for a sign of life; was Lydia there after all? Then they saw movement, and the whaleboat coming out to them and

> I at last saw my dear wife pale with excitement and with plain traces in her face of the effect of her many trials. I cannot tell you of our meeting when I led her into the *Ripple's* cabin. For a long time, speech was impossible and we could only weep together. We comforted ourselves with the precious words of comfort from him who is the Father of mercies.[61]

The waiting was over at last but a deep well of grief remained.

---

61   Brown to Chapman, 28 March 1880 in Brown, Letter Book, 1876–1880, ML A1686-3 CY 2772.

11. 'I wish I was twenty years younger'

New Britain, New Ireland 1880

'We hope for better times now,' George Brown wrote, in a long letter to his friend Benjamin Chapman. It had been harrowingly difficult to go back to the empty house at Kinawanua. Lydia, worn out from the many months of anxiety, grief and heavy nursing work, was now unwell herself. Benjamin Danks assured Brown that 'but for her Mrs Danks must certainly have died as he was utterly unable to help at times. They both say that they often thought that the intense sorrow when Wallis died would seriously affect her health. She seemed beyond comfort.'[1]

With a rare opportunity to send mail away with Captain Ferguson, Brown quickly set about learning from Danks and the teachers everything that had been happening during his long absence. He learned that the people were still violent, still cannibals, still 'clothed in sunshine', and their languages were still mysterious. Few had much interest in the message brought by the mission team. There were the newer issues of the labour traffic and the 'sale' of local land to traders. Brown asked the advice of the mission Board: 'Do we exceed our duty if we advise our people not to go as labourers on Samoan plantations?'[2] He had argued against the great land sales to foreigners in Samoa, and Lydia's father had done the same in New Zealand; now he saw it happening again. Villagers were parting with their land for plantations now owned by outsiders. It could only end in grief, he believed, and wrote, 'We tell them it is not right to impoverish themselves and deprive their children of the means of subsistence for the sake of a musket.'[3]

'I intend to give myself heart and strength to the language. I have not forgotten any, I think, and knowing that my stay here now must necessarily be short I purpose doing all I can,' he went on.[4] He thought Danks was 'a good-hearted sensible fellow with no starch and not afraid of dirtying his hands. May he

---

1   George Brown to William Fletcher, 27 March 1880, in George Brown, Letter Book, 1876–1880, ML A1686-3 CY 2772.
2   Brown to Chapman, 29 March 1880.
3   Ibid.
4   Ibid., 28 March 1880.

long be spared from fine gentlemen and kid gloves.'[5] Danks had also made rapid progress with the language. Now it was Brown's goal to translate the Gospel of Mark for the people of the Duke of York language group as quickly as possible. Then he would be free to take Lydia and his surviving son to be reunited with the rest of their family. As he wrote, 'I feel more than ever I did the intense desire to make the Mission here a successful one. We certainly can show more signs of progress and power than any which I or anyone else can see in the Solomons Group.'[6]

Captain Ferguson and the *Ripple* sailed on 30 March 1880. Now that all his correspondence was on its way, Brown was ready to sit down to his translation task without interruption. Or so he thought. The day after the *Ripple* sailed for the Solomon Islands they had unexpected visitors. A boat was dragged up on to their shore with three haggard strangers and one of their teachers from New Ireland. As they came to the house with a plea for help, the mission families were astonished. Their guests were speaking in French.

* * *

On the far side of the world, while George Brown was struggling to return to his home near the equator, other voyagers had been approaching that region from the north. A party of French, Belgian, Dutch and other European colonists, persuaded by the mendacious propaganda of one Charles du Breil, Marquis de Rays, had sailed from Flessingen, Holland on the ship *Chandernagore* in September 1879 with a view to establishing a colony on New Ireland. The vision they were offered was very tempting; escape from the political, religious and commercial crises of France and its neighbours in the 1870s to a tropical paradise where a model colony was to be founded. They would find, it was said, a seaport and new planned town, cheap and fertile land where the 'benefits of Christianity and our civilization' would be offered by the great Catholic missionary orders.[7] It was all a fantasy. Neither de Rays nor anyone known to him had ever seen the coast of New Ireland. He had built a phantom world from a point in a map, guided by a description by a sailor who had visited in a good week in 1823. Gullible and hopeful, some 150 people paid their money and set out. The signs were not good, even before they left Europe. When they landed at what would be called Port Breton, on 16 January 1880, they found no town but a narrow strip of arable land ringed by a rocky mountain range. When they sought an alternative place, some of them moved around the coast to a place described as 'sand and mud' or a 'brackish bog'.[8] Instead of welcoming chiefs,

---

5   Brown to Horsley, 9 November 1880.
6   Brown to Chapman, 29 March 1880.
7   J.H. Niau, *Phantom Paradise: The Story of the Expedition of the Marquis de Rays*, Sydney: Angus & Robertson, 1936.
8   Ibid.

they met people from a cannibal culture who were not inclined to hand over their land. Instead of pleasant streets with the beginnings of a city, they had to put up their own makeshift humpies. Food was short. There was little sense of genuine community as these were people from many places of origin and several languages, all striving to survive. Their ship departed without warning, taking the medicines with it. Health quickly deteriorated as people were struck down with malaria, dysentery and tropical ulcers. It was a catastrophe. In desperation, some had set off to try to find another place to settle—and had vanished forever. Others met a Fijian teacher on New Ireland, and the teacher brought them to Brown and Danks.

They called together some of their teachers to act as the crew and set off in the mission whale boat in an attempt to rescue any other survivors. It was a long, hot, hard pull for the crew across the channel. To their relief, they caught up with the *Ripple*, that had been delayed, and together they travelled on to the eastern coast of New Ireland. It had taken most of two days to reach the colonists. Ben Danks went ashore in driving rain. Brown was ill and incapacitated so stayed on board. Some men of the colony were desperate to leave. They were hungry and sick, living in little huts with minimal equipment, filthy and in a wretched state, with 'bandaged legs, all emaciated, sunken-eyed and mere skeletons.'[9] There was a rush for the boats, every man fighting for the right to board the *Ripple* and to be taken away to some sort of safety, where there was food and medicine. Foreseeing possible problems in the future, Brown insisted that the men asking for shelter sign a formal petition requesting refuge, and about forty men signed; Brown did not want to be accused, as a British Protestant, of interfering with a French Catholic colony.[10] He was assured that the remaining colonists were expecting fresh supplies soon, though he could not have known that one ship had already sailed from Barcelona with another soon to leave, bringing many more potential colonists to the precarious enterprise.

---

9   Danks, unpublished manuscript, quoted in Niau, *Phantom Paradise*, p. 33.
10   *Sydney Morning Herald*, 10 August 1881, quoted in Rosemary Harrigan, *They Were Expeditioners: The Chronicle of Northern Italian Farmers – Pioneer Settlers of New Italy with Documentation of the Marquis de Rays' Four Expeditions to New Ireland Between 1879 and 1881*, Werribee, Victoria: Rosemary Harrigan, 2006. p. 18; George Brown, *George Brown: Pioneer-Missionary and Explorer: An Autobiography*, London: Hodder and Stoughton, 1908, pp. 357–58.

Figure 11. Men of colony of Marquis de Rays, Port Breton, New Ireland 1880.

Source: George Brown photograph collection: Australian Museum V 6381.

The *Ripple* arrived back in Port Hunter during the night and in the morning Lydia saw her husband being carried up the hill to the house. He was a very sick man. Not only was George ill, he had brought with him forty-one men, many of whom were very ill with tropical ulcers, dysentery and malaria. One of them died that day and others were on the verge of death. With Brown bedridden for the first days after their arrival, it fell to Danks and the women to make arrangements, with the valuable help of the teachers and their wives. When it came to building two places to accommodate the men, one for the able bodied and another for the very sick and infectious, Danks explained, 'the poor fellows were so weak and broken-spirited by the privations which they had passed that we could get little or no help from them in this; so the labour fell upon our teachers and as many natives as we could hire.'[11]

Their clothes were badly soiled rags and Lydia soon organised for the teachers' wives to sew clean garments. Lydia had a lot of experience in caring for the bodily needs of her sick family and friends but now she was faced with the needs of a great many strangers. The rank odours, the stench of tropical ulcers, the pitiful state of helpless men, many of them young, assailed her. She did her best, in schoolgirl French learned in Auckland, to communicate with desperate

11   Danks, unpublished manuscript, quoted in Niau, *Phantom Paradise*, p. 35.

men cut off from the lands of their birth in Europe. At first the mission group expected that the refugees would care for each other but few of them had any loyalty to the others; many did not even have a language in common. Mission supplies of medicine and food were shared, with some help from local traders. Brown recognised the weight being borne by his wife; 'they were fed from our own table. This was no little tax on Mrs Brown, and also upon our resources.'[12] An Australian newspaper reported, 'The worst cases were removed to the mission premises, so as to be under the direct care of the missionary ... and more suitable food ... [the care of the very sick] became an almost unbearable burden to the Mission family, as but one only of his comrades could be persuaded to go near and help him in his dying state.'[13]

Ten men died, six were drowned and some lost their minds. Most of these were young men who, in their dying, were aware of a woman speaking their names and, in awkward French, offering the comfort of a mother. Sickly survivors began complaining as weeks passed; Brown wasn't providing enough tobacco, they said, and they were far too fragile to become gravediggers. Some found employment with nearby traders and others seemed to be settling in at Kinawanua, reluctant to return to their own colony. The mission supplies were running out. The European guests had been in the care of the missionaries for almost seven weeks and now Lydia Brown herself was ill with malaria. In late May several sea captains from German trading companies worked together to insist that enough was enough and any man who had not found employment elsewhere must return to the colony. On 25 May they transported seventeen colonists from Port Hunter back to New Ireland. Hernsheim reported that they found the new settlement in a 'most deplorable and disorganised condition.'[14] There was a little wooden store, five or six 'mere hovels', and scattered from the beach to the store was a disarray of machinery and equipment, lying in careless abandonment exposed to the elements.[15] A supply ship that arrived in April carried tons of bricks for public buildings and boxes of glass with gothic window frames but not enough food, tools or planting material.[16] The enterprise was collapsing into a ludicrous swindle, with the imminent arrival of two more shiploads of émigrés only adding to the disaster.[17]

Flames from burning huts rose near the beach at Port Hunter as the buildings that had housed the diseased colonists were destroyed. Fresh graves lay near the resting places of little Mabel and Wallis, with markers echoing names from

---

12   Brown, *George Brown: Pioneer-Missionary and Explorer*, p. 359.
13   'From a correspondent at Port Hunter 29 (19?) May 1880,' in the *Sydney Morning Herald*, 21 June 1880, quoted in Harrigan, *They were Expeditioners*, p. 20.
14   Ibid.
15   Ibid.
16   *Sydney Morning Herald*, 14 April 1880, quoted in Harrigan, *They were Expeditioners*, p. 21.
17   The *Genil* sailed from Barcelona in March 1880 and the *India* left Barcelona in July 1880 with 340 more colonists.

distant Europe.[18] There was relief when the last of the men had left the mission but the experience was not forgotten by any of them. At least one man wrote a letter of appreciation from New South Wales a year later, 'I owe you my life'.[19]

* * *

Once the distraction of the reluctant colonists was removed, Brown was able to turn his attention to his two main goals for the rest of the year. He hoped to make progress on his translation work and to try to establish the very young Christian community as a church with indigenous leadership. For some time Brown had believed that missionary endeavour was most effective when it used the strengths of indigenous agency. There was still a place for 'foreign' mission staff, he told the Conference early in 1880, but he expected converts in New Britain to preach to their own people. They should be trained for this work, as leaders in Fiji, Tonga and Samoa had been trained, but he pictured them speaking of God to their neighbours in natural and heart-felt ways long before they had formal instruction.

The first three local men were commissioned as lay preachers by Brown on 13 April 1880. His good companion Peni Lelei was from Duke of York Islands, Ilaita Togimamara was from New Britain and Petero Topilike was from New Ireland. Although Brown could not have predicted this, all three men would continue as devoted lay preachers to the end of their lives. Knowing that his own time in the region was coming to an end within months, Brown was delighted to report a few weeks later on 'the happiest Sunday I have spent in the mission field.'[20] A regular tour around the mission stations had brought him to Diwaon where, two years earlier, the Fijian Teacher Livai had been killed, dismembered and eaten. The preacher for the day was one of the newly appointed lay preachers, the local chief Ilaita Togimamara. Brown's first encounter with Ilaita had been in 1875 when he had attempted to come ashore on New Britain where no trader then dared to live; Ilaita had been among those who threatened his life that day and had challenged him with the question 'Are you not afraid?'[21] Now Brown sat and watched the same man preach from the text, 'The earth is full of the goodness of God.'[22]

> I was really astounded and delighted as I sat and heard him. His language was good, and he spoke earnestly and well, without the slightest hesitancy, and yet without any appearance of assumption. Oh! How different his language sounded to our poor attempts. The natives

18 Brown, Letter to the Editor, *Sydney Morning Herald*, 21 June 1880.
19 M.L. Bocquet to Brown, 1881, Wesleyan Methodist Missionary Society Correspondence and Papers, vol. 1, ML CY 1365.
20 Brown, *George Brown: Pioneer-Missionary and Explorer*, pp.380–81.
21 Brown to Chapman, 14 June 1880.
22 Psalm 33:5, King James Bible.

listened with ears, mouths and eyes. I never saw such an attentive congregation. My heart was very full as I sat and listened, and I felt as if I would like to get up and run away somewhere into the bush out of sight and hearing of everyone but God. It was a rich reward for all our labours and trials.[23]

He went on, 'I am more than ever convinced that our great help must come from the people themselves.'[24] He admitted that he tended to be an optimist, but not even at his most hopeful had he dared to expect to hear such a sermon from Ilaita, or profound prayer from Peni. 'I wish I was twenty years younger, or that I could get a thorough, good overhaul in some dock or other, and get reclassed for a few years yet. But there I must leave all this, and just wait and do what He marks out for me.'[25]

* * *

It was a relief to have some encouragement. In other areas things were not easy. Bad feeling continued between tribal groups and between traders and local people, resulting in more violence and murders. Sickness continued to dog the whole community. Brown was less at ease with the expatriate community than he had once been. His neighbour Herr Blohm, the manager for Hernsheim, was sometimes irritated with him because of his attitude to the labour trade. Theodor Kleinschmidt the scientist accused him of being more interested in his collections than in conversions, although Brown declared that, since his return to the islands he had spent less time on Natural History than on 'reading the *Sydney Morning Herald* before breakfast.'[26] He had a running confrontation with the trader Thomas Farrell, recently arrived in the area with his Samoan-American partner Emma Coe Forsayth; Farrell disagreed with his negative attitude to the labour traffic and accused Brown of cheating legitimate traders by acquiring vast quantities of tortoiseshell for sale through the agency of mission teachers. This infuriated Brown who demanded to know the source of such a rumour and wrote angrily that he had 'never sold a pound of tortoiseshell either directly or *indirectly* and I have never bartered it or traded it in any way.... I am a plain outspoken man.... I have always found it to be the best plan.'[27] These prickly relationships confirmed his opinion that anyone who attempted pioneer mission work was dubbed a 'fool' but when the work became established and the region became safer for other outsiders, he would then be called a 'knave'.[28]

---

23 Brown to Chapman, 14 June 1880.
24 Ibid.
25 Ibid.
26 Ibid., 23 August 1880.
27 Brown to Farrell, 7 May 1880.
28 *Weekly Advocate*, 7 February 1880.

Now that the Danks had moved to New Britain, the colonists had left and few white neighbours came to visit, Lydia Brown was often alone at home. She did not like it. She had often travelled with George in the past. Brown told Chapman that

> since our little ones were taken, the house is too lonesome for my dear wife when the little boy and I are away, and so now we do as we did nearly twenty years ago, before the children came, and often go together to visit the stations. The teachers like it and so do the people, and we also enjoy it. So all are pleased.[29]

Lydia joined George, with eight-year-old Geoffrey Brown, on a journey to New Ireland, leaving the comparative comfort of Kinawanua on 22 June 1880. It began well enough. They crossed St George's Channel in the steam launch and for several evenings stayed with mission teachers on the western coast, and with a white trader. Then George was keen to explore further. He had heard that it was possible to cross New Ireland at a certain point where a narrow isthmus divided the west from the east coast. It's not far, he was told. They climbed the steep western ridge through tropical bush, strangers moving into unfamiliar territory where recent murders had been reported. Brown would later admit that he 'did not feel very comfortable'.[30] After several hours of walking in hot sun, it was clear that the eastern coast was much further away than they had supposed. Lydia began to realise that the leaden weight in her legs, her aching head and the whistle and gasp of labouring lungs was now mixed with the signs of an attack of malaria. 'Mrs Brown walked bravely on for several miles,' Brown would tell Chapman later. 'She held out as long as she could but at last consented to be carried on a rope slung to a pole, and borne by two natives.'[31] Clinging to the pole in the misery of fever, she was carried on through scattered villages where the people 'had never seen a white man [so] our appearance caused no little sensation … [they were] especially interested in Mrs Brown and our little boy.'[32] At last they reached the more level lands on the eastern shore and a village community where they were given food and the use of a yam house where they could sleep.

---

29 Brown to Chapman, 14 June 1880.
30 George Brown, *A Journey Along the Coasts of New Ireland and Neighbouring Islands*, from Proceedings of the Royal Geographical Society and Monthly Record of Geography, April 1881, pp. 1–8.
31 Brown to Chapman, 16 June 1880.
32 Brown, *A Journey Along the Coasts of New Ireland and Neighbouring Islands*, p. 5.

Figure 12. Lydia Brown and women, New Ireland 1880.

Source: George Brown photograph collection: Australian Museum V 6392.

The yam house was soon surrounded by very curious people, astonished at their first close sight of a white man, woman and child. Lydia did her best to rest surrounded by staring people, spears and axes in every hand and a rising volume of agitated voices in a language she did not know. 'Mrs Brown was much alarmed.'[33] Brown himself was quite relaxed and asked the convert and lay preacher Petero to reassure the people that they meant no harm. 'Ask them to look at my wife and my boy Geoff, and tell me if a man brings his wife and a boy like that when he comes to fight.'[34] The realist Lydia knew that things could go very wrong. Geoffrey was only a child, she herself was ill, they were in a strange and less than welcoming village twenty-five kilometres from the steam launch. Every rustle or creak in the darkness might be only a rat, a gecko or a big cockroach, or it might be a murderer creeping toward them. 'Mrs Brown was still frightened by the tales she had heard,' Brown would tell Chapman later.[35] Their mission lads stayed awake and 'kept watch all night. There was not the slightest necessity of doing so, but I had long given up attempting to convince them when they preferred being frightened and uncomfortable.'[36]

---

33   Brown to Chapman, 16 June 1880.
34   Brown, *A Journey Along the Coasts of New Ireland and Neighbouring Islands*, p. 6.
35   Brown to Chapman, 16 June 1880.
36   Ibid.; Brown, *A Journey Along the Coasts of New Ireland and Neighbouring Islands*, p. 7.

The next day through pouring rain they set out again for the west coast, Lydia suspended most uncomfortably from the rope and pole and jostled along by carriers. Even when they finally reached their steam launch again, Brown was not ready to set off for home. People had brought him some remarkable wooden masks and wood carvings of hornbill, snakes and iguanas, so Lydia waited while he bargained for these prizes. He was delighted to buy a skull for his collection 'for a few beads', the result of a cannibal feast. If Lydia Brown pointed out to her husband that the existence of such an artefact might explain some of her anxiety, it was not recorded.[37]

* * *

It had been unrealistic to think that the translation of the Gospel of Mark could be completed before they left the islands, given the many interruptions to the work. Brown told a friend, 'I am kept very busy indeed and can do but very little indeed translating. However I am getting a fair knowledge of the language and so shall be able to do something in the Colonies if spared.'[38]

In the final months, as they waited for the arrival of the new missionaries, the Reverend Isaac Rooney and his wife and family from Fiji, and the ship that would take them back to Australia, George Brown threw himself into his work, trying to achieve as much as possible before it was too late. The latest plan was for their older children to join them in Sydney and for Brown to continue his translation work there. Lydia Brown was torn in several directions. She longed to see and hold again her five older children but she was leaving the graves of her two little ones. She longed to see her parents in Auckland as well as women whose friendship had sustained her through their letters over the years. Sydney would be unfamiliar, even though it could be a place to bring together her surviving family. And what of Emma Danks? Emma was pregnant now and who would help her when her time came? To Brown's consternation, Lydia suggested to George that she should stay on with Emma until another mission wife arrived to be her companion.[39] Lydia began preparations to leave with a troubled heart.

In July, Brown sent much of his artefact collection and correspondence away with his friend Captain Alex Ferguson on the *Ripple*. A month later the *Ripple* returned to Port Hunter. The Browns looked forward to their mail and to seeing their friend again. The flag on the *Ripple* was at half-mast. Who had died? A weeping local chief brought the news of disaster. Brown went on board and was led by speechless mate and crew into the cabin. The blood of his friend Alex Ferguson stained the walls and ceiling. Gouges from axe blades scarred

---

37   Brown to Chapman, 16 June 1880; Brown, *A Journey Along the Coasts of New Ireland and Neighbouring Islands*, pp. 1–8.
38   Brown to Henry Reed, 1 September 1880.
39   Brown to Chapman, 23 August 1880.

walls. Arrow heads and bullet holes studded the craft. Seven crew members who still lived bore tomahawk wounds that gaped horribly. Alex Ferguson and three others were dead, murdered on 9 August in an attack while trading in the Solomon Islands. With great difficulty, the survivors had fought off their attackers and managed to get up steam to make their way to Port Hunter. Shocked and heartbroken, Brown was faced with the care for the wounded and the grim task of sewing up and dressing many wide axe wounds that had been neglected for days. One badly wounded man died several days later, but the others recovered. Ferguson had been widely respected and trusted in the region and both traders and local people mourned for him. George and Lydia Brown grieved for the loss of a man who had walked with them through their darkest times. In his desecrated cabin, as a last sign of their friendship, Brown found all their mail, newspapers and parcels waiting for them, and a tin of biscuits marked as a gift for Lydia.[40]

* * *

It was just over five years since George Brown had first arrived in the area with the pioneer group of teachers. Despite illness, conflicts and his long absences, there were encouraging signs. Visits from two British men-of-war in August and October gave him the opportunity to visit less accessible regions in western New Britain and the northern tip of New Ireland. One captain wrote a letter of commendation to the naval Commodore, J.C. Wilson: 'It is my decided opinion that the Mission is doing unmixed good wherever its influence is felt.'[41] He spoke highly of the Fijian, Tongan and Samoan teachers, 'a most respectable and worthy body of men' whose language skills, example and influence for good in situations of conflict and tension had helped to avoid further problems.[42] Mission teachers, Brown and Danks had all participated in ceremonies of reconciliation between previously warring groups, using traditional symbolism and gift exchange. Cannibal practices seemed to be waning in some areas. More people were asking to be prepared for Christian baptism; on 19 September 1880 Brown baptised another group of fourteen people. Small schools, inadequate and simple though they were, had been established on most of the mission stations. A little book, the first of its kind in the region, had been translated with a simple alphabet and numerals, catechism and fourteen hymns; the schools were using it. Brown's assessment at the time was that 'our work is in a good state and I am not afraid to be judged by comparison with any other Mission for our five years work.'[43]

---

40 Brown, *George Brown: Pioneer-Missionary and Explorer*, pp. 370–78.
41 Lieutenant de Hoghton, *HMS Beagle*, to Commodore J.C. Wilson, 4 December 1880, quoted in Brown, *George Brown: Pioneer-Missionary and Explorer*, p. 391.
42 Ibid.
43 Brown to I.F. Horsley, Hotham, Melbourne, 9 November 1880.

Figure 13. Group at Urukuk; Pacific Island teacher and wife with Lydia and Geoffrey Brown 1880.

Source: George Brown photograph collection: Australian Museum V 6384.

The schooner *John Hunt,* the replacement for the mission ship *John Wesley,* arrived at Port Hunter on 2 December 1880 prepared to take the Browns and their party away to Australia. Brown's replacement, Isaac Rooney, had been delayed. Only days later, Emma Danks went into labour. With many years of experience in helping his wife and neighbours through childbirth, Brown was confident that, between them, he and Lydia would be able to support Emma to a safe delivery but Emma's labour went on and on. Fearing that the lives of mother and unborn child would be lost, Brown organised a crew of the strongest teachers and other men to row the whaleboat sixty miles from Port Hunter across the Channel to Port Breton on New Ireland. He knew that a French doctor had arrived at the colony with the *India* and sent a message pleading for this man to come to help them. In a feat of great courage and endurance, the teachers rowed against contrary currents, striving with the oars for forty-eight hours until at last they brought Dr. Goyon safely to their landing place. By the time Dr. Goyon came hurrying into the house at last, the baby had been born, coming into the world alive two days earlier. But Emma Danks was near death. Helpless and horrified, the Browns and Ben Danks had done everything in their power but it had not been enough. Something was very wrong. George Brown had asked Danks whether, if the doctor did not come that evening, he should attempt a surgical procedure that he had never tried before. It would be an act of desperation but Emma was dying. Their relief when the whaleboat was sighted at last was extreme. Dr. Goyon took charge and did what needed to be done. Emma's life was saved, and that of her baby boy. Danks recorded in his diary that 'the doctor was as generous as he was handsome, for he would take no remuneration for his trouble and his great service.'[44] The good doctor assured Brown that this act of mercy was a small repayment for the kindness of the Brown and Danks families to the sick colonists.

* * *

It was almost time to go. In the middle of the flurry of packing boxes and dealing with the procession of people who came to greet him, it occurred to Brown that Lydia was 'often in tears and strangely apathetic about our packing.'[45] She admitted at last that she felt that she must stay with Emma Danks until the new missionary Rooney arrived with his family. Emma herself wrote,

> I cannot attempt to give you the least idea of the love and kindness of Mr and Mrs Brown. If I had been their own child they could not have done more; night and day they were with me, doing all in their power, and in such distress when they thought I must die. Mrs Brown has been so good to my dear baby, and has done everything for it. How I shall miss her no one knows.... [She] offered, if Mr Brown would let her, to remain with me until Mr Rooney came.... Here she has been three or four years away from her dear children, and yet she was willing to remain some time longer, to comfort and help me. Not one in a thousand would have thought of such a thing, much less propose it.[46]

Brown knew that he was running out of time to record a world that was rapidly changing. He brought out the cumbersome photographic equipment he had bought from a departing scientific photographer who had declined to stay in the area in 1875. Now he set about photographing people and places. One series captured forlorn groups of colonists on New Ireland, where two more shiploads of newcomers had swelled their numbers. During the final days, for the first time, he recorded his own family; Lydia and Geoffrey seated in a group with a Fijian teacher and his wife and child, surrounded by young men and women of the place; Lydia and Geoffrey standing beside the memorial headstone marking the place where she laid her beloved Mabel and Wallis. There was also an image of Lydia seated on the ground, bareheaded, her wide-brimmed straw hat with the dark hatband on her knee. If she had been in Sydney or Auckland she

---

44 Danks diary, quoted in Niau, *Phantom Paradise*, p. 36.
45 Brown, *George Brown: Pioneer-Missionary and Explorer*, p. 396.
46 Emma Danks letter, published in the *Weekly Advocate*, 26 February 1881, quoted in Brown, *George Brown: Pioneer-Missionary and Explorer*, p. 397.

would have been dressed in black, layers of dark fabric in the elaborate fashion of the day. At Kinawanua she sits quietly among shadows, face averted from the camera, in a simple long pale dress, her hair dressed in the smooth style of her youth, the central figure among naked village women gathered around her with their babies, staring at the photographer. There was no need for Lydia Brown to wear mourning. Her exhaustion, grief and anxiety were all there in her tired face.[47]

* * *

The great farewell took place on New Years Eve 1880. Danks wrote,

> I wish you could have been present with us during the past few days, and seen the natives as they trooped up to Mr Brown's house, bringing pigs, fowls, spears, clubs and other things which they count valuable, and laying them at his feet, without seeking any return; and many of them with tears in their eyes giving expression of their regret at the prospect of parting with their 'best friend'.[48]

On the day of the farewell, before it was daylight there were the squeals of many pigs under the butcher's knife, thud of wood being chopped for the fires, cheerful shouts as people relished the drama of a great festivity. Smoke rose from many cooking fires. While the food steamed in the pits of hot stones and leaves, the Fijians danced and speeches were made. Brown made a speech, encouraging the people to follow the *lotu* of Jesus Christ and reminding them that he and the teachers had not come to trade or to acquire their land but to teach them 'to walk in the good, straight road.' He said with feeling, 'Don't forget me when I am gone from you. I shall never forget you, and I will always pray to him who made us all, and ask him to give you all good things.'[49]

Despite everything that could have brought the whole enterprise undone, somehow they had survived. Somehow through the grace of God, in spite of himself, something remarkable was happening. Brown looked out across the great crowd of gathered people, some five hundred of them, and recognised people from the villages of the Duke of York group, others from the villages of New Britain and from across the Channel on New Ireland. That they were together at all was remarkable but they had come almost entirely unarmed. Danks noted that night that this crowd was, 'sitting together in Mr Brown's

---

47   Photographs: Australian Museum Archives, published in Osaka National Museum of Ethnology catalogue of Brown Collection, p. 21; Australian Museum Archives AMS 318 V6388; Brown, *George Brown: Pioneer-Missionary and Explorer*, p. 406.

48   Danks, the *Weekly Advocate*, 26 February 1881, 12 March 1881, quoted in Brown, *George Brown: Pioneer-Missionary and Explorer*, pp. 398–405.

49   Danks, *In Wild New Britain*, p. 147.

yard, assembled there for the express purpose of bidding Mr Brown goodbye. Not a dozen weapons were to be seen, except what were brought by them to Mr Brown as presents. These are sober facts which speak for themselves.'[50]

As the people finally made their way home again, bearing trophies of pork and poultry and leaving behind gifts that would form part of Brown's growing collection of treasured objects from the islands, they went peacefully, 'by far surpassing the most sanguine expectations of our most sanguine brother,' as Ben Danks put it.[51]

* * *

At midnight that night, the missionary community would have held their Watchnight Service. Following the pattern set down by their founder John Wesley, George and Lydia Brown would have read together the words of covenant with God, placing themselves into God's hands for the unknown future. As leader, Brown would have read, 'Christ has many services to be done; some are easy, others are difficult; some bring honour, others bring reproach.... Yet the power to do all these things is assuredly given us in Christ, who strengthens us.'[52] And together they would have said the old words, quietly, perhaps with tears, perhaps with rising hope, 'I am no longer my own, but Thine.../ I freely and heartily yield all things to Thy pleasure and disposal.'[53]

The *John Hunt* sailed on 4 January 1881. Duke of York Island and Kinawanua dropped below the horizon. George Brown would return there more than once. Lydia Brown never did.

---

50 Danks, the *Weekly Advocate*, 26 February 1881, 12 March 1881, quoted in Brown, *George Brown: Pioneer-Missionary and Explorer*, pp. 398–405.

51 Ibid.

52 Rupert E. Davies, *Methodism*, Middlesex: Penguin Books Ltd., 1963, p. 90.

53 Ibid.

12. 'A vagabond streak'

Australasia, United Kingdom, North America 1881–1886

It was the time in between, the hinge on which past and future turned. Much later, when the time came for George Brown to record his own story, the period of six years spent in Sydney, from when they disembarked from the mission ship on 2 February 1881 until early 1887, barely counted in his memories. Years of living were condensed to a few pages. The period spent establishing the New Mission was the time to which he had looked forward through the preceding years in Samoa and the time to which he would always look back in the years that followed. It had been a period of intense effort and extreme challenge. Now he faced years of talking about it and being shaped by it.

When George and Lydia Brown arrived in Sydney Harbour on that summer day in 1881, he was a seasoned forty-five-year old ready for the next stage of his ministry. She was a woman who had been through fire but was now ready to begin again. After three years apart, their great joy was to have their whole family under one roof. Not everyone was there, of course. Two small graves lay at Kinawanua not far from the water's edge and Lydia's parents and brothers and sisters were only as close as the tiny photographs in the little rose-pink album their children brought from New Zealand. Their four girls, Lizzie, Amy, Monica and Claudia with their brother Fred, were all with them once more, all maturing, with Lizzie and Amy, at nineteen and seventeen, already young women. Perhaps it took some time for them to feel truly at home with each other. Too much had happened while they had been apart and their father, in particular, may have seemed at first a respected, distracted though affectionate stranger. The city of Sydney was unfamiliar to all of them and Lydia may have found the tall sandstone buildings, speeding wheeled carriages and smoking steam trams daunting. Soon, however, they were settled in a narrow terrace house in Surry Hills not far from the harbour. As the last trails of smoke from the bushfire season drifted away it was time to arrange for their children's education for the new school year. Despite local debate on whether or not higher education might be dangerous to the health of girls, George and Lydia enrolled their daughters in Miss Baxter's excellent Argyle School for girls in nearby Albion Street, Surry Hills, with Miss Lizzie preparing for matriculation and the hope of university studies at the University of Sydney in 1882.

Figure 14. Peni Lelei and his wife, Duke of York Islands 1880.

Source: George Brown photograph album: Australian Museum V 6418.

Invisible threads still bound them to the people and issues of the Pacific. The work of translation tied Brown's mind to the language of the Duke of York Islands as he worked with Peni Lelei and Timot each day. Lydia worked in the house beside the Samoan couple who had been with her for years. She hung her curtains from long island spears and decorated her home with shells and woven baskets. Whenever Brown was invited to speak in Sydney churches he retold the stories of the islands; the tales polished in the telling, bringing back into his mind the people and the place now seen from the safety of distance. News from the islands, carried by shipping, was heard with keen interest: the health of Ben and Emma Danks; the arrival of the new missionaries Isaac Rooney and then Rickard; the latest troubles with men recruiting labourers; more German traders buying land, more conflicts; more illness. When public debates about the future of those large islands near the equator grew warmer and more strident, Brown began writing letters to the newspaper, under the nom de plume *Carpe Diem* with his opinion that the colonial power of Great Britain rather than Germany should be exercised in that region. His links with the scientific community of Sydney were through his collection of island artefacts and he was gratified that a number of items were at the Australian Museum. Some special pieces were on display in the Exhibition at the splendid Garden Palace in the grounds of the Botanical Gardens; sadly these were destroyed later in the conflagration that consumed the whole Garden Palace Exhibition on 22 September 1882.[1] Even their connection with the colonists from the ill-fated enterprise of the Marquis de Rays continued in Sydney. A large party of French and Italian migrant families, in despair at the failure of the colony, abandoned the settlement with its poor huts and pointless piles of bricks for an imagined cathedral, and attempted an escape which took them through great trials to New Caledonia and on to Sydney. Before leaving for northern New South Wales where they were to establish a successful settlement, a number of them called on the Brown family in Sydney to share their stories. Despite having their feet on Sydney streets, the minds and hearts of George and Lydia Brown were still firmly located in a distant place, a place of fear and tears but precious, nonetheless.

* * *

There was unfinished business to attend to before Brown could feel completely free. The Methodist General Conference was to be held in Adelaide in May 1881 where men from all the colonies would meet. He knew that, whether he liked it or not, they would debate his actions in 1878. He was already regretting some unguarded letters he had sent out following the 'New Britain Affair' and criticism in the colonial press had made him feel 'rather fightable…. I am tired of keeping quiet,' as he told a friend.[2] The criticism of two men in particular had wounded him. The widely respected President-General of General Conference the Reverend John Watsford had written public statements, and former missionary in Fiji the Reverend Joseph Waterhouse had, he understood, published anonymous criticisms in the Fiji *Argus*. Brown told a colleague in Fiji:

> I hope to be at General Conference and then we will have it out and Joe too will have his whack. The two men are very different. I respect one and despise the other. I mean to have the whole affair out. I could not do it before the trial in Fiji. I can now.[3]

He wrote that, while he did not regret his actions, he did regret the necessity for them and went on,

> I mean to expose J.W. and his *Argus* leaders and test the opinion of my brethren as to the propriety of our acts and then be guided by their decision. I certainly won't trouble them long if they think they have

---

1   George Brown, *George Brown: Pioneer-Missionary and Explorer: An Autobiography*, London: Hodder and Stoughton, 1908, p. 128.
2   Brown to Horsley, 9 November 1880, in Brown, Letter Book, 1876–1880, ML A1686-3 CY 2772.
3   Brown to F. Langham, 23 August 1880, in Brown, Letter Book, 1876–1880, ML A1686-3 CY 2772.

reason to be ashamed of me. We saved our Mission [and many lives] and that will be comfort enough for me until 'that day' when the final decision will given.[4]

Brown set off for Adelaide with his New South Wales colleagues ready to confront Watsford and Waterhouse and he looked forward to meeting his beloved uncle Thomas Buddle again. It was not to be. Joe Waterhouse would never 'have his whack' after all. By the time Brown and his colleagues reached Melbourne they were shocked to hear news of a shipwreck. Joseph Waterhouse was dead, drowned in the wild seas that engulfed the steamship *Tararua* off the southern coast of the South Island of New Zealand on his way to the Conference, on 29 April 1881. One hundred and thirty-one people had perished, and among the dead were five senior Methodist men who had been on their way to the Wesleyan Methodist Conference.[5] Thomas Buddle and other New Zealand Methodists stayed to deal with the crisis. Brown and the others sailed from Melbourne to Adelaide, passing through wild storms along a southern coastline notorious for shipwrecks. It was a sober gathering in Adelaide as five names on the roll were marked with a neat cross—drowned.[6]

* * *

Brown chafed as he waited through days of other church business. He was pleased when his friend Benjamin Chapman was re-elected as General Secretary for Missions. Chapman had been wrestling with a number of challenging issues during the past three years, not only in New Britain but also in Fiji, Samoa and Tonga, and was looking very weary. However, with his reputation at stake, Brown waited anxiously for Chapman to raise the matter of his actions three years earlier. When at last the time came, the first speaker to express concern over the 'New Britain affair' was John Watsford, former missionary in Fiji who had just completed his term as President General. Watsford expressed mixed feelings—Brown was his dear friend who had almost certainly saved the life of his daughter Emma Danks—but he believed Brown 'was not infallible … even if he stood alone in the opinion, in his judgment the course pursued was a mistake, and he hoped that such a mistake would never be repeated.'[7] Another speaker said that although the 'character and reputation of Mr Brown were very dear to him, the character and reputation of the Church were even dearer still.' The question, he said, was not one of character but of policy.[8] The debate was

---

4   Ibid.
5   Lost at sea with the *SS Tararua*: the Reverends J.B. Richardson, Conference President; John Armitage, Conference Secretary; Joseph Waterhouse, formerly Fiji District; and Mr E. Connall and Mr Mitchell, lay representatives.
6   Minute Book, Wesleyan Methodist General Conference Minutes, May 1881, ML Methodist Church 580.
7   *Weekly Advocate*, 4 June 1881, reporting on General Conference sessions of 17 May and 18 May 1881, with acknowledgement to the *Adelaide Star*.
8   Ibid.

now on. Should Brown, who had already been through church and civil courts in NSW and Fiji, be tried all over again? Men shouted Points of Order. Brown rose to try to defend himself, telling his story over again. At the heart of his defence was the question: 'You all tell me what I should *not* have done. What should I have done? No one answers that!'[9] After long and painful debate it was decided to affirm an earlier decision by the NSW Conference. This satisfied everyone but Brown who, after a sleepless night, asked for the matter to be reopened. The statement still contained the words 'we can never sanction the use of military measures in our missionary enterprises.' Brown pleaded that he had not used 'military measures'; he believed 'that this was a crisis in his life ... with the construction that he put upon the resolution he could not think himself justified in continuing in his position. He could not carry on his work with that resolution unexplained.'

The search for a form of words went on, words that protected the Church from accusations of sending out militant missionaries, armed and violent against native races, but gave comfort to a valued member who was hovering on the verge of resignation. At last they added a statement reaffirming the principle

> which underlies all our missionary operations—that military enterprises cannot be sanctioned in their conduct—it records its judgment that in the present case Mr Brown acted in defence of the Mission teachers and their families, has not violated the regulations which govern our Mission work, and retains the full confidence of this Conference.[10]

'Has not violated the regulations ... retains the full confidence....' indeed. A great weight of anxiety was lifted. At last he was free to go on with his work and his ministry without the shadow that had darkened his way for three years. He had not lost the respect of his peers, after all.[11]

* * *

As May moved into June, Lydia Brown faced her first winter in many years. It was a dark period. Her husband was often away. Smallpox broke out in the streets around them in Surry Hills, introduced by shipping and carried in the very inadequate systems of sanitation in the growing city. News of illness and death seemed everywhere. Waterhouse, drowned; Barnabas 'Ahongalu in Samoa, dead; scientist Kleinschmidt in the Duke of Yorks, murdered; chief To Pulu, ill with measles; Minnie Rooney, young missionary wife on her way to New Britain to join Ben and Emma Danks, dead from malaria. Closer still,

---

9   Ibid.
10   Minute Book, Wesleyan Methodist General Conference Minutes, May 1881, ML Methodist Church 580.
11   *Weekly Advocate*, 4 June 1881.

Lydia's sister Lizzie's husband William Fletcher was dying after a long illness and died not long after George Brown returned from Adelaide.[12] William and Lizzie Fletcher were their closest family in Sydney and the loss was felt keenly.

* * *

Although George Brown meant to give his full attention to the work of translation in Sydney, there were always distractions. Travelling to speak about the New Mission, attending meetings, writing political and scientific letters and meeting with friends. Despite these other demands, with the help of language informants Peni Lelei and Timot, Brown continued work on the translation of Mark's Gospel. According to Danks this was 'of necessity slow work, made slower by the Deputation work put upon him at the same time in the Colonies. Then, too, the knowledge of the language on the part of all was yet imperfect.'[13] The language was unlike any of the Pacific languages known to Brown and was only one of many languages in the region.[14] It was challenging but they pressed on.

One Monday morning in September 1881 Brown was shocked and saddened to read the news that his good friend and mentor Benjamin Chapman had just died after a very short illness. Not only had Brown lost a valuable friend but now he was asked to help the President of Conference with mission matters as well as travelling to three colonies as a mission speaker until they appointed a new General Secretary. Squeezing translation work into every free moment, Brown and his co-translators managed to complete their work just after Christmas 1881. When the little book was at last in his hands, the dimensions of a postcard, he knew that the words of the Gospel of Mark were likely to be flawed as the words made the uncertain journey from one language to another, but were a gift from the heart from those who had done their best with it. The next year more translation work was possible, this time helped by the presence of Ben Danks, who was in Sydney for some months recuperating from illness. This work included a catechism, short scripture selections from the Gospels, prayers and a collection of hymns written by Brown and Danks.[15]

* * *

It was no surprise that his church appointed him to a circuit once his translation task was complete. Early in 1883 Lydia Brown supervised the move from their latest terrace house on Upper William Street to the Parsonage at the Methodist

---

12   William Fletcher died 20 June 1881, Joseph Waterhouse died 29 April 1881, To Pulu died in February 1881. The smallpox epidemic in Sydney began in June 1881, Theodor Kleinschmidt died April 1881, Barnabas 'Ahongalu died 9 May, Minnie Rooney died on 13 June 1881.

13   Benjamin Danks, *New Britain Mission: A Brief History*, Sydney: Australasian Wesleyan Missionary Society, Epworth Press, 1901, p. 22.

14   Brown to Chapman, 7 February 1879, published in the *Weekly Advocate*, 5 April 1879.

15   George Brown and Benjamin Danks, *A Buk Na Wetiri U Ra Lotu ma ra Buk na Niluluk*, Emerald Hill: Donaldson & Hartley, 1883.

Church in Bourke Street, Darlinghurst, complete with all their exotic masks, clubs, spears and mats. The work in Bourke Street Church was going to present a very different challenge, with a large congregation of prosperous middle-class people, many with large households and a lively community of children and young people, gathering in the splendour of a fine sandstone building with Doric columns and balconies for the crowds. Before he began the new work George Brown kept a promise to his wife and took her to New Zealand to see her parents and other family members; she had not seen them for seven years.[16] The visit was a rich time of reunion. Not long after they arrived home in Sydney, however, Lydia realised that at the age of forty-four she was pregnant again.

For George Brown, the world was lived in two spheres. While he busied himself with the congregation at Bourke Street, with all its enterprises, growth and Sunday School of four hundred children, he could not help letting part of his mind attend to the island world that had been his for so long. His children were now all at school and university, absorbed into the opportunities and enrichment of their local society. In the islands to their north, young people were being recruited unwillingly as labour on distant plantations; Rooney had recently written of 105 lads taken from New Britain to Samoa as labourers, some of whom 'had been with our teachers and had been sold by their parents for muskets etc.'[17] The people at Bourke Street were enthusiastic about the new congregation begun that year, in the developing suburb of Randwick, while in the north teachers were beginning new congregations in remote places that Brown had explored. In Sydney, Brown was now a member of a number of church committees, including the group to plan for the first Methodist secondary school for girls in Sydney, to be built at Burwood. At the same time he was part of the Committee on Tongan Affairs, which was to continue to struggle with the issues of church conflict in distant Tonga.[18] As discussion in Sydney town was of release of land for new suburbs along the Parramatta and Cooks Rivers, Brown was absorbed in debates on land and property as it affected traders, planters and villagers in the north and east, beyond the colonies of Australasia—a tug-of-war between nations vying for access to the potential of the islands.

A painted tin crown perched incongruously on the head of the chief To Pulu; the memory struck Brown as significant. When the German ship *Ariadne* had visited the Duke of York Islands in 1878, a crew member had fashioned a mock crown out of tin and painted it with the colours of the German flag. It was presented to To Pulu, a man wealthy in local valuables, and he was 'crowned' as King Dick. Ben Danks had observed more recently, 'That crown has undergone

---

16 Wesleyan Methodist Missionary Society (WMMS), Board Minutes, 10 January 1883 in Wesleyan Methodist Missionary Society Correspondence and Papers, vol. 1, ML CY 1365.
17 Isaac Rooney, Letter, 25 August 1882, in the *Weekly Advocate*, 18 September 1882.
18 *Weekly Advocate*, 2 February 1884.

a change, and now it represents English colours, by whom changed I cannot say. But nationalities do not trouble Dick much—all white men are good or bad, just as they serve his purpose or no.'[19]

German colours or British? French or American? The debate was gaining pace and passion with many interested parties in the colonies giving their opinions. Should the people of New Britain and New Ireland, or the people of the great island of New Guinea, or the New Hebrides or the Solomon Islands for that matter, be left alone? Ought they to come under the jurisdiction of the Western Pacific High Commission? Did they need protection from unscrupulous traders in labour? Or were they needed as a source of labour for growing agricultural and other industrial needs in the colonies? Were the people of the islands, like To Pulu, interested in using the traders, missionaries and explorers for their own purposes, and did not care from whence they came? Under the cloak of *Carpe Diem*, George Brown wrote a series of letters to the *Sydney Morning Herald*; it was his opinion that the people of the northern islands would welcome annexation or a protectorate 'for their own protection' and that the abuses of the labour trade 'could only be remedied by the establishment of an authorised authority in the different groups.'[20] The authorised authority he had in mind was the British Foreign Office. After a series of dramatic moves and counter moves throughout 1883 and 1884, it was the German flag that was raised over the region of New Britain, New Ireland and the north-eastern coast of New Guinea in November 1884. Brown was disappointed and angry, blaming the shillyshallying of the British Foreign Office which allowed German pressure without insisting on German responsibility.

* * *

For Lydia Brown, the period when the family was all together in Bourke Street, Darlinghurst was rare, precious and brief. It was the only period during their marriage when her husband was likely to sleep at home in his own bed. Her children were with her, all busy with studies and interests and with their house crowded with friends. Her daughters were better educated than she had been and were interested in the growing influence of women through organisations like the Young Women's Christian Association, and the new Woman's Christian Temperance Union. It was a time of prosperity in the community where anything seemed possible. Her Lizzie graduated from the University of Sydney as one of the first two women graduates there, listed among the 'Honour men' in Classics; Lydia remembered teaching her little girl her first lessons in half-built houses in distant Samoa.[21] After years of isolation, Lydia was near to women friends once

---

19 *Weekly Advocate*, 15 March 1881.
20 *Carpe Diem*, 4 December 1883, *Sydney Morning Herald*.
21 For the story of Mary Elizabeth Brown, see Margaret Reeson, *A Singular Woman*, Adelaide: OpenBook, 1999.

more. She loved to fill her home with guests and to offer hospitality to all; her husband told her once that he had seen a splendid dining room 'large enough and broad enough even for you.'[22] There was grief, too, at that time. A tiny boy was born at their Wesleyan Parsonage on 9 January 1884.[23] They called him Fletcher, in memory of their dear friend and brother-in-law William Fletcher. He lived for three days. When an album of family photographs of the extended Wallis family was presented to Lydia's parents James and Mary Anne Wallis to honour their Golden Wedding, the images of three of her children, Mabel, Wallis and Fletcher, were not there.

* * *

For so long George Brown's focus had been on the southern hemisphere and the islands of the western Pacific. Now a dream of going 'home' to England after thirty years became possible. He had permission to take leave from his work at Bourke Street Methodist Church as well as his many committees, and also the honour of being one of the commissioners for the New South Wales exhibit at the Colonial and Indian Exhibition in London later in 1886. Lydia would stay in Sydney maintaining their home for the rest of the family; they would have to move house yet again. Brown's hopes were to meet his sisters and step-mother again, to make his mark within British Methodism and to connect with the scientific community. He set off with high expectations, a collection of exotic limelight images and a human skull among the artefacts in his luggage. When he sailed from Sydney on the 3000-ton steamship *Mariposa* on 22 April 1886 his daughters Lizzie and Amy were already living and working in Brisbane. The Brown family was scattering once more.

* * *

By the time he sailed at last up the Thames in late June 1886 he had sailed across the Pacific Ocean, the Atlantic Ocean and travelled across North America from San Francisco to New York by rail. He had left London as a rebellious nineteen-year-old lad and returned as a fifty-year-old tourist, wide-eyed at the famed sights of the city. It was quite overwhelming and he told Lydia that he was 'very busy running about every day and I am almost tired of this big, big city.... I shall not be at all sorry to be back in Sydney again. I am tired of travelling about this big world of ours.'[24] It seemed strange to see the familiar objects from New South Wales in the vast Colonial and Indian Exhibition in South Kensington where they had become exotic. To his disappointment, he soon realised that because it was summer it was almost impossible to arrange any opportunities to speak in public; public meetings for churches and for scientists were held

---

22   Brown to Lydia Brown, 21 July 1886, in Brown, Letter Books, 1886–1887, ML A1686-4 CY 2810.
23   *Weekly Advocate*, 19 January 1884.
24   Brown to Lydia Brown, 2 July 1886, from London.

in the winter months. As an unknown person from the colonies, he had little chance to be heard, even though he had been able to secure a speaking role at the annual British Wesleyan Methodist Missionary Meeting at the end of July. He told Lydia, 'That is all I want. Let me have a chance at talking and I am pretty certain that the tale I have to tell will take with English Methodists.'[25] In the meantime he set off to visit France and Switzerland and then to crisscross England, seeing regions of his homeland that he had never known. He visited his half-sisters; Anna married to a Church of England vicar in rural Lincolnshire and Emily living with his step-mother in Barnard Castle, County Durham. These women were all virtual strangers to him but he valued the chance to be with them once more. 'I am very glad that I have come,' he told Lydia.[26]

* * *

The British Wesleyan Methodist Conference began late in July 1886 and at first the unknown visitor from the colonies found it rather dull. When the Missionary Meeting began, with crowds curious to hear heroic tales from India or China or the West Indies, he knew that they would never have even heard of New Britain. Brown was to be the third of six speakers, each to tell their missionary story for a maximum of twenty minutes. The first two speakers, however, did not know when to stop. When Brown rose to speak, he used his astute understanding of audiences. Plunging straight into a gripping word picture of their first landing on New Britain, he soon had their rapt attention.

> I was in the midst of telling them one of the most exciting incidents connected with our mission, when Waruwarum wished to take one of his wives from under our care for the purpose of cooking her, to which proceeding we strongly objected, when I noticed that my allotted time had expired. I stopped suddenly and stated that I must defer the completion of my story till some other time. There was at once great excitement in the audience, and cries from all parts for me to 'go on'.[27]

Despite this urging, he told them that he would not take up the time of the speakers still to follow. Predictably, he soon found himself being invited to speak in many places all over the country and the unknown man would be soon very well-known.[28]

* * *

Once the round of autumn and winter meetings began, George Brown was constantly in transit, using the extensive railway system to carry him around

---

25 Ibid.
26 Ibid., 21 July 1886.
27 Brown, *George Brown: Pioneer-Missionary and Explorer*, p. 411.
28 Ibid.

the country to speak in churches and to scientific bodies. His tales of exotic places captivated his audiences and people began to suggest that he write a book. Brown warmed to that idea and told Lydia, 'If ever I do write a book this visit of mine will do much to further the sale of it. I mean to set about that work as soon as I get home.'[29]

For a man whose early education in a small rural town had been limited, Brown relished his new opportunities to rub shoulders with Oxford professors, colonial governors and knights of the realm as he dined in such company and addressed their scientific organisations. In Oxford he donated a skull and other items to the new Pitt Rivers collection and although he assured Lydia that after 'a day of bigwigs I should much prefer being quietly at home with my dearly loved ones,' the recognition and admiration of the scientific community was very gratifying. At a meeting of the Geographical Club at London University, for example, he spoke, 'and kept them roaring with laughter every now and then. I felt quite at home.... It was no trouble at all for me to speak and I have no fear of dignitaries when I am talking about matters about which I know more than any of them.'[30]

Even in England, though, he could not escape reference to the 'Blanche Bay Affair'. At a dinner party he met a fierce critic of his actions, Secretary of the Aborigines Protection Society, anti-slavery campaigner and journalist Frederick Chesson. Their host invited Brown to tell the story of the events of 1878. To Lydia he wrote later, 'I told my story and Mr Chesson admitted that he had long seen the matter differently especially since he had seen Sir Arthur Gordon on his return. Then Sir William said, "Oh and did Sir Arthur Gordon distinctly approve of what Mr Brown did," and Chesson had to say "Yes." Poor fellow, he must have felt uncomfortable.'[31]

A dark winter descended over England while in Sydney Lydia watched purple jacaranda blossom against a sky of clear cerulean blue. Her household was in yet another house, this time in the dusty building site of the new suburb of Paddington, while they waited for Brown to return.[32] Brown, living in the dense fogs that settled over London 'like a thick dark yellow cloud of smoke and soon you can scarcely see your way,'[33] discovered a deep sense of homesickness. He had always thought of himself as English, but now 'I love the sunny south the best now as a place to live in,' he wrote and, observing the thrashing of the Australian cricketers in England that year, 'I am an Australian here and always stick up for them.'[34] He was missing his family deeply, not least because he was

29 Brown to Lydia Brown, 30 September, 19 November 1886.
30 Ibid., 25 November 1886.
31 Ibid., 5 November 1886.
32 During 1886 Lydia Brown resided at 4 Radford Terrace, Brown Street, Paddington.
33 Brown to Lydia Brown, 25 November 1886, from London.
34 Brown to Lydia Brown, 17 August 1886, from Paris.

absent while Amy was being courted by a young man. He told Monica and Claudia, 'You must take the broom handle to any young fellow who may come prowling around while I am away and if that doesn't do Mother can give you my revolver or one of the Fijian clubs perhaps would be best. And see here, mind you keep clear yourself.'[35]

From the far side of the world he wrote loving letters to his children, assuring his sons of his pride in them both as they grew into 'great and good Christ-like men.'[36] To his daughters he wrote, 'I am proud of our girls, distinguished as they are for Learning, Flirting, Painting, Music and other Fine Arts to say nothing of Teaching and Scone and Rock Cake making.'[37] He was trapped in an endless series of commitments in England, with many uncertainties about future appointments in the United States and finding it hard to finalise travel plans for the homeward journey, but now he was turned toward home and Lydia. He told her how much he longed to be with her and concluded, 'God bless you, my own good dear wife. You have been a great blessing to me and you are dearer than ever as time goes on … as ever, my dear old woman, your loving husband Geo Brown.'[38]

The key question that hung over Brown as he concluded his time in England was: where would Conference appoint him in 1887? He had been learning some things about himself as he travelled. Observing the very quiet rural village where his sister Anna's husband was rector, he wrote, 'I should not like to be shut up in such a place.'[39] In his travels he had been impressed by what he had seen of the effective use of lay people as evangelists as well as the work of women in the church; 'It is amazing how some of these Methodist ladies do work. I have been quite surprised.'[40] Rumours had begun to filter through to him that, with the failing health of the new General Secretary for Missions, the name of George Brown was being mentioned for that role. He told Lydia about the rumours and asked,

> Have you heard anything about where we are likely to go next year? You do not say a word about it so I suppose you have not done so.... I do not object to a Circuit but would object to go far into the country. Between you and me I do not care to lift a finger for the Missionary Secretaryship but I do not see how I could refuse it if appointed.[41]

---

35   Brown to Monica and Claudia Brown, from Boston, USA, 7 January 1887.
36   Ibid.
37   Ibid.
38   Brown to Lydia Brown, 9 December 1886.
39   Ibid., 5 July 1886, from Miningsby, Lincolnshire.
40   Brown to Lydia Brown, 19 November 1886.
41   Ibid., 17 September 1886.

After many delays, George Brown sailed from the English port of Liverpool on 11 December 1886. The experience had taught him much but now he wanted to go home. The homeward journey proved to be one hazard after another; a gale during the Atlantic crossing, delays and frustration in New York and Boston, fierce winter snow storms blocking his rail journey across Canada and a painfully slow vessel from Vancouver to San Francisco. He feared he would miss the *Mariposa* and was profoundly relieved when he was safely on board and heading west across the Pacific. A letter from home told him that almost all of his family, including Lydia, had been away from home at times during the summer and wrote, 'I wonder what folks think of us. They must think there is a vagabond streak in my composition that has descended to the children and even infected the wife.'[42]

While he was at sea, Conference was meeting and his future had been decided. Perhaps, as the ship approached Auckland, he dreamed of an appointment that would permit him to sit at his own table for dinner, enjoy the conversation of his own family, sleep in his own bed, write his book and stop this relentless, endless travel.

The *Mariposa* docked in Auckland. He soon learned the news from Sydney. Conference had appointed him as the new General Secretary of Missions. His first journey in the role was already planned. In January the former missionary and now Premier Shirley Waldemar Baker in Tonga had survived an assassination attempt. The new General Secretary must travel to Tonga as soon as possible.

---

42 Brown to Monica and Claudia Brown, 7 January 1887.

13. 'One of the toughest morsels'

New South Wales, New Zealand, Tonga, Fiji 1887–1890

'I am counting the days,' George Brown wrote, as he travelled home to his family early in 1887. By March he was home again at last with his 'dear old woman' and his six children. Now Lydia could hand back to George her anxieties over his financial affairs, and there was news of Lizzie teaching at Brisbane Girls Grammar, Amy's engagement, Monica's art, Claudia's romances, Fred and Geoffrey's studies. His new role meant still another house move. Lydia seemed to be packing up all their belongings almost every year. This time they moved to a handsome house in the new suburb of Randwick. She had not forgotten other homes. On a brass plaque at their new home at 6 Wood Street, Randwick, with its leadlight windows and iron lace, was the word 'Kinawanua', a memory of that other home on a ridge overlooking the St George's Channel and in sight of the huts of cannibals.

It was soon clear that any dream of staying home and writing a book had been pure fantasy. Brown began work at the Mission office at 415 George Street, Sydney on 7 April 1887. He was already familiar with the office, the Board and the broad work of the Wesleyan Methodist Missionary Society in the Pacific and had visited each of their fields of work. It had been part of his world since 1860. Over the years he had sent enthusiastic, miserable and angry letters to that office. Now he was sitting in the uneasy office chair with other men's letters on his desk. Of all the responsibilities before him, the most urgent was the conflict in Tonga. The new High Commissioner in the region, Sir Charles Mitchell, had appealed to the Wesleyan Methodist Conference in New South Wales and Queensland to attempt to reunite the fractured Methodists in Tonga. Brown had been appointed, with two others, to travel to Tonga in July as a delegation to attempt to deal with a complex and difficult situation.[1]

The lives of two men, the Reverends George Brown and Shirley Waldemar Baker of Tonga, had followed many parallel paths. Baker was a year younger than Brown and both Englishmen had arrived in the colonies before they turned twenty. They each were ordained and began their missionary lives with the Wesleyan Methodist Missionary Society in 1860, Brown in Samoa and Baker in Tonga. Baker's wife had come from Brown's home town of Barnard Castle.

---

1 George Brown, *George Brown: Pioneer-Missionary and Explorer: An Autobiography*, London: Hodder and Stoughton, 1908, pp. 422–23.

Both were men of strong personality and strong opinions and experienced long-distance tussles with the Mission Board. Brown knew of the breakdown of trust between Baker and his colleagues in Tonga during the 1860s. Although they never served in the same field, Brown and Baker met at intervals over the years and kept up a friendly correspondence. When Brown was in Sydney in 1874 to promote his vision for the New Mission, Baker was also in town and returned to Tonga to encourage a substantial gift from the annual fund-raising of the Wesleyans of Tonga to support the new enterprise; people criticised Baker's aggressive methods of fund-raising, but appreciated the funds.[2] Brown knew of the good work Baker was doing on a Constitution for Tonga, which was enacted in 1875, and perhaps envied the way in which the missionary Baker was able to advise the Tongan King George Tupou so that Tonga was able to maintain its independence. In Samoa in the same period, rivalry between competing chiefs had made it almost impossible for them to take a united stand against colonial powers. The influence of Baker with the Tongan King was increasing, causing anxiety among Methodist leaders in the colonies and irritation for the civil authorities at the Western Pacific High Commission.[3] Baker was under attack on many fronts. George Brown had had his own serious problems in 1878 and 1879, and perhaps he had a certain fellow feeling for Baker who was also under attack from armchair critics. Both Brown and Baker could have been in the mind of the High Commissioner Sir Arthur Gordon when he described Wesleyan missionaries as 'those eager, irrepressible, maladroit, bustling, tiresome persons who are forever offending prejudices and getting into hot water.'[4]

By the time Brown found himself seated in the General Secretary's chair in 1887, his path had crossed with that of Baker a number of times during the previous decade. He had been note-taker for a deputation investigating Baker in Tonga in 1879 while on his way to face court in Fiji. Then, after the dismasting of the mission ship, he had been an unwilling participant in the Conference of 1880 where Baker was severely censured. The Conference decided that in 'reference to his interference with the politics of Tonga, Mr Baker has gone beyond the bounds permitted to our missionaries'[5] and he was ordered to 'rest' for a year in New Zealand, away from Tonga. King George Tupou of Tonga was offended that a distant council had withdrawn his advisor. A year later Brown and Baker met again at Conference. Baker was still in trouble with his Church. In defiance of the demands of the 1880 Conference, he had returned to Tonga, taken up office

---

2   Noel Rutherford, *Shirley Baker and the King of Tonga*, Melbourne: Melbourne University Press, 1971, p. 85.
3   J.K. Chapman, *The Career of Arthur Hamilton Gordon: First Lord Stanmore 1829–1912*, Toronto: University of Toronto Press, 1964, pp. 284–85.
4   Sir Arthur Gordon, speech to the London Society for the Propagation of the Gospel, quoted in the *Weekly Advocate*, 23 June 1883.
5   W.G.R. Stephinson, 'Preface,' in *The Secession and Persecution in Tonga*, ed. J.B. Waterhouse, Sydney: Wesleyan Book Depot, 1886, p. 4.

with the King as Minister for Foreign Affairs and Comptroller of Finances, and continued to influence significant decisions. By midyear he had been appointed Premier. In December 1880, the King issued a Proclamation:

> I, George Tupou … having made up my mind that my people and country shall be entirely free and independent, and having thoroughly resolved that Tonga should have an independent Church, take this opportunity of publishing my intentions so that the leaders of the Church in Sydney, the missionaries and the whole world shall see that I am determined to have the separation.[6]

In an era when international commercial and political interests were active in the Pacific region, those with insight knew that many of the island groups, sooner or later, would become protectorates or be annexed by a colonial power. One of the few regions to be able to withstand pressure from outside was Tonga. Flags were being raised—and torn down—over more than one coveted piece of land in those years but the painted tin crown in the colours of Germany or England worn carelessly by To Pulu in the Duke of York Islands would never be accepted in Tonga. It was a serious error of judgement on the part of the several Wesleyan councils in 1881 to fail to understand the desire for independence in Tonga or the internal rivalries that existed between British and Tongan church leaders. The response of the decision-makers in the Australian colonies was too slow, unwise and unhelpful. They forced the resignation from ministry of Baker, demanded the withdrawal of J.B. Watkin who supported the King and appointed J.E. Moulton, who was in bad odour with the King at the time, as Chairman. When news of this reached Tonga, there was a furious reaction. An attempt by General Conference to transfer the Wesleyan work in Tonga from the control of the Mission Board to the control of the Conference of New South Wales and Queensland was also rejected. A telegram was sent to the President General from S.W. Baker in May 1881 demanding an independent District and the reinstatement of Watkin. It concluded, 'Grant this, peace. Reject, one secession. Don't be deceived. Secession will be universal and popular.'[7]

The fabric of the Wesleyan connection was wearing very thin in Tonga. Over the next few years, the signs of increasing tension multiplied and division hardened between those who supported Moulton and those who agreed with the King. Differences of opinion about the scene in Tonga had spilled far beyond the local setting as Methodists in NSW, New Zealand and Victoria came to different conclusions about who was in the right. Attempts to find a compromise failed, and Baker told Brown in 1884, 'I think that nothing but secession will bring the

6   A. Harold Wood, *Overseas Missions of the Australian Methodist Church Vol. 1, Tonga and Samoa*, Melbourne: Aldersgate Press, 1975, pp. 166–67.
7   S.W. Baker to President General Of Wesleyan Methodist Conference, 29 May 1881, in *The Secession and Persecution in Tonga*, ed. Waterhouse, p. 6.

Sydney Conference to its senses and should the General Conference not yield to the wishes of their Melbourne brethren, I will go for it with all my might and that means something.'[8]

On 14 January 1885, in the presence of King George Tupou, a formal decision was made to secede and establish the Free Church of Tonga with Watkin as its first minister. The people of Tonga would now be independent, not only from the control of any colonial power, but they would would also have their own independent Church, based on the doctrines and polity of the Wesleyan Methodist Church. Those who were reluctant to accept this were threatened with the loss of land and dismissal from senior government positions. 'Will you be in the free church or the enslaved church?' they were taunted, and told to transfer membership, allegiance and property.[9] A large number of people resisted this demand. Yet another deputation from General Conference attempted mediation but failed. The deputation observed, 'On every side we hear "Tupou is King but Mr Baker rules".'[10] Their recommendations, which included transferring both British combatants Watkin and Moulton out of Tonga, were later rejected by Conference.

Not long before Brown left Sydney for his trip to England in 1886, disturbing documents relating to events in Tonga were published and distributed in Sydney.[11] They described a sorry scene of persecution. Those Tongans who still remained loyal to the Wesleyan Church were said to belong to 'the Church that has to wait for orders from somewhere else.'[12] There were tales of floggings and imprisonment, loss of property and employment, threats and banishment. The King, who had spent some months in the northern islands of the group, returned to Tongatapu in July with an intimidating fleet of sixty canoes and 1,800 armed men. It became almost impossible to disobey the King's wishes.

One tropical evening in Tonga in January 1887, while Brown was in the depths of a frozen winter on the train journey across Canada, Baker was driving in the buggy with his son and daughter. On the Beach Road on the coastal fringe of the town of Nuku'alofa, the buggy lamp shone on armed assailants. Baker's son went to speak to the men but was shot and wounded. His daughter Beatrice jumped down to go to her brother while Baker tried to control the frightened

---

8   Baker to Brown, 31 May 1884, in Rutherford, *Shirley Baker and the King of Tonga*, p. 242.
9   J. Moulton to NSW & Queensland Conference, 3 February 1885, in *The Secession and Persecution in Tonga*, ed. Waterhouse, pp. 16–17.
10   Report of the deputation (J. Watsford, F. Langham and W.T. Rabone) appointed to visit Tonga by the 1884 General Conference, 16 May 1885, in *The Secession and Persecution in Tonga*, ed. Waterhouse, pp. 81–85.
11   J.B. Waterhouse (ed.), *The Secession and Persecution in Tonga*, 1886.
12   Elizabeth Wood-Ellem (ed.), *Tonga and the Tongans: Heritage and Identity*, Alphington, Vic.: Tonga Research Association, 2007; Siupeli Taliai, 'Ko e Kau Fakaonga,' in *Tonga and the Tongans: Heritage and Identity*, ed. E. Wood-Ellem, Melbourne: Tonga Research Association, 2007, pp. 147–60, p. 147; Gareth Grainger, 'Fakaonga Exiles,' in *Tonga and the Tongans: Heritage and Identity*, ed. E. Wood-Ellem, Melbourne: Tonga Research Association, 2007, pp. 161–77, p. 162.

horse, but Beatrice was trampled, wounded by another gunshot and left permanently paralysed. Baker escaped but was very alarmed.[13] He had known that he had enemies in many places and there had been other plots to kill, or capture and deport him. Although the group of assassins proved to be escaped convicts, there was suspicion that perhaps some discontented Wesleyans had been behind it. In the wake of the shooting, the reaction of the King, no doubt encouraged by Baker himself, was extreme. The Wesleyans were targeted in violent reprisals. The weeks that followed the shootings were terrifying. Men were executed and more executions were threatened. There was lawlessness, with floggings, plunder of property and imprisonment. Churches were closed, and Tupou College with its few remaining students was disbanded.[14] Only a stubborn handful of Wesleyans remained and a month after the assassination attempt a hundred of them left Tonga to seek asylum on the island of Koro in the Fiji group.

Brown and two colleagues arrived in Tonga late in July 1887. After two weeks of intensive meetings with all the parties, he returned to Sydney very despondent. Neither party was prepared to compromise. He reported that there was little hope of 'this grievous wound being healed so long as Mr Moulton remains in Tonga.'[15] To Brown's great disappointment and despite days of debate in Conferences both in Sydney and later in Melbourne, the recommendations brought by Brown and his colleagues were rejected. The church in Tonga was not given status as an independent Conference and Moulton was not transferred on the grounds that he was needed by the remnant group. Moulton, who was present for the debate in Sydney, declared, 'If they removed him, whom would they send in his place? ... There was only one man in this Conference who had the necessary qualifications and that was the Rev. George Brown. If they would send Mr. Brown down he would ask the Conference to withdraw him.'[16]

By the time the matter was debated in Melbourne it was clear that the conferences in the other colonies were very dissatisfied with the decisions of the New South Wales and Queensland Conference.[17] As debate raged over whether, or how, there could be reunion of the churches in Tonga 'on honourable terms', or whether it was possible for the Wesleyan Methodists to entertain the idea of organic union with other Methodist Churches in Australasia (such as the Primitive Methodists, or the Bible Christians), it seemed quite possible that the General Conference itself was at great risk. Rather than creating a climate of

---

13   Wood, *Overseas Missions of the Australian Methodist Church Vol.1 Tonga and Samoa*, p. 189.
14   J. Egan Moulton, *Moulton of Tonga*, London: Epworth Press, 1921, pp. 101–02; Grainger, 'Fakaonga Exiles,' pp. 165–72.
15   Brown Report to NSW & Queensland Conference, January 1888, in Wood, *Overseas Missions of the Australian Methodist Church Vol.1 Tonga and Samoa*, p. 196.
16   *Weekly Advocate*, 4 February, 11 February 1888.
17   Ibid., 12 May 1888.

union they were heading for a split. In front of a crowded gallery of onlookers, a tense debate raged for two days. At last, to the relief of everyone but Brown, Moulton was persuaded that for the good of everyone he should transfer to Sydney from Tonga and continue his scholarly work on Bible translation—on the condition that George Brown was appointed to Tonga in his place. Although Moulton declared 'that Mr Brown was regarded in Tonga as a Baker-ite,' he believed that Brown could be trusted; he was 'a thorough missionary,' 'a most capable man' and 'Mr Baker would have in Mr Brown one of the toughest morsels to deal with that ever he had.'[18] Brown denied that he was in Baker's, or anyone else's, camp and pointed out that the act of appointing him as Special Commissioner to Tonga was most unlikely to resolve the profound problems there. Even so, he was prepared to be obedient to Conference. His brethren were overjoyed at this solution and sang, 'Praise God from whom all blessings flow' with tears in their eyes.[19] Brown was not so sure.

An urgent telegram was sent to Lydia Brown in Sydney. Was she willing to go to Tonga with him? Once more she faced a hard choice; to be with her husband or to be with her children. But these days her children no longer needed her so much; Lizzie was in Brisbane, Amy was newly married and the others were competent adults. Her reply was read aloud to the meeting in Melbourne. She had written, 'If you think it is your duty to go, I am willing.'[20]

If Brown was reluctant to be appointed for a long period in Tonga it was only in part because of the obvious difficulties of the task. Sydney in 1888 was a vibrant, prosperous and interesting place as they celebrated the centenary of the colony. It was disappointing to be away. He had been welcomed back into the respect of his peers and had even been a nominee for the role of President that year, albeit with a grand total of three votes. As General Secretary for Missions, his responsibility was far wider than the narrow issues of Tonga. In Samoa, political battles were raging between three colonial powers, Germany, the United States of America and Britain, while traditional Samoan chiefs wrestled for power as loyalties shifted. Fiji was changing and volatile; some suggested that the original population was a dying race because of epidemics, and officials, planters, missionaries and other foreigners were vying for power over land and people. What had once been known as the 'New Mission' in New Britain and New Ireland had been established now for thirteen years and was making progress. He wanted to visit them all to encourage them, in particular to promote the agency of indigenous leaders. In recent times he had tried to promote the wider use of lay agents in missionary work but this had been rejected. Single women were beginning to offer for missionary service and although this was a novel concept

---

18   Ibid., 26 May 1888.
19   Ibid., 19 May 1888, 26 May 1888.
20   Brown, *George Brown: Pioneer-Missionary and Explorer*, p. 438.

to many, Brown was starting to see possibilities for it. In his own household he witnessed the intelligence, energy and ability of his adult daughters. His wife had always worked beside him in challenging missionary places; she had been not only wife, mother, hostess and housekeeper but also nurse, secretary and voice of reason. Benjamin Danks, newly returned to Australia, had recently spoken publicly of his great admiration for Mrs Lydia Brown, 'a good, brave, noble Christian lady.'[21] Perhaps employing women in mission work was not such an outrageous idea.

That was not all. Instead of being sent to deal with an intractable problem in Tonga, he wanted to be free to begin something new. Through contacts with island traders he had heard a remarkable story. A Solomon Island man who had been taken to Fiji as a labourer had been converted to Christianity while working in Fiji. Now he had returned home as a lay preacher and was a pioneer missionary among his own people.[22] Brown had passed through the Solomon Islands and knew their beauty and the violence of their people. At the Conference in Sydney in 1888 he had pointed out that, 'Within a few days sail of this Australian coast were large islands, such as the Solomons and the Admiralty Group, which were inhabited by teeming thousands of people to whom the first tidings of the Gospel of Christ had yet to be proclaimed.'[23] But at that time no one was listening and he had no clear plan. The conflict in Tonga cast its shadow over everything.

George and Lydia Brown sailed from Sydney in June 1888, travelling slowly first through New Zealand and then Fiji. In New Zealand, Brown was not impressed by the lack of interest in his missionary meetings and commented that, 'Unless something is done very soon the Missionary Collection, like the Moa, will have to be added to the extinct species in New Zealand.'[24] Lydia was thankful to spend time with her elderly parents. They were a little surprised to find S.W. Baker in Auckland. His daughter, injured in the assassination attempt, lay paralysed in their Auckland home and needed constant care so Baker travelled frequently between his family in Auckland and his duties as Premier in Tonga. He and Brown had several friendly conversations; Brown thought he seemed lonely and isolated from his Methodist friends in Auckland. Passing through Fiji in July, they were touched to meet an old friend from the pioneer group to the New Mission, Ratu Livai Volavola, and excited by the presence in the Training Institution of four young men from the Duke of York Islands. Brown was becoming restless as time went on and they waited for their ship. He wrote to Moulton, 'I often get fainthearted about the whole affair.... I would feel much

21 Benjamin Danks, quoted in the *New Zealand Herald*, 9 July 1887.
22 *Missionary Notices Wesleyan Methodist Missionary Society, UK, Sixth Series Vol. III*, March 1888, p. 49.
23 *Weekly Advocate*, 11 February 1888.
24 Ibid., 8 August 1888.

happier if I were now on our way to start a new Mission in the Solomons or any other savage group. However we must do our best.'[25] In a later letter he added, 'I dread the journey more and more as time draws near. I will do what I can, with God's help, and if I fail, why, I must fail.[26]

George and Lydia Brown landed at the wharf in the chief town of Nuku'alofa on 7 August 1888. Coming from the relative sophistication of the Sydney of the 1880s, the town must have seemed very small. Lydia was familiar with similar towns; early Auckland, Apia and Levuka. In each place the foreign residents lived in sometimes uneasy relations with the original people of the place. She knew that a community like this was small enough for the foreigners to all recognise each other but big enough for distinct parties to form; small enough for gossip to travel fast but big enough for foreign residents to imagine themselves superior to the local people; small enough to be isolated from the rest of the world and big enough to believe that the whole world was centred on them. The newcomers were in the middle and yet on the edge of affairs. They were known, but were still outsiders, unlike those who had lived in the area for many years. They were identified with the Wesleyan Methodist Church in Australasia but also known as old friends of the Bakers. In a divided community, perhaps observers wondered which side they were on. Within days of their arrival the Moulton family left Tonga, amid great signs of grief from their supporters.

It was time to begin work. Inevitably there was suspicion of Brown's motives. The Free Church suspected that anyone from the Australian Methodist Church had come to interfere with their autonomy. The Tongan Wesleyans had heard a rumour,

> that I was coming down to sell some of the churches to the Free Church, to burn the remainder, and to pass over all lands, etc, to the Free Church Conference.... [I told them that] I was sent to promote peace and goodwill among all parties ... there was no truth whatever in any report that I was going to extinguish our Church ... on the contrary I was certain that I expressed the feelings not only of the Conference but of the Methodist Church everywhere that our Church should remain in Tonga for ever and ever.[27]

Foreign residents were not sure that they could trust him. In attempting to walk a middle path in a divided community, George and Lydia Brown were known to dine with, play tennis with and worship with the opposition. He was said to have

---

25   Brown to Moulton, from Sydney, 12 June 1888, in Brown, Letter Books, 1888–1889, ML A1686-5 CY 2810.
26   Brown to Moulton, 9 July 1888.
27   George Brown, *Report by the Rev. George Brown, Special Commissioner of the Australasian Wesleyan Methodist General Conference to Tonga*, Australasian Wesleyan Methodist General Conference, Sydney 1890, reports of December 1888 and 26 April 1889.

'a sharp rat-terrier look.'[28] Alert, watchful, and though he spoke words of peace they were not sure about him. Even so, things seemed to be becoming calmer and the excesses of the previous year were not repeated. As for his relationship with Baker, who continued to come and go from New Zealand, Brown continued to meet him for 'square talks' and told President Lane, in Sydney, 'He talks very freely with me and I think is willing to do what he can. I have not yet got from him what his wishes are. Mr Baker is a "big fish" and it won't do to try to land him too soon. I do not wish to frighten him at the beginning.'[29]

Language caused Brown to stumble. Although he believed that he spoke functional Tongan, some statements he made in a public meeting were misunderstood and caused outrage among the members of the Free Church. Of several remarks that gave offence the most damaging was that he had declared that the division of the past few years was 'in my opinion, the work of the Devil, who had caused it and was using it for his own purposes.'[30] The reference to 'the Devil' was taken to be a slur against the Free Church, or S.W. Baker, or even the King himself. The fragile peace was disrupted. Although Brown did his best to reassure the Free Church that he had been misunderstood, there was little sign that things were improving. As the months went by it seemed to Brown that although Baker and Watkin made promises of easing the limitations on the remnant Wesleyans there was no action. Brown began to despair that any reunion was possible and decided that the divided churches should make up their minds to 'work side by side in peace and harmony.'[31]

At the end of 1888 George Brown returned to Sydney to report to Conference. Lydia remained in Tonga, assuming that he would only be gone for a month or two. A family friend wrote admiringly of her as one who 'remains patient and steadfast at her post' as she had done in New Britain,

> and she does this sort of thing after a quiet, matter-of-fact fashion, as if it involves no more self-sacrifice than an interview with the butcher and the selection of the daily joint. And when she comes home again she will just step into her vacant place as quietly as if she had only been visiting a neighbour round the corner of the street, instead of making a sacrifice which brings tears into strong men's eyes whenever they think about it.[32]

---

28 Rutherford, *Shirley Baker and the King of Tonga*, p. 207.
29 Brown to G. Lane, 7 September 1888.
30 Brown, Australasian Wesleyan Methodist General Conference, *Report by the Rev. George Brown, Special Commissioner of the Australasian Wesleyan Methodist General Conference to Tonga*, First Report, December 1888, p. 6, Printed Sydney 1890 NLA N 287.09961 BRO.
31 *Weekly Advocate*, 1 December 1888.
32 *Spectator*, 4 January 1889.

They were not to know what that sacrifice would mean. By the time her husband had returned at last to Tonga in May 1889, Lydia knew that her first grandchild had been born to Amy, and had died days later on his great-grandfather Wallis' eightieth birthday.[33] She had been too far away to cradle the child or to comfort Amy.

For the early months of 1889, Brown travelled in New South Wales, Victoria and South Australia, speaking at church meetings about the scene in Tonga. With him on these public platforms were two of the exiled Wesleyans from Tonga, the Reverend Tevita Tonga and his wife Rachael. Tevita Tonga was one of the men most loyal to Moulton and to the original Wesleyan cause and his wife Rachael was a member of the Tongan nobility, intelligent and articulate. To colonial audiences, usually preoccupied with the continuing drought, the threats of commercial recession and debates about excluding Asians from the colonies, their stories were dramatic. They told tales of persecution, flogging, humiliation and exile as they tried to raise funds for the support of their troubled church. This disturbing news sped round the colonies and deepened antipathy toward the people of the Free Church and in particular toward the Reverend Shirley Waldemar Baker. At the time, it may have seemed a legitimate and reasonable approach. However, by the time Brown returned to Tonga in May 1889, he discovered the damage that had been done.

Days before Brown arrived back in Tonga, having visited the Tongan exiles at Koro in Fiji on his way, Baker sat down to write a letter from his Auckland home. 'Sir,' he began abruptly, dispensing with his usual friendly greeting to 'My dear Geo.'[34] He was feeling bitter and betrayed. Over the months he was becoming more and more isolated, under attack on all sides. Observers like the colonial officer Sir John Thurston noted the 'violent and often unwarranted hostility with which Mr Baker has been pursued by his opponents both clerical and lay,'[35] and Brown had told the President George Lane, 'We have to look at this sad affair from both sides ... both Mr Watkin and Mr Baker feel sore about some of the things which have been said and written about them in the colonies.'[36] But now even his trusted friend Brown was blackening his name in the colonies. Baker wrote,

> I was very surprised and also grieved to find from the papers to hand from South Australia about your sayings and doings there relative to myself and especially to read a leader of the *Advertiser* dated March 29 1889 concluding with this remark. 'Of this we are sure should the Revd George Brown tell the tale in London which he has told in Adelaide and

---

33   Monica Brown's Birthday Book. James Wallis Dinning was born 15 April and died 18 April 1889.
34   S.W. Baker to Brown, 11 May 1889.
35   Rutherford, *Shirley Baker and the King of Tonga*, p. 161.
36   Brown to President Lane, 6 October 1888.

produce as his witnesses Mr and Mrs Tonga such a storm of feeling might speedily be raised as would not only render Mr Baker's residence in Tonga impossible but drive him to seek shelter for his dishonoured head in some corner of the planet where his name has never been heard.'[37]

Baker charged Brown with 'being guilty of a most base, mean and dishonourable action and that you have been guilty of lying and acting a lie.'[38] Brown had not witnessed any of the events he was declaiming in the colonies, he argued, and Tevita and Rachael Tonga were unreliable witnesses. Baker was outraged at what he described as 'exaggerated statements made on the Wesleyan platform in the Colonies bringing tears from the eyes of the audience and squeezing money out of their pockets.'[39] The man with the pen felt cornered. In Tonga he was being blamed for the excesses of others, in fear for his life from enemies. Even the King, whom he had served loyally for so many years, seemed to be losing confidence in him. In the colonies his name was an anathema. Now even one of his oldest friends had betrayed him. In a passage that he would later regret, he concluded,

> I should certainly have thought you who escaped a felon's cell at Suva because I was made your scapegoat—for it is well known the understanding between the officials of the British Government and Messrs Chapman and Hurst that if I were not sacrificed and recalled you would not escape, but if I were recalled you would be let go free on the charge of having murdered the innocent women and children of New Ireland in your murderous raid made upon them—would have acted more honourably to an absent friend but I was fool to think that in your desire to raise money you would ever think of the injury you were doing to the character of an absent friend. I am, Sir, your obedient servant, Shirley W. Baker.[40]

Copies were made of this letter and sent to key leaders in the Wesleyan Methodist Church in Australasia. Brown saw the original later in May. The war of letters had begun.

Once, they had been friends. Now every word scratched onto paper was loaded with hurt and disappointment. In a first response Brown told Baker,

> I only wish to remind you that for years I, with some others, have endured much pain in my endeavours to present your conduct to the

---

37 S.W. Baker to Brown, 11 May 1889.
38 Ibid.
39 Ibid.
40 Ibid.

Conferences in the most favourable light.... I had good hopes that the wrongs which our people suffer would be removed. I endeavoured in every way possible to work with you and through you.[41]

In a private letter to his cousin Tom Buddle in Auckland seeking legal advice, Brown wrote, 'You will be astonished at the calmness of my reply.... I have been astonished at it myself. Had I consulted my own feelings and inclinations I would have gone down and horsewhipped him in the streets but I kept my soul in patience from the sheer contempt which I feel for the fellow.'[42]

Did he have a strong case to sue for substantial damages for libel, he asked Buddle. In a very long letter of self-justification to the President General he listed again all the problems in Tonga and defended himself against the attacks of Baker. If anything, he insisted, he had been too gentle with Baker and 'the White residents were openly saying "Mr Brown might as well have stayed in Sydney" and some of our people were disposed to think that they were going to be handed over to Mr Baker whether they wished it or not.' Now Baker had no good word to say for him, even mentioning his 'carroty beard' as if ginger whiskers were a sign of ill will.[43] It was clear that Brown was no longer in the mood for conciliation.

The remaining months in Tonga until they left in September 1889 were frustrating. Brown was an angry man and now was sure that he was wasting his time. Baker had said that he was unwilling to take any action to facilitate the union of the two churches as long as Brown remained in Tonga. Brown had caused offence in several settings, inadvertently or otherwise; a letter addressed to King George Tupou critical of Baker's influence was seen as insulting. He had achieved neither a reunion nor an honourable withdrawal of the Wesleyans. The continuing irritation of having competing congregations worshipping almost side by side in the same village was causing petty complaints about disputed property, loud singing and noisy prayer meetings. His dreams of promoting a New Mission in the Solomon Islands were being smothered under the weight of curt letters, sharp conversations and threats of legal action. There was no longer the violence in Tonga of earlier years, but a visitor observed that the local people 'had lost heart, somewhere or somehow.'[44] It was some small comfort to know that the British authorities in Fiji disputed Baker's accusation of collusion between colonial officials and church leaders over the New Britain affair of

---

41 Brown to Baker, 1 June 1889.
42 Brown to Thomas Buddle Jr., 17 June 1889.
43 Brown to J.C. Symons, 19 June 1889.
44 'A Journalist on Tongan Affairs,' *Sydney Morning Herald*, reprinted in the *Weekly Advocate*, 6 April 1889.

1879. Sir John Thurston described it as being, 'without foundation in fact … is mendacious and slanderous in the highest degree, whether as regards yourself or such officers.'[45]

It was as well that George Brown had his wife Lydia beside him through this time. On occasions, he had said that 'a canoe needs an outrigger' and a missionary needs a wife to give needed balance and stability. He spoke with feeling, knowing that without Lydia he would be in danger of being capsized in the dangerous seas of conflict. Lydia's chief responsibility from May 1889 until late that year was the care of her husband. Her man with the carroty beard, now greying, was not a happy man and often in pain with rheumatism. He felt constrained by the small scale of the islands of Tonga when there was a whole world beyond.

The end came quickly in September 1889. A formal approach by Brown asking for a meeting with the leaders of the Free Church to attempt to work out a plan for reconciliation was met with a reply in the form of a Minute from the Free Church Conference. It stated baldly,

> That no further communication will take place between the Free Church of Tonga and the Rev. G. Brown, Special Commissioner of the General Conference in connection with church matters, owing to the action taken by the Rev G. Brown during his deputation tour through the Australian colonies and also on account of the irritating letter he wrote to his Majesty the King of Tonga on the 6th June 1889.[46]

Within days, Baker tried to apologise for his savage letter that had referred to a 'felon's cell'; 'I beg leave to apologise for said letter and withdraw the same.'[47] Brown wasn't having it. He shot a reply straight back. He was pleased to see the apology but was not willing to accept the withdrawal of the letter without time to consider the implications.[48] Lydia was not there to offer any wisdom; she had just heard news of the serious illness of her father and left immediately with the mail steamer *Wainui* for New Zealand. Brown planned to leave on its next trip. He had already begun his very long and detailed report. He had never had very high expectations of success and would conclude his report, 'I am sorry that I have not been able to secure the "honourable and lasting union of the two Churches", but trust that something has been done towards the conservation of our work, and the promotion of the welfare of the Tongan people.'[49]

---

45   J.B. Thurston to Brown, 9 September 1889, from Fiji. Enclosures included an official communication by HE Sir Arthur Gordon on 12 November 1879 and an extract from the *Fiji Times*, 15 November 1879.
46   J.B. Watkin to Brown, 9 September 1889.
47   Baker to Brown, 11 September 1889.
48   Ibid.
49   Brown, Australasian Wesleyan Methodist General Conference, *Report by the Rev. George Brown, Special Commissioner of the Australasian Wesleyan Methodist General Conference to Tonga*, 1890.

He was not sorry to leave. He had told the Wesleyans that he may or may not return in 1890, but he knew that he now had a perfect opportunity to escape the confines of Tonga. An invitation had come to the Board of Missions, with the possibility of a fresh beginning in a new region. The only disappointment was that it seemed that the Solomon Islands would have to wait.

14. 'The other end of the telescope'

Australasia, British New Guinea, Tonga, Samoa 1890

The map spread before him. The islands of the western Pacific Ocean were studded against blue; the familiar names of Fiji, Rotuma, Samoa and Tonga, the less known New Caledonia and New Hebrides, his old home in the cluster with New Britain and New Ireland and the long chain of the Solomon Islands where he had imagined another New Mission. Lying just south of the equator was the great dragon shape of New Guinea trailing a wide scattering of smaller islands behind its long tail to the east. George Brown had rarely imagined New Guinea as a site for a new Wesleyan Methodist mission. Old friends from the Samoan years, London Missionary Society (LMS) men W.G. Lawes and James Chalmers had begun work on the southern coast of New Guinea in 1874 and 1877, following the first islander pioneers, and the last thing he wanted was a repetition of conflict between the LMS and the Wesleyans in Samoa. With the echo still in his ears of Tongan congregations in the same village trying to out sing each other, Brown wanted to avoid competition between missions and churches.

Now a direct invitation offered another possibility. The Governor of British New Guinea was inviting the Wesleyan Methodist Missionary Society (WMMS) to consider beginning a new work in his region. Invisible across the map were recent lines of demarcation. Colonial powers—British, German, Dutch and French—had marked out regions now under their authority. One such region was British New Guinea, the south-eastern section of the great island with the small eastern islands first charted a hundred years earlier by the Frenchman Bruny D'Entrecasteaux and his compatriot Louis De Bougainville. Sir William Macgregor was the Governor of the newly annexed dependency in his first appointment in the role. George Brown had met Macgregor at intervals since the younger man, a Scot and doctor, first arrived in Fiji in 1875. Macgregor had observed the work of the Wesleyan Methodist Mission in Fiji. Since his appointment as the first administrator of British New Guinea in 1887, Macgregor had faced the daunting task of governance of the people of a thousand miles of coastline, hundreds of scattered islands and a mysterious and inaccessible inland. He believed that his governance would only be effective if there was a deep sympathy and intimacy with the indigenous people. In his years in the role he would resist significant establishment of British-owned plantations, create progressive labour laws, make it his business to travel widely across his new and very raw community to establish the rule of law and encourage local people to maintain their traditional villages and agricultural practices.[1] In 1889, however, as he considered a strategy for this task, it seemed to him that the work of missions could pave the way for his own goal, the work of 'civilization'. It was clear that the London Missionary Society, despite being established in the area for years, was understaffed and with many deaths from disease among their workers, now had only one worker in the entire western region, 'holding the fort with a single sentry'.[2] Macgregor pictured having four separate missionary societies—the London Missionary Society, the Catholic Sacred Heart Mission, the Australian Board of Missions of the Anglican Church and the Wesleyan Methodist Missionary Society—each taking responsibility for a designated region, and he wrote 'I may be able to see our long line of savagery attacked simultaneously by the four missions. I am looking forward to this.'[3]

Before George Brown left Tonga late in 1889, he knew of the invitation. He also knew that if the Methodists declined Macgregor's offer, then the Governor had said 'some other Church will be asked to do so.'[4] Macgregor was interested in recruiting any reliable missionary organisation and had no special commitment to the Methodists. Brown, in his role as General Secretary, was enthusiastic. It was not the Solomon Islands as he had imagined, but it was an open door—and it was British. After the frustration and confinement of the Tongan experience, any new opportunity was appealing. Compared to the expanse of British New Guinea on the map, the Friendly Islands of Tonga were mere specks on the ocean.

It was one thing to imagine a new Mission. Before a New Mission in British New Guinea could become a reality, the men who made the decisions through the colonial conferences would have to agree to it. From the time he left Tonga in late September 1889 until the New South Wales Conference in late January 1890, Brown travelled at a relentless pace—New Zealand, Fiji, New South Wales, Melbourne, by train, ship and coach—speaking about Tonga, New Britain and now the new possibility in British New Guinea. By the time the Wesleyan Methodists of New South Wales met in the heat of summer for their annual Conference, a major debate considered whether or not regular attendance at the traditional Methodist Class Meeting was an essential element of Methodist membership, or whether a new flexibility could be allowed; Brown was so rarely at home that he risked being cut off the membership roll if they kept their own rule. His focus was on promoting the New Mission rather that church polity. Despite the warnings of some who foresaw increasing instability in the

---

1 R.B. Joyce, *Sir William Macgregor*, Melbourne: Oxford University Press, 1971, pp. 20–22, 40, 68, 83, 197.
2 'Notes from New Guinea,' in *Weekly Advocate*, 29 March 1890.
3 William Macgregor, Journal, 4 June 1890, in Joyce, *Sir William Macgregor*, p. 173.
4 *Weekly Advocate*, 7 September 1889.

economic climate and suggested that they should withdraw from one of their older mission fields in order to begin something new, the decision was made to recommend to General Conference that the invitation from Macgregor should be accepted.[5]

If he was honest with himself, George Brown must have seen the invitation to British New Guinea as a dignified escape route from the frustrations and stagnation of Tonga. Yes, it would offer the gospel of Jesus to people who had never heard that name. Yes, it would build fine cooperation with the British administration with the encouragement of Sir William Macgregor who expected 'very valuable results from a religious, political and commercial point of view'.[6] It would also be a fresh task with purpose after the failures of his efforts in Tonga. There was still no escaping the problems of Tonga. The Sydney Wesleyan Methodists were still smarting over a sense of betrayal that a Church they had nurtured now wanted to separate from them; one wrote, 'Our foes were they of our own household. Serpents nurtured in our bosom have bitten us.'[7] Further troubled debate about Tonga consumed the people at Conference. The details of that debate, with the full text of a sequence of letters exchanged between High Commissioner Sir John Thurston and Shirley Waldemar Baker, were published in both the *Sydney Morning Herald* and the Methodist *Weekly Advocate*, spreading all the mess and muddle of failed relationships, accusations of libel, self-justification and stiff apologies before the public gaze.[8] It was not edifying. Conference did not believe that Brown had completed his task in Tonga, despite his fifty-page report, and directed him to go back to Tonga as soon as possible. They hoped that his visit would coincide with a visit to Tonga by the High Commissioner. By the end of March 1890 Brown was back in Tongatapu. The trip proved to be a waste of time. Nothing had changed. The exiles were still refused the right to return home. Freedom of worship was still restricted. Distrust, unease and rumour plagued the general society. When Brown discovered that High Commissioner Thurston was not due in Tonga until late May, he left Tonga again, unsatisfied, and arrived back in Sydney on 8 May. The meetings of General Conference had just begun.

Not for the first time, George Brown found himself a focus of controversy among his colleagues from the colonies of Australasia. Some supported his actions in Tonga and others believed that he had made some serious blunders. The men from Victoria were particularly critical. Far from building a climate of reconciliation, they said, Brown's public meetings in Victoria with the dramatic witness of Tevita and Rachael Tonga had just made matters worse, and his letter to the

---

5   *Sydney Morning Herald*, 30 January 1890 and 7 February 1890.
6   *Weekly Advocate*, 19 April 1890.
7   *Weekly Advocate*, 18 January 1890.
8   *Sydney Morning Herald*, 4 February 1890, 6 February 1890; *Weekly Advocate*, 24 May 1890.

King had been very unwise. They strongly opposed the suggestion that the Conference request Thurston to use his influence in the matter, on the grounds that it was a mistake to ask the State to sort out problems for which the Church should take responsibility. Brown urged them to ask for Thurston's mediation; another direct approach to King George Tupou was unlikely to help, he said, as 'Mr Baker was the King of Tonga, Upper House, Lower House and everything else.'[9] It was a very uncomfortable debate for Brown. As well as questioning his actions in Tonga, the discussion moved to suggesting that someone other than Brown should be appointed as Special Commissioner to Tonga. Brown responded with some irritation. He had not expected the appointment to continue, he said, nor desired to be reappointed for another year. He went on, 'He would prefer to see someone else appointed. He had had to bear a great deal in connection with the work in Tonga.... He did not wish for the position and he hoped the conference would make other arrangements.'[10]

He could have saved his breath. The meeting immediately voted to appoint him once again as both General Secretary of Missions and Special Commissioner to Tonga, with a vote of thanks and much applause. Perhaps he took himself off home to grumble privately to Lydia. At least they had agreed to ask for the intervention of the High Commissioner.

Two days later George Brown was back in the conference spotlight. Having made his report on the general state of their missions in the established regions, he put to the gathering the invitation to British New Guinea, with the support of several colonial Conferences. Macgregor, he said, spoke of a region of four hundred islands almost untouched by Christian missionaries, with an intelligent island people, skilled builders and gardeners who would make 'good subjects of the Government if their rights are respected.'[11] Brown knew that the people in the colonies were concerned about local issues; drought and recent flooding in Queensland, industrial unrest, threats of strike action, miners and shearers and waterside workers in tension with employers, the hazards of land speculation and rumours of the insecurity of the banking system. Some debated the possibility of a federation of the colonies across Australia. Brown's focus was to the north and east. He told the gathering that he understood why they might hesitate at this time, but, 'in the face of the most prudential reasons the Church has sent, and will continue to send, abroad the messengers of light and peace to every dark and peace-less spot of God's earth.'[12]

There was almost no debate. Brown's friend Lorimer Fison moved that they agree with the Board's plan and that Brown be sent to discuss it with Macgregor

---

9   *Weekly Advocate*, 17 May 1890.
10   Ibid.
11   *Weekly Advocate*, 29 March 1890, quoting Sir William Macgregor.
12   Editorial, *Weekly Advocate*, 19 April 1890.

in Port Moresby.[13] The members agreed with the new vision and immediately began to promise funds from their own resources. They also decided to establish a missionary magazine to report on the new venture.[14] Even as they were riding this wave of enthusiasm an urgent message came. Governor Macgregor planned to sail to the eastern islands within weeks. If Brown could reach Port Moresby in time he could travel with him to see the proposed region for the New Mission.

George Brown had been home for only a week since his Tonga trip before Lydia was packing his tropical whites again. Port Moresby was so far away and they both knew how long the journey might take. This time, armed with his photographic equipment, he rushed to take advantage of the recent railway link with Brisbane, catching the express train north, then sailing by steamship to Cooktown and on with *SS Hygea* to Port Moresby. His wife saw him go with the old gleam of excitement in his eyes as he headed for uncharted territory. She would have to wait and hope, praying that his enthusiasm would not outstrip his strength and health, but knowing her man, she knew that he was now being set free to do what he loved best. As he travelled north, some friends urged Methodists in the colonies of New Zealand and Australia to pray for Brown. They wrote:

> George Brown is something more and something better than a fearless, ready, steadfast man. The lion heart in him is as soft as the heart of a child. It is full of the tenderest sympathy ... which has won him the respect and affection alike of chief and serf among the Natives, of men of high places among ourselves, as well as the veriest beachcomber in the islands of the sea.... He could not do a mean thing to save his life, and he does great things without thinking them to be great. There are men who do little things and magnify them; George Brown looks at his doings through the other end of the telescope.[15]

Travelling north in haste hoping to catch the Governor, Brown may have pondered why he was making this effort. Some would say that he was a restless empire builder, seeking new worlds to conquer, for the thrill of exploration. Some might say he was escaping from the challenges of Tonga and the limits of an office desk in Sydney. There was some truth in all of those impressions. Yet at heart he was a man who was a missionary, who saw the possibility of transformation in the most unlikely people and their communities. He did not preach a message of hellfire and damnation. In later life he would recall his own

---

13   *Weekly Advocate*, 17 May 1890.
14   Ibid. Mrs Ellen Schofield sent an immediate letter with an initial donation of £500 with further gifts to be made annually. Ebenezer Vickery urged four friends to match his offer of £250 immediately and £100 per annum for five years.
15   *New Zealand Methodist*, 21 June 1890; statements by the Reverends Rainsford Bavin of New Zealand and Lorimer Fison of Melbourne.

experience of coming to faith as a young man in Auckland and discovering 'the pardoning love of God … new life, new thoughts, new desires, and a new purpose in life.'[16] As a man who had boundless affection for most of his fellow human beings, his understanding of God was as a God of love. He once wrote to his young daughters in New Zealand:

> I hope my dear girls that you will read your Bibles carefully and form your own opinion about God's character and God's dealings with us as individuals as well as communities. Take for the very foundation of your opinion that blessed truth that God is love and be assured that any doctrine that anyone may preach that is inconsistent with or irreconcilable with that must be false…. When I was a boy the plan was to frighten children into being good or to pretend to be so by the fear of hell.[17]

Before he began his work in the Duke of York Islands in 1875 he wrote of 'bringing the glorious gospel of our Lord Jesus, with all its privileges and blessings, and with the responsibilities which it entails upon those who receive it.'[18] The changes which he dreamed of seeing were not only the individual responses, but also a transformation that might re-shape a community. His thoughts, when making first contact with the people of a village on New Ireland, were that 'the reception of the religion of Jesus will soon produce peace and order where now all is discord and confusion.'[19] Peace in place of conflict, safety in place of danger, kindness in place of cruelty, calm in place of fear, mutual respect in place of distrust; these hopes fitted well with Macgregor's goal of civilisation. Brown had witnessed other societies that had been transformed. He believed that it could happen again.

* * *

He was not too late, after all. The *Hygea* arrived in harbour in Port Moresby on 9 June 1890. His arrival was timely. The Governor had not yet left on his tour, and the key players for a discussion of future mission work in British New Guinea were all now in Port Moresby. Compared with the size and comparative flatness of the island of Tongatabu in the Friendly Islands, this was a very different land with some ninety thousand square miles as well as four hundred offshore islands. Beyond the smooth steepness of hills rising from the waters of the port towered range upon range of mountains to the horizon and to east and west as far as the eye could see. Marine villages fringed the shore, delicately poised

---

16   George Brown, *George Brown: Pioneer-Missionary and Explorer: An Autobiography*, London: Hodder and Stoughton, 1908, p. 18.

17   Brown to children, from Duke of York Island, 16 December 1878, Brown, Letter Book, 1876–1880, ML A1686-3 CY 2772.

18   Brown, *George Brown: Pioneer-Missionary and Explorer*, p. 87.

19   Ibid., p. 136.

on stilts over the water and, on the hillsides the glint of sun on corrugated iron roofing marked the houses of the few Europeans. Old friends London Missionary Society missionaries, the Reverend William G. Lawes and Mrs Fanny Lawes, welcomed him. They had all been together as young newlyweds and raw missionaries in Samoa from 1861. Brown met the Reverend Albert Maclaren, representative of the Anglican New Guinea Mission, as well as new LMS men, F.W. Walker and H.M. Dauncey, and was disappointed that another old LMS friend, James Chalmers, affectionately known as Tamate, was not in Port Moresby at the time. For the first few days they enjoyed each other's company, hiked in the bush, picnicked on the beach, visited local village communities and worshipped in both the tiny 'English' church and with village congregations. Brown was busy taking photographs as he was fascinated with the people and distinctive architecture of the place.

* * *

In the sticky heat of the governor's residence in Port Moresby on 17 June 1890, with his guests gathered round a wide map of the land, Governor William Macgregor laid out his plan. Around the table were Lawes, Walker and Dauncey of the London Missionary Society, Anglican Albert Maclaren of the Australian Board of Missions and George Brown of the Wesleyan Methodist Missionary Society. Significantly, the leader of the fourth mission in British New Guinea was not there. Bishop Henry Stanislaus Verjus of the Catholic Sacred Heart Mission declined the invitation to join them in any kind of comity agreement. He believed that as the Catholic Church was the 'true Church of God', any concept of spheres of influence would divest her of her right to teach all men.[20] The Sacred Heart missionaries had begun their work at Yule Island and Mekeo to the west of Port Moresby in 1885,[21] following the LMS who had been in the region since the arrival of the first Rarotongan workers in 1873. Macgregor knew that he was dealing with men of strong character and would describe all the leaders of the four missions at the time as 'remarkable men'.[22] George Brown was the oldest present, a fifty-four-year-old explorer, scientist and church leader. Lawes was a fifty-year-old missionary scholar, translator, teacher and wise leader, with long experience in Samoa, Niue and New Guinea. Maclaren was a fellow Englishman in his late thirties, new to New Guinea—a godly and ascetic High Church man with a powerful sense of call and Christian duty. The absent leader, Bishop Henri Verjus, was the youngest of the quartet, an Italian-born thirty-year-old who had struggled against great obstacles to establish a Catholic Mission in British New Guinea, known for his passionate desire to see the conversion of the

---

20 Joyce, *Sir William Macgregor*, p. 173.
21 John Garrett, *To Live Among the Stars: Christian Origins in Oceania*, Geneva: World Council of Churches Publication, 1982, p. 231.
22 Sir William Macgregor, Address given to the London Missionary Society Centenary Meeting, Edinburgh, 11 March 1895, NLA PETH pam 2450.

villagers, sometimes expressed as being 'avid for martyrdom'.[23] As a Christian man himself, Macgregor respected and understood the work of the missions. His role was to govern a society that was spread along more than a thousand miles of coastline, divided, isolated, often brutal, and at risk from unscrupulous labour recruiters. A few years later he would tell an audience in Edinburgh that he believed that 'missionary work is a most important aid to Government work … the principles of Christianity are taught by them all, and this supplies the groundwork on which the armed constable and the village policeman can operate with special advantage.'[24]

It was as well that the men representing their missions had already established friendly relationships. They were all aware that over previous months there had been some awkward misunderstandings among them. As each mission had had very little contact with the others, each had made assumptions about their future areas of influence. Now it became clear that all three Protestant missions had presumed that they would be working in some of the same areas, even though 'no rights of any kind have been acquired by either Church'.[25] Maclaren, for example, had written to a friend in disappointment, 'My object in coming over to New Guinea is to see Sir William Macgregor with reference to our mission, and I am sorry to find that the Wesleyans have taken possession of our centre of work, so that we shall have to seek a new field…. Now we shall have to go to the mainland.'[26] The spectre of the unseemly and debilitating brawls between missions in Samoa frightened them. On no account could they risk putting any of their mission enterprises in that situation in the future. For the sake of the people of the place compromises were worked out. The task was so vast that no single missionary body could hope to cover the whole country, even if they had great resources of men and money. None of them did.

The record of their gathering began: 'We regret the misunderstanding that has arisen with respect to the field of labour to be occupied by the respective Societies.'[27] and went on to outline the detail of how the misunderstandings had occurred and the proposed new boundaries for the work of each group 'so as to use to the best advantage for the native population the force available for mission purposes, and to prevent as far as possible further complications re missionary boundaries.'[28] Macgregor insisted that government policy demanded that in any

23   Garrett, *To Live Among the Stars*, pp. 238–42.
24   Macgregor, Address given to the London Missionary Society Centenary Meeting, Edinburgh 11 March 1895.
25   *Weekly Advocate*, 21 December 1889.
26   Albert Maclaren, letter written 26 February 1890, quoted in Frances M. Synge, *Albert Maclaren, Pioneer Missionary in New Guinea: A Memoir*, Westminster (England): Society for the Propagation of the Gospel in Foreign Parts, 1908.
27   Minutes of the meeting of 17 June 1890, Port Moresby, quoted in Brown, *George Brown: Pioneer-Missionary and Explorer*, p. 468.
28   Ibid.

one village only one grant of land for a church would be given. With recent memories of the crowding of church buildings in Tonga, with dueling prayer meetings, Brown was glad to hear it. The decisions of that day, decided among friends and confirmed by the respective mission boards, would set a pattern of denominational allegiances that continue into the twenty-first century in those regions of contemporary Papua New Guinea.

* * *

To his great delight, Brown was invited to travel with the Governor and his new Anglican friend Albert Maclaren on the government steamship *Merrie England* to see for themselves the districts marked out for them on a map. They left Port Moresby on 23 June 1890, steering east. Brown was in his element. He was seeing new places and people, tramping with mates through unfamiliar territory, searching for new birds and shells, teasing children by dragging his dentures out. He captured photographic images of proud people adorned with shell, bone and tattoo who gazed steadily at the strange figure under the black cloth. With Macgregor he discussed their mutual enthusiasm for botany, geology, politics, map-making and languages; with Maclaren he shared thoughts about their future mission and theology, and with ship's captain, government officers and a travelling naturalist discussed everything under the sun. Macgregor's main aim for the journey was to survey the region and to bring justice to those who thought they could escape the law because of isolation. The *Merrie England* sailed in a great sweep across seas where Brown had never been. From the tiny island of Samarai they sailed east through the islands of the Louisiade Archipelago, north to isolated Woodlark, west to the Trobriands and south again through the larger islands of the d'Entrecasteaux group. In every place Brown observed everything and kept detailed notes. In many places it seemed that the *Merrie England* and its party were among the first Europeans to contact the islanders. Brown noted that the area 'was said to be very unhealthy, but it is certainly very beautiful.'[29]

---

29 Brown, *George Brown: Pioneer-Missionary and Explorer*, p. 478.

Figure 15. George Brown with group of men on Woodlark Island/Murua 1890.

Source: George Brown photograph album: Australian Museum V 6578.

Beautiful or not, even after five weeks of travel Brown was still not satisfied that he had found the place best suited for their first mission in the area. Macgregor left him with the ship *Hygea* to explore the D'Entrecasteaux Islands more closely, while the governor took Maclaren in the *Merrie England* along the north-east coast of the mainland to see his proposed region for work. On a very hot day Brown took the ship's boat and with a crew rowed towards a small island that lay between two much larger islands. He had been warned by Macgregor that the people there were known to be treacherous, indeed 'among the worst' he knew in the whole country, and to be careful. With his usual disregard for such warnings, Brown landed. A crowd of people came out to stare at the strangers. Rather than adding his skull to the collections he saw in neat rows outside some of their houses, they seemed quite friendly, and escorted him to several well populated villages; the crowd of onlookers following like a long trail of particles attracted to a magnet. This island seemed to him to have everything he needed; a location within reach of other major islands, a large population, fertile land and a people who seemed prepared to welcome him. The model of establishing a new mission on a strategic small island as a bridgehead to larger populations was a familiar one.[30] The island of Dobu, between Goodenough and Fergusson Islands, would be the new centre for the Wesleyan Methodist Mission. It was 4 August 1890, almost exactly fifteen years since he had first landed in the Duke of York Islands.[31]

* * *

Lydia Brown may well have been thankful that her husband was thousands of miles away when she heard the latest news from Tonga. Shirley Waldemar Baker had been deported. British High Commissioner Sir John Thurston had travelled to Tonga, assessed the situation, made a decision and sent Baker on his way. Lydia missed her husband, but was sure that it was best that he was busy elsewhere when Thurston arrived in Tonga. The questions surrounding affairs in Tonga had gone far beyond the internal wrangling of a fractured Church. Thurston had jurisdiction only over British residents, but the entanglement of local politics, the authority of the King, ancient Tongan clan loyalties and divisions, international trade and finance, and the relationship of this island kingdom to colonial powers had become knotted together in the person of Premier Baker. Was his influence benign and helpful for the good governance of the Friendly Islands, or not? The relationship between Baker and the remnant of Wesleyans was only one part of a greater whole. Thurston arrived in Tonga on 25 June 1890. He met with deputations of leading Tongan chiefs, traders, government officials, church leaders from the Free Church, Wesleyan Church and Catholic Church, and with the King and his relatives. From every part of the community he heard consistent stories of serious criticism and dissatisfaction with the Premier. Secular affairs had been mismanaged. Promises had not been kept. Freedom had not been permitted. Advice had been suspect. Confidence was lost. Divisions had been deepened. Although for twenty years Baker had provided advice to the King and promoted the independence of the island kingdom, the relationship between Premier and aged King was now tainted, and the whole edifice of government was teetering on the verge of collapse. What had once been valuable to the kingdom had been lost. Thurston found that the King had just dismissed Baker as Premier, willingly or under pressure from others. A group of chiefs voluntarily made sworn statements that 'Mr Baker was the sole cause of the trouble, poverty, and wretchedness in Tonga, and that great disturbance would arise if he remained: they therefore begged his Excellency to take him away at once.'[32] Now, in the light of all the evidence, Thurston told the Colonial Office 'that the Premier, both feared and hated, was

---

30 Examples include: Manono between Upolu and Savai'i in Samoa; Duke of York Island in the channel between the more populated New Britain and New Ireland; Nusa Duwa Island off Munda on the island of New Georgia in the Solomon Islands.

31 Brown, *George Brown: Pioneer-Missionary and Explorer*, pp. 471–88.

32 Letters from E.E. Crosby, J.A. Bowring describing events in Tonga between 25 June and 5 July, in the *Weekly Advocate*, 9 August 1890.

unworthy of longer credit or confidence.... I felt that Mr Baker's presence was unquestionably dangerous to the peace and good order of the islands.'[33] On 5 July, Thurston told Baker that he was to leave Tonga for two years under a Pacific Order in Council as a British subject whose presence in the region was dangerous to peace and order. Baker sailed from Tonga on 17 July 1890, a humiliated and broken man.[34]

Days later, unaware of distant events in Tonga, Brown returned to the little government island of Samarai where he rejoined Magregor and Maclaren. As they sailed back to Port Moresby, Brown told the Governor of his selection of a site for a New Mission and assured him that he would be able to bring all his long experience to the task of recruiting staff and raising funds. Both he and Maclaren were now ready to return to Australia to inspire their respective Churches with the vision, a daunting but exciting prospect. On their way south, when they landed in Cooktown in far north Queensland, a telegram was waiting for Brown. To his astonishment, he learned that dramatic changes had been happening in Tonga: Baker was gone, the King had granted full civil and religious rights to the Wesleyan people, and the Tongan exiles in Fiji and Tofua were on their way home. His attention was now divided between new opportunities and the possible resolution of a long-running difficulty.

Lydia Brown was warned. Before her husband landed in Sydney from British New Guinea on 29 August, she knew that the Wesleyans in Tonga, the High Commissioner and his church friends were all urging him to return to Tonga as soon as possible. The small German steamer *Lübeck* was in Sydney Harbour, due to sail for Tonga and Samoa within days. So Lydia made her preparations. George whirled into Sydney, rushed into the mission office for a few days, as always, grateful for the support in the home office of the Reverend Jabez B. Waterhouse, had hasty reunions with his family, learned that their married daughter Amy was pregnant again, checked and repacked his photographic equipment, arranged for his latest photographic images to be transferred into slides for projection, slept in his own bed for five nights after three months absence, and was away again when the *Lübeck* sailed on 4 September. This time Lydia sailed with him.

* * *

It had not been planned. The voyage together lasted for only eight days. Even so, the passengers on the *Lübeck* discovered that they were in the company of a remarkable little group. George and Lydia Brown met fellow passengers

---

33   Thurston to Colonial Office, 31 July 1890, quoted in Deryck Scarr, *Viceroy of the Pacific; The Majesty of Colour: A Life of Sir John Bates Thurston*, Canberra: the Australian National University Press, pp. 238–41.
34   A. Harold Wood, *Overseas Mission of the Australian Methodist Church, Vol. 1 Tonga and Samoa*, Melbourne: Aldersgate Press, 1975, pp. 202–03.

on board: the Reverend James and Mrs Lizzie Chalmers, who were travelling for Mrs Chalmers' health; the Reverend Archibald Hunt and Mrs Hunt, also from the LMS and transferring from British New Guinea to Samoa, and the novelist Robert Louis Stevenson with his wife Fanny. Stevenson had bought a property in Samoa. The men were quickly attracted to each other. The older women, at first glance, had less in common: recently re-married widow Lizzie Chalmers was newly from England; unconventional divorcee Fanny Stevenson had been adventuring around the Pacific and the quiet Lydia Brown. Though their journeys had been very different, they soon learned that each had married an exceptional man, had lost children, had left adult children behind and had experienced life far beyond the limits of suburbia.

Stevenson and his wife had a rather cynical view of missionaries and churchmen in general, and may initially have been alarmed at the thought of spending this voyage with nowhere to escape from piety. However he would soon write to his mother,

> Chalmers and Brown are pioneer missionaries, splendid men, with no humbug, plenty of courage, and the love of adventure: Brown the man who fought a battle with cannibals at New Britain, and was so squalled over by Exeter Hall.... Chalmers, a big stout wildish-looking man, iron-grey, with big bold black eyes.... I have become a terrible missionaryite of late days: very much interested in their work, errors and merits.[35]

Each of the men was a storyteller, in writing and speaking. Brown was still full of his latest adventure in British New Guinea and poured out tales with the bloom and gloss of a wonderful story told for the first time. The sparkle and colour of the islands shone, reflected in his eyes as he told of first contact and his dreams for the future. Even Lydia had not heard many of these stories before. As the storm buffeted the ship, the four couples met in the smoking room, usually reserved for gentlemen. Chalmers recalled, 'We spent many happy hours in it with our new friends. Oh! The storytelling of that trip. Did that smoking room on any other trip ever hear so many yarns? Brown surpassed us all, and the gentle novelist did well.'[36]

By the time the *Lübeck* reached Tonga, Stevenson had a proposal. He would like to write the story of Brown's life. Brown must have been tempted. A book by the writer of *Treasure Island* and *Kidnapped* would surely publicise the work of mission. Regretfully, Brown declined; his work was so demanding that there was no free time to sit and be interviewed by a biographer. It is possible that he may have feared having his life magnified into something more akin to a novel, with himself as a pirate-cum-hero wielding a righteous sword against a cannibal

---

35 Brown, *George Brown: Pioneer-Missionary and Explorer*, pp. 63–64.
36 Lovett, *James Chalmers*, pp. 351–52.

foe, rather than himself as a fallible man stumbling through the perplexities of unknown cultures. The writer was disappointed, saying 'Well, Brown, if we cannot do it now, we must just wait,' but promised his writing gifts whenever the time was right.[37]

* * *

Sitting cross-legged on woven mats, George Brown met with King George Tupou. They were on the verandah of his house on the Tongan island of Ha'apai. Lydia Brown was with them as they talked, and marvelled at the new ease and freedom of the conversation. The problem of the letter from Brown to the King that had given offence was now behind them. The exiles had returned home, humble in their most ragged mats, and the King was reconciled with his daughter who had been among them.[38] The King told Brown that he had made it clear at a number of public meetings that the Kingdom of Tonga now had three recognised churches, the Free Church, the Wesleyan Church and the Catholic Church. There must, he insisted, be 'perfect freedom of worship everywhere' and the unholy division and conflict was to end.[39] It was hard to realise that so recently there had been such bitterness and even physical violence between members of the churches. Many problems still remained to be solved. Questions of property and church land were still waiting for resolution and the hurt of damaged relationships was still tender. Yet it seemed that the remnant Wesleyan Church had survived the storm.[40]

Brown's two key preoccupations, the fragile Wesleyan Church in Tonga and the New Mission in British New Guinea, intersected through his photography. Most evenings after dark a sheet onto which he projected exotic images of New Guinea from his limelight lantern, was suspended between trees. The people were amazed and delighted and when an appeal was made for volunteers from the Wesleyan Church to serve in the New Mission there was a strong response. Six couples were chosen and Brown would write, 'Our visit has cheered our people very much, and my lectures and views are making quite stir enough to convince the most sceptical that the Wesleyan Church in Tonga is not dead, but is very much alive.'[41] Even the King had no objections to the Wesleyans going to New Guinea and said, 'Of course they can go! Who will hinder them? Let them please themselves!'[42]

---

37 Brown, *George Brown: Pioneer-Missionary and Explorer*, pp. 62–65; Fletcher, *Black Knight of the Pacific*, p. 140.

38 Gareth Grainger, 'The Fakaongo exiles from Tonga to Fiji 1887–1890,' in *Tonga and the Tongans: Heritage and Identity*, ed. Elizabeth Wood-Ellem, Melbourne: Tonga Research Association, 2007, pp. 161–77.

39 'Tonga', in *Weekly Advocate*, 6 December 1890.

40 *Weekly Advocate*, 29 November 1890.

41 Ibid., 8 November 1890.

42 Brown, quoted in the *Weekly Advocate*, 6 December 1890.

The plan was for George and Lydia Brown to leave Tonga in early November, visiting their old home of Samoa on the way back to Sydney. Although he was troubled with a painful rheumatic knee he rarely seemed to rest—attending meetings, working on correspondence and filling any spare moment with photography. He was brought to a sudden halt when, on the way home from a final District Meeting, the buggy in which he was riding accidentally overturned and he was thrown out. A badly sprained or broken ankle did not stop him from insisting on leaving Tonga as planned, however, and they sailed for Samoa on 12 November 1890.

Brown farewelled his Tongan friends with satisfaction even though there was disappointment. As far as he could see, he had completed the task as Special Commissioner but he had not brought true reconciliation to the fractured churches. The Wesleyan District Meeting had sent a message to the President of General Conference in gratitude for his work, saying 'Truly, language fails us to set forth the momentous work your representative accomplished.'[43] He knew, however, that he left behind him a church still split in two, with unresolved issues and a legacy of hurt and loss of trust. The Wesleyan Church had not been utterly crushed, but neither did the Free Church see a future where they would again be part of the world communion of Methodists.[44] The damage to the people of Tonga had been great and would not easily be forgotten. So much of it need never have happened if only the original desire of the Church in Tonga for autonomy had been understood and accommodated by the leadership in distant Sydney. If only…. Years later he would write that, on reflection, 'I always regard the work that I did in Tonga as the best which I have been able to do for the Methodist Church.'[45] He added a wistful note on what might have been, if his former friend Baker had made other choices before the whole edifice of his power and leadership in Tonga had crumbled into his sad exile, loss and disappointment, 'He might have brought about the reunion of the Tongan Church, he could have secured for this united Church everything for which the Free Church contended, and he could, by a course of wise and conciliatory action, have rehabilitated himself to a considerable degree with the conference of our Church; but…'[46]

* * *

Visiting Samoa together was a little like coming home. Just over thirty years earlier, in October 1860, a young redheaded George with his slim little bride Lydia had left the small safety of the mission ship *John Wesley* and gone through the darkness to their Samoan home. Now in their fifties, George's beard was

---

43   *Weekly Advocate*, 29 Nov 1890.
44   Brown, Report to Conference 1891, quoted in *George Brown: Pioneer-Missionary and Explorer*, p. 459.
45   Brown, *George Brown: Pioneer-Missionary and Explorer*, p. 460.
46   Brown, *George Brown: Pioneer-Missionary and Explorer*, pp. 460–61.

grey, Lydia was stouter and the old *John Wesley* had been wrecked years ago. Everywhere they went they were overwhelmed with memories. The grave of dear friend Barnabas 'Ahongalu, the towering tamarind tree they had planted as a seedling, the low stone fence where once they had watched men carrying headless bodies during the days of war, the houses George had built. Lydia remembered where each of her older children had been delivered, swiftly or slowly and sometimes frighteningly, into the hands of their father, the rooms where they had taken their first steps and had their first lessons, the beaches where they had swum with Samoan children. Now other people lived in the houses, other voices called through the rooms, other women governed the households. Her babies were gone, grown to adulthood in another land. They travelled from village to village, memory to memory. At each place a procession of singing women came to welcome them with garlands of fragrant flowers, heaping gifts of food, fine woven mats and local *tapa* cloth at their feet. Curious children stared at these strangers and were told by their elders that these were indeed honoured old friends. Men made long orations in welcome and recalled past deeds, grown more dramatic in the telling.

By the final day of their triumphal tour around Savai'i, Lydia was weary. At sunrise she clambered into the open mission boat with George. The oarsmen bent to their oars and she waved goodbye to the mission community who had gathered on the water's edge at Saleaula. This had once been home, but was home no longer. Sixteen years ago she had been carried away from that same spot, with tears blurring her eyes and her children huddled around her, to be taken on board the mission ship to leave Samoa forever. She could still feel the wrenching hurt of that time and the pain of her husband as he left a place where he had worked so hard but where it seemed he was leaving under a cloud of criticism and personal conflict. At the time, even his dream of a New Mission had been uncertain. Now she was ready to go home to Sydney. From sunrise until after dark she sat with aching joints in the open whale boat riding over the unimaginable depths of the ocean.[47] The renewed love of the Samoans had been a balm for old hurts and a reassurance that their work there had not been wasted. That night she agreed with George that she would return to Sydney by the next mail steamer while he went on to Fjji to recruit more new people for the new Mission.

Brown had been away from home almost all of 1890. Perhaps Lydia Brown imagined that the new year of 1891 might be different.

---

47   J.W. Collier, Letter to Editor, Samoa, *Weekly Advocate*, 3 January 1891.

15. 'A doubtful experiment'

New South Wales, Victoria, British New Guinea, New Britain
1891

Sitting at his own dinner table on New Year's Eve 1890, George Brown was a beloved visitor. He had missed Christmas at home yet again, this time at sea between Auckland and Sydney. Over the previous ten months he had spent a total of sixteen days in Sydney. That summer evening, the Brown family attended the traditional Wesleyan New Year's Eve Watchnight and Covenant Service at their local church at Randwick. This new year of 1891 was still a mystery for George Brown. All he knew was that his life must now take a new direction. The period of focus on Tonga was over. The New Mission in British New Guinea was ahead; he would administer this enterprise but another man would be the leader of the pioneer party. He imagined that he was likely to continue in the role of General Secretary of Foreign Missions. There was also a rumour that he would be a nominee for the next President of Conference in New South Wales and Queensland but in the past he had gleaned an embarrassingly meagre number of votes. It was true that some of his colleagues did not approve of him. As midnight approached on New Year's Eve, he heard the familiar words: 'Christ has many services to be done; some are easy, others are difficult; some bring honour, others bring reproach…. Yet the power to do all these things is assuredly given us by Christ, who strengthens us.'[1] With the voices of his friends and family around him, Brown joined the refrain in the familiar old words. 'I am no longer my own but Thine. Put me to what Thou wilt, rank me with whom Thou wilt….' All he knew was that the mysteries of 1891 were in God's hands.[2]

When the Board of Missions met in January for the first meeting of the year, there were conflicting emotions. There was enthusiasm about the New Mission and the recruitment of experienced missionary the Reverend William Bromilow to lead a large team of Fijian, Tongan and Samoan workers. On the other hand, realists among them were anxious about the timing of such a grand enterprise. The speculation of the boom years was beginning to collapse, banks were becoming increasingly nervous and strikes were crippling maritime and pastoral

---

1 Rupert E. Davies, *Methodism*, Middlesex: Penguin Books Ltd, 1963 p. 90. The 'Covenant Service' was instituted by John Wesley in Great Britain in the eighteenth century for the use of Methodists.
2 Ibid.

industries.[3] There was potential for advances in mission work, but Brown's trusted right-hand man in the mission office, the Reverend Jabez B.Waterhouse, was gravely ill. To Brown's grief, Waterhouse died a week later and Brown would have to face a complex year without his brotherly help.[4]

The rumours were increasing. It was hinted publicly that one of the candidates for the role of President of Conference was a missionary 'whose name is today familiar as a household word throughout Australasia.'[5] This posed a dilemma for both George and Lydia Brown. As he had not taken seriously the idea that he might be elected, he had accepted an invitation to travel to Melbourne during the period of Conference to speak at a fundraising event in support of the New Mission.[6] Lydia was also torn. Her daughter Amy was due to give birth in the New South Wales country town of Oberon where her husband Benjamin Dinning was the Methodist minister. Should Lydia travel to Oberon to help Amy, or be with George during the pressures of Conference? There is no evidence as to where Lydia Brown chose to be on 3 March 1891. On that day in Sydney, her husband George was elected by a large majority to the role of President of the Wesleyan Methodist Conference in New South Wales and Queensland for 1891 and her daughter Amy gave birth to a baby boy in Oberon about 124 miles away. Within a matter of days, George Brown had been relieved of his responsibilities in Tonga, made a rail journey to Melbourne and back. He became a grandfather and, in the words of an observer, he had 'gathered up the reins of the Methodist coach as one accustomed to the situation.'[7]

It had never been a foregone conclusion that Brown would one day take his seat as President of Conference. He had always known that there were mixed opinions about him. It was said,

> An impression was abroad at one time that a life devoted to pioneer work as a missionary had so interfered with the acquirement of technical Methodist information and the development of a business faculty as to make Mr Brown's election to the Presidential chair a doubtful experiment. And there can be no doubt that this impression has delayed the honour which Mr Brown has long deserved, and which has at length been accorded him.[8]

However, before the weeks of Conference were over, it was warmly reported that Brown as the President of Conference 'has put to flight the fears of many, and has exceeded the expectations of others, by the exhibition of splendid business

---

3   *Weekly Advocate*, 10 January 1891.
4   Ibid., 7 February 1891.
5   Ibid., 21 February 1891.
6   Ibid., 14 March 1891.
7   Ibid.
8   Ibid.

qualities in connection with the functions of his high office... [he has] insight into the nature of things, an accuracy of judgement, and a talent for smoothly accelerating the business of the Conference.'[9]

The Methodist coach did not accelerate at a great pace, it had to be admitted. The meetings ran for almost three weeks. After years of focus on issues of the communities of the islands of the Pacific, Brown found himself presiding over debate on many issues specific to New South Wales and Queensland.[10] A great deal of time was spent on issues of church property, with debate over leases, land purchases, debt on new buildings, trusts and regulations.[11] There was also debate on Local Option (the right for local regions to influence the practice of the liquor trade), the 'needless multiplication' of Protestant churches in thinly settled rural districts,[12] an enhanced role for the lay members of Conference, the increasing demand for an active role for women within the church, and the harsh reality of social unrest.

One task for the new President was to prepare a Pastoral Address. Underneath all the ordinary concerns of Methodist congregations was the knowledge that the world they were all living in was very unstable. For many it was a year of what Brown called 'great commercial trial'. While the Methodists were meeting in Sydney, in Queensland strike action by shearers was becoming increasingly violent; dissatisfied unionists were burning the Queensland Premier in effigy.[13] In his Pastoral Address Brown urged Methodists to be in sympathy with that movement which 'aims at securing by legitimate means truer social adjustments.'[14] While having no sympathy for violence and lawlessness, he acknowledged that

> there is an element of unrest whose characteristics are in harmony with the principles of the Sermon on the Mount, which favours a more equal distribution of the good things of this life. It reminds us of the 'all things common' usage of the early Church. Millionaires and beggars cannot live side by side in a pure Christian atmosphere.... Let us not sacrifice men in the interests of material progress.... The Kingdom of Jesus must increase though material progress decrease.[15]

* * *

---

9   Ibid.

10   The following year, in 1892, Queensland became a separate Conference, but in 1891 New South Wales and Queensland were a single Wesleyan Methodist Conference.

11   Minutes of the Australasian Wesleyan Methodist Conference of NSW and Queensland: 1891, ML 287.1/7 CY 1365.

12   *Weekly Advocate*, 21 March 1891.

13   Manning Clark, *Manning Clark's History of Australia*, abridged by Michael Cathcart, Melbourne: Melbourne University Press, 1993, p. 383.

14   George Brown, 'Pastoral address,' *Weekly Advocate*, 21 March 1891.

15   Ibid.

The voices of women were silent in Conference, as they had no representation there. However it was becoming very plain that women had voices and wanted to be heard. A Women's College had just been opened at the University of Sydney.[16] Women formed associations to work for fairer working hours for shop girls,[17] for the right to vote and in support of temperance. Women wanted better education and the opportunity to work and serve beyond their home. George Brown knew from experience in his own family the worth of educated women and the great worth of the role his own wife had played through years in missionary endeavour. In 1888, Brown had failed to persuade the church of the value of using the agency of both lay men and women in missionary service. By 1890 they were willing to explore the possibility of offering opportunities for 'the Christian zeal of our sisters in these southern lands',[18] although a request from New Britain for a woman worker was rejected. It was clear, however, that the climate of opinion was changing. Other missionary organisations were now employing single women, including Methodist women, and their own Central Methodist Mission in Sydney had recently employed women to visit prisons, the disadvantaged and the sick in the inner city. Younger people favoured the idea but more senior people were dubious. The church journal declared that it was a great pity that their own women had to seek a place to serve outside their own Church: 'Surely modern Methodism is capable of sufficient expansion and adaptation to give scope for the realisation of its ancient ideal, a work for everybody, and everybody at work!'[19]

George Brown assured the Conference that he believed that 'a large field for female missionary work was open to their Society ... New Britain and New Guinea offered practically unlimited scope for this particular kind of labour.'[20] Fearing that there was enough opposition to the concept to shut the door for women entirely, Brown proposed a convoluted process. He suggested that a Ladies' Auxiliary be established to raise funds for potential future work by women missionaries—and won the day with a unanimous vote in favour.[21] It was a first step.

During March 1891, while the Methodists were meeting in Sydney, another group of men was also in Sydney to debate a matter of great importance. Some of the most distinguished men from the colonies of Australasia had gathered for

---

16 Clark, *Manning Clark's History*, p. 369.
17 *Sydney Morning Herald*, 14 February 1891.
18 Australasian Methodist Conference Minutes of New South Wales 1891, quoting General Conference Minutes for 1890, ML 287.1/7.
19 *Weekly Advocate*, 7 March 1891.
20 Ibid., 21 March 1891.
21 Ibid., 21 March 1891. W. Moore, J.E. Moulton and A.J. Small pointed out problems, but voted for the resolution. See the Australasian Methodist Conference Minutes of New South Wales 1891, ML 287.1/7.

the National Australasian Convention, working toward a potential federation.[22] Few of the Methodists had travelled as widely as Brown across the colonies of Queensland, New South Wales, Victoria, South Australia and New Zealand and for years he had been arguing for common action and a common policy for defence. He had participated in a sequence of Wesleyan Methodist General Conferences, a version of colonial federation, where men from the various colonies made decisions about common goals. Aware of the Convention meeting nearby, the Methodists spoke of the 'supreme question of Australasian Federation', and declared that 'the coming week or two will give a colour and direction to the national life for years—perhaps centuries—to come.'[23] They were disappointed, however, by the secular nature of the Convention, and while they affirmed the concept of 'One People—One Destiny,' added that, 'It is none the less regrettable that there should be no public recognition of the Divine Being in the attempt to lay what we all hope will prove to be the foundations of a great and glorious Australian Dominion.'[24]

A message was sent from the Methodist Conference to the Convention, assuring them of the deep interest of their Church in the question of federation: 'We trust that under divine guidance you may be led to conclusions which will advance the best interests of Australasia.'[25] In the end, the Methodist Conference was long over and all their people had gone home before the Convention completed its work on a proposed draft for a federated Australia in mid-April. Even then any action on their thoughtful efforts would be delayed, obstructed and amended. Federation was still ten years in the future.[26]

* * *

Once Conference was over, Brown needed to demonstrate that his election had not been a 'doubtful experiment'. As President for the year, he would be a member of many committees, preaching, visiting, writing and having special influence.[27] His preaching had a colourful turn of phrase. He startled one congregation by announcing that he was there to report the rumoured death of the Devil, but even if it proved true that the Devil was dead, he said, 'his extensive business was still carried on, with some branch concerns in the low parts of Sydney,'

---

22 Zelman Cowen, 'Is it not time?' The National Australasian Convention of 1891, in Patricia Clarke, *Steps to Federation: Lectures Marking the Centenary of Federation*, Melbourne: Australian Scholarly Publishing, 2001, pp. 33–35.
23 *Weekly Advocate*, 28 February 1891.
24 Ibid., 7 March 1891.
25 Ibid., 14 March 1891.
26 Cowen, 'Is it not time?' in P. Clark, *Steps to Federation*, pp. 36–37.
27 During his Presidential year Brown was a member of, or chairman of, the following committees: Board of Missions, (Protection of) Privileges Committee, Examining Committee, Sunday School Union, Newington College Council, Ladies College Burwood Council, Provisional Theological Institution, Affiliated College Committee (with aim of establishing a College within University of Sydney), Centennial Thanksgiving Fund Committee, 'The Methodist' publication Committee.

that showed more 'devildom' than many remote mission regions.[28] Early in the year he moved up the city street from the offices at 415 into new premises at 381 George Street, in a prime city location almost opposite the new and elegant Strand Arcade.[29] The Mission Office had been given a fine room on the first floor overlooking the busy street, sharing the property with the large Book Depot, committee rooms and the office of the *Weekly Advocate*. This suited Brown well. For years he had been writing for the church journal and secular newspapers and now he planned to begin a new magazine to promote the latest New Mission, to be titled *The Australasian Missionary Review*. His written offerings may have been thought too generous; a Board Minute once instructed him to 'read a brief extract' of a long report to Conference, with the words 'brief extract' heavily underlined.[30]

* * *

There was no shortage of stories for the church papers during May 1891. 'The churches in this city have been fairly taken by storm,' one wrote effusively, while there were excited references to 'a Missionary Invasion' and an 'avalanche of gatherings'.[31] As well as other notable visitors and events, a large party of men and their families had arrived in Sydney on their way to pioneer the New Mission in British New Guinea. It was a time of intense activity in the Mission Office.

The pioneer missionary team was far larger and their departure was being orchestrated on a far grander scale than had been attempted before. A ship to take the party to the northern islands had to be chartered and staff finalised. A schooner, two whale boats and the pre-fabricated components of two houses, along with tools, trade goods and supplies had to be funded and purchased. About seventy islander men, women and children had to be accommodated for several weeks in the city and provided with warm clothes. The presence in Sydney of so many people from Tonga, Samoa and Fiji was a novelty, and at first a source of some amusement and condescension as they visited many congregations. Their singing, dancing and style of prayer charmed and intrigued those urban dwellers who had never visited the Pacific. Then a new respect began to grow. These people were intelligent, articulate, physically imposing men and women whose Christian faith was more authentic than that of many suburban church-goers.[32] They were willing to risk their lives for the gospel.

---

28   Letter to the Editor, *Weekly Advocate*, 25 April 1891.
29   381 George Street was located between Market and King Streets. In an earlier period, the building had housed a photographic and artist's studio.
30   Minutes of General Missions Committee of Australasian Conference of Wesleyan Methodist Church, 5 December 1888, ML MOM 2 CY354.
31   *Weekly Advocate*, 25 April, 10 May, 23 May 1891.
32   Ibid., 16 May, 23 May 1891. 'In a physical sense they are fine specimens of the *genus homo*, and we are glad to be able to say that their mental qualifications are equal to their physical development. They have delighted and impressed many of our city congregations.' See *Weekly Advocate* 23 May 1891.

They were themselves vivid evidence of the change that was possible. If their own islands could hear and respond to a gospel of peace, grace and forgiveness, despite histories of violence and cruelty, could not the same happen in the islands of British New Guinea?

At one of the many special meetings where Brown and the islander men spoke, in the very large new Methodist Church at Waverley, the place was crowded. One Fijian speaker noticed that the building was lit by a number of chandeliers suspended from the high ceiling, some larger than others. One remained unlit. He spoke of the simple coconut oil and wick in a coconut shell used to light the houses in his home village and pointed with respect to the illumination of the chandeliers. He had been told, he said,

> that the oil had been brought there in long pipes, and he pointed to where he supposed the hidden pipes might be. So the gospel had been brought to Fiji, and the unseen Spirit had supplied the oil for the true light that shone there. Then throwing himself forward and pointing straight to the large chandelier which was radiating its light all around, 'There' said he, 'that is England' and he pointed to some of the lesser lights, 'that is Sydney; that is Tonga; that is Fiji,' and then suddenly pointing to the unlit chandelier, 'There' said he, 'That is New Guinea!'[33]

Town-dwellers who came to be entertained and amused went home sobered and challenged. One wrote of how moved he had been to meet the island missionaries. 'I am not naturally emotional,' he wrote and added that he was determined to take practical action to support their work, on the scriptural grounds that faith without works was dead. 'Some Christians seek to fulfil the scripture by combining their faith with someone else's works.'[34]

For several weeks the island visitors were the talk of Sydney. A group photo of them all appeared in an illustrated newspaper.[35] They appeared in crowds in churches and city streets. Sixty of them descended on the Zoo in Moore Park, to be astonished at the bear pit and the elephants.[36] Two ferry loads of people sailed up the Parramatta River for a great picnic at Fern Bay, and a party of Samoans braved a tram ride to Randwick to visit Lydia Brown at her home, 'Kinawanua', where she greeted them in their own language. George Brown was able to go home in the evenings, but he was distracted with the many demands of final preparations for their journey. The enterprise was proving very costly. He knew that there was growing unease in the wider community as the impact of

---

33   *Weekly Advocate*, 23 May 1891.
34   Ibid., 10 May 1891.
35   *Town and Country Journal*, 23 May 1891, reference in *Weekly Advocate*, 30 May 1891.
36   *Australasian Methodist Missionary Review*, July 1891. Sydney's first zoo was located in Moore Park between Anzac Parade and Cleveland Street.

financial calamities overseas and local strikes began to affect the economy; would the widespread financial woes leave this new missionary enterprise crippled by impossible debt? Lydia Brown did her best to provide a stable household to support him, and offered hospitality to islander and white missionary alike. She preferred the role of friend and mother to that of public figure. It is likely that William and Lilly Bromilow, with ten years mission experience in Fiji, as well as the other new missionaries, were guests in the Brown home during their weeks in Sydney. Brown had recently written that 'I think that no men are more brotherly than missionaries: and I know no men—or women either, for that matter—who can talk more or sit up longer to do it than old missionaries when they meet together in the Islands.'[37]

Figure 16. Mission Team ready to leave for New Britain and British New Guinea 1891. Front: the Reverend W. Brown, Mrs W. Brown, Mrs Lilly Bromilow, the Reverend S. Fellows; Back: the Reverends J.T. Field, R.H. Rickard, George Brown, W.E. Bromilow, J. Watson and Mr Bardsley.

Source: James Colwell, *Illustrated History of Methodism: Australia 1812–1855; New South Wales and Polynesia 1856–1902*, Sydney: William Brooks & Co., 1904, p. 418.

---

37 *Weekly Advocate*, 21 February 1891.

At the Farewell service for the missionary party at the Centenary Hall on 18 May 1891, a close friend of the Browns, the Reverend Lorimer Fison, made a speech. Fison told the gathering that, 'the Mission party were a fine contingent, with a fine man (Bromilow) at their head, who had a fine woman at his head. There were some women specially made by God for missionaries' wives. Mrs Bromilow was one, George Brown had got hold of another, and he knew of a third [his wife].'[38]

Lydia Brown may have found it embarrassing to be singled out as being 'specially made by God' for a wife of a missionary. She knew, however, that her own background as the child of missionaries was unusual—'I lived among the Maoris [sic] as long as I could remember.'[39] Not every woman found this role natural or even possible. For some, only loyalty to their husband—and the practical impossibility of escape because of the isolation of their mission location—kept them there. More than one man had returned to Australia much earlier than expected because his wife was ill or very unhappy. When, a week later, Lydia said farewell to the missionary families as they boarded the *Lord of the Isles* on 27 May to sail for British New Guinea, she wondered if they understood what they were facing. This hopeful party was going to an alien place with a language they could not speak, with diseases they might not resist and to a people who had no reason to welcome them. Some of them would never see their homes again. Her husband was travelling with them, excited but already exhausted and unwell, anxious about everything that might go wrong. With prayers and tears, the ship pulled away from Moore's Wharf at last and voices blended from ship to wharf as they sang together, 'Jesus, Lover of my soul … / Hide me, O my Saviour hide, / Till the storm of life is past; / Safe into the haven guide, / O receive my soul at last.'[40] Their last sight of the barquentine was its three masts standing proud as it disappeared toward the Sydney Heads and out of the harbour into the open ocean.

After the extreme activity of the previous few weeks, there was a sense of anti-climax. The Mission office 'seemed strangely silent … the contrast between the bustle and confusion of the preceding three weeks and the now unnatural calm was very marked.'[41] An observer noted, after the ship had sailed, 'Such a large party has never before, to our knowledge, gone forth at one time to initiate an enterprise like this, and we pray that their success may be in proportion to their numbers.'[42]

* * *

---

38 *Australasian Methodist Missionary Review*, 1 June 1891.
39 C. Brunsdon Fletcher, *The Black Knight of the Pacific*, Sydney: Australasian Publishing Co. Pty. Ltd., 1944, p. 65.
40 Charles Wesley, 'Jesu, Lover of my soul', 1707–1788.
41 *Australasian Methodist Missionary Review*, 1 June 1891.
42 Ibid.

After a rough voyage north, the *Lord of the Isles* reached at last their destination, the small island of Dobu between the larger islands of Normanby and Fergusson. As they approached on 19 June 1891, the wind dropped and they were becalmed within tantalising reach of their goal. It was a great relief when the government steamer *Merrie England* came into sight, with the Governor, Sir William Macgregor, and they were towed to a landing place. Macgregor had promised Brown 'You may depend on my doing all in my power to aid your people in every possible way.'[43] The Governor was in the area to investigate the murder of a Chinese trader in the region where the Methodists planned to go and reflected that 'it is a good thing that I shall be first at Dobu with a large force.'[44] Macgregor was understandably anxious about the wellbeing of this pioneer party and noted in his diary his concern for the families, particularly the young children among them, who had 'come to brave the unknown dangers of this new country of evil character and its actual hardships and dangers, all for Christ's sake! They have indeed a courage equal to the best.'[45]

Now they needed to negotiate for a place where they could settle. Macgregor was a key to the negotiations with the village leaders, requesting a particular site and allowing time for them to debate it. The presence and authority of the Governor was important as it was clear that both the Methodist and the Anglican missions were part of his strategy for the wider region. As soon as a site was negotiated, a period of intense work began while the *Lord of the Isles* was still in the area. Several men of the pioneer team had practical skills. Building material was unloaded and in steamy heat and torrential downpours they worked to build a secure place. Brown used the time to visit villages and meet local leaders, despite feeling ill. It was hard to guess whether acceptance of an alien presence by the local people was just a temporary mask while the Governor and his police were in their district. Noting his first impressions, he wrote,

> The people are very friendly, and we never see arms, either in their canoes or in their villages. We have a grand district, with plenty of people and openings for Mission work on every side.... I am inclined to think too that we shall find a more suitable opening for female agents in these Groups, than we have in any of our older districts, but it is too early to speak positively about this.[46]

---

43 Macgregor to Brown, 5 April 1891, Wesleyan Methodist Missionary Society Correspondence and Papers, ML CY 1365.

44 Sir William Macgregor, 13 June 1891, Manuscript Diary, 14 November 1890–14 April 1892, NLA mfm G 23005.

45 Ibid.

46 George Brown, letter, 22–23 June 1891, published in the *Australasian Methodist Missionary Review*, 1 August 1891.

At dawn on 14 July 1891, Brown sailed on with *Lord of the Isles* to visit his old region of New Britain with new staff for that area. As they left the pioneer group behind, Brown recorded in his journal his relief that this great enterprise was safely begun.

> I have been feeling very unwell lately, but this morning all sense of bodily weakness and pain seemed to leave me, as my heart was full of devout thanksgiving and gratitude to God for his great goodness to us all. I have felt deeply the great responsibility of this voyage, and have had many fears and much anxiety at times; but now I have no other feeling than great thankfulness.[47]

Far away, to the south, a small schooner the *Dove* sailed toward Dobu. The *Dove* was a new vessel for the use of the New Mission, paid for by many small donations from Methodist children around Australia. Lydia Brown almost had the honour of launching her, but the church philanthropist Mrs Ellen Schofield was the one who flung the bouquet of white flowers on their blue ribbon against the bow as she slid into the harbour.[48]

* * *

For the first time in over ten years, George Brown sailed once more into the St George Channel. 'The change which has taken place here since the days when we landed is such as no stranger can possibly appreciate,' he wrote.[49] The region was now a German colony with German language and German place names; what he had known as New Britain was now Neu Pommern. In the place where once a handful of isolated traders had feared for their lives, plantations and substantial trading enterprises flourished. The Methodist missionaries had been joined by the Catholic missionaries of the Sacred Heart, who arrived in the area in 1882; this created a new set of challenges as the German Foreign Office had decreed that both Catholics and Methodists were free to work in the Gazelle Peninsular though in separate areas.[50] Brown's old friend, the Samoan-American woman, 'Queen Emma' Forsaythe, welcomed him to her grand establishment near the centre of German administration at Herbertshoe.[51] The area was almost unrecognisable. Children were in schools, people wore trade clothing, housing imitated that of the men from the South Seas, plantations replaced jungle and

---

47 George Brown, Journal, 14 July 1891, quoted in Brown, *George Brown: Pioneer-Missionary and Explorer: An Autobiography*, London: Hodder and Stoughton, 1908, p. 493.

48 Methodist Mission Board Minutes, 15 June 1891; *Australasian Methodist Missionary Review*, 1 August 1891. The *Dove* sailed for New Guinea on 4 July 1891.

49 Brown, Journal, 20 July–1 August 1891, published in the *Australasian Methodist Missionary Review*, 2 November 1891.

50 J.L. Whittaker, N.G. Gash, J.F. Hookey and J.R. Lacey (eds), *Documents and Readings in Papua New Guinea History (Pre-History to 1889)*, Milton, Queensland: Jacaranda Press, 1979.

51 R.W. Robson, *Queen Emma: The Samoan-American Girl who Founded an Empire in 19th Century New Guinea*, Sydney: Pacific Publications, 1965.

cannibalism was disappearing. More profoundly, there were other signs. It was not simply that communities had built churches and were going through the forms of Christian worship. Fear was being replaced by trust. Brown laughed with men who remembered the time when he first visited a village and was threatened with a spear; 'nowadays they go without fear to places to which it needed a lot of persuasion and some bribing to get them to venture when I first visited them,' Brown wrote.[52] Generosity was replacing avarice. Brown was deeply moved when a community brought gifts of chickens, sugarcane, yams and coconuts. He recorded, 'If anyone had ventured to predict such a scene a few years ago, he would have been laughed at by all who knew these people, for the idea of present giving was one which was very far away from their customs … [this was] a further proof of God's truth to change the whole nature of men everywhere.'[53] Most satisfying of all the changes were signs that local people were taking leadership in this new Christian community. Men, like his old friend and fellow translator Peni Lelei, were as much pastors to their people as any of the Fijian or Tongan men.[54] This was truly becoming a church of the people of the place. If such changes were possible in New Britain, he believed, there was good hope for the future of the new work in the eastern islands of British New Guinea.

In all the memories stirred by his return to this region, the face of a younger Lydia was always there. Sitting in an open boat off New Britain alone with a local crew, soaked to the skin and uncomfortable, he recalled earlier times, and 'could scarcely imagine that so many years had passed, and that I was not again a missionary, with my good wife waiting for me at Duke of York.'[55] Ten years after he had sailed from Port Hunter with Lydia in tears, he landed once more in the Duke of York Islands and climbed the hill to Kinawanua past the graves of his children. So many once had walked that hill with him; the island teachers, sea captains and traders, Ben and Emma Danks, his murdered friend Alex Fergusson, the deluded immigrants from Europe, chiefs and followers. Their house was still there. Lydia had suffered so much in that place that perhaps it would have hurt too much to ever return.

The return voyage south to Sydney was surprisingly dangerous. The chronometer of the *Lord of the Isles* was faulty and during a five-week passage they were repeatedly alarmed to find themselves almost aground on reef or rocks as they passed through the Coral Sea and the Great Barrier Reef. Brown 'never had

---

52   Brown, Journal, 20 July–1 August 1891, published in the *Australasian Methodist Missionary Review*, 2 November 1891.
53   Ibid.
54   Peni Lelei died early in 1895 in the Duke of York Islands. The notice of his death stated that he was one of the first converts, 'bright, intelligent … very earnest in preaching gospel to his own people.' See the *Australasian Methodist Missionary Review*, 5 February 1895.
55   Brown, Letter, 14 July 1891, published in the *Australasian Methodist Missionary Review*, 2 November 1891.

more narrow escapes from shipwreck, and never experienced a more anxious time at sea than I did on this voyage.'[56] It was September by the time he reached home, exhausted and unwell after several bouts of malaria and bronchitis.[57] The colonies, in particular New South Wales and Queensland, had been embroiled in industrial action almost the whole time he had been away, and now angry unionists marched with banners through Sydney. The economy was crumbling. Friends were dying; before the year was out they had news of the deaths and illness of several of the islander missionaries so recently farewelled, and a missionary woman being cared for by Lydia died in their home.[58] The newly established New Guinea Mission begun by the Anglicans at Dogura in British New Guinea was also facing great trouble, with almost all their staff ill with malaria; Albert Maclaren and his colleague Copland King had been farewelled in Sydney in August, but by 27 December 1891 Maclaren was dead. Brown grieved for his friends, shaken by reminders of the fragility of human life.

George Brown passed on the responsibility of the role of President in March 1892. All around them society was in pain. More and more people were out of work and in serious financial distress. In February and March 1892, banks were closing their doors against desperate depositors whose entire savings were lost. Ordinary working people, as well as those who had thought themselves secure, found themselves humiliated, hungry and homeless. Against this background, the Wesleyan Methodists met in Conference. As his final act as President, George Brown presented his Retiring Address. Some aspects of their Church he affirmed. They were willing to modify church polity, to exercise 'the power of adaptability to changing circumstances' without compromising the central truths of classic doctrine.[59] They had embraced change, he said, in less central areas like church music and whether or not a preacher could be bearded; to a hall filled with be-whiskered men he teased that 'the possession of a big beard was not inconsistent with soul-saving power.'[60] More importantly, they were now considering new opportunities for ministry by women and beginning to work for a potential union of the several branches of Methodism. He was glad that they were opening the way for greater participation by laymen in decision-making as he did not believe 'that we use to its full extent the services of the intelligent Christian laymen in our Church for the advance of Christianity, and for the good of humanity.'[61] The spiritual life that Brown offered was a

---

56   Brown, *George Brown: Pioneer-Missionary and Explorer*, p. 495.
57   Brown arrived back in Sydney on 6 September 1891.
58   *Australasian Methodist Missionary Review*, 1 December 1891. Miss Marian Crosby had accompanied her brother, the Reverend Ernest Crosby, from England to Tonga between 1884 and 1891. Miss Crosby died on 8 October 1891.
59   Brown, 'Retiring address at end of term as president,' in the *Methodist*, 5 March 1892.
60   Ibid.
61   Ibid.

life as 'a living likeness of God' rather than conformity to a particular form of Christianity. In England he had seen hedges clipped into the shapes of peacocks and urns, he said, but for 'true spiritual life'

> it is not necessary that this life should be trimmed into the shape of a Methodist peacock or a Presbyterian urn. Nor do we feel it right that we should put any man on a pedestal, and say, That is the man to whom all should conform, even though that man be John Wesley, John Knox, Dr Parker or General Booth.[62]

In the light of contemporary events, Brown suggested that 'we do not exercise that power in the politics of our country which we ought, as a Church, exercise.' He added, 'We, who believe in the power of the Gospel of Christ to exalt and bless the nation, cannot with impunity be indifferent to the principles and life of our legislators.... We are men and we are citizens, and all that concerns a man or that affects the land that we love, must be of interest to us.'[63]

The symbols of the office of President were handed to another man at last. Now there would be space for something new.

---

62   Ibid.
63   Ibid.

16. 'Rev. Dr. Georgium Brown'

New South Wales, South Australia, Western Australia, Samoa, Tonga
1892–1895

Names…. He had been plain George, 'Geo' to close friends, 'Palauni' to the Samoans, the Reverend George Brown. Now his name appeared in Latin on a splendid certificate—*Georgium* Brown, Fellow of Royal Geographical Society,' and the citation '*Propter magnum scientiam Literarum Sacrarum in comitus publicis*….'[1] He had been awarded an Honorary Doctorate in Divinity by the Wesleyan Theological College, McGill University in Montreal, Quebec, Canada on 6 April 1892. As a youth he had spent two years in Canada and had been involved in a shooting accident there with a romantic rival; if the shot had not gone wide he might have spent years in a Canadian jail. That fiery youth would never have dreamed of academic honours. Even if there were some raised eyebrows over his many scientific and political interests beyond the church, it was plain that his broad interests were taken seriously. A month later a selection of his photographs was sent to the Chicago Exhibition as representative of the Pacific region.[2] For a man who had always regretted what he saw as his inadequate education, this recognition must have been a source of great satisfaction. The runaway sailor, failed ship's cook and almost criminal had transmuted into the Reverend Dr. George Brown.

Not everyone viewed George Brown in a heroic light. Some members of the Board questioned how well he was fulfilling his role as General Secretary for Missions. There were hints in the Board Minutes that his long absences from the office had caused frustration; he was rarely present at meetings, work and decisions had to wait until his return, and there was an acerbic note at one point, hoping that the Tonga work would soon prove useful 'so that he may return at an early date to attend to his Secretarial duties.'[3] People admired his energy and enthusiasm for the New Mission in British New Guinea and worried about 'the unreasonable demands made on the General Secretary's time and strength, imperilling his health.'[4] However, some were irritated that so much of his time was focussed on a narrow range of work—Tonga and its troubles, New

---

1   The framed certificate is held in the Archives of New South Wales Uniting Church.
2   Minutes of General Missions Committee of Australasian Conference of Wesleyan Methodist Church, ML MOM 2 CY354, 25 May 1892.
3   Ibid., 25 May 1892, 23 April 1889, 11 November 1889.
4   Ibid., 15 December 1891.

Britain as it developed, the new enterprise in British New Guinea—while other demands seemed to be ignored or neglected. The appointment of a Chinese catechist to work among Chinese labourers and shopkeepers in Darwin received little publicity or support.[5] There was no sign of any Methodist interest in work among the Aboriginal people anywhere in the Australian colonies, despite regular information about those communities in the newspapers and the work of other churches.[6] There would be future criticism of 'this inexcusable neglect'.[7] When the Board was asked by Methodist mission staff in Fiji to recruit a catechist from India to work among the thousands of Indian labourers who now lived in Fiji, the response was delayed.[8] There was a plea from Solomon Island Christians who had worked in Fiji, asking for missionaries to their own islands; this, too, was postponed indefinitely. It was clear to the Mission Board and to Brown himself that the opportunities for new work were almost endless. They were also overwhelming.

It was not reasonable to lay all the blame for inaction on the focus of General Secretary Brown on the people of the Pacific islands. The times were very hard. Banks were failing, strikes were crippling, the numbers of unemployed were increasing. Finding little sympathy from government, groups speaking on behalf of those facing penury appealed to churches. When a delegation approached the Methodists asking for help for those seeking employment and in dire financial need, Brown was with the group who met them.[9] He believed that

> the business of the church is to concern itself with all that affects man's welfare, either temporally or spiritually, that it has to do with the bodies as well as with the souls of the people, and that in so doing we are but following the example of Him who had compassion on the multitude because they had nothing to eat.... It is only that as we fully recognise the truth that love to God must be accompanied by love to our fellow men, that we realise the importance of all work, and all efforts for the welfare and happiness of our fellows.[10]

As if in defiance of the anxieties of wider society, several new and vigorous movements were emerging. Women were becoming more visible and outspoken, expanding educational opportunities for girls and women, and advocating suffrage for women, temperance, rights in the work force and sex education.

---

5   Ibid., 24 March 1893.

6   *Sydney Morning Herald*. For example, on 21 October 1892 it reported on plans for a school near Walgett, fishing equipment for Port Stephens, a new manager for Warangesda and activity in Grafton.

7   Joseph Bowes, 'The Australian Aborigine,' in *A Century in the Pacific*, ed. James Colwell, Sydney: William H. Beale, 1914, pp. 151–74, p. 172.

8   Minute Book of Wesleyan Methodist Conference, New South Wales, 1892–94, 1892, ML 287.1/7.

9   *Methodist*, 10 March 1982. W.G. Taylor of the Central Mission and Richard Bavin were with Brown in this task.

10 George Brown, 'Retiring address at end of term as president,' in the *Methodist*, 5 March 1892.

On this rising tide of opinion, the Methodists had begun debating whether women could participate in the courts of the church. Brown had been trying to persuade the Board to employ single women for several years, and he published a letter from William Bromilow in the new missionary magazine. Bromilow, writing from British New Guinea, argued, 'We all think there is a splendid field for women to work among their coloured sisters here. The native women have considerable influence, own property, possess the power of witchcraft, and have quarrels among themselves which the men are powerless to check.'[11] To Brown's satisfaction the Board of Mission decided to employ single women in their mission fields in February 1892, with not a single voice of dissent.[12]

The great crowd that overflowed beyond the Centenary Hall in York Street in February 1892 numbered in the thousands. They listened with open hearts to a challenge to serve the living God and before they left that place over a hundred women and men had offered for missionary service.[13] Two women were chosen as the first in what was seen as a daring experiment; Eleanor Walker and Jeannie Tinney were appointed to join the New Mission in British New Guinea with the Bromilows.[14] On the day of their farewell on 11 April 1892 a group of women met to form a Ladies Missionary Auxiliary, with the goal of supporting Eleanor and Jeannie with prayer, regular correspondence and practical financial and other help.[15] Lydia Brown and her sister Lizzie Fletcher were among them, along with other wives of former missionaries. Both sisters were invited to speak, but at the last minute Lydia decided that public speaking was not for her. The formal launch of the Missionary Auxiliary was a grand occasion in the Centenary Hall in May, with a large attendance. This group was committed to their new task and when the first meeting of the Executive was held in the city on a miserable wet wintry day, eighteen of them splashed through puddles to attend. Though Lydia was unwilling to speak publicly, and was happy to defer to Mrs Moore as president, she was appointed treasurer.[16]

* * *

After the great excitement of establishing the new work in New Guinea, the meetings of the Board of Missions now seemed rather mundane. There were

---

11   William Bromilow, Letter, 28 October 1891, published in the *Australasian Methodist Missionary Review*, 6 January 1892.
12   Minutes of General Missions Committee of Australasian Conference of Wesleyan Methodist Church, ML MOM 2 CY354, 8 February 1892. The men who made this important decision were: the Reverends W. Clarke, George Brown, S. Wilkinson, W.H. George, J. Clifton, R. Bavin, J. Oram, J.E. Moulton, B.J. Meek and Messrs R.H. Ducker, R.S. Callaghan, E. Dawson, W.A. McClelland and Dr. O'Reilly.
13   *Methodist*, February 1892.
14   Eleanor Walker had been working with the Central (York Street) Mission in Sydney and Jeannie Tinney was from the Lydiard Street Methodist congregation in Ballarat, Victoria.
15   Minutes of General Missions Committee of Australasian Conference of Wesleyan Methodist Church, ML MOM 2 CY354, 4 April 1892.
16   *Australasian Methodist Missionary Review*, 5 Sept 1892.

always anxieties about money and Brown was forced to write to the staff in the field rejecting their requests for more funds. Their needs were real. The limits were equally real.[17] There were disappointments. News from the field reported illness even among the healthiest staff, indiscipline in some regions and rumours of unfortunate friction between clergy and lay staff; the Board realised that they needed clear regulations to cover these relationships.[18] On a happier occasion, the Board welcomed the Indian catechist from Lucknow, John Williams, on his way to begin work among the Indian migrant labourers in Fiji.[19] It was a daunting task, and perhaps even the worthy Board members may have wondered what a single person could do, even with fluency in Urdu and Hindi languages, attempting something new among thousands of people with their own, mainly Hindu, views of the world.

* * *

No single grand project occupied Brown over the next few years. He was active in many spheres, within his Church, as General Secretary of Missions and with his friends in the sciences. As he was now more often in Sydney, he had been appointed to almost every committee that existed under the banner of Wesleyan Methodism in the colony; in 1893 he was a member of thirteen Conference committees.[20] Of particular interest was membership in the committee promoting union of the several branches of Methodism that had splintered away from the original body over the early part of the nineteenth century.[21] The task was to 'promote the organic union of the various branches of the Methodist Church' by working with the other churches, and if it seemed likely to succeed 'to prepare a draft scheme as a possible basis of Union.'[22] Brown himself believed that 'one of the most cheering signs of the times is the steady growth of opinion in its favour.'[23] When travelling in Canada in 1886 he had been told of the success of a similar union of Methodists there. In North Queensland he had been troubled by the 'great waste of men and money' caused by disunity and said that 'I, for

---

17   Minutes of General Missions Committee of Australasian Conference of Wesleyan Methodist Church, ML MOM 2 CY354, 8 February, 29 February, 18 July, 21 July 1892.

18   Minutes of General Missions Committee of Australasian Conference of Wesleyan Methodist Church, ML MOM 2 CY354, 6 June 1893.

19   Ibid., 20 June 1892.

20   For example, in 1893, Brown was a member of the Board of Missions, (Protection of) Privileges Committee, Examining Committee, Newington College Council, Ladies College Burwood Council, Provisional Theological Institution, Affiliated College Committee (with the aim of establishing a College within the University of Sydney), Centennial Thanksgiving Fund Committee, the *Methodist* publication committee, Discipline Committee, Methodist Union Committee, Executive of the Church Sustentation and Extension Committee, Book Committee. See Minute Book of Wesleyan Methodist Conference, New South Wales, 1892-94, ML 287.1/7.

21   Don Wright and Eric G. Clancy, *The Methodists: A History of Methodism in New South Wales*, Sydney: Allen & Unwin, 1993, pp.47–55. By the 1890s, branches of Methodism found in New South Wales included Wesleyan Methodist, Primitive Methodist, United Methodist Free Church, Lay Methodist.

22   Minute Book of Wesleyan Methodist Conference, New South Wales, 1892–94, ML 287.1/7, 1892.

23   *Methodist*, 12 March 1892.

one, hope to live long enough to see this growing desire an accomplished fact in this fair land in which we live.'[24] A year later in 1893, Conference recorded 'its deep and solemn conviction that, in the interests of Christ's Kingdom in these colonies, an organic union of the several Methodist Churches is desirable.'[25] A Joint Committee prepared a draft Basis of Union and sent this document out for comment to all the Quarterly Meetings and District Meetings across New South Wales.[26] However, to the disappointment of the working group, it seemed that Wesleyans in New South Wales were not persuaded about the value of union. Reluctantly, the Conference of 1894 had to record that 'it is thought that the Churches are not yet ripe for such a union.'[27]

* * *

News of unresolved problems between missionary colleagues in Samoa reached Sydney. Brown was asked to visit that region and left Sydney in April 1893.[28] At that time, Samoa was in the throes of continuing instability, with tensions between the 'Three Powers'—Great Britain, Germany and the United States— over colonial authority in the region, as well as longstanding conflicts over traditional authority between rival Samoan leaders Mata'afa and Malietoa Laupepa. As he travelled around the communities of Samoa in the course of dealing with church business, Brown remembered their history of fluid alliances. Near the end of his visit, Brown met with his friend Robert Louis Stevenson at Vailima on the island of Upolu. Stevenson was writing about the simmering conflicts of Samoa for the British press and reported,

> Dr George Brown, the missionary, had just completed a tour of the islands. There are few men in the world with a more mature knowledge of native character, and I applied to him eagerly for an estimate of the relative forces. 'When the first shot is fired, and not before,' said he, 'you will know who is who.'... There are too many strings in a Samoan intrigue for the merely European mind to follow.[29]

Stevenson renewed his offer to write Brown's biography. Again Brown postponed the offer until a more convenient time. Stevenson's sudden death in 1894 cut off this possibility.

It would have been a relief for Brown to reach Tonga. The island nation that had seen so much sadness in previous years was now calm. There were still challenges

---

24 Ibid.
25 Minute Book of Wesleyan Methodist Conference, New South Wales, 1892–94, ML 287.1/7, 1892.
26 Ibid., 1893.
27 Ibid., 1894.
28 Ibid., 1893.
29 Robert Louis Stevenson, *Vailima Letters: Being Correspondence Addressed by Robert Louis Stevenson to Sidney Colvin, November 1890- October 1894*, London, Methuen 1895.

ahead. The people were still in mourning for their aged and venerated King George Tupou who had died at the age of ninety-six years, to be succeeded by his nineteen-year-old great-grandson.[30] Brown reported that 'Everything was quiet in Tonga and civil liberty was enjoyed by all.'[31]

* * *

While her husband travelled during the winter of 1893, Lydia Brown learned of the death of her aged mother Mary Anne Wallis, far away in Auckland, and welcomed another grandson, a second son for Amy. Lydia was thankful that she had been able to visit her parents the previous year.[32] Amy and Ben Dinning were now stationed at Richmond on the outskirts of Sydney so, with her husband away, Lydia was free to be with Amy and help with the new baby. As well as her commitment to the needs of her family and local church community, Lydia Brown continued to take a personal interest in the families and single women who had gone from Australia and New Zealand to work in the island communities across the Pacific. Letters and parcels of supplies were flowing between the concerned women of the Ladies Auxiliary and the women in the field.[33] Early impressions were that the single women were finding their place and beginning useful work among the local women. The Mission Board was very encouraged.[34]

* * *

Brown returned from the tropics in June 1893 to a bleak colony. It would be described as a year of 'extraordinary calamities and financial disasters, which have caused suffering, direct or indirect, to the whole colony.'[35] Failed banks, unemployment, political struggle, lost crops, severe flooding and bankrupted businesses touched everyone. Financial loss among their church members had its own impact.[36] Brown was back in time to observe the formal establishment of the Australasian Federation League on 3 July 1893 in the Sydney Town Hall, note support for the new political movement, the Labor Electoral League, and hear fierce public debate over political representation with some demanding 'One Man – One Vote'. The spectre of unemployment sharpened the demand for protection for local workers with 'the total exclusion of all Asiatics and other

---

30 A. Harold Wood, *Overseas Missions of the Australian Methodist Church Vol. 1, Tonga and Samoa*, Melbourne: Aldersgate Press, 1975, pp. 205–06.

31 *Australasian Methodist Missionary Review*, 4 July 1893.

32 Leslie Langham Dinning, born 17 May 1893. Monica Brown's Birthday Book.

33 *Australasian Methodist Missionary Review*, 4 August, 4 October 1893.

34 Minute Book of Wesleyan Methodist Conference, New South Wales, 1892–94, ML 287.1/7, 1893.

35 Ibid., 1894.

36 Rev. Joseph Spence, quoted in the Minute Book of Wesleyan Methodist Conference, New South Wales, 1892–94, ML 287.1/7, 1894. The Conference rejected a request from the recently separated Conference of Queensland for financial help on the grounds of the 'seriously embarrassed condition of its own Church Property trusts.'

aliens whose standard of living and habits of life are not equal to our own.'[37] All around there was great unease. People were even beginning to suggest that fractured colonial society was faced with a choice: federation or revolution.

* * *

Shaking and instability were not limited to the colonies. In the area of New Britain early in 1894, where earth tremors were commonplace, a severe earthquake shook the region. The new young missionary wrote from Kinawanua to tell Lydia Brown of their fears of a tsunami and worry that the cliff-top mission house 'would have fallen over the precipice'.[38] It was still standing, though there was much damage across the Duke of York Island. The missionary wrote sadly, 'The grave where your dear little children were buried sank down and the tombstone was thrown down, and fell on the iron railing and was broken.'[39] Lydia could picture the place, the sacred spot among tall tropical trees where she had so often gone to weep and remember. Now it was desecrated, muddied and broken. Not even the graves of her children were secure.

The family was to move yet again. The elegant terrace house in Randwick was rented and now George was considering building a house of his own. His collection of artefacts and documents continued to grow, and he dreamed of building a house with more space. Suburbs were springing up along the new railway line running north of Sydney Harbour where once orchards and small farms had been hidden in bushland. Families that had once lived close to the city on the harbour began to move north. Brown decided to buy a block and build a family home in the new suburb of Gordon near several other Methodist families. The house would be called 'Kinawanua'. That other cliff top house, shaken by earthquakes, anxiety, depression and grief, could never be forgotten.

While their new house was under construction, Brown planned a journey to the west, sailing to Adelaide in April 1894 and then on to Albany and Perth in Western Australia. Lydia decided to travel with him, despite having an injury that kept her on crutches for a period. During the five weeks while Brown travelled widely to visit churches in Western Australia, Lydia stayed with friends in Adelaide until her husband returned there for the three-yearly General Conference.[40] Memories of that other General Conference in Adelaide in 1881 were difficult. Then some colleagues had accused him of murder. Now

---

37   Stuart Macintyre, 'Corowa and the voice of the people,' in *Steps to Federation: Lectures Marking the Centenary of Federation*, ed. Patricia Clarke, Melbourne: Australian Scholarly Publishing, 2001, pp. 39–53, p. 48.
38   Rev. William Brown, Letter, 15 February 1894, published in the *Australasian Methodist Missionary Review*, 5 July 1894.
39   Ibid.
40   *Australasian Methodist Missionary Review*, 4 August 1894. Among other places, he visited between 26 May and 1 July 1894 Albany, Perth, York and Beverley.

he returned with honour as Dr. Brown. He had never forgotten the emotions of that time and when addressing newly ordained young ministers warned them that they would probably experience times of

> depression and of doubt, times when the world will seem strangely out of joint, and you are tempted almost to doubt the existence and over-ruling power of a good, loving, wise God. There may come to you experiences so painful and so mysterious that you are unable to reconcile them with your ideas of justice and of right. In these times you will have to wait, to suffer and be strong.... You will need that higher courage, which comes from perfect loyalty and perfect love to Christ. You will have to be fearless in the discharge of plain duties, even should your actions entail the pains of misrepresentation, unpopularity or loss of friends. You will have to stand fast in the faith against the assaults of open enemies and false friends.[41]

The focus in 1894, however, was not on the crimes of George Brown but on the issue of whether or not the Wesleyan Methodists should move to a union with the other smaller communities of Methodists. Brown was a committed member of the New South Wales panel appointed to work with other Methodist bodies 'to promote a spirit of unity ... that oneness of spirit and practical fellowship which is absolutely necessary for Organic Union.'[42] For twelve hours they debated the issue in Adelaide and finally decided, 'that union with the other branches of Methodism in these Colonies, practically identical in belief and teaching with itself, sprung from the same spiritual stock, and separated from it merely by difference in ecclesiastical order, would be for the glory of God and the advancement of Christ's Kingdom.'[43]

Even though he feared that New South Wales would be slow to ratify this, Brown now thought he would probably live to see Methodist Union come to pass.[44]

A group portrait of the Brown family was taken around the time of Claudia Brown's wedding in May 1895. In the photographer's studio they are arranged formally, unsmiling, and even the two little grandsons have kept very still. Each one is linked with an arm around a shoulder, a hand reaching to touch. The four-year-old grandson leans back in his grandfather's arms with a hand on his grandmother's knee. This is a rare moment when they are all together. Lizzie

---

41 Brown, 'Charge to ordinands,' in the *Methodist*, 12 March 1892.
42 Minute Book of Wesleyan Methodist Conference, New South Wales, 1892–94, ML 287.1/7, 1894.
43 General Conference resolution re Union, quoted in James Colwell, *Illustrated History of Methodism: Australia 1812–1855; New South Wales and Polynesia 1856–1902*, Sydney: William Brooks & Co., 1904, p. 610.
44 In 1895, Brown worked on the Methodist Union Committee with clergy, J.E. Carruthers, Spence, W. Clarke, Pincombe, R. Sellors, G. Lane, J. Austin, R. Bavin, Maddern, J. Woolnough, P. Clipsham, W. Rutledge and twelve laymen.

has returned to live in Sydney, the Dinnings are in town briefly from their country appointment and George Brown is at home for once. The new house at Gordon has been finished ready for the wedding and the newlyweds will be living not far away in the new suburb of Lindfield. All of Lydia's children who have survived are now adults, all beloved. In the midst of the fragility of human life, with news of deaths and loss around them, this moment early in 1895 has been captured.[45]

Figure 17. Brown family 1895. Back: Geoffrey Brown, Benjamin Dinning, Mary Elizabeth (Lizzie) Brown, Fred Brown, Monica Brown, Percy Slade, Claudia Brown. Front: Amy (Brown) Dinning, Leslie Dinning, Lydia Brown, Alan Dinning, George Brown.

Source: Brown Family Album, per favour of Miss Nancy Joyce.

* * *

Tolerant he may have been, able to accommodate a wide range of theological opinions and happy to enjoy the company of knighted gentleman, cannibal chiefs, small children or crusading women. Tolerant George Brown was not when his beloved mission work was under attack, most particularly when that attack came from a Roman Catholic Cardinal. Cardinal Moran gave an address

---

45   The original of this photograph is in family possession. It has been published in Margaret Reeson, *A Singular Woman*, Adelaide: Open Book Publishers, 1999, p. 158.

in Sydney in June 1895 in which he compared unfavourably the efforts of Anglican and Protestant missionary organisations with those of the Catholic Orders. Not only was Brown outraged. The speech struck at the heart of all those working for organisations such as the Church Missionary Society, the Australian Board of Missions, the London Missionary Society, the Presbyterian Missionary Society and the Wesleyan Methodist Missionary Society. In the Methodist Centenary Hall, 'packed from floor to ceiling on Sunday afternoon,' in July 1895, the Anglican Primate Dr. Saumarez Smith used his authority to control the audience as 'applause swelled strong in the bosom of the auditory' and Brown made a long speech that the secular press described as a 'formidable controversial' address.[46] The Catholic Church, he conceded, must be given credit for taking seriously the need for missions to the heathen centuries before the Protestant churches. However, he examined the history of Catholic missions of long standing in South America, China, India and Japan and asked, 'Does there exist now, after three and a half centuries, a powerful Native Church?' 'No,' he declared.[47] In many cases, local tribes had been wiped out, or had returned to their original beliefs. Giving examples from the Pacific, he assured his audience that strong 'Native churches' had been established by Protestant missions, where the people of the place participated in leadership and had made the church their own. In the Pacific, he announced, the priests had almost always followed the earlier Protestant missionaries, when the region was deemed safe. The Protestants had not fought among themselves nearly as much as the Cardinal had suggested and he listed the various benefits brought to island communities by the Protestant missions, with Bible translation and the gift of an 'open Bible' a significant blessing. His audience loved it. It would have done nothing to endear Brown to the Catholic community in Sydney.[48] Combative speeches and outraged responses were to continue for years.[49]

* * *

Both Lydia and George Brown were very busy with their pens. Lydia kept up a wide correspondence with extended family members in New Zealand and New South Wales, as well as regular pastoral letters to missionary women across the Pacific. Her caring motherly approach brought understanding of their remote situations, and she passed on news of mutual friends; the babies, the weddings, the illnesses. Letters from the islands often carried requests for items for women's activities—school supplies, or '2 yards of print or turkey red (double width) hemmed at both ends'[50]—and she did her best to find these things. Her

---

46   *Australasian Methodist Missionary Review*, 5 July 1895.
47   Ibid.
48   Ibid.
49   For example, Cardinal Moran made another critical speech in 1899 that prompted a large gathering of Protestants in Sydney Town Hall.
50   For examples, see *Australasian Methodist Missionary Review*, 4 August 1893, 4 October 1893.

letters always carried the promise of prayer. George Brown did not much enjoy being bound to his desk at 381 George Street, Sydney, but perhaps remembered the hurt he had experienced when his own letters from Samoa had not been answered quickly. From the desk he understood the difficulties of writing with wisdom concerning the many challenges being faced in distant places. As well as business correspondence, he wrote frequently for church and scientific journals. His life was busy as church leader, fund raiser, committee member, public speaker and active member of his new local congregation; in 1895 he and son-in-law Percy Slade were among the signatories for the certificate of title for land bought near Lindfield Railway Station for a new Methodist Church.

In July 1895, Lydia's aged father the Reverend James Wallis died in Auckland. He was the oldest surviving Methodist minister in the colonies of Australasia, having been ordained over sixty years earlier. He was greatly respected, with strong appreciation for his years in Māori communities. At his funeral his old friend, the Reverend H.H. Lawry, spoke of 'the lifework of his departed friend, laying special emphasis on the care and fidelity with which he trained his family in the fear of God. In both the work of the public ministry and of the home, God had crowned his labours with success.'[51]

As the century came closer to an end, organisations for women and for youth grew stronger. In the churches, groups like the Christian Endeavour, the Mutual Improvement Societies, the Band of Hope and the Woman's Christian Temperance Union were flourishing. Large numbers of younger people gathered for local meetings and from time to time met in great combined events in the city. The women of the Brown family had a special interest in their new Ladies Auxiliary supporting women missionaries. The two single daughters, Lizzie and Monica, now invested much energy into this, with Monica taking responsibility as Secretary of the group. In a time when there were robust debates about whether a woman could represent her church community at the annual Conference, a correspondent to the church journal wrote,

> Should not women as well as men have opportunity of exercising their gifts and graces? Are the domesticated Marthas to be everlastingly applauded for their cuisine, and the congenialities with which they set the table, and the spiritual, the intellectual and the philosophical Marys to be undervalued…? At the Lord's table, in the prayer meetings, in the work of the Church, and in the hope of heaven, woman is equal to man, and on a level with him. Why, then, should she not be his associate in Conference?[52]

George Brown agreed.

---

51 *Methodist*, 20 July 1895.
52 William Hill, Letter to the editor, in the *Methodist*, 11 May 1895.

Lydia Brown may well have seen herself as a 'Martha', a traditional home-centred woman with hospitality and personal relationships at the heart of her world. Lizzie and Monica were both equally competent in domestic matters as they were in leadership, management, music, art and teaching. Her married daughters Amy Dinning and Claudia Slade, also gifted and educated women, were both expecting babies and Lydia looked forward with delight to having her arms full of grandchildren.[53] Her husband would go on travelling, she knew, visiting his widely flung people and taking their story across the colonies. He was already considering two new projects. For herself, she preferred to stay home in her new house and help with the babies.

---

53   Stanley Dinning was born on 19 November 1895. Mabel Slade was born on 8 September 1896.

17. 'Sanctified audacity'

New South Wales, British New Guinea, New Britain, Fiji, Tonga, Solomon Islands 1896–1900

The region where once George Brown had met curious and hostile villagers was changing. The curves of coastline on the maps were familiar but the place names had become German. New Britain was now Neu Pommern. Duke of York was Neu Lauenburg. German colonial authorities were in charge. Priests and nuns from Europe, with the Sacred Heart Mission, had been in the area since 1882. In Australia, the Methodists realised that to maintain their place in that region it would be strategic to recruit a German agent. It was decided in 1896 to appoint a 'German Methodist Minister of good standing and ability,' and George Brown began the task of communicating with his counterparts in Germany.[1] By the middle of the year the Reverend Heinrich Fellmann had been selected. Brown wrote to Fellmann explaining that his aim in asking for a German missionary was to forge a strong link with the colonial authorities and to strengthen the status of the Wesleyan Methodist Mission in Neu Pommern.

> The Roman Catholics seem to be able to do as they please and are openly trying to force us out of the land where we have done so much for God and the people there.... We want to assure [the German Colonial authorities] that we are extremely anxious to help them in every possible manner in their efforts to promote the well being of the native race.... We ask for no privileges which are not granted to the Roman Catholics. We simply wish to do the work God has given us to do and we never attempt to interfere with the politics of the secular government of the country.[2]

* * *

Competing voices vied for Brown's attention. Messages from each of their fields of mission continued to ask for more resources or suggested new initiatives. In Sydney, the gentlemen of the Board of Missions shook their heads pessimistically in the light of the continuing financial stress. At home, the Brown family was conspicuous at the opening of the first small Methodist Church near Lindfield Railway Station on 19 April 1896; Brown preached, Lizzie played the organ,

---

1 Minute Book of Wesleyan Methodist Conference, New South Wales, ML 287.1/7 CY 1365, 1896.
2 George Brown to Heinrich Fellmann, 3 August 1896. In the private collection of Dr. Ulrich Fellmann.

Lydia and Monica helped with hospitality and a pregnant Claudia hoped that her baby would be the first to be baptized in the new church.[3] This would be the home congregation for George and Lydia Brown for the next seven years.

That same month, in Suva, Fiji, a group of indentured labourers from the Solomon Islands approached the leaders of the Methodist Mission with a plea. They had been converted to the Christian faith while they were in Fiji, they explained, but although they had asked more than once for missionaries to go to their people in the Solomon Islands, the Methodists had always hesitated, wanting to avoid competition with the Melanesian Mission of the Anglican Church in that chain of islands. The men from the Solomon Islands were not satisfied. The Melanesian Mission was working hundreds of miles from their north-western homes, they said, and added that although the Melanesian Mission was a 'true religion' it was a 'slow religion' and had still not reached their home in Guadalcanal after many years. Their request was passed on to George Brown and the Board of Missions.[4] Brown welcomed this approach. He had been raising the question of a new work in the Solomon Islands for years.[5] Even so, it was not the only demand on mission resources. Requests and complaints arrived on his desk daily from the other mission Districts. He needed to visit the work in British New Guinea and Neu Pommern and grumbles about the limitations of the missionary efforts among the Indian labourers in Fiji were growing louder.[6]

* * *

In December 1896, the young German minister, Heinrich Fellmann, arrived in Sydney. With him was his twenty-year-old bride, Johanna. Taking the newly-weds into their home, George Brown was impressed with the quality of the young man and enchanted with his bride, soon calling her his 'dear little *Tochter*'.[7] Lydia Brown took Johanna Fellmann to her heart immediately. Johanna was beautiful and intelligent, fluent in English and French as well as her native German—and profoundly homesick for her parents, Matthaus Class, Wesleyan minister, and his wife Sophie, far away at home near Stuttgart, Germany. Lydia understood. At a similar age, she too had left her family a week after her wedding and left her home country to travel with her new husband to a foreign land. Unlike Johanna, Lydia had grown up in a missionary household in a Māori community. Johanna had recently graduated from an international school for young women in Europe.[8] The adjustment, not only to Australia but to Neu Pommern, was going to be profound.

---

3   Geoffrey Stacy, *A Cloud of Witnesses: at Tryon Road Uniting Church 1896-1996,* Sydney: Lindfield Tryon Road Uniting Church Centenary Committee, 1996.

4   *Australasian Methodist Missionary Review,* 4 July 1896.

5   John F. Goldie, 'The Solomon Islands,' in *A Century in the Pacific*, ed. J. Colwell, Sydney: William H. Heale, 1914, pp. 559–85, p. 565.

6   A. Harold Wood, *Overseas Missions of the Australian Methodist Church, Vol. III, Fiji-Indian and Rotuma*, Melbourne: Aldersgate Press, 1978, pp. 10–12.

7   Brown to Johanna Fellmann, 18 February 1897 (Private collection).

8   Ulrich Fellmann, 'Missionarsfrau Johanna Fellmann geb. Class und die wesleyanischen Methodisten,' *EmK – Geschichte,* Quellen, Studien, Mitteilungen, vol. 25 (2004): 5–11.

Figure 18. Rev. Heinrich and Johanna Fellmann, Sydney 1897.

Source: Fellmann Family Album, per favour Dr. Ulrich Fellmann, Aachen, Germany.

The Brown family did their best to make the young couple welcome. They discovered that Heinrich's twenty-sixth birthday was on Christmas Day and celebrated it with him in the strangeness of summer heat. In Sydney, there were shopping trips, social calls, church meetings, and a train journey into the Blue Mountains to walk with George and Lydia Brown through ancient sandstone rocks and bush of eucalypt and acacia, so remote from the linden and spruce of their homeland.[9] Lydia Brown was worried to see how often Johanna suffered from severe headaches; new spectacles helped, but Lydia felt that the young woman's pain was linked less with eyestrain than with homesickness, the strange territory of a new marriage, a different language and an alien hemisphere. Much later Brown would remind Johanna, 'Do you remember our talk upon the veranda one day when you said, O Doctor, ten years seems to be such a long time before I shall see my Mother again.'[10]

On their last night together at Gordon, 28 January 1897, as the family gathered over their meal, George Brown told the tale of the tragedy of their family loss in 1879, when Lydia faced the deaths of their children in the cannibal islands without her husband. Lydia Brown may have regretted her husband's timing as insensitive.[11] Johanna offered the family her 'Poetry Book', with the loving messages inscribed in it by her family and friends in distant Germany. The Brown family each added their own words of blessing. Lydia wrote 'In the centre of the circle of God's love I stand....'[12] She treasured her own Autograph Book with its freight of memories.

Many missionary couples had been welcomed into their home over the years, and many had become deep and lifelong friends. This young pair touched the Browns in a particular way. After Heinrich and Johanna sailed north to their future home, George Brown wrote to Johanna of returning to the house after seeing them off and finding himself with tears in his eyes as he looked into their empty room. He joked gently about the 'German cakes made by the *kleine frau* that used to tease me so much,' and added, 'I thought of the dear good little girl who had come from the Fatherland with her dear husband to help him in his great work and I felt that she had crept into all our hearts and endeared herself to us.... We often talk about you both and think and pray about you and for you.'[13]

---

9   Photographs of family group with Fellmanns, and Lydia Brown with the Fellmanns in the Blue Mountains; Fellmann family photo album, in possession of Dr. Ulrich Fellmann, Aachen, Germany.
10   Brown to Johanna Fellmann, 28 November 1902. Series of personal letters in possession of Brown's great granddaughter, Miss Nancy Joyce, Sydney.
11   Ulrich Fellmann (ed.), *Von Schwaben in den Bismarckarchipel: Tagebücher der Missionarsfrau Johanna Fellmann aus Deutsch-Neuguinea 1896–1903*, Harrassovitz: Verlag, 2009, entry for 28 January 1897.
12   Lydia Brown, entry in Johanna Fellmann's Autograph Book, 28 January 1897. The Autograph Book is in the private collection of Dr. Ulrich Fellmann.
13   Brown to Johanna Fellmann, 18 February 1897.

The friendship between the Brown and Fellmann families, that had begun between a homesick young bride, her husband and a welcoming family in Sydney, was to continue unbroken into the next generations for over a century.

* * *

It was six years since George Brown had visited British New Guinea and New Britain. He left for the north at the end of May 1897. He had suggested to his daughter Monica that she should travel with him this time, 'as I am getting very old now and they ought not to let me go alone.'[14] He was in fact a very active sixty-one-year-old and Monica declined. His journey took him first to Port Moresby and then the small eastern island of Samarai where he was met by William Bromilow. For two weeks they sailed in the mission schooner *Dove*, visiting isolated mission stations in the eastern islands that had been pioneered since his previous visit.[15]

Brown and his companions arrived at the central island of Dobu on 9 June. The large new mission schooner *Meda*, purchased after intense fundraising, had arrived, bringing another party of teachers from Fiji. He planned to sail on to New Britain in her soon. Brown was moved to visit Dobu again, the place that he had selected in 1890 as a site for future mission work. He wrote, 'This has been one of the most memorable days in my life.'[16] Where once there had been wild bush and a suspicious and indifferent people, he found houses and gardens, a church, small hospital and school, housing for teachers and students and a mission community of about one hundred people. By coincidence, Brown's arrival coincided with the sixth anniversary of the landing of the pioneer group. Now he watched as canoes came across the water from nearby Normanby Island with people coming to worship. The church was packed with people. The singing was sweet and tuneful, the many young people enthusiastic, the prayers and messages brief and lively, the congregation attentive. He later wrote,

> As I looked on the large congregation and contrasted the sight with that which we saw on our first landing I felt deeply grateful to God. My eyes indeed were so full of tears that I could not read the words of the hymn. During the opening services I had the privilege of baptizing ten adult converts, who after a long trial and careful teaching and supervision were received into full membership of our Church. I have now, therefore,

---

14 Ibid.

15 George Brown, Journal, 7 June 1897, published in the *Australasian Methodist Missionary Review*, 6 November 1897.

16 Brown, Journal, 10 June 1897.

baptised converts in six different languages. I preached to the people from Romans 10:12 'There is no difference between the Jew and the Greek: for the same Lord over all is rich unto all who call upon him.'[17]

That evening, weary after a long day of preaching, meetings and a boat trip to Fergusson Island for a service held under the shade of trees, Brown saw the last of the canoes disappear under a sunset sky. He was tired but elated. The missionary team was an impressive group of people. They had 'a strong love for all' and shared Brown's belief in the core of Christian faith; 'the blessed story of God's love to them, and to man everywhere.'[18] The mission Sisters, who had come to this place as an experiment, were proving very valuable members of the team.[19] The Fijian, Samoan and Tongan teachers were good people and Brown repeated his opinion that 'we could never have made the progress which we have made but for the invaluable help of our native agents.'[20] Even though he knew that this could also be a place of doubt, disappointment, disease and conflict, at that moment he was profoundly thankful for what he saw. The investment of 1891—what Bromilow called the 'sanctified audacity'[21] of beginning mission work in such a place—was bearing fruit.[22]

* * *

The telegram came as a shock. In the warmth of her winter fireside, Lydia Brown had been imagining her husband in the tropics. The telegram painted an alarming picture. The brand new mission schooner *Meda* had been wrecked on a reef, and Brown and Bromilow were thought to have been on board.[23] The distance between her and her man was immeasurable. Was he safe? There was no way of making contact. There was nothing she could do but wait and pray with the support and care of her family, and her friends in the new congregation at Lindfield.[24] It was a week before another brief message arrived, this time from George himself and passed on by a passing vessel. The *Meda* was wrecked but he and Bromilow and the others were all safe. Again Lydia settled herself to wait. She, with her friends, would pray for the safety of the travellers – and for courage for herself.

---

17   Ibid., 13 June 1897.

18   Ibid., 13 June 1897, in the *Australasian Methodist Missionary Review*, 6 November 1897.

19   At this time, the mission sisters were: Eleanor Walker, Jeannie Tinney, Emily Newell, Minnie Billing and Julia Benjamin.

20   Brown, Journal, 10 June 1897, in the *Australasian Methodist Missionary Review*, 6 November 1897.

21   W.E. Bromilow, quoted in speech to Missionary Society, 28 Feb 1898, in the *Australasian Methodist Missionary Review*, 7 March 1898.

22   Brown, Journal, 13 June 1897, in the *Australasian Methodist Missionary Review*, 6 November 1897.

23   *Brisbane Courier*, 24 July 1897. The *Meda* ran aground on 15 June 1897. More detail on the wreck was published in the *Australasian Methodist Missionary Review*, 6 November 1897.

24   The first anniversary of the Lindfield Methodist Church was celebrated on 16 May 1897. See Stacy, *A Cloud of Witnesses*.

* * *

The loss of the *Meda* was a serious blow. Brown was forced to wait in the eastern islands of British New Guinea for another vessel. While he waited, he endeared himself to the staff by his willingness to travel anywhere with them. On one occasion, walking back from an inland village in the heat, sudden tropical darkness fell when the party was an hour's walk from home. 'So I had to consent to be carried, as I was footsore and lame and could not see the track.'[25] Two men made a litter, hoisted him precariously shoulder high and set off at a good pace over the rough coral track in the deep dark, while Brown nervously braced himself, expecting a heavy fall. Bromilow described the day when he and Brown sat on the ground at the centre of a crowd of villagers, sharing their meal of boiled bananas and yams taken hot from a clay cooking pot, adding, 'The Doctor has not forgotten how to adapt himself to circumstances.'[26]

The weeks were passing, however, and George Brown knew that he was long overdue in New Britain. There was no way of letting the small mission community in the now-German colony know that the *Meda* was lost. After two months in British New Guinea, Brown decided to risk travelling on to New Britain in the little fourteen-ton schooner, *Dove*. He reached New Britain safely on 31 July 1897. The Methodists there had given up waiting for him, believing that he had returned to Australia. Johanna Fellmann, at home in the mission house at Raluana, 'could not at first recognise the strange old man in a long oilskin coat and a queer hat, who was coming up the path to the house, but as soon as she did so, I got a most hearty and loving welcome, and there was enough excitement to satisfy anyone.'[27]

For George Brown, this was like coming home. From the mission house he could see the sweep of the bay with the distinctive shapes of the Mother and Daughter volcanoes, the dark volcanic sand, the familiar faces of the people. But there were great changes, too. Brown noted that, 'scene after scene of the early days presented itself to me. I could scarcely realise that I was in the same land in which I had lived more than twenty years ago.'[28]

The presence of traders, explorers, scientists, plantation owners, missionaries and colonial authority in the islands was shaping a different society. Expansive, ordered plantations were in the control of outsiders. Once no white man dared land unless he was heavily armed, but now a German colonial authority ruled the region. Brown, with the Fellmanns and their colleagues William Chambers

---

25   Brown, Journal, 23 July 1897, published in *Australasian Methodist Missionary Review*, 7 February 1898.
26   William Bromilow, letter published in *Australasian Methodist Missionary Review*, 6 November 1897.
27   Brown, Journal, 31 July 1897, published in *Australasian Methodist Missionary Review*, 7 February 1898.
28   Ibid., 1 August 1897.

and John Crump, were entertained by German hosts.[29] Brown was driven along well-made roads lined with plantations of coconut and cotton, bright shrubs and telephone lines between substantial houses.[30] It was hard to believe that these were places where 'wild, boisterous, excited men and women crowded around us on our first visit,' naked, armed, aggressive, demanding trade goods.[31] Now he saw thatched schoolrooms and church, and Johanna Fellmann's mission house was elegant with potted palms, Chinese screen and solid furniture from Germany.[32] It was no longer a region ruled by fear. Cannibalism was fading away.[33] Brown observed that,

> The appearance of the people here, as in New Guinea, is wonderfully altered.... The change is indeed a very marvellous one, and we have in New Britain another proof of the great truth that 'if any man be in Christ Jesus he is a new creature, old things are passed away and all things are become new.'[34]

Children and youths with no memory of Brown's time in the islands stared at this grey-bearded older man with curiosity. It was hard for them to imagine a time before the traders, before the Methodist or Catholic missionaries, before the plantations. They knew the name of George Brown, if not the man, from the newly established training institution for converts in the Duke of York Islands, George Brown College.[35] Most of the old people who, armed with slingshots and axes, had seen this white man first step on to the dark sand and bleached coral of their shore were now gone. When Brown showed his old lantern slides of the people from the past, the audience cried out 'the dead are alive again tonight'.[36] Brown had been the pioneer but his time in the islands had been limited and interrupted. The sustained work had been done by men like Danks, Rooney, Rickard and the South Sea Island men. He noted in his journal, 'I felt very thankful, indeed, to God for giving me the privilege of seeing the grand work which has been done here by the earnest, devoted men who have laboured here, and whose work He has so signally blessed.'[37]

In a region where George Brown had experienced some of his most extreme challenges and most shattering times of depression and grief he was once more able to travel with the present mission staff. The Duke of York language came

---

29 Brown, Journal, 3, 4, 5 August 1897.
30 Ibid., 20 August 1897, published in the *Australasian Methodist Missionary Review*, 4 June 1898.
31 Ibid., 31 July 1897.
32 Fellmann, *Von Schwaben in den Bismarckarchipel*, pp. 244–45, 254.
33 Brown, Journal, 9 August 1897, in the *Australasian Methodist Missionary Review*, 4 May 1898.
34 Ibid., 1 August 1897, in the *Australasian Methodist Missionary Review*, 7 February 1898.
35 Rev. J.A. Crump was responsible for the Training Institution, George Brown College. Land was selected for this property on Brown's 1897 visit and it was established in 1898 at Ulu, Duke of York.
36 Brown, Journal, 12 August 1897, in *Australasian Methodist Missionary Review*, 4 May 1898.
37 Ibid., 1 August 1897 in the *Australasian Methodist Missionary Review*, 7 February 1898.

back up to the surface of his memory and he 'had no difficulty whatever in finding the words to speak to them again of the love of God.'[38] Returning to Kinawanua, he remembered 'those dark days when I and one very dear to me had to pass together through the deep waters of affliction, and what then appeared as hopeless sorrow.'[39] He could never forget Kinawanua, a place of hopelessness and hope, despair and redemption.

* * *

It was time to go. Brown knew, much as he loved this region, that he could only be a visitor. Other challenges waited for him back at his office in Sydney. Although Johanna Fellmann pleaded that he should wait for the commercial steamship *Titus*, he insisted on sailing for the hub island of Samarai on the little *Dove* at the end of August 1897.

There were times during the slow journey home, when he wondered if he would ever reach his own front door and Lydia's welcome again. As he spent days in a dead calm with a choice of the insufferable heat of the little cabin or the unshaded deck,[40] he worried about the mountain of mission correspondence that must be accumulating on his office desk in Sydney. Lashed by torrential rain, he wondered what dire news his mission treasurer would have for him. After waiting in vain at Samarai for the steamer, Brown risked the hazardous passage of the Great Barrier Reef to Cooktown in the *Dove*. During the interminable five weeks it took to make the journey south to Sydney, Brown worried about all the work he ought to be doing. Fiji was one area on his mind. In the early months of the year he had been working with his Board on the longstanding issue of providing a ministry among the growing number of indentured Indian labourers on the plantations in Fiji, as well as those who had settled there. The initial appointment of an Indian catechist had ended after two years. An impassioned appeal at Conference had resulted in an application from a woman, Miss Hannah Dudley, who offered to go; Hannah Dudley had previous experience of work in India and spoke an Indian language.[41] He and his Board had debated over several months whether it was right to send one woman, with no companion and few resources to support her, to attempt such a task among 10,000 Indian people. He had interviewed Miss Dudley.[42] Just before he had left Sydney in

---

38   Ibid., 8 August 1897, *Australasian Methodist Missionary Review*, 4 May 1898.
39   Ibid.
40   Ibid., 27–30 August 1897, in *Australasian Methodist Missionary Review*, 4 June 1898.
41   Morven Sidal, *Hannah Dudley: Hamari Maa, Honoured Mother, Educator and Missioner to the Indentured Indians of Fiji 1864–1913*, Suva: Pacific Theological College, 1998, pp. 1–6.
42   The Finance Committee of the Board received the application at their meeting on 17 March 1897, ML CY354.

early May the Board had decided to engage Hannah Dudley as a Missionary Sister but he did not know what had happened in the months since then.[43] He arrived home at last on 4 October. He had been away for almost five months.

* * *

Lydia Brown welcomed home her husband with relief. Monica was glad she had chosen not to go with him. With her daughters, Lydia found it best to go on with her own life in his absence. There was plenty of family news to share: Fred's wedding planned for February 1898 to Eva Bloomfield; Geoffrey's studies and his courtship of Ada Price; Lizzie was learning to use a typewriter, Monica working hard as Secretary of the Ladies Auxiliary and as a public speaker. Lydia often caught the train to visit Claudia. Her grandchildren delighted her and Brown teased that if Amy's children had lived nearer to Sydney 'we would never have Mrs Brown at home.'[44] The community of Methodists in the new congregation at Lindfield, friends in her neighbourhood of Gordon and the scattered missionary community all gave Lydia a sphere where she could give and receive love. For her family she remained the secure anchor of their world.

George Brown now had to drag his mind back to everything that had been going on in his absence. It was hard, at first, to feel at home on a crowded city street. Work was continuing on the building site between the church offices and the Town Hall where workmen and artisans created dust and noise raising the splendid domes, stonework and stained glass of the Queen Victoria Building. The financial depression continued and his mission treasurer brought him grim reports of dwindling resources made worse by the wreck of the new ship *Meda*. Public debate continued about the possibility of a Federation of the colonies and church debate still struggled over the question of union of the several streams of Methodism. Brown took an active interest in both issues and was irritated when, after more than twenty years of debate on Methodist Union, the Wesleyan Conference in NSW in 1898 still failed to reach a conclusion.

As he had predicted, his desk was piled with work to be done, with urgent pleas from every mission region for more financial resources and stern warnings from his Finance Committee that he must reduce spending as their debt was becoming more and more alarming. It had been very different in 1891 when he had been able to arrange substantial resources for the New Mission in British New Guinea. While he had been away, the Ladies Auxiliary had committed their members to supporting Hannah Dudley in Fiji and had given her a fine farewell in August, but Brown was anxious about the rather loose arrangements

---

43 Minute Book of Wesleyan Methodist Conference, New South Wales, ML 287.1/7 CY 1365, 5 May 1897.
44 Brown to Johanna Fellmann, 24 February 1898.

that had been made.[45] When General Conference met in Auckland at the end of the year, there was considerable criticism of the contrast between the vast resources poured into British New Guinea and what seemed an inadequate and half-hearted effort in Fiji, and the Board was instructed to address the needs of the Indians in Fiji 'on a more aggressive and comprehensive scale'.[46] In the face of the criticism, it was a comfort to hear that, while visiting Sydney, Sir William Macgregor had said publicly of the Methodist mission in British New Guinea 'that there was no better conducted mission in the world … he could testify from personal knowledge that they were not simply inspired by a temporary enthusiasm but that they worked as well today as when they first landed.'[47]

'The Board thinks I must visit some of the Districts each year,' Brown wrote.[48] He had no objections. Despite the inevitable hazards of travel and the fact that he would often become ill far from home, Brown valued the opportunities to speak face to face with mission staff rather than through the filter of letters. It was true, however, that every time he went away the regular work of the Missions office was neglected. It was a great relief to him when his old friend and colleague, Benjamin Danks, who had shared some of the worst moments of his time in New Britain, was appointed to the role of Organising Secretary for Foreign Missions. Lydia and George Brown welcomed the Danks family from Victoria with an 'At Home' at 'Kinawanua', Gordon, on 7 May 1898.[49] The bond between Lydia Brown and Ben and Emma Danks was very strong. The younger couple held Lydia in very high regard. The two families would continue to be close friends and colleagues for the rest of their lives.

In 1898 George Brown was able to visit New Zealand, Fiji and Samoa. In Fiji there were some tense meetings with newer staff and a difficult encounter with Hannah Dudley.[50] Brown met with other mission staff and Miss Dudley; 'our unanimous opinion was that if we are to do any real work here, we shall have to adopt other and more effective means,' he wrote,[51] but ambitions to provide more staff were being thwarted by lack of funds.[52] Despite assuring her that he admired her work, Brown left Hannah Dudley disappointed that there were no

45   Minute Book of Wesleyan Methodist Conference, New South Wales, ML 287.1/7 CY 1365, 19 August 1897.

46   Wood, *Overseas Missions of the Australian Methodist Church, Vol. 111, Fiji-Indian and Rotuma*, p. 12.

47   Minute Book of Wesleyan Methodist Conference, New South Wales, ML 287.1/7 CY 1365, 28 January 1898.

48   Brown, letter to Johanna Fellmann, 14 September 1898.

49   *Australasian Methodist Missionary Review*, 4 June 1898.

50   The Reverend Frederick Langham served as Chairman of the Fiji Methodist District from 1869 until 1895. In 1898 the new chairman was the Reverend W.W. Lindsay, with H.H. Nolan, A.J. Small, W.A. Burns, Jennison, W. Slade and J. Bathgate as colleagues.

51   Brown, Journal, 14 July 1898, in the *Australasian Methodist Missionary Review*, 6 December 1898.

52   Ibid.

funds available to employ her sister to help her.[53] It was not an easy journey. Brown was ill with flu as he travelled by sea and land to visit remote places and after a very long and poorly timed journey on horseback and on foot through the central mountains of Viti Levu he admitted that he had 'often been tired in my life but I was never so utterly tired out as I was during those last two miles.'[54] Then it was on to Samoa, a place of so many memories shared with a young Lydia, and more sea and land travel. At Satupa'itea, where they had established their first home together, he opened a fine large church and witnessed the largest communal feast he had ever seen. His camera captured many images of the occasion, including thirty carriers bearing his own portion away after the formal distribution of food; his personal share of ten pigs, a thousand head of taro, a great many bunches of bananas and two roots of kava was 'a very fair dinner for one man'.[55]

Travel was as natural as breathing to George Brown but he knew that many Australians rarely left their home district. If only they could see for themselves the way in which the gospel of Christ was transforming societies, he thought, they would be inspired to be generous and the financial woes of the mission would be over. An idea took shape and an advertisement appeared for a 'Winter Excursion' to visit the mission enterprises of the Wesleyan Methodist Church in Australasia. It would leave Sydney in June 1899 for a round trip through British New Guinea, Kaiserwilhelmsland, Neu Pommern and the Solomon Islands, with George Brown as tour guide.[56]

The steamship SS Moresby sailed from Sydney Harbour on 18 June 1899 with what Brown described as a 'very miscellaneous collection' of missionaries as well as a small group making the Winter Excursion. With Anglican, Lutheran, London Missionary Society and Methodist missionaries there were also a group of Roman Catholic nuns, brothers, a priest and two Bishops. An old friend who had once travelled on another long voyage with George Brown would write of him that, 'he had captured all whom he met; the captain on the bridge, the seaman in the forecastle, commercial travellers, passengers, women, children … where ever he touched he left his mark. He found God in everything; all loved him.'[57] If there was a time when this might be tested, it was now.

---

53   Hannah Dudley had been shocked to discover that a person she had employed to care for the little ones had been abusing some of them.
54   Brown, Journal, 20 June 1898, in the *Australasian Methodist Missionary Review*, 6 December 1898.
55   Ibid., 13 July–6 August 1898, in the *Australasian Methodist Missionary Review*, 4 April 1899. Photos of this event are in the photographic Album of George Brown, held at the Australian Museum, Sydney.
56   'Winter Excursion,' invitation from Australasian Methodist Missionary Society, signed by Brown, to the public to join a tour of Society's mission fields in the South Pacific, departing Sydney, 1 June 1899, returning Sydney, 14 July 1899, Petherick Room, NLA JAFp BIBLIO F6291a.
57   Dr. Fitchett, speaking after Brown's death at the Methodist General Conference, quoted in the *Methodist*, 26 May 1917.

Only days before they sailed, Brown attended a special meeting of the Board of Missions to discuss serious confrontations between Roman Catholics, Methodists and other Protestants, in Fiji, Samoa and Sydney.[58] Ever since he had witnessed a violent encounter between Scots Protestants and Irish Catholics in Montreal when he had been a young sailor in Canada in 1853, he had been aware of the depth of antagonism between these branches of Christianity.[59] Over the years he had debated with Catholic missionaries and bishops in Samoa, Fiji and New Britain. Recently, the French Bishop Julien Vidal in Fiji had been sharply critical of the Methodists there. The Irish Cardinal Moran in Sydney had outraged the Protestant community by writing in scathing terms of what he saw as the failures of most Protestant missions in the Pacific. No love was lost between the groups. Public debates and immoderate letters to the newspapers fuelled the fire. Among other statements that incensed the Methodists was the accusation by Cardinal Moran that a new translation of the Bible into Fijian, recently completed by Brown's friend Frederick Langham, was 'a book of lies, for many parts are absent from it, and very much is misinterpreted, but in the Catholic School they will be able to read the true original, they will hold the Sacred book in their hands in English.'[60] Now Brown discovered that he would have the company of both Bishop Julien Vidal from Fiji and Bishop Broyer from Samoa on board *SS Moresby* for many weeks, and there would be no escape.

The *Moresby* sailed north into tropical waters, while in Sydney the furore between Catholic and Protestant increased in volume and acrimony. Protestants were challenging Cardinal Moran to substantiate his allegations against Protestant missionaries in Samoa.[61] Brown, however, had found some common ground with his Catholic fellow passengers. Within days of the public debates in Sydney, near Port Moresby Brown and a large party from the visiting ship accepted the gracious hospitality of the priests and nuns at the Catholic Mission on Yule Island. The whole community had gathered for a Retreat and Brown was impressed—and envious—to meet fifteen priests, sixteen lay brothers and twenty-one nuns. He enjoyed a long conversation with Archbishop Navarre; Navarre had arrived in New Britain not long after Brown had left there in the early 1880s.[62]

---

58 Minute Book of Wesleyan Methodist Conference, New South Wales, ML MOM 203 CY 3305, 7 and 14 June 1899.

59 George Brown, *George Brown: Pioneer-Missionary and Explorer: An Autobiography*, London: Hodder and Stoughton, 1908, pp.12–13. In Montreal in 1853, the Orange Order organised speeches by the fiercely anti-Catholic and anti-Irish former priest Alessandro Gavazzi, resulting in a violent confrontation between the Scots and the Irish.

60 *Australasian Methodist Missionary Review*, 6 July 1899.

61 Ibid.

62 Brown, Journal, 9 July 1899, in the *Australasian Methodist Missionary Review*, 6 October 1899; Brown, *George Brown: Pioneer-Missionary and Explorer*, p. 507; John Garrett, *To Live Among the Stars: Christian Origins in Oceania*, Geneva: World Council of Churches Publication, 1982, pp. 237–38.

The ship sailed on. They visited the Methodist work in British New Guinea, landed Pastor Flierl and his party at the Lutheran Mission at Simbang, and reached New Britain in late July, much later than expected. Here again there was ambivalence about the relationship between Catholic and Methodist missionaries. Fellmann and Chambers recently had been involved in a court case over land claimed by both Catholics and Methodists. Yet Heinrich and Johanna Fellmann told Brown of the great kindness of Catholic Bishop Louis Couppé when Johanna had been dangerously ill with malaria the previous year.[63] By the time Bishop Vidal and his party left the ship, on an island near Guadalcanal in order for the Bishop to establish his pioneer missionary group in the Solomon Islands, Brown had been in their company for thousands of miles. Brown recorded their landing without rancour, adding that there was no sign of any Protestant missionary work in the western Solomon Islands.[64] Neither Brown nor Vidal would have been aware that only days before the two men had parted there had been a very large, noisy and acrimonious 'United Protestant Demonstration' in Sydney Town Hall, where representatives of many missionary societies expressed their indignation about accusations against their Societies by Cardinal Moran.[65] The grand 'Winter Excursion' came to harbour in Sydney again on 22 August 1899. They had travelled for nine weeks over 6,000 miles.

Brown had much to ponder. Of all the regions he had seen during that voyage, the area that stayed in his mind was the Solomon Islands. He had visited, unwillingly, that string of islands in 1880 as he struggled to return to Lydia following the court case in Fiji. This time he had returned once more to the beautiful region of Roviana Lagoon. He could not get out of his mind the pleas of the men from the Solomon Islands who had met with him in Fiji the previous year. The spokesman had said, 'Why, sir, when we first asked for a teacher, [British] New Guinea was heathen, and now we hear of the great success there, whilst our people are heathen still.'[66] It was true. Twenty years earlier he had tried to contact a principal chief in the area but his advances had been rejected. It was the same this time. Principal chief Ingava made it clear that 'for one reason or another, neither he nor his people want missionaries to live here.'[67] Brown wrote in his journal that the Roviana people

> are all head hunters and still make raids on neighbouring islands to obtain these ghastly trophies, especially when a new *tambu* house is

63   Fellmann, *Von Schwaben in den Bismarckarchipel*, p. 255.
64   Brown, Journal 10 August 1899, in *Australasian Methodist Missionary Review*, 6 November 1899.
65   *Australasian Methodist Missionary Review*, 7 August 1899. Protestant Missionary Societies represented included Anglican, Presbyterian, Methodist, Congregational, London Missionary Society, Baptist and Council of Churches.
66   Brown, Journal, 10 August 1899, in the *Australasian Methodist Missionary Review*, 6 November 1899.
67   Ibid., 3 August 1899, in the *Australasian Methodist Missionary Review*, 6 November 1899.

being built, or a canoe launched.... I wish that our Church would give some of us the opportunity of beginning Christian work amongst them. It would be a glorious work to win these souls for Christ and I am sure it can be done.[68]

* * *

'I must hurry to write to you,' wrote Lydia Brown as she began a letter to Johanna Fellmann, 'for I know you will be disappointed if there is no letter from me.'[69] The next ship to leave for New Guinea and Neu Pommern was due to leave very soon and the women of the Brown family were busy with their correspondence. Lydia Brown had the official role of Corresponding Secretary for the Ladies Auxiliary. She knew the missionary wives and single women well. Many of them had visited her home. She understood from her own experience the value of a simple letter. Invisible webs of care and friendship were being woven, threads that would cross oceans and bring comfort to other women, linking them in ways that went beyond the deliberations of Board meetings or the columns of financial figures that ruled their world. The letters spoke of babies and growing children, of the anxieties of pregnancy, of understanding what it was like to be alone at home while a husband was away for weeks at a time. There was always news of mutual friends.

The place and value of the women, married and single, as part of the Methodist missionary work was constantly being brought to the attention of George Brown by the women in his private world. Lydia's place had always been central and he valued the practical contribution made by many missionary wives.[70] Their single daughters were intelligent, educated and capable women. Lydia wrote of them, 'Monica is as energetic as ever and so is Lizzie, who is very conscientious in all her work.'[71] Not everyone saw the value of a wider role for women in church and community. Voting rights for women were still being debated in the community,[72] and women could still not take a seat in the Conference of the Methodist Church. Although other Protestant missions employed women, and missionary nuns worked in the Pacific, very few Methodist women had been employed until the end of the nineteenth century. In earlier days, an isolated Lydia Brown had waited hopefully for mail and now she was determined to send regular letters to women who were teaching women and girls, offering health care, caring for orphaned and neglected children and instructing young people

---

68 Ibid.
69 Lydia Brown to Johana Fellmann, 24 September 1900.
70 An example is Mrs Heighway in Fiji; *Australasian Methodist Missionary Review*, 6 September 1900.
71 Lydia Brown to Johanna Fellmann, 1 March 1904.
72 Suffrage for women was granted in 1902 in both NSW and the Commonwealth of Australia.

in the Christian faith. Some had discovered that life in a missionary setting was more mundane and ordinary than they had imagined. One mission Sister told Lydia,

> I have just been trying to imagine how great a difference there must have been between your first impressions of mission life in New Britain many years ago and mine here in Dobu during the last three months.... Dr Brown has told of the terrible hardships you had to meet in your isolated position, in the midst of cannibalism and savagery, and how the trials were intensified by the infrequent intercourse with the colonies. How very unlike that is to our position here.[73]

It would not be cannibals who disturbed such women, Lydia knew. It was more likely to be illness and isolation, the periodic abrasions of living with other women, the frustrations of having little voice in making decisions, the hurt when relationships within a small community went awry and lack of recognition.[74] From her suburban home on the northern outskirts of Sydney Lydia Brown now reached out to distant women. She knew that her own name had not been forgotten in the islands; the newly established college on Ulu Island for training local leadership was to be called Lydia College, and in New Guinea a mission boat was named the *Litia*. She still remembered what it was like to live where the younger women now lived, even though she was now an ageing grandmother.

'The others are gone to bed,' wrote the quiet woman, 'and I still have a letter to write to one of the Sisters in New Guinea, so I will wish you goodbye for this time. You take care of yourself and with God's blessing all will be well. Give my love to your husband and to your own dear self, in which my family unite. Believe me, dear Mrs Fellmann, Yours very sincerely, S.L. Brown.[75]

* * *

There must have been many times, as the century moved to its close, when being in the Mission office gave George Brown a very bad headache. He was being dragged in many directions. They should employ more staff—and withdraw staff because of their catastrophic debt. He needed to travel—and he needed to be available in the city office. He was invited often to promote mission work in city and rural congregations—and he was advised to care for his health and stay home. Some people accused him of timidity and lack of faith while others accused him of recklessness in the light of the debt. It was all impossible. In his

---

73 Sister Edith Lloyd to Lydia Brown, 19 February 1899; Sister Julia Benjamin to Lydia Brown, 20 March 1899, in the *Australasian Methodist Missionary Review*, 6 May 1899.
74 Annual Report of Australasian Methodist Missionary Society for 1897–98. In formal reports, male missionaries were listed by name but the single women were not (NLA N 266.7 MET).
75 Lydia Brown to Mrs Johanna Fellmann, 24 September 1900.

report for 1898 he stated, 'There was never a time in the history of our Mission when the success of our great work was more evident than it is today, and never had we more pressing demands for help than we receive from our mission districts by every mail ... but the Board is powerless because the necessary funds are not furnished.'[76]

By 1900, despite every effort by the financial managers and the mission fundraisers to stem the tide, they had gone even further backwards. It broke George Brown's heart. Every mission District sent requests for help to maintain good work and begin new and urgently needed enterprises. Brown admitted to feeling 'very sad and troubled as he read letter after letter.' He was 'sometimes sorely tried and dispirited.'[77]

His report for 1900 was ready to be presented. It was a difficult report to bring to the Annual Meeting and of all the duties of the Board, he admitted,

> The most painful of all is to be compelled to refuse the most pathetic appeals for help, knowing at the same time that the assistance sought is sorely needed.... If the funds necessary for the carrying out of Christ's command be not given, then the work cannot be done, and the Church itself must accept the responsibility attaching to such a failure.[78]

Brown knew that he must offer leadership in being disciplined, but found that he couldn't help himself. His heart was fighting with his sense of what was probably sensible. In the face of pessimism and despondency, even though it made no sense, he made a speech.

He felt himself growing old, but he would count it one of the honours of his life if they would commission him to found a new mission in the Solomon Islands.[79]

---

76 *Australasian Methodist Missionary Review*, 7 March 1898.
77 Ibid., 8 January 1900.
78 Annual Report of Missionary Society, in the *Australasian Methodist Missionary Review*, 10 March 1900.
79 Ibid.

18. 'Something of the vagabond'

New South Wales, Queensland, Samoa, Fiji, Norfolk Island, Solomon Islands 1900–1902

'To do all my work properly,' wrote one of his mission staff, 'I ought to be able to divide myself into two men.'[1] George Brown understood what he meant. The people under his care were taking on impossible workloads; travelling, counselling, mediating, preaching, teaching, learning languages, translating Scripture, wrestling with small craft at sea and house building on land, establishing plantations to support their work or planting gardens for the survival of their families. Many of them worked in lonely isolation or were embroiled in local tensions. Some of the most able men and women, exhausted by malaria and other tropical diseases, sent apologetic letters to the General Secretary admitting that their health had reached the point where they must leave the tropics or die there.[2] It was a challenge to fill the vacant places and Brown accepted the offer of a lay missionary couple from England.[3]

At the beginning of a new century, Brown could have wished to be more than one person. In the wider community, he took an active interest in important public decisions on Federation, a 'White Australia' policy, voting rights for women, the labour movement, and the role of the international powers in the Pacific. The newspapers were full of news of the Boer War in South Africa.[4] In China, foreigners were under attack in the Boxer uprising and Lydia Brown was especially anxious for her niece who was a missionary there. She wrote to her women correspondents of the 'terrible times' for missionaries and Chinese Christians, as well as the 'sharp struggle' of the Boer War. There were hints that economic prosperity could be returning. Brown continued to take an active part in the affairs of the worldwide scientific community.

* * *

George Brown relished the fact that his work demanded frequent travel. He told one audience, 'I have been going about a good deal of late years and I like

---

1 Heinrich Fellmann, in the *Australasian Methodist Missionary Review*, 4 June 1900.
2 Ibid., 4 June 1900.
3 Ibid., 4 May, 6 July, 8 December 1900.
4 *Sydney Morning Herald*, 24 January, 7 February, 21 February 1900.

it. I have something of the vagabond in my nature.'[5] He loved the energy of the packed bag, the ship moving away from the wharf, the first sight of another coastline. As well as island travel, Benjamin Danks had organised a grand plan for visiting every Australian colonial centre with speakers on mission issues, with many appointments for Brown.

In 1900 a regular journey took Brown first back to Samoa and then on to Fiji. Samoa had recently become a German 'possession', with German colonial authority, and was slowly recovering from the years of internal wars and epidemics. In Fiji he visited Hannah Dudley who had been joined by her mother and sister in a volunteer capacity. Brown was impressed with the progress she had made despite inadequate space and support. It was clear to him, however, that the task was too great for one person and would appeal, 'Will the Church send a duly qualified man for this work? An experienced missionary from India is needed for it.'[6]

During October George Brown travelled with two representatives from the Board around the Methodist circuits of Fiji, meeting all the missionaries in their places. They all gathered at last at Rewa for the annual District Synod meetings and a group photograph was recorded.[7] During their Synod a party of Fijian chiefs approached the Mission House in ceremonial dignity. The chiefs carried a handsome whale's tooth. They came, they said, to express their sorrow and repentance for the murder of the Reverend Thomas Baker over thirty years earlier in 1867. The people of the place had not only killed him but eaten his body. Chief Ratu Beni Tanoa of Naitasiri spoke on their behalf, 'We have heard that he was murdered in our province under our rule ... the story remains and attaches to us and we are ashamed before you, our elders ... we cannot bear it.... We wish, sirs, to make atonement for that which our fathers did.'[8]

In humility the whale's tooth, a significant cultural symbol, was presented to Chairman A.J. Small with the wish that the evil of the past might be 'buried, forgotten, never again mentioned.' Small received the fine tooth and assured the Fijian chiefs of the forgiveness of the Methodist Church. Brown, who witnessed this, was asked to carry the symbolic tooth to Sydney to be cared for in the Missionary Museum.[9]

The deputation from the Board of Missions had been sent to the Fiji District Synod that year to carry a proposal from the Board and the Conference concerning a Constitution. Within that Constitution was a section that was to

---

5   *Australasian Methodist Missionary Review*, 9 April 1901.
6   Ibid., 12 February 1901.
7   Ibid., 4 March 1901. In photograph: Front row, W. Heighway, W. Slade, George Brown, A.J. Small, George Lane, R.S. Callaghan, T.J. Wallis. Back row, J.C. Jennison, W.A. Burns, W. Brown, C.E. Williams, H.H. Nolan.
8   *Australasian Methodist Missionary Review*, 8 December 1900.
9   Ibid.

cause division. No doubt influenced by Brown, the Board believed that the time was ripe for greater participation by lay Fijian Methodists in the decision making of the Fijian Church. The white missionaries thought that such a move was premature and ill-advised. Brown was disturbed by their reaction. He had very potent memories of the problems in Tonga. A plan for lay representation had been incorporated into a Constitution for Tonga as early as 1875 but when the Tongan aspirations for independence were denied by the distant Board in Sydney the result had been a tragic division. The separated new church called itself 'Free'—free of the perceived bonds of subjection to the authority of the remote white leadership. He did not want to see the same thing happening in Fiji. It did not seem unreasonable to Brown that a small step be taken in moving toward greater self-reliance within the Fiji Methodist Church. In a private meeting with the Fijian and Tongan men who had been ordained, he learned that their main concern was transparency rather than representation. They explained, 'The missionary contribution is not clear. The people want to know how these [funds] are disbursed. Let it be placed before the people and they will be pleased, and seek to meet expenses. Do not hide anything from us.'[10]

The Fiji District Synod dismissed the idea of lay representation. Brown and his deputation colleagues had been persuaded that delay was inevitable. Much more training and preparation would be needed. Brown reported, 'We feel convinced from our observations and intercourse with the Native Ministers and officers, that at present they are not competent to take full charge either of circuit finances or district management, and that all steps in the direction of fuller self-government must be taken with caution and deliberation.'[11]

* * *

With the new century, change and renewed confidence was in the air. Within weeks of the formal inauguration of the Commonwealth of Australia on New Year's Day 1901, the Wesleyan Methodist Conference in NSW at last, after some twenty years of consideration, decided on union with two smaller Methodist bodies in New South Wales—the Primitive Methodists and the United Methodist Free Church. Other strands of Methodism in the other colonies had already decided to unite at some point between 1896 and 1900 while the Wesleyans in New South Wales dawdled.[12] When at last, after yet another long debate, a decision for church union was made late one evening in February 1901, there was great jubilation. George Brown had worked for this result for years, chairing a group to prepare the way for union when he had been President of Conference,

---

10 'For members of conference only. A personal statement. By Rev. Dr. George Brown D.D.,' 1905, NLA Ferg/6162.

11 Ibid.

12 James Colwell, *Illustrated History of Methodism: Australia 1812–1855; New South Wales and Polynesia 1856–1902*, Sydney: William Brooks & Co., 1904, p. 611.

ten years earlier. On a rainy autumn afternoon at the end of April 1901, Brown had the satisfaction of witnessing the moment when the Presidents of three branches of Methodism each signed the Plan of Union in the presence of their communities. One speaker mentioned the critical moment ten years previously under the leadership of Brown when the Wesleyans had resolved to give this matter serious consideration; this had set them on the path to union, he said.[13] The new united Methodist Church would celebrate their first Conference in NSW at the beginning of 1902.[14]

* * *

Renewed confidence was felt in the Mission office at 381 George Street. News was encouraging from several spheres of influence. Samoa was peaceful again. New schools for girls, and energetic practical work in community health, were making a difference in Fiji. The NSW Conference of 1901 approved a Constitution of the Fiji District, with a detailed structure for the future to provide for an increase of the self-governing power of the District;[15] although there would be a delay in bringing in the section that provided for lay representation, Brown persisted with his vision, 'Our ideal for Fiji is a self-governing Church; but our native agents are not ripe for it yet. Our work is to prepare them for it.'[16]

New Britain was celebrating twenty-five years of missionary work with great signs of health despite considerable challenges.[17] To the astonishment of the Board, the financial situation in 1901 was a dramatic improvement on previous years. Instead of a debt, they found that donations had improved so much that they now had a surplus and could confidently employ new staff.[18] The Board began to appeal for missionary laymen who could serve in education, health and training.

The unexpected buoyancy of funds gave Brown the freedom to talk about the Solomon Islands once more. Early in 1901 he began to mention the invitation from traders in the area of Roviana Lagoon for missionaries to come to their area of the western island of New Georgia. In theory, the Melanesian Mission of the Anglican Church was responsible for mission work across the hundreds of miles and countless islands of the Solomon Island chain. Since the days of Bishop George Augustus Selwyn, the grand vision for the Melanesian Mission had

---

13   *Methodist*, 4 May 1901.

14   Ibid., 6 March, 10 March, 17 March 1900, 9 March 1901; Colwell, *Illustrated History of Methodism*, pp. 609–12.

15   *Methodist*, 23 March 1901.

16   Report at Foreign Missionary Meetings at NSW Conference 1901, in *Australasian Methodist Missionary Review*, 9 April 1901.

17   New Britain Synod Minutes 30 October 1900, in *Australasian Methodist Missionary Review*, 8 December 1900, 8 January 1901.

18   Report of Annual General Meeting of Mission Society, 28 February 1901, in *Australasian Methodist Missionary Review*, 4 March 1901.

encompassed some 2,800 islands spread across an impossibly endless ocean.[19] In practice, their work was found only in the south eastern sector. Brown asked, 'Rubiana [Roviana] is part of a field occupied by another mission, but if they cannot occupy it, what then? Rubiana is for the present closed to us by the "honourable understanding"—but if that Mission indicates they can't work there, then [I am] anxious for the Methodist Mission to do so.'[20]

* * *

Over the family dinner table and in the intimacy of their home George Brown told his stories and shared something of the pressures of his work. The women of his family who remained at home, his wife Lydia and his two single daughters Lizzie and Monica, were all constantly in touch with the issues of his work. It became clear to them that he needed help. In the past Lydia Brown had helped him by taking responsibility for copying long letters by hand, or passages from his original journal to be sent away for publication. Times were changing. Women were now working in wider spheres and Brown himself had spoken of the 'fitness of devoted consecrated womanhood for Evangelistic work among the women of heathen races'[21] and his 'fervent praise of the work which devoted Christian women are doing in our day.'[22] Why, then, should Miss Mary Elizabeth Brown not work for her father? Lizzie Brown had given up her teaching role, but was a well-educated single woman approaching forty who was free to offer her new skills in using shorthand and a typewriter. Lizzie began to travel into the city office with her father, at first as a volunteer. It was not long before the Board recognised the value of her work and arranged to pay her a salary as a member of staff, backdated to January 1901.[23]

Lydia Brown's world was centred on her home and family, and her wandering man was always drawn back into the circle of her love. Her former life in Samoa and in the Duke of York Islands seemed a world away, even though reminders of those days were always around her in the collection of shields and shells, carved masks and baskets that infiltrated the whole house in suburban Gordon. News had come that the 'old historic house' at Kinawanua had been pulled down.[24] She tried to picture it—the timbers that had sheltered their family and many guests, the verandah where she had watched the channel for a sign of George's return from the punitive raid, the room where her beautiful Mabel and Wallis had died, leaving their playthings behind to mock her, the attic store room where she had locked herself, weeping for the deaths of her children. The

---

19   David Hilliard, *God's Gentlemen: A History of the Melanesian Mission 1849–1942*, St. Lucia: University of Queensland Press, 1978, p. 7.

20   Report of Foreign Missionary Society 1901, in *Australasian Methodist Missionary Review*, 9 April 1901.

21   *Methodist*, 9 March 1901.

22   *Australasian Methodist Missionary Review*, 12 Feb 1901, 9 April 1901.

23   Minutes of Wesleyan Methodist Missions Board, May 1898–July 1906, MOM 203 CY 3305, 17 April 1901.

24   *Australasian Methodist Missionary Review*, 19 February 1901.

house had taken so long to build, and she had waited for it wearily, managing her household in the rudimentary hut where the tropical rain leaked through the leaf roof and rodents scuttled behind the woven walls. Now, after little more than twenty years, it was seen as 'historic', had been demolished and all its components carried off in the whale boat to be rebuilt on Ulu Island to serve the new training centre there. All that was left, she heard, was the flight of concrete steps, rising up to nothing, and a chimney. That life, that part of her world, had vanished, and Lydia knew that she would never visit it again. Even her name, she thought, had disappeared; the new training centre on Ulu, briefly called 'Lydia College', had somehow become George Brown College instead. That had been another life. Now she was a vigorous woman in her sixties, happily helping with her grandchildren in a city that had been home now for over twenty years.

In the summer of 1901 she had the rare delight of having her whole family gathered around her. George was at home for a change. Amy and the Reverend Ben Dinning with their five young children had just moved to Penrith on the outskirts of Sydney, Claudia and her family lived in a nearby suburb and her sons Fred and Geoffrey and their wives also lived nearby. To have them all crowded noisily around her table and to be able to care for them all was a deep joy. With some fidgeting and family negotiations at last they all lined up for family photographs with the newest baby on Lydia's lap and the older children at their feet. That day another photograph was taken of Grandmother Lydia with nine grandchildren clustered around her, the bigger boys looking uncomfortable, squirming little girls and squalling infants. At their heart sat Lydia, still and calm, the only figure in sharp focus.[25]

The Mission office was crowded again with the bustle and confusion of a new group of mission staff preparing to leave for their appointments. It was early May 1901. Many of those due to be farewelled were going out for the first time. George Brown had preached at the Ordination service for five young ministers.[26] His sermon was based on God's call to the young and hesitant Gideon, called away from his familiar duties to risk something challenging. 'Have I not sent you?' asked God of Gideon.[27] Brown spoke from his heart and out of his years of experience. You will be tempted, he said, to think you should have stayed home. He described the troubles of his own earlier years when he had questioned his call to the work. You, too, will be discouraged, he said, and sick and depressed. 'When I was a young man I took for my motto "Trust in the Lord with all thine heart and lean not to thine own understanding" and I commend the same to you … I read Bushnell's sermon on every man's life a plan of God.'[28]

---

25 Photograph in Brown family collection held by Miss Nancy Joyce.

26 J.A Walsh, M.K. Gilmour (to British New Guinea), W.E. Bennett, T.W. Butcher (to Fiji), W.H. Cox (to New Britain) were ordained at Centenary Hall, Sydney, 23 April 1901.

27 Judges 6:14, King James Bible.

28 Notes from sermon preached by Brown on 23 April 1901 at Centenary Hall, York St, Sydney, in *Australasian Methodist Missionary Review*, 8 May 1901.

Figure 19. Lydia Brown with grandchildren 1901.

Source: Brown family album, per favour Miss Nancy Joyce.

He urged them to look after their health, to exercise and avoid the lethargy of 'sofa disease', to keep their minds active and care for their spiritual lives, to spend time with the local people and learn their language, listening with respect to their views and not being too hasty in trying to bring change. Above all, he said, his chief instruction was to 'Love the people!'[29]

There had been alarming rumours. No one wanted to believe them. The news was confirmed on 9 May 1901, a day when in Melbourne a vast audience of dignitaries and ladies in splendid hats witnessed the Duke of York opening the first Federal Parliament, and in Sydney the large party of missionaries assembled for their valedictory service before they sailed to their appointments. On Easter Day 7 April 1901, the Reverend James Chalmers, known across the Pacific as Tamate, with his colleague Oliver Tompkins, had been clubbed to death, beheaded and their bodies had been eaten. They had been visiting the island of Goaribari on the western coast of British New Guinea.[30] George Brown was shocked and deeply grieved. Chalmers had been a dear friend, a man after his

---

29   Ibid.
30   Richard Lovett, *James Chalmers: His Autobiography and Letters*, London: Religious Tract Society, 1914, pp. 473–83.

own heart who had shared so many of his own visions. Like Brown, Chalmers had put himself in harm's way more than once when meeting unwelcoming strangers. Chalmers' name was legendary and news of his death went around the world; his old friend William Lawes writing that it was 'almost impossible to translate Tamate into black and white.'[31] On the day that they heard the news of Chalmers' violent end, Brown faced the group of new mission staff about to leave for British New Guinea, German Neu Pommern and Fiji. It was a sombre occasion. Brown tried to be confident; he must allay any fears that nervous people might have, he said, as 'the place to which they were going was just as safe as Sydney—most of it was, at any rate.'[32] But others spoke in solemn tones of martyrdom, and sorrow, and the profound loss of their friends in the London Missionary Society. By the time the meeting concluded the whole company stood in silence and then, with quavering voices, sang the farewell song 'God be with you till we meet again.'[33]

Undeterred, Brown continued to pursue his goal of taking the Christian gospel to the western Solomon Islands. Within a week or so of the departure of the missionary party, Brown was in Brisbane to attend the triennial General Conference. Among several themes concerning the mission enterprises of the Methodists was a Conference resolution to approve the new constitution for the Methodist Church in Fiji with 'larger powers of self-government' and with 'lay representatives enfranchised in the highest local Church court, the Fiji District Synod,' despite the misgivings of the mission staff in Fiji.[34] There was serious interest in the Solomon Islands. The debate was vigorous but in the end Brown was persuasive. On the grounds that the Melanesian Mission had still not reached the western region of the Solomon chain after fifty years, Brown was given the authority to plan for a new mission, on condition that there be 'a satisfactory arrangement with our Anglican friends, so that neither now nor in the future should there be any conflict or competition.'[35]

When he learned that Charles Woodford, Deputy Resident Commissioner for the Solomon Islands was in Sydney in June 1901, Brown acted quickly. He called a meeting of the Board of Missions and invited Woodford to attend. Woodford assured the Board that there were densely populated areas in the western islands where neither Melanesian Mission nor Catholic Marists had established work, and he urged the Methodists to begin something in those areas. He described the intricate local systems, the head-hunting and disease that had decimated the population and the power of rival chiefs with their fleets of war canoes. These days, he said, with the presence of representatives of the Western Pacific High

---

31   Ibid., p. 486.
32   *Methodist*, 18 May 1901.
33   Ibid.
34   Ibid., 1 June 1901.
35   Ibid., 1 June 1901.

Commission and Fijian police, there was little to fear.[36] Woodford intended to sail shortly for the Solomon Islands and urged them to send Brown with him to explore the possibilities for a new work.[37] The Board agreed and a week later Brown was at sea with *SS Titus*, on his way to the Solomon Islands.

* * *

There is no record of what his wife Lydia thought. Not only had her husband set off through a fierce gale that was battering shipping, but her eldest daughter Lizzie had sailed with him. As Lizzie was his private secretary and assistant, she intended to keep records of meetings and help with the beginnings of a book her father intended to write. If they survived the storm at sea, they were moving into the territory of head-hunters. It was said that their friend Chalmers had been deeply depressed after the death of his wife and may have even welcomed martyrdom but that was not true for Brown. All Lydia could do was pray for the safety of those she loved.

The first step was to visit Norfolk Island to meet Cecil Wilson, Bishop of Melanesia and responsible for the work of Melanesian Mission. They were ferried to the rocky wharf and driven past the ruins of the one-time penal colony up to the fine establishment of the St. Barnabas complex, almost a small township clustered around the central stone church.[38] Their model of mission was very different from that of the Methodists. On Norfolk Island they had established a strong base where young men were brought from the northern islands to be educated and trained in the Christian faith by British and Australian staff. Each year a party of the most promising young men were taken back to their home regions with the aim of bringing Christianity to their own people. In time, they recognised how difficult it was for a young person with no local authority and a thin veneer of western ideas and manners to have much influence over a community he had left some years earlier.[39]

---

36   Alan R. Tippett, *Solomon Islands Christianity: A Study in Growth and Obstruction*, London: Lutterworth, 1967, p. 152; Martin Zelenietz, 'The end of headhunting in New Georgia,' in *The Pacification of Melanesia*, ed. Margaret Rodman and Matthew Cooper, ASAO Monograph 7, University of Michigan Press, 1979, pp. 104–07; Judith Bennett, *Wealth of the Solomons: A History of a Pacific Archipelago, 1800–1978*, Honolulu: University of Hawai'i Press, 1987, p. 107.

37   *Methodist*, 22 June, 29 June 1901.

38   Raymond Nobbs, *St Barnabas and the Melanesian Mission Norfolk Island*, Sydney: Macquarie University Australian History Resources Centre, 1990, p. 4.

39   David Hilliard, *God's Gentlemen: A History of the Melanesian Mission 1849–1942*, St Lucia: University of Queensland Press 1978, pp. 8–9.

Figure 20. Missionary party before departure for British New Guinea, New Britain and Fiji in May 1901. Back: George Pearson, W.E. Bennett, J.A. Walsh, J.A. Crump, T.W. Butcher, W.H. Cox, M.K. Gilmour; Middle: Mrs Gilmour, Mrs Bennett, Benjamin Danks, George Brown, Miss Newell, Miss Benjamin; Front: Mrs Butcher, Mrs Pearson.

Source: The *Australasian Methodist Missionary Review*, 8 May 1901.

Brown was eager to discuss his own plans with Bishop Wilson. Correspondence had passed between them about the request of Solomon Island men for missionaries, but without any resolution. Now they could speak directly.[40] Bishop Wilson was reluctant to relinquish part of his bishopric responsibilities to another Church but it may have been an unequal contest. Brown was twenty-five-years older than the gentle and cautious Bishop, had far more experience in the Pacific and was a forceful personality in pursuit of a long-held dream. Brown also had the support of British Commissioner Woodford. They studied the maps together. Wilson questioned Brown's choice of the Roviana area of New Georgia; it was a region famously unwilling to receive missionaries. Brown insisted that there was no other mission organisation in that region 'so we are not going to labour on any other society's foundations.'[41] Bishop Wilson felt obliged to

---

40 *Australasian Methodist Missionary Review*, 6 December 1898, 8 July 1901.
41 *Methodist*, 6 July 1901.

accept the Methodist intention, as a start, to explore the western area.[42] A new 'gentleman's agreement', unwritten and unsigned,[43] now marked an invisible line on the sea, identifying parts of the western Solomon Islands as a sphere where the Methodist Mission could work.

The *SS Titus* reached the beautiful Roviana Lagoon of New Georgia on 26 July 1901. The traders were welcoming but the local chiefs much less so. The principal chief Ingava was giving a great feast that day to celebrate the completion of a new house. Things were changing already, trader Frank Wickham explained. If the new house had been opened only a few years ago, it would have meant a raid on another village for heads to be incorporated into the ceremony. The influence of the Resident Commissioner was having an effect, and these days such raids were carried out in clandestine fashion, out of sight of the colonial authorities, rather than in the great days of old when Ingava would take five hundred men to capture slaves. Even with this concession there was still no enthusiasm to have resident missionaries and Brown decided to proceed with caution. For ten days he visited villages and explored the area, talking through an interpreter with village leaders.

It seemed to him that it should be possible to acquire a small piece of land on an island in the lagoon, to use as a mission base, and win the confidence of the people over time before attempting to establish anything larger on the island of New Georgia itself. One evening, he arranged for a large sheet to be suspended between two palm trees, set up his magic lantern and projected images of the people of New Britain, British New Guinea and Fiji, as they had been in the past and as they were now. In the darkness Brown could hear the gasps of astonishment as image after image magically filled the white sheet. He hoped that they would make the connection that he intended—that the Christian gospel had made the difference. They probably did not. Yet, for those with eyes to see, it was all there; change was coming to their people and the absence of fresh human heads at the opening of the chief's house was just one sign of the beginning of the decay of a complex social system that had served them, for good or ill, for generations. By the end of August, Brown and his daughter were home in Sydney and when he learned that a trader was prepared to sell a little island in the Roviana Lagoon just off the coast of New Georgia, he bought it.[44]

* * *

In his enthusiasm, George Brown may have been premature. In January 1902, Bishop Wilson visited Sydney and met Brown to continue their debate about

42   Tippett, *Solomon Islands Christianity*, p. 38.
43   Hilliard, *God's Gentlemen*, p. 23.
44   Minutes of Wesleyan Methodist Missions Board, May 1898–July 1906, ML MOM 203 ML CY 2810, 7 March 1902.

spheres of influence. Brown held that the Methodists would prefer to work in Guadalcanal or Malaita, because of the direct links with men who had worked in Fiji, but would be willing to work in the New Georgia group in keeping with the 'honourable understanding that no Protestant Mission should interfere with the work of another sister Society.'[45] Bishop Wilson was hesitant. He had been appealing for funds for a replacement for their mission ship the *Southern Cross*,[46] so that he could visit the more remote regions of his diocese and feared that the Anglicans would not understand if he were to relinquish some of that area. Wilson said,

> I should not regard it as an unfriendly act if you occupy New Georgia, but I should regard it as an unfriendly act if you were to occupy Guadalcanal or Mala[ita].… New Georgia is the last place in which I should think of taking up mission work, and I should certainly not take it up at all if you had a strong and effective mission work there.[47]

By the time the men parted, Brown felt free to report to his Board that while the Bishop for prudent reasons was not willing to give the Methodists official consent to begin work in New Georgia, 'he was personally not at all disinclined to do so.'[48] Lizzie Brown's notes of the meetings with Bishop Wilson were duly typed and added in this new form into the Minute Book,[49] and the formal decision to begin a new Mission in the New Georgia area of the Solomon Islands was made.[50] It was possible to report to the Methodist community that, 'we shall not in any way whatever interfere with any kindred society…. We shall be fellow-labourers with them, but in a distinct and separate group.'[51]

* * *

Although Brown's focus in the early months of 1902 was on his new project in the Solomon Islands, there were many other things to take his attention. The first Conference of a united Methodism was celebrated with great optimism and hope in February and Brown was pleased when one commentator noted that a sign that the Union would be stable and blessed was that 'it should be characterised by an intense Missionary spirit.'[52] The new mission schooner the *Litia* was launched. In Samoa there were fresh problems and in Fiji there

---

45   Report on meeting in January 1902 between G. Brown and Bishop Cecil Wilson; Minutes of Wesleyan Methodist Missions Board, May 1898–July 1906, ML MOM 203 ML CY 2810, 9 April 1902.

46   The Melanesian Mission used a series of mission ships, over many years, each called the *Southern Cross*.

47   Report on meeting in January 1902 between G. Brown and Bishop Cecil Wilson; Minutes of Wesleyan Methodist Missions Board, May 1898–July 1906, ML MOM 203 ML CY 2810, 9 April 1902.

48   Ibid.

49   Ibid.

50   Minutes of Wesleyan Methodist Missions Board, May 1898–July 1906, ML MOM 203 ML CY 2810, 4 September 1901. The work in the Solomon Islands was planned to begin in March 1902.

51   *Australasian Methodist Missionary Review*, 4 March 1902.

52   *Methodist*, 3 May 1902.

was no softening of attitudes about lay representation. When Brown took his place as part of the great Conference photograph he was very aware of the many excellent Australian laymen in their number.[53] In society, women had been awarded the right to vote in the next federal election and the wheels had been set in motion to transfer the responsibility for British New Guinea to the newly Federated Australia.[54] At home, Lydia was constantly busy with their local church planning to build a Methodist church in Gordon and with her growing family; two more grandchildren had just been born.[55] Central to Brown's mind at the time was the preparation for another New Mission. Two young ministers had been appointed as pioneer missionaries, John Goldie and Stephen Rabone Rooney, and island teachers had been recruited from Fiji and Samoa. By the end of April 1902 everything was ready.

The farewell was a grand occasion. Missionaries were ready to travel to many places, including the new team for the Solomon Islands.[56] Monica Brown organised a dinner for five hundred and the hall was crowded for the final speeches of farewell. Tributes were made to the courage of the new team, to Brown who was to travel with them and to 'his family in consenting to such a lengthened separation, at a time of life when the less arduous labours of his office might have been permitted him.'[57] When, at last, George Brown rose to speak on behalf of the whole missionary group the entire audience rose to their feet in thunderous applause.[58]

It was one thing to be borne up by the warmth and security of a great hall packed with supporters. It was different when they stood in the rain on Circular Quay ready to board SS Titus on 3 May. Brown knew that the responsibility for this group was his. Not all of them would return home. There would be illness, the hazards of childbirth and possibly violence. He was taking an inexperienced team to a place with an uncertain welcome. There were tears as Helena Goldie and Lydia Brown parted from their husbands; an observer would write, 'No one could witness the partings on that wharf without feeling that faith and love to God triumphed over the dearest ties.'[59] A photographer captured an image of the group on the rain-washed wharf.[60] The faces are sober, unsmiling, apprehensive Fijian and Samoan women, their men, Brown and Danks with some other

---

53   Colwell, *Illustrated History of Methodism*, p. 606.

54   The process began in November 1901 and was completed in September 1906. See, Raymond Evans, Clive Moore, Kay Saunders and Brian Jamison, *1901 Our Future's Past: Documenting Australia's Federation*, Sydney: Macmillan, 1997, p. 224.

55   Inaugural Meeting of the Gordon Methodist Church Trust, 5 October 1901.

56   *Australasian Methodist Missionary Review*, 6 May 1902. Thirty-one Australian, New Zealand, Fijian, Samoan and Solomon Island men and women were named as they left for several mission regions.

57   Ibid.

58   Ibid.

59   *Australasian Methodist Missionary Review*, 6 May 1902.

60   Photo, *Town and Country Journal*, reprinted in the *Australasian Methodist Missionary Review*, 7 July 1902.

church leaders and arranged in the foreground Goldie and Rooney, young men preparing to face a great unknown. An onlooker was overheard to say, as they all moved away to board the *SS Titus*, 'I'm a bit of a heathen myself but this has moved me very much. Brave people these.'[61]

The above is a Photo. of the Mission Party sent out by the Methodist Missionary Society of Australasia.—*May, 1902.*

Figure 21.Missionary party before departure for Fiji, Samoa, New Britain and Solomon Islands 1902. Back: Rabone Rooney (Solomon Islands), C.O. Lelean (Fiji), Benjamin Danks, E.W. Caust (Rotuma), John Goldie (Solomon Islands). Front: C. Doley (New Britain), Mrs Lelean, Mrs Doley, George Brown, Mrs Caust, Mrs Neil, E.G. Neil.

Source: The *Australasian Methodist Missionary Review*, 4 June 1902.

Brown, though outwardly confident, would later assure a critic that 'the three weeks spent aboard the *Titus* on the voyage from Sydney to New Georgia were amongst the most anxious I have ever spent.'[62] In those earlier adventures as a pioneer in New Britain and British New Guinea,

61 *Australasian Methodist Missionary Review*, 6 May 1902.
62 Ibid., 5 January 1903.

We went to a people who were indifferent to our work, but in New Georgia we went to natives who did not wish us to go, and we knew before we went that they did not want us. I have known the head-hunters of New Georgia for many years and 27 years ago they told my dear old friend Captain Ferguson, and myself, that they would have nothing to do with missionaries. I well knew when I visited them last year that if I had asked permission to start a mission I would have got a positive refusal, and so we did not ask but simply went.[63]

MISSION PARTY ON WHARF, PRIOR TO EMBARKING OF MISSIONARIES AND NATIVE TEACHERS FOR NEW GEORGIA.
[From Block kindly lent by Town and Country Journal.]

Figure 22. Mission party on wharf before sailing for New Georgia, Solomon Islands 1902. John Goldie and Rabone Rooney in centre front.

Source: The *Australasian Methodist Missionary Review*, 7 July 1902.

In the late afternoon of Friday 23 May 1902, the steamer came into Roviana Lagoon. The sudden tropical sunset was not far away and they chose to stay on board overnight, but in the morning his old friends the traders Norman Wheatley and Frank Wickham were quick to provide boats to transfer people and cargo to land. That night George Brown began his first letter to Lydia.

To my own dear wife, We got here yesterday at ½ past 4 o'clock just three weeks from Sydney and we were all right glad to get here. As you

---

63   Ibid.

can imagine we have all been very busy indeed on this the first day here, and I for one am very tired. So far as I can tell at present our prospects are very good … I have visited the island which I bought in Sydney, Nusa Zonga, and find it rather small but I am hoping to get a piece inland very soon. At any rate we won't meet with any pronounced opposition and this is a good thing. Some white men, not any of the traders here, have been trying to set the chiefs against any Missionaries coming here at all but they have not succeeded in doing so though they have of course done something to unsettle them by their stories … altogether we are in good spirits.[64]

The next day was Sunday and Brown joined the group for a service of worship. Once again he read scripture and preached before a group of curious local onlookers, bemused by the odd activities of newcomers. That night he added to his letter to Lydia.

I am not feeling very bright tonight and that is a sure sign that I must take a little medicine. I have decided to erect the small house which I brought down on Nusa Zonga the island which I bought in Sydney. We shall know more about the place where we are to have the head station as we know more of the people and have time to look about.[65]

After the relative calm of the Sabbath, the practical work began. Cargo was unloaded and stored in a large copra shed, timber for houses, provisions, equipment—'There is an awful pile of stuff,' wrote Brown.[66]

More importantly, they needed to make careful contact with the local men of authority, the chiefs. The power of these influential men would make the difference between disaster and a secure environment for the work they hoped to do. Brown wrote to his friend Benjamin Danks. He told him of meeting with Ingava and other chiefly men,

The results are just as I expected they would be, that is that we shall receive no opposition from the Chiefs or from the people. They do not receive us with any enthusiasm or cordiality simply because they do not know for what purpose we have come and also because they have been frightened by stories told them by some white men in order to prejudice their minds against us.… We shall have to exercise great care and prudence in all our dealings with them especially in these early days in order to remove this impression.… I often felt very anxious whilst we were on the steamer especially as we got near the Solomons but most of my fears have proved to be groundless.[67]

---

64 Brown to Lydia Brown, 24 May 1902. In family collection, held by Miss Nancy Joyce.
65 Ibid.
66 Ibid.
67 Brown to Danks, 26 May 1902.

The early weeks were engaged in exploration, negotiation and building the beginnings of trust as well as temporary bush buildings. Brown spent time with the chief Gumi, 'a very intelligent man,' suggesting that one day the new arrivals would hope to purchase a portion of land on the coast of New Georgia within range of Nusa Zonga. He had learned to offer time, respect and caution when negotiating with island leaders. He warned the Fijian and Samoan Teachers of

> the trouble which may be caused by any assumption of superior power or by the appearance of any overbearing conduct on their part. I told them very earnestly that the greatest power in the world was that of love, that we can only hope to win the people by proving in every way that we love them and that we have come here because God loves them and that Christ died for them.[68]

An invitation to travel with Commissioner Woodford to visit the vast northern coral atoll of Ontong Java delighted Brown and he was happy to explore the remote villages there. On his return to Roviana after a very rough voyage, he suggested to his team that they might include Ontong Java, over 250 miles of ocean to their north, in their sphere. They were not enthusiastic; they had barely begun at Roviana.[69] In his absence, however, Goldie and Rooney had identified a piece of land on New Georgia with a fine outlook across Roviana Lagoon. With careful negotiation between the white missionaries and the local chiefs, land was bought.[70] In time it would become the site of a significant church property known over one hundred years later as Munda. The local name, Kokenggolo, meaning fragrance of a local flower, was a fitting title for a place that would slowly permeate a damaged society with healing.

* * *

Far away in her Sydney home, Lydia Brown read the letters that had arrived at last from her George. During their long years of marriage they had been apart as often as they had been together, still linked by their love and the thin web of letters. As he travelled he knew that she was not anchored to a single place in his absence. He had written to 'Mrs Brown, "Kinawanua", Gordon or Lindfield, Chatswood, St Leonards or Penrith,' the locations of each of her children. Family love and loyalty drew her wherever she was most needed at the time and with new babies and active older children she was often away from home. It was hard not to be anxious for her husband. At sixty-seven he was not always well and the demands of first contact in the islands were great. She remembered the days

---

68   Ibid.

69   *Australasian Methodist Missionary Review*, 6 November 1902. See John F. Goldie, 'The Solomon Islands,' in *A Century in the Pacific*, ed. J. Colwell, Sydney: William H. Heale, 1914, pp. 559–85, pp. 578–80.

70   George Brown, *George Brown: Pioneer-Missionary and Explorer: An Autobiography*, London: Hodder and Stoughton, 1908, p. 531.

in the Duke of York Islands when spears were there for the business of dealing death, not domesticated into curtain rods in suburban Gordon, and clubs were bludgeons, not curios to be dusted. Now she pored over his letter, searching for the personal words in among the mission information.

> I for one am very tired ... our prospects are very good.... I am not feeling very bright tonight ... I am well and hearty and full of hope.... It will be uphill work at first but it will be alright in the end.... You must not worry about me, I shall be well cared for. We have come here because God sent us and he will preserve us I am sure.... I often think of you all and pray for you as I know you do for me. May God our Father keep and bless you all abundantly. With lots of love to your own dear self I am, my dear loving old wife, your affectionate husband, Geo Brown.[71]

Now she had to wait, yet again, to welcome him home.

* * *

After nearly two months in the Solomon Islands, George Brown said goodbye to the pioneer group, joined the visiting steamer once more and turned his face to home. He left a vulnerable little group, with great hopes but little so far to encourage them. Brown prayed with them before he left, urging them that 'if they would be men of power, to be men of prayer.' 'We must labour patiently and faithfully,' he said, 'remembering that God measures not as men do, and the Master's "Well done" was to the faithful, and not merely to the successful servant.' Together, they heard the words of Scripture, 'Peace I leave with you, my peace I give unto you: not as the world giveth, give I unto you. Let not your heart be troubled, neither let it be afraid.'[72]

To Danks he wrote,

> We will all do our best by God's help to make this Mission as successful as the older ones have been. We are proud of them and some day I hope we shall be proud of this the New Georgia Mission. It is very little and very weak at the present but it will grow as the others have done.[73]

Winter was nearly over when the SS *Titus* came into harbour in Sydney once more. There were new grandchildren to meet and visitors to greet. It was hard to focus on the regular work of the Mission office or the local excitement as the Methodists at Gordon saw the ground cleared for their new church building. When the crowd gathered on 13 December 1902 to witness the formal laying of commemorative stones and pray for the future ministry at that place it seemed only fitting that one of the three stones was being laid, not by the well-known Dr. Brown, but by his loved wife, Lydia.[74]

---

71 Brown to Lydia Brown, 24 May 1902.
72 *Methodist*, 6 September 1902; John 14:27, King James Bible.
73 Brown to Danks, 26 May 1902.
74 Organ of the Willoughby and Gordon Methodist Church, *Messenger*, 1 Feb 1907.

19. 'The Venerable General Secretary'

New South Wales, Fiji, Victoria, South Australia, Solomon Islands, New Britain, Papua 1903–1906

'It is to be deplored,' a writer announced in 1902, 'that so little aggressive work is done by the Foreign Mission enterprise … it gives a little relief to know that the Society's operations are to embrace the Solomon Islands.'[1] George Brown was furious – and hurt. Had decades of effort gone unnoticed? He wrote a long defensive reply setting out the work of the Society over the years across the Pacific. When the Mission Board asked Brown to prepare a short pamphlet explaining the range of Methodist missionary work for distribution, he did it with some satisfaction.[2]

Whether or not new work was being attempted, there was work to be done in the established regions. There were continuing problems in Fiji, and Brown was sent once more in 1903 as a Commission with two colleagues, the President General Reverend George Lane and the Honourable William Robson, to investigate. Not for the first time, there were serious tensions in Fiji between the Catholic Mission and the Methodists, as well as ongoing issues between Methodists and the British colonial government over land and property. Tension was building between mission staff in Fiji and the Board in Sydney over the new Constitution, approved at the 1901 General Conference. The missionaries in Fiji were still offended by the clause about lay representation. They had already voted against it once, in October 1901, and were no more persuaded in 1903.[3] It was not an easy visit.

Using his long relationships with colonial authorities and with the missionaries, Brown, Lane and Robson travelled widely around the island group. Brown was delighted to meet with his old friends from the pioneer group to New Britain nearly thirty years earlier, Ratu Livai Volavola and Aminio Baledrokadroka, men he loved and valued.[4] His appreciation of men like these had influenced his

---

1 *Spectator*, 21 November 1902.
2 George Brown, *A Brief Account of Methodist Missions in Australasia, Polynesia and Melanesia, their Past History, Present Conditions and Future Possibilities*, Sydney: Methodist Missionary Society of Australasia, 1904; *Australasian Methodist Missionary Review*, 4 March 1904.
3 Rev. Dr. G. Brown, 'For Members of Conference Only. A Personal Statement.' 1905, NLA Ferg/6162. The Fiji District Synod decision was made on 10 October 1901.
4 Photograph of Brown with Ratu Livai Volavola and Aminio Baledrokadroka, in the *Australasian Methodist Missionary Review*, April 1906.

opinion about the representation of Fijian lay men in decisions about their own finances. The missionaries, it was clear, believed that the local people were not ready for this new responsibility. There were suggestions of possible corruption, undue influence of chiefs and incompetence. Within months of the visit of the deputation, the Fiji Synod once more voted firmly against it.[5] There would be further fruitless debate on the matter at the New South Wales Conference in March 1904.[6]

The tension between Catholic and Methodist Churches in Fiji had been intensified shortly before the visit of the Commission. Over the years, Brown had witnessed in a number of places the way in which island leaders could use allegiance to a particular brand of religion as a tool to manipulate their own ends. Early in 1903, a Fijian high chief, offended by the Methodists, had chosen to withdraw his allegiance from them and take his entire large community with him to join the Catholic Church. As a sign of this new loyalty, the group gave up their Methodist hymn books, catechisms and Bibles. In an action that was according to their own official procedure but insensitive to those who valued that material as sacred, this literature was taken away and burned, an action that was witnessed by some who were still loyal to the Methodists. This caused great outrage, and the story spread as far as the colonies. It was said that some of the books that were destroyed included the new translation by Brown's friend and contemporary Frederick Langham published only a year earlier.[7] Having heard the evidence, Brown and his colleagues reported to the Board that although they accepted that the unfortunate incident had happened as described, it was not appropriate to pursue the matter further.[8]

By the time the deputation returned to Sydney and reported their findings to the Board, there was a new reason for grief. Frederick Langham, Bible translator and veteran missionary, had died in London on 20 June 1903. It was a sombre Board meeting. There was rebellion in the ranks of their missionaries in Fiji, illness and discontent in some other fields, and news from the Solomon Islands spoke of the illness and deaths of some of the pioneer team. A brighter moment was the news that the special copy of the new translation of the New Testament in the Kuanua language of New Britain had been presented to the German Kaiser Wilhelm by Heinrich Fellmann while in Germany on furlough.[9]

* * *

---

5 Brown, 'For Members of Conference Only'. Fiji District Synod decision was made on 14 October 1903.
6 Minutes of Wesleyan Methodist Missions Board, May 1898–July 1906, ML MOM CY 2810, 6 January 1904; *Methodist*, 13 March 1904.
7 Frederick Langham, letter published in the *Australasian Methodist Missionary Review*, 6 October 1902.
8 A. Harold Wood, *Overseas Missions of the Australian Methodist Church, Vol. 11, Fiji*, Melbourne: Aldersgate Press, 1978, pp. 256–57.
9 Minutes of Wesleyan Methodist Missions Board, May 1898–July 1906, 6 August 1903.

No one could have foreseen the changes that would happen in their family in March 1904. Lydia Brown had often been with her daughters Amy and Claudia during pregnancy and childbirth, and supported her sons' wives as well. The four youngest little ones were toddling and crawling happily. Lydia loved all her grandchildren dearly, and took a genuine interest in the children of all the missionaries. On 1 March Lydia Brown wrote to Johanna Fellmann of her children, and then wrote of her own daughter Amy's latest pregnancy. Amy's husband the Reverend Benjamin Dinning was staying with Browns during the Conference, but, wrote Lydia,

> Poor Mrs Dinning is very near her time of trial and she will be glad to get her husband back. It is an awkward time to be laid up.... They are put down for Tamworth on the northern line. I am sorry they will be so far away from us, but still I hope to be able to visit them once at any rate.[10]

She told Johanna about each of her children and grandchildren, the colds, the teething and other ailments, the constant houseguests. Lydia mentioned her visits to Penrith to help Amy and the comfort of having Lizzie and Monica at home, 'though they have to be away from me so much, but I am better off than a good many mothers. I am able to see all my children and grandchildren occasionally, what would your dear mother give for a sight of you sometimes.' She concluded 'I find I have anxieties as a grandmother and I suppose it will be so to the end.'[11] Tamworth seemed a long way away, hundreds of miles to the north, but at least Amy's latest little one would be born before they moved.

Amy Dinning gave birth to her second daughter and her seventh baby at Penrith on 8 March 1904. Lydia was probably with her at the time, and would not have been home the next day when George came home to Gordon with the news that the Board had granted him leave of absence 'to engage in literary work'.[12] The publication of the short pamphlet on their missions had suggested that it was time for a more substantial piece of writing about the history of their mission, and Brown was the man to do it. He was beginning to hint at retirement, and the Board was happy to appoint the very capable Benjamin Danks to the role of Acting General Secretary when his leave of absence began.

Leave of absence was quickly forgotten. The news from Penrith was disturbing. Amy was not recovering. Lydia knew very well the hazards of childbirth. She had watched helplessly as other women suffered and faded from life, beyond her medical skills to help. But this was her daughter Amy; Amy the singer, busy wife and mother, leader among the women and children of her church. This

---

10   Lydia Brown to Johanna Fellmann, 1 March 1904.
11   Ibid.
12   Minutes of Wesleyan Methodist Missions Board, May 1898–July 1906, 9 March 1904.

was not possible, not right. Yet Lydia watched and knew. The doctors affirmed that Amy was dying and there was nothing they could do. The family gathered. Friends travelled to see her and, through their tears, gently sang familiar hymns around her bed with Amy's voice joining in. Lydia held her hand and heard Amy's quiet prayers for her husband, her little ones, her newborn baby. George baptised the baby girl, at Amy's request, and laid the newborn, head still wet with the waters of baptism, in the curve of his daughter's arm as she stroked the infant head and whispered the new name, her own name, Amy Eadith.

Amy Dinning died on 17 March 1904. Her baby daughter Amy Eadith was nine days old. George and Lydia Brown were heartbroken. The funeral, on Amy's fortieth birthday, was a very big one, with a crowded church in Penrith before funeral trains carried them back to Gore Hill Cemetery. Hundreds of letters of condolence poured in. No one knew how to comfort the grieving family. There were so many reasons why this was a meaningless and mysterious death, and platitudes did not help. Among the sounds of weeping Lydia heard the tiny cry of a motherless baby. One thing was certain. Ben Dinning must leave Penrith very soon with his older children for his new appointment in Tamworth, and Monica had offered to go with him to help for some months. Amy's infant daughter was coming home with Lydia.[13]

* * *

The funeral flowers drooped and decayed. Printed leaflets in memory of Amy Dinning were sent out in response to the overwhelming mountain of condolence messages. Black-bordered notepaper matched the bleak grief of Lydia's heart. A tiny child needed her, and Lydia Brown with the help of her daughter Lizzie cared for the baby through sleepless nights and weary days. In a letter to a friend she wrote,

> It has been a terrible blow to us and a loss to her family and the whole Church. Never more will we hear her lovely voice singing with such feeling all those lovely pieces, and she was so good and kind to everybody and such a gentle nature. Her poor husband misses her terribly.... It has all been such a mystery to us that Mrs Dinning should have been taken away in the midst of her usefulness. We never expected her death.[14]

At the April Board meeting his friends offered their formal condolences to George Brown and his family. They felt for him, but this was not the only serious illness and risk of death before them. News of the illness and forced retirement of staff seemed to be a constant feature of their meetings—European and Pacific Island missionaries, their wives and children. They agreed that it was vital that new

---

13   *Methodist*, 9 April 1904.
14   Lydia Brown to Johanna Fellmann, 14 November 1904.

mission staff should have rigorous medical checks before they were accepted for service, but even the fittest people could have an accident or be laid low with malaria or tropical ulcers. The latest news from the Solomon Islands mentioned their own share of poor health among staff and local people, but Helena Goldie, who had now joined her husband, wrote cheerfully, despite the challenges of their context. She said that the chief on Roviana Island had refused to receive an Island teacher but she had persuaded her husband to let her go,

> hoping it would lead to something greater. I just go in a small boat I borrow from Mr Wickham, and only take children with me, and even then the first time I went the people who were able all ran away. It was a very cold welcome even though they came back afterwards. They said that they were afraid of me, but I laughed at them, saying I was a very little woman for them all to be afraid of. The next Monday the chief ran to meet me, and the welcome felt very much warmer. I held the sewing class, and did what I could for about thirty sick people, and going home was caught in a squall, and the boat nearly went to the bottom. We were glad to get home.[15]

When Lydia Brown heard news of Helena Goldie and Ray Rooney's bride who had joined him in 1903, she thought of these young women and others like Johanna Fellmann. They were all in their child-bearing years in remote and isolated places; if Amy could die following childbirth in Penrith, with a doctor at hand, what of these other young women when their time came?

* * *

At home, Lydia cared for a tiny baby and the many houseguests who travelled through, while George was frequently out or away from home for meetings and speaking engagements.[16] In May 1904 he attended General Conference in Melbourne where his close friend and colleague the Reverend George Lane concluded his term as President-General. Once again they debated the Constitution and increased powers of self-government for the church in Fiji and once again made no progress, sending the matter back to Fiji.[17] To Brown's pleasure the Conference confirmed that he could take one year of leave to complete his 'Reminiscences'. He had been able to report that the first chapter was already written.

* * *

---

15   Helena Goldie, letter of 20 March 1904, in the *Australasian Methodist Missionary Review*, 6 May 1904.
16   Brown addressed the New South Wales Presbyterian Assembly Foreign Missions Night; reported in *The Messenger of the Presbyterian Church of New South Wales*, 20 May 1904.
17   *Methodist*, 4 June, 11 June 1904. General Conference in Melbourne began on 26 May 1904 and was held in the Wesley Church, Lonsdale Street.

It was not an easy year. In August 1904 George and Lydia Brown were shocked by the sudden death of their friend George Lane. Painful correspondence from Fiji continued to arrive on the desk of Brown as General Secretary. Mission funds were dwindling again and an ambitious plan for Brown to travel across several States on a speaking tour was arranged. Two Fijian men, the Reverend Taniela Lotu and layman Ratu Niko Rabuku, arrived in Sydney to travel with him. At a public meeting of Methodists in Sydney in September 1904, with Brown interpreting for Taniela Lotu, the two Fijians spoke with feeling of contemporary issues in their Fijian Methodist Church. Little was said of the controversy over lay representation, but as the audience listened to the godly old Taniela and the imposing layman Rabuku many were persuaded that men like these ought to have a greater voice in their own church.[18]

'Dr Brown has been away from home for such a long time,' wrote Lydia Brown. He had been travelling for two months in Victoria and South Australia with the two Fijian visitors, trying to raise funds for a Special Appeal Fund for missions but was disappointed with the response. Lydia did miss him. Her heart still ached with the grief of losing her beloved Amy and she admitted that she 'could not take an interest in anything. I trust the Lord is now giving me more resignation to His will. I know that He does all things well and by and bye we will see the reason for all these afflictions.'[19] In her more honest moments she confessed to her friend Johanna Fellmann that as the first anniversary of baby Amy's birth and mother Amy's death approached, she was struggling to make sense of her loss.

> This month brings it all before us again so vividly.... The past year has been a very sad one to all of us and I think life will never be the same again. How I miss her precious weekly letters … now all is so silent. If I could really believe that it had been God's will for her to die I would be more resigned but I cannot help feeling that her death was untimely. She did not expect to die and none of us did either.... There is so much mystery connected to the unseen world. We must patiently wait until we will understand it all.[20]

It was not that she did not have plenty to fill her days. Her house, as always, was full of guests and Baby Amy was a delight but demanded a lot of attention. She wrote, 'I am thankful for my own good health and for the healthy baby. She is a great pet with us all and is quite an advertisement for a bottle-fed baby. Lizzie is perfectly wrapped up in her and would almost break her heart to lose her. The little darling is getting very interesting.'[21]

---

18   *Methodist*, 24 September 1904.
19   Lydia Brown to Johanna Fellmann, 30 November 1904.
20   Ibid., 7 March 1905.
21   Ibid.

Figure 23. George Brown with Benjamin Danks, Taniela Lotu and Ratu Niko Rabuku, Sydney 1904.

Source: Brown family album per favour of Miss Nancy Joyce.

The Brown household was still in a state of change. George Brown had arranged for the purchase of another house in Gordon, nearer the railway station for convenience and with a large room to house his ever-increasing collection of artefacts and library but, as Lydia wrote, 'We are wanting to move into our other house near the station but we must get rid of this place first.'[22] Lydia Brown had another worry on her mind as well. Daughter Claudia was expecting another baby and after the shock of losing Amy her mother could not bear to think of another loss.

By March 1905 George Brown was home from his interstate travels. Conference was a stressful time, as Brown was involved in another confrontation over lay representation in Fiji. On behalf of the missionaries in Fiji, C.O. Lelean contended that the idea had been hatched by the Board in George Street, Sydney and was a danger to the work of God as men who could not manage their own small affairs could not be expected to deal with financial business; though a worthy goal for the future, it ought to be postponed. Brown countered that delay was even more dangerous; admission to the full privileges of the Church was a 'matter of right and justice,' he said.[23] Another significant report was brought to that Conference; discussions had begun between the Presbyterian General Assembly, the Congregational Union and the Methodist Church about the possibility of a future Church Union.[24]

While George Brown was distracted with mission matters, Lydia Brown supervised a family move to a slightly smaller house in Gordon. She wrote that 'it has been a great work moving especially with all the curios.'[25] Claudia had produced a fifth daughter safely and Lydia did her best to help her when she could. Lydia was thankful that she was a healthy woman as, at the age of sixty-seven, she had the constant care of small Amy Eadith who was just learning to walk—'and my two daughters being so much away from home at their duties leaves me very much tied, but I would not part with the little darling. She is part of her dear Mother.'[26] Lydia continued to write loving pastoral letters to the women missionaries, aware that many lived in places where violence was common. She was shocked by a massacre of ten Catholic missionaries in the Baining area of New Britain late in 1904, with five nuns murdered—'I do feel so sorry for those poor sisters.'[27]

* * *

---

22   Ibid., 30 November 1904.
23   *Methodist*, 11 March 1905, 19 March 1905.
24   *Methodist*, 19 March 1905.
25   Lydia Brown to Johanna Fellmann, 7 March 1905.
26   Ibid., 9 May 1905.
27   Ibid., 30 November 1904; *Methodist*, 12 November 1904.

For years people had said to George Brown, 'You must write a book.' The Mission Board had urged it and now the General Conference had given him time to work on it. His diaries, his political letters, his correspondence as General Secretary and with scientists of many stripes around the world, and his enthusiasm as editor and writer for the *Australasian Methodist Missionary Review* provided him with a mass of documentation to help his memory. As he approached his seventieth birthday later in 1905, he was aware that men of his generation were dying, suddenly or in a slow decline, and a fresh urgency came to him. He carried in his memory a body of knowledge that he believed he must pass on. Lydia Brown told a friend, 'I suppose this year Dr Brown will be leaving the mission office as he really intends to write his book. It will be strange for him and Lizzie to be away from the office.'[28]

It seemed so difficult to let go the work that had consumed him for so long. He had great confidence in his successor Benjamin Danks, and his intention was to return to his role as General Secretary once the year of writing was over, but even so he found it hard to relinquish the daily connection.

If Brown was to write his book, where was he to work? The distractions of his private household, and the mission office with its new technology of telephone and cable, made them unsuitable. He decided to escape by taking a sea voyage to revisit the three regions that he had himself pioneered, refresh his memories and focus on writing in a quiet setting. Miss Lizzie Brown would travel with him again as his private secretary and typist. The voyage would be a holiday after illness and the stress of responsibilities. On a bright cool winter afternoon, a crowd of some two hundred Methodists met at Parbury's Wharf on Sydney Harbour on 7 July 1905. An anonymous benefactor in New Zealand had donated a 108-ton yacht to the Methodist Mission for use in their Pacific work and they crowded on deck to dedicate her. The Board had decreed that the yacht should now be named the *George Brown*. That evening George Brown and his daughter Lizzie embarked on the *SS Moresby*; the *George Brown* would follow them north.[29]

* * *

'I cannot realise that I am out of the office, even for a time,' wrote George Brown cheerfully, as they sailed north. 'Miss Brown, for a wonder, has kept fairly well. I am first class so far as health goes.'[30] Lizzie Brown observed that 'Father soon cast off his worried looks. The sea seems to cast a magic spell over him.... I shall be glad to be settled on the little island of Nusa Zonga and get to work' on the

---

28   Lydia Brown to Johanna Fellmann, 7 March 1905.
29   *Australasian Methodist Missionary Review*, 4 August, 4 October 1905.
30   Brown, Letter, 10 July 1905, in the *Australasian Methodist Missionary Review*, 4 August 1905.

book. [31] Before they moved on beyond the last place of regular contact with the rest of the world, at Gizo, Brown wrote, 'I feel so thankful that there is no cable or telephone in the Solomons. I hope to appreciate them by and bye, but not now. I hope to get to work on my book next week. That is going to be my work every day I hope until the yacht [the *George Brown*] arrives.' [32]

The Browns, father and daughter, settled on the little island of Nusa Zonga and a pattern of writing began. 'I keep pretty steadily at work every morning and so I am making very fair progress. Of course a good deal of time is taken up with sorting out my papers and reading up old books, letters etc to refresh my memory.' [33]

Lizzie Brown was relieved that the island in the Roviana Lagoon was so small that her father could not escape far from his task, although he usually found time for a sail at sunset. Distractions were few and so he could report to Danks, 'You will be glad to know that we have got on remarkably well with the book. We have, I am sure, done twice as much as we should have been able to do at Gordon.' [34] When a canoe or other small craft was available he made the crossing to the large island of New Georgia to visit the developing site of the mission at Kokenggolo. A mission house had been built on a hill overlooking the Lagoon. Children were being attracted to the mission and one day Brown and Lizzie witnessed about sixty children and youth delighting in a grand Sports Day, complete with swimming and diving races and an excited tug of war. [35] Ray Rooney and John Goldie were full of hope for the future despite many challenges. They had decided late in 1904 to expand their borders by stationing Rooney on the island of Choiseul. [36] Goldie wrote, 'History may repeat itself here – the history of Fiji, Samoa, New Britain and New Guinea. What God has done in these places he can and will do for the Solomons. My dream is not a wild one.' [37]

For his peace of mind, it was as well that Brown was not connected to the rest of his work by cable or telephone. Isolated on tiny Nusa Zonga in the Roviana Lagoon, he did not read the letters of complaint that reached the mission office from Fiji, describing the proposed Constitution as the 'tyranny of needless

---

31   Mary Elizabeth Brown, Letter, 17 July 1905, in the *Australasian Methodist Missionary Review*, 4 September 1905.

32   Brown, letter, 22 July 1905, in the *Australasian Methodist Missionary Review*, 4 September 1905.

33   Brown to Danks, from Nusa Zonga, 7 August 1905.

34   Brown to Danks, in the *Australasian Methodist Missionary Review*, 4 November 1905; *Methodist*, 11 October 1905.

35   *Australasian Methodist Missionary Review*, 4 October 1905.

36   Solomon Islands District Synod resolved on 25 November 1904, 'to include in the bounds of the District the large island of Choiseul, and to constitute it as a separate Circuit,' in the *Australasian Methodist Missionary Review*, 4 April 1905.

37   John Goldie, *Australasian Methodist Missionary Review*, 4 March 1905.

legislation'.[38] Nor was he aware that, to the astonishment of Chairman Small in Fiji, Hannah Dudley had resigned and departed without warning to work for the Bengali Mission in Calcutta, taking seven young Indian girls with her.[39] He did not read of the challenges facing their missionary in the Chinese quarter in Cairns; this man commented on the community of Chinese, Singalese, Japanese, Malay and Kanaka residents, a group that 'almost sends a red-hot advocate of a "White Australia" into a fit of convulsions, who longs for a political besom [broom] to sweep the whole thing off the face of the sacred soil of the continent.'[40] News of the deaths of more of his old friends did not reach him. His focus was on the islands of the Solomons, Neu Pommern and New Guinea. His world had narrowed to the villagers of the lagoon and the memories awakened by his old letters and papers.

Early in September they joined the passing steam ship *SS Moresby* and went on to visit the other regions where he had been a pioneer. By the time they reached the region that had been known as British New Guinea, Lizzie Brown was ill with malaria and the writing project came to a temporary halt. This area was now called Papua, and was under Australian colonial responsibility. Tropical diseases were a significant problem for their mission people in the area. Travelling on to Neu Pommern they were welcomed by the mission staff and other old friends. There was much to encourage Brown, and he reported warmly of Heinrich Fellmann that he 'has done splendid work for the Mission and enjoys the confidence and esteem of both the German officials and the foreign residents and the natives.'[41]

* * *

At home in Sydney, Lydia Brown waited until she had her household settled in bed and began a letter to Johanna Fellmann. It had been a very busy day with seven grandchildren to mind and she was weary. She admitted that she had been worried for her husband and daughter but had just heard that they had arrived safely at Dobu. 'I hope we shall now soon see our wanderers home and I hope they will come back with renewed vigour for whatever work may be before them,' she wrote. Lydia wrote of Wallis Danks. Wallis, the baby who had been born to Emma Danks at Kinawanua with such drama in 1880, was now a young man, an ordained minister and had recently gone as a missionary to his birthplace. Lydia wrote,

---

38   *Methodist*, 2 December 1905.
39   Morven Sidal, *Hannah Dudley: Hamari Maa, Honoured Mother, Educator and Missioner to the Indentured Indians of Fiji 1864–1913*, Suva: Pacific Theological College, 1997, pp. 80–90; the *Australasian Methodist Missionary Review*, 4 September 1905 reported that Miss Dudley had resigned on 24 July and gone to join the Bengali Mission in Calcutta. In time she returned to continue work in Fiji.
40   *Australasian Methodist Missionary Review*, 4 September 1905.
41   Ibid., 4 November 1905.

I want to write and thank Wallis for attending to the graves of my precious children … give my love to him and thank him from me. It was a sad time for me when I had to see my darlings buried out of my sight, but even that was not so hard as losing my precious Amy in the midst of her usefulness. God's ways are mysterious, but doubtless He will make it plain by and bye and I must not murmur but what grieves me is that I could not have done more to help her with her family, but God knows how willingly I would slave for my dear ones.[42]

Rev. J. C. Jennison. Rev. W. Brown. Rev. H. H. Nolan.
Rev. W. A. Burns Rev. C. E. Williams.

Rev. W. Slade. Rev. A. J. Small. Rev. Geo. Lane. Rev. T. J. Wallis.
Rev. W. Heighway. Rev. Dr. Brown (Chairman). Mr. R. S. Callaghan.

THE FIJI DISTRICT SYNOD, AND MEMBERS OF THE RECENT DEPUTATION.

Figure 24. George Brown with visiting deputation and members of Fiji District Synod 1901. Back: C.J. Dennison, W.A. Burns, W. Brown, C.E. Williams, H.H. Nolan. Front: W. Heighway, W. Slade, G. Brown, A.J. Small (Chairman), George Lane, R.S. Callaghan, T.J. Wallis.

Source: The *Australasian Methodist Missionary Review*, March 1901.

George Brown and his daughter Lizzie arrived back in Sydney early in November with the *Prinz Waldemar*. They had been away for four months. Within weeks Lizzie was able to tell a friend that she 'felt quite well again now and ready to go on with writing the book.'[43] Very little work would have been

---

42 Lydia Brown to Johanna Fellmann, 27 October 1905.
43 Mary Elizabeth Brown to Johanna Fellmann, 22 November 1905.

done on the book at that time, however. Brown discovered that, while he had been happily meeting with other mission staff in the northern island groups, in Fiji many of the Methodist missionary staff members were very unhappy. They objected to the directive of General Conference that the new Constitution for Fiji Methodists must be brought into effect in 1906—which included the right of each Quarterly Meeting to elect a layman as their representative to the Financial District Synod. They had been protesting for at least the past five years that this was premature, and believed that 'a burden was being placed on the shoulders of the missionaries that was well-nigh impossible to be borne.'[44] Not every missionary in Fiji felt this way, but the men who were not rebelling against the directive were all about to leave Fiji for retirement, furlough or sick leave. The scale of the problem emerged when they attempted to work on the plan for ministerial appointments in Fiji for 1906. A number of Tongan and Fijian Native Ministers had recently died, several Australian ministers were going on leave—and most of the rest announced that they wanted to transfer back to Australia or New Zealand. Their Chairman, A.J. Small, was horrified. He sent an urgent cable to Sydney: 'Station sheet practically blank situation serious strongly advise you summon me Sydney immediately to confer with the Board.' The reply came back: 'Cable main facts of situation.'

Small tried again. It seemed to him that it was imperative that he speak with the Board personally. The steamship *Hauroto* could provide timely passage. This time, on 31 October 1905 he cabled, 'Twelve signed memorial requesting recall self Heighway retiring strongly desire explain matters may I come and return *Hauroto*.'[45] To his great frustration, the only reply was a cable saying: 'Board awaits mail write fully.'[46]

A week after arriving back in Sydney, Brown attended a very disturbed Board meeting. There was little interest in his latest travel tales. A series of letters had arrived from Fiji, with a Memorial signed by ten men.[47] They asked to be 'recalled to the Home Work on the grounds that they cannot conscientiously administer that part of the new constitution relating to the admission of Lay Representatives to the Financial District Synod.'[48] The Board was shocked. They knew that there had always been resistance to the inclusion of Fijian laymen in decision making but they had never dreamed of a mass resignation of staff. The names of the signatories were all familiar to Brown. He had visited them all, been entertained in their isolated homes, laughed with their children and witnessed their good work. They were his friends. To lose so many gifted and

---

44 *Methodist*, 2 December 1905.
45 Minutes of Wesleyan Methodist Missions Board, May 1898–July 1906, 11 November 1905.
46 Ibid.
47 The Memorial to the Board was signed by H.H. Nolan, C. Bleazard, C.O. Lelean, J.C. Jennison, J.W. Burton, W.R. Poole, Wm. Bennett, R.O. Cook, Cyril Bavin and W.T. Butcher.
48 Minutes of Wesleyan Methodist Missions Board, May 1898–July 1906, 11 November 1905.

able people would be a disaster. At one level, George Brown understood their frustration. Memories of his own struggles with the Mission Board had been revived while he had been re-reading his own records of struggles in Samoa and New Britain. Then he had acted according to his own lights and been rebuked by the Board of the day. He knew what it was like to see a local scene very clearly and doubt whether a remote body of men meeting somewhere in a distant city could possibly imagine the issues he was facing. He understood the tension between the island-centred staff and the New South Wales-centred Board, the intimate understanding of a local scene against the long experience of a broad history of a region, the engaged parochial view opposed by an educated wide view. A.J. Small had written that to wait for organic growth was wiser and that 'to chisel out a new constitution in Sydney may be a fine achievement from a sculptural point of view but it won't breathe.'[49] Even so, Brown remained determined to pursue this issue.

The Board struggled, and then did what Boards do. They set up a small sub-committee, including Brown, to try to draft a response.[50] Repeatedly the sub-committee and the Board met during December. Line by line, clause by clause of their draft was debated, criticised, revised, ripped up and sent back for more work.[51] Finally a much manipulated letter was drafted; it expressed 'surprise and regret at the attitude of the Brethren ... but after long and painful consideration, it declines to recommend any course which would interfere with the action of the [General] Conference.'[52] There was a plea for signatories of the Memorial to reconsider their attitudes and postpone their retirements from mission work.[53] By now, inevitably, news of the dispute had spread across Methodism in Australasia and everyone had an opinion. It was said that the influence of George Brown on the Board was so powerful that his stubbornness was at the root of the conflict, in effect responsible for forcing good men out of Fiji.

Brown was very distressed. He wrote a long confidential statement for members of the New South Wales Conference. He wrote 'as an old missionary who loves Fiji and the men who labour there.' These men, he believed, 'would never accuse me of seeking to drive them from Fiji.' He had no wish to be embroiled in controversy, for 'the subject is too painful, and I am neither able nor willing to bear the strain.'[54] Almost his entire long ministry had been spent in the service of the mission enterprise and

---

49 Small to Brown, 8 February 1905, in Wood, *Overseas Missions of the Australian Methodist Church, Vol. 11, Fiji*, p. 280.

50 Minutes of Wesleyan Methodist Missions Board, May 1898–July 1906, 15 November 1905.

51 Ibid. In addition to meetings of the sub-committee, the full Board met to debate the draft on 6, 11, 15 and 18 December 1905.

52 Minutes of Wesleyan Methodist Missions Board, May 1898–July 1906, 18 November 1905.

53 Ibid.

54 Brown, 'For Members of Conference only.'

during all those years I have always enjoyed the love and esteem of my brethren in the mission field, and though the brethren in Fiji deplore the action taken by the General and Annual Conferences which I and others have advocated, I rejoice in the assurance that I retain their love, though they cannot all accept my judgement on this important matter. But with advancing years I cannot any longer endure and bear the pain to which I have been subjected. Letters are being sent from another State to myself personally and to ministers of our Church, in which, as stated publicly 'the most scandalous statements' are made against me, in which I am charged with being solely responsible for the action taken by the Conferences, with driving our missionaries out of Fiji and other similar charges. These charges I indignantly deny.[55]

He continued that no one could say that the process had been hasty. The issue in regard to Fiji had now been brought to five annual Conferences and two General Conferences, with three deputations visiting Fiji, since 1900. Point by point, he argued against the objections of the missionaries in Fiji. He saw little sign of any preparation for future self-government. He could not believe that in a Church that had been established for seventy years and had thousands of Fijian lay preachers, catechists and teachers that not a single reputable lay person could be found who could be nominated; if that were so it would be 'the most serious reflection which has ever been made on the value of our work in Fiji, and on the labours of the noble men and women who have laboured there, and I for one would bow my head in shame if I believed it to be true.'[56]

He saw the inclusion of laymen in decision-making as an act of justice and essential for the health of their work in Fiji, and although he recognised the need for training in the principles of self-government and self-support and believed that the Fijian Church would need missionary leadership for some years yet, 'I do, however, contend that a beginning should be made … and that it should be done at once.'[57] In the rapidly changing context of Fiji at the beginning of a new century, the risks were too great if they delayed. He concluded that in his opinion the best policy to pursue in Fiji

is that we should make our Church in Fiji the Church of the people of Fiji, that the people should feel that they do not belong to the church of the missionaries or of the people of Sydney or Australia, but that they and their Church in Fiji form part of the great universal Church of Christ, and that they are responsible to God for its continued success.[58]

* * *

---

55   Ibid.
56   Ibid.
57   Ibid.
58   Ibid.

There were days, as the new year of 1906 began, when George Brown felt old and tired. It was not just that he had marked his seventieth birthday in December, or that people sometimes referred to him as the 'venerable General Secretary' or that his whiskers and hair, once gingery, were snow white. He felt that there were so many weights on his shoulders, so many signs of instability in his work, so many disappointments. Despite their best efforts and the most heart-felt appeals, the response to the major appeal for funds had been disappointing. Acting-General Secretary Benjamin Danks put the situation bluntly, 'Is our Church staggering under a burden it ought not be called upon to carry, or is she evidencing a degree of inattention to her call that is blameworthy?'[59]

Almost every region where they had mission work was going through periods of significant social change and stress. Even the most committed of the mission staff were often forced to resign because of illness.[60] Many of the women missionaries whom he had championed were finding that the rigours of a tropical climate, or the equally debilitating effects of unhappy relationships in an isolated community, were too much for them and were giving up. There were complaints from discontented staff about conditions.[61] Although the disgruntled men in Fiji had chosen to delay their retirement from the field after all, the problems there still festered. The many Board meetings were often stressful. George Brown still retained his love for the work of mission, and when invited to speak publicly it was reported that this 'worthy father' had kept his audience 'at the one moment convulsed with laughter, and the next brought to the soberest consideration of the claims and necessities of our work.'[62] Even so, there were times when discouragements cast a cloud over his usual optimism. The idea of retirement was beginning to appeal. Danks was doing a fine job as Acting-General Secretary. Brown's contemporaries were dying and a new generation was taking their place, men and women who were more familiar with a legendary old man than with the human George. He had lost none of his relish for life but was anxious to complete his book, to write on other themes, to travel beyond the Pacific and to spend more time on his keen interest in the scientific world.

He had seriously underestimated the time it would take to write his book. There were so many distractions and other responsibilities. There was also an immense archive of documents that he had created over the years. He wavered between writing a history of Methodist missions in the Pacific, a compilation of observations on Pacific culture or an autobiography. On what matters would it be best to keep silent? The manuscript was already becoming longer and longer,

---

59 *Australasian Methodist Missionary Review*, 5 March 1906; Annual Report of Mission.
60 Ibid.
61 Minutes of Wesleyan Methodist Missions Board, May 1898–July 1906, 6 October, 7 November, 5 December 1906.
62 *Australasian Methodist Missionary Review*, 4 April 1906.

and very unwieldy, though far from complete. With some embarrassment he asked Conference for a second year of leave to complete the work and, with some reluctance, leave was granted.[63]

* * *

The year 1906 was a year of natural disasters. Bushfires roared across New South Wales.[64] Earthquakes and volcanic eruptions of catastrophic proportions shook San Francisco, Italy, Tonga and New Zealand.[65] In Samoa a volcano on the island of Savai'i was erupting again and molten lava was slowly pouring down toward the eastern coast near Saleaula, engulfing villages, farms and plantations in its path. The house that George had built of stone in Saleaula in 1868 was now deeply embedded in a barren waste of lava some ten feet deep. Villagers had been forced to flee as the lava moved on out across the beach, out as far as the reef, leaving desolation in its wake and destructive waves to trouble the coastline.[66] If ever Lydia Brown considered visiting again any of her former homes in Samoa, Tonga or New Britain, she decided against it. Almost every home where she had once lived was now gone; collapsed, demolished and relocated or engulfed by lava. Her good friend Emma Danks had recently travelled back to New Britain to visit her son Wallis. Lydia was happy for her. Emma wrote that she was 'enjoying myself immensely. It is a great treat to be here, and to see some of the boys and girls of our day, now men and women with their children around them; living good lives themselves and working for God. We sowed in tears but see what a good harvest has been gathered in.'[67]

For herself, Lydia knew that she would never go back. As a very private person, she may have been surprised to see her own portrait in the *Australasian Methodist Missionary Review,* her smooth hair still quite dark in the simple style she had worn since she was a bride and her soft grandmotherly features framed in the lace yoke of her dress. As Acting-General Secretary, Benjamin Danks had done what her husband could not have done and written a public appreciation of the woman who had nurtured him and his wife through the loneliness, illness and grief of their first years in the islands. Although, he said, Dr. Brown was widely known and valued,

> His good wife, one of the most unassuming and modest of women, is not so generally known. Those, however, who have been honoured with her friendship realise what a Mother in Israel she is, and know that by her patient self-forgetfulness and her strong, willing endurance of

---

63 *Australasian Methodist Missionary Review*, 4 August 1906.
64 *Methodist*, 13 January 1906.
65 *Australasian Methodist Missionary Review*, 4 September 1906.
66 Ibid., 4 May 1906.
67 Ibid.

hardships for the Master's sake, she has strengthened and cheered her husband in his great work ... the story of her life there and the suffering she had to bear has yet to be written ... she is greatly respected and loved by all who know her.[68]

Several factors worked together to help George Brown to decide to announce his retirement. On the one hand he found himself embroiled in a war of words with the Bishop of Melanesia, Cecil Wilson, over boundaries. The Bishop was not happy. In the Solomon Islands John Goldie's action in establishing his colleague Ray Rooney on the island of Choiseul and purchasing land for a mission property on the northern atoll of Ontong Java gave offence.[69] From the Bishop's vantage point this was a sign that the Methodists were not keeping to their boundary agreement and was 'an abominable breach of trust.'[70] A stiff letter from the Bishop to Brown 'requesting that the doctor should definitely define the limits of our Missionary work,' was discussed at a Board meeting just after Christmas 1906. Brown offered his response and had the support of the Board, but it was clear to him that serious questions still lingered in their minds. It would be resolved in the end, particularly as the Melanesian Mission was unable to provide enough workers to establish their own work there, but not without tension.[71] The other major issue facing the Board at that time was the unhealed sore over lay representation in Fiji. Seven years after the question had first been raised, they were still arguing. In 1907 the matter was still a live issue and would be for years to come.[72] The Board itself was deeply divided over how to proceed. The best they could do was to urge the Fiji District 'to consider the whole question of the extension of self-governing powers and self-sustaining responsibilities of the Fiji Methodist Church' and report in three years time.[73] It was exhausting and dispiriting. Brown was wearying of fighting the same battles year after year. He believed that he had other work to do before he faced his own end.

Two months later the Reverend Dr. George Brown presented the Board with notice of his retirement. He intended to finish his work as General Secretary at General Conference in June 1907.[74]

---

68 *Australasian Methodist Missionary Review*, 5 November 1906.
69 Ibid.
70 David Hilliard, *God's Gentlemen: A History of the Melanesian Mission 1849–1942*, St. Lucia: University of Queensland Press, 1978, p. 138.
71 Alan R. Tippett, *Solomon Islands Christianity: A Study in Growth and Obstruction*, London: Lutterworth, 1967, p. 358.
72 William E. Bennett, 'Fiji,' in *A Century in the Pacific*, ed. James Colwell, Sydney: William H. Beale, 1914, pp. 439–506, p. 474.
73 Minutes of Wesleyan Methodist Missions Board, 1906–1909, 22 February, 25 February 1907.
74 Minutes of Wesleyan Methodist Missions Board, 1906–1909, 17 April 1907.

Figure 25. Lydia Brown 1906.

Source: The *Australasian Methodist Missionary Review*, 5 November 1906.

20. 'Grand old man of Methodist Missions'

Australia, South Africa, United Kingdom, Solomon Islands
1907–1912

Applause broke out as the entire Conference stood to honour the Reverend Dr. George Brown. Memories of George Brown as a thorn in the side of Conference, or as an embarrassment to the worthies of Methodism seemed to have faded with his announcement of retirement. After a missionary career spanning forty-seven years and many fields, the words of appreciation flowed. He was, they said, their 'grand old man of Methodist Missions ... full of missionary enthusiasm and possessed of a unique knowledge of the Polynesian races ... a trusted leader in all our missionary forward movements, and a brother beloved and revered by all the missionaries on the field ... enjoyed the confidence and affection of the native races in all the Districts under our care.'[1]

They wished him 'a prolonged and restful eventide.'[2] Brown was not planning a restful eventide, however, and assured them that he had 'not lost one particle of love for mission work and would do all he could to carry on the work.'[3] He was given a formal designation as Honorary General Secretary with Benjamin Danks as his successor as General Secretary, and retained his seat on the Board of Missions. During the period of transition which would last into 1908 he would continue to participate in meetings and all the general work of the Board, would write more letters to the press under his nom de plume 'Carpe Diem' on the politics of colonial rule in the Pacific region and would go on writing his autobiography. However, when the mission ship *George Brown* sailed for New Britain in July 1907, it was Benjamin Danks who sailed with the ship, not Brown.

During that final year before formal retirement, a collection was made across the nation for a gift for Dr. and Mrs. Brown 'in the coming eventide of their lives.'[4] It was true that the sun was setting for people who had been dear to him. When he learned of the death of an old friend, Lorimer Fison, Brown wrote of his sense

---

1   Minutes of Methodist Missions Board, 1906–1909, 17 April 1907.
2   *Methodist*, June 1907.
3   Ibid.
4   *Australasian Methodist Missionary Review*, 4 December 1907.

of loneliness at the loss of almost the last of his friends from the early years of missionary work, men who had mentored and ministered to him, challenged and comforted him over the years. The reminders of mortality gave urgency to Brown as he thought of everything he still wanted to achieve.

The book manuscript was still incomplete but he had a publisher. As soon as he could relinquish the responsibilities of office in March 1908, he planned to carry his book to London where the publishing house of Hodder and Stoughton would help him with publication. It was twenty years since he had last been to England and he was excited about the prospect. Lydia made it clear that she would not make the journey with him; her little granddaughter Amy Eadith was now a four year old and needed her at home. Their daughters Lizzie and Monica would be his travelling companions and Lizzie would go on working with the unwieldy manuscript.

A new challenge was before the Board that year. In 1906, while visiting London and the British Methodist Missionary Society, the President General of the Methodist Church in Australasia, the Reverend Dr. W.H. Fitchett had been asked whether his church would consider accepting responsibility for a mission district in Jabalpur Province in North India. Fitchett offered to visit that region while he was on the way home to Australia and wrote that 'there is wakening a sense that we ought to take some part in the Christianization of India. God has signally blessed our missions in the South Seas; may we not expect that He will open the way for us for service in one of the greatest fields of Christian work on the planet?'[5]

The Board of Missions did not warm to the idea at first. Their finances were already very tight. The region in North India was unrelated to the places of origin of the Indians now living in Fiji. In addition, the work that the British mission hoped to pass to them was unlike their usual model of mission; it was based on an orphanage with the hope that the children would be converted to the Christian faith. The Australian Methodists were prepared to accept new work in India on condition that it should be evangelistic, located in a region from whence the indentured labourers in Fiji had come and would provide training for future staff who would work in Fiji among the Indian population.[6]

* * *

Every three years since 1881, George Brown had attended the Methodist General Conference as it gathered leaders from all the colonies to meet in one of their cities. In June 1907, General Conference met in the familiar space of the Centenary Hall in Sydney. He presented his final report as General Secretary

---

5   Minutes of Methodist Missions Board, 1906–1909, 5 February 1908.
6   Ibid.; *Australasian Methodist Missionary Review*, 4 March 1908.

and was encouraged when the meeting resolved that it was their 'distinct duty and privilege to maintain our missions in the Pacific in thorough efficiency and as opportunity offers, determines to extend them to the islands that are not at present evangelized.'[7]

With renewed financial buoyancy and under pressure from Fitchett and the Victorian Conference, General Conference directed the Board to pursue a plan for Australian mission staff to prepare for work in India. The recurring theme of lay representation in Fiji was still a live issue. The missionaries in Fiji, despite their threats of resignation in 1905, were still at their posts. Conference assured them that their faithful work in the rapidly changing social conditions of Fiji was recognised but insisted that the principle of lay representation must be adopted in 1908.[8] Brown participated in the long and keen debate and saw, in the end, an overwhelming majority vote to grant the new Constitution to the Methodist Church in Fiji, 'conferring the right upon each circuit to send a Lay Representative to the Fiji Financial Synod.'[9] The Methodists in Samoa were now asking for similar rights.[10]

The people of the Methodist Church farewelled George Brown handsomely, offering him glowing speeches and gifts. A speaker hoped that 'your dear wife, Mrs Brown, may be spared to you in health and strength for many years.'[11] In his reply, Brown said that he was 'thankful for the past days, rich in happy memories, and he owed much to his wife, who had been through times of stress and danger with him.'[12] Perhaps he recalled an old tale from the Samoan years where someone had dared to imply that Brown might be tempted to beat his wife. One who knew them both well wrote later, 'The idea of anyone attempting to beat Mrs Brown, who though exceedingly quiet and good tempered was full of feminine fire of the right kind, was sufficiently amusing; but that her husband who loved her and leaned upon her, should take to the stick was the greatest joke on record.'[13]

With warm applause in his ears, Brown took his seat at the end of the recognition of his retirement.[14] The old man and his old wife had survived. He had loved and leaned on Lydia through it all. Danger from cannibals, disease and at sea,

---

7   Minute Book, Methodist Church General Conference, 1890–1913, ML Methodist Church 581.
8   Ibid.
9   *Australasian Methodist Missionary Review*, 4 March 1908.
10 Ibid., 4 February 1908.
11 Ibid.
12 Ibid.
13 C. Brunsdon Fletcher, 'George Brown and the Pacific,' *Royal Australian Historical Society Journal and Proceedings*, vol. 7, pt. 1, 1921: 1–54, p.39.
14 *Australasian Methodist Missionary Review*, 4 April 1908.

danger from errors of judgement and the sharp sting of criticism; they had arrived at the moment of retirement with honour, after all. A letter from one of the younger missionaries in Fiji at that time touched him. J.W. Burton wrote,

> I sometimes think that we younger fellows are not as considerate as we might be. Never mind, Doctor, though we often make you the butt of our complaints—perhaps often unjustly—we all love you personally and I know your warm heart is glad because of that. We shall be sorry when a new General Secretary takes your place.[15]

* * *

If he had thought this was an end to his work, George Brown might have been filled with grief at the stripping away of many things that gave his life meaning. It was not. As he planned to sail for England, he anticipated a life full of interest. He would complete his manuscript. He would organise his museum and home library and write other scientific papers and perhaps books. He was still a member of the Board of Mission. In London he would visit the British Methodists and negotiate the most appropriate way for Australian Methodists to begin new missionary work in India. The final annual report he presented as General Secretary of Missions included a potential beginning. The list of missionary appointments now included: 'India. Two to be sent.'[16]

* * *

Since 1905, 'Father's book' had loomed large in the Brown family. There was such a wealth of material to be arranged. Brown had always encouraged others to keep their archival documents and had been very diligent in keeping his own. Now he had access to a vast archive as well as his own memories. With Lizzie's help, he had arranged it into chapters covering the large themes and contexts of his life; England, Canada and New Zealand, then Samoa, New Britain, Tonga, British New Guinea and the Solomon Islands. His selections had been, to a degree, self-serving. He had left out most references to his immediate family, though that may well have been at the insistence of his wife and daughters. He had conflated to a single paragraph many years of inter-mission conflict over the resumption of the Wesleyan Methodist Mission in Samoa in 1857, concluding,

> I have always felt that the question as to whether it was expedient to resume the Mission after the lapse of so many years might at one time have been fairly questioned ... but the position I took up was that I was sent to Samoa by the Conference to take charge of our people in that group, and that it was my duty to be a loyal servant to the Conference.[17]

---

15 J.W. Burton to George Brown, c.1908, ML MSS 263/1 *7-939c; CY 3405.
16 *Australasian Methodist Missionary Review*, 4 April 1908.
17 George Brown, *George Brown: Pioneer-Missionary and Explorer: An Autobiography*, London: Hodder and Stoughton, 1908, pp. 29–30.

He ignored completely the years of dissension between himself and his brother-in-law J.W. Wallis, barely mentioned his own deep depression and frequent illnesses and reduced fourteen years of work in Samoa to a series of adventurous tales about coastal travel, hurricanes and tribal warfare. The five years of the beginning of the New Mission in New Britain had been the central point of his life, despite the fact that he had been away from the region for many months during that period; compared to a single paragraph about troubles in Samoa he devoted six chapters to events related to New Britain. Brown believed that he needed to justify his actions in 1878 and wrote in great detail, admitting that he had been intemperate in his reaction to criticism. 'I am older now and I hope that I am a wiser man than I was at that time.'[18] His writing on the three-year period of trying to make peace in a divided Church in Tonga threatened to overwhelm the whole manuscript; in the end he was persuaded to cut out a large portion of this material.[19] The vivid tales of the beginnings of the two new missions in British New Guinea and in the Solomon Islands were taken almost verbatim from journal entries and articles he had written at the time. Some themes were missing by choice. Endless debates over representation and inclusion, the long struggles for funding, difficulties, disappointments, the struggles of the work among the Indian population of Fiji, the newest proposal for an Australian work in India; there was no room for these in his book. His audience, he may have believed, would respond to his famous tales of cannibal chiefs and escapes from shipwreck but would find the sorry stories of failure or frustration too depressing. The weighty manuscript was still not finished but he assured his daughters that they would complete it during the long voyage to London.

* * *

In March 1908, George Brown sailed for England with his daughters Mary Elizabeth and Monica. After years of sea travel in small vessels in the arc of the Pacific, Tasman and Coral Seas, this time he was travelling on the *SS Suevic*, a comparatively new and luxurious steam ship of 12,500 tons. Lydia Brown moved in with her daughter Claudia and Percy Slade and their family of little girls. Lydia knew that her help in that busy household would be valued. As so often before during their married life, her link with her husband would be through letters. As the *Suevic* steamed west along the southern coast of Australia, Brown looked forward with enthusiasm to his first opportunity to visit the ports of Durban and Cape Town in South Africa and meet once more his relatives, church friends and colleagues in the scientific world in England. Even so, he admitted to Lydia that 'I cannot say that I enjoy going to sea as I once

---

18 Brown, *George Brown: Pioneer-Missionary and Explorer*, p. 271.
19 The original manuscript version is held in the Mitchell Library, ML A 4096-97.

did,'[20] and discovered that a combination of rough weather and little privacy meant that his grand plan of finishing his book during the voyage was doomed to failure. Brown was missing Lydia more than ever. Writing during the voyage, he told Lydia,

> I have been thinking over the years we have spent together and I often feel very thankful to God for giving me such a dear good wife and one who has been such a help to me in my work. I know how you disparage yourself and often talk as if you were of little use in the world but this is not so. People often speak kindly of the work which I have done but no one knows so well as I know it that, if I had not been blessed with the wife I have, a lot of that work would never have been done. This is a simple fact. You have let me go to the work to which God called me without murmuring and this has enabled me to do that for which men praise me today. You and I however know that the praise is not to us but to the loving Father who has blessed and strengthened us in the work which he gave us to do.... It seems to me indeed that I think about you oftener this time than I have ever done before though I scarcely see how that is possible. God bless and keep you my own dear wife.[21]

Eight weeks after leaving Sydney, Brown and his daughters reached London. He visited his publishers on 22 May 1908 and discussed his manuscript. Methodists in London welcomed him. Invitations to speak at church functions began to come in and a new generation found themselves entertained and moved by his storytelling, his humour and his evangelistic fervour. An English observer wrote of a degree of hero worship that surrounded Brown and noted that Brown aimed at 'self-sustaining native churches, both as to men and to means. Christianity was not to be an exotic, kept by expensive European machinery but was to root itself in the soil and adapt itself to the climate. He had a great love for the Polynesian people and resented the name "savage".'[22]

Carrying the bundle of manuscript with them in their baggage, Brown and his daughters caught the train to the north to spend time in his old home town of Barnard Castle on the hillside above the River Tees, with his half-sister Emily Brown and Dixon cousins. Lizzie was prepared to continue to work with her father on the book but first she had to catch him. On board ship his excuse had been lack of privacy. Now he had a busy itinerary and was constantly travelling. With some frustration Lizzie complained to Johanna Fellmann, who was in Germany on furlough at that time. Until her father returned to Barnard Castle to complete the revisions of the manuscript, she and Monica would not be free to

---

20   Brown to Lydia Brown, 15 April 1908.
21   Ibid.
22   Joseph Nettleton, *The Foreign Field of the Wesleyan Methodist Church Vol. IV 1907–08*, London: Wesleyan Methodist Mission House, 1908, pp.193–98.

visit the Fellmanns.[23] At last the manuscript was completed and was published in London late in 1908 to some fanfare among the Methodists. A presentation copy was sent, with compliments, to Kaiser Wilhelm as a sign of respect as so much of the story was located in the regions now part of the colonies of Germany. It was a handsome large book bound in red covers, rich with photographic plates and a map of the Pacific with many of the island regions coloured Empire pink. A dedication read simply: 'To My Wife'.

* * *

In a Sydney of summer heat and drought, Lydia Brown thought of her husband and daughters in the bitter cold of a northern winter. She was content and busy living with Claudia Slade and her family but watched eagerly for letters from England. She told a friend, 'Everyone wonders at Dr Brown being so full of life and energy and my dear daughters have improved very much in health, the change and rest have done them both good. They are just beginning to talk about coming home.... I hope before very long we will again be united.'[24]

George Brown and his daughters were not ready to return to Australia yet. Brown would admit later that he was 'so busy and going about so much in England.'[25] They visited relatives and friends, met the scientific community and both George and Monica Brown were invited to speak in churches. He told Lydia, who had always declared that she could never speak in public, 'If you cannot talk in public you can and do talk to people by the gently loving life you live.'[26] It was an exciting time to be in England, with suffragist marches, the opening of the vast Franco-British Exhibition and a chance to be at the centre of Empire. For Brown, as he was selling his book, it was a time to see the Pacific from the perspective of London, islands that were fabled, very far away and only a minor part of the global vision of the Methodists. It was gratifying to be described as one 'known all over the world as one of the intrepid pioneers of missions in the Southern Seas'[27] but sitting among the many hundreds gathered in the Royal Albert Hall for the 'Great Methodist Missionary Meeting' on 3 May 1909, Brown knew he was only a small part of a wide panorama of Methodist missions around the world.

George Brown and his daughters did not sail for Australia until 29 July 1909. Once more they sailed with the *SS Suevic* along with nearly five hundred other passengers, passing through dangerous winter storms as they crossed the Indian

---

23   Mary Elizabeth Brown to Johanna Fellmann, Barnard Castle, 1908. Private collection.
24   Lydia Brown to Johanna Fellmann, 30 January 1909.
25   Brown to Lydia Brown, 6 August 1908.
26   Ibid.
27   Wesleyan Methodist Missionary Society, 'Review of George Brown D.D., *Pioneer Missionary and Explorer: An Autobiography*,' in *The Foreign Field of the Wesleyan Methodist Church*, no. 56, vol. 5 (April 1909).

Ocean; it was feared that they would have to take to the lifeboats.[28] Two other passenger liners were lost that winter on that route to Australia, but yet again George Brown arrived safely home, landing in Sydney on 17 September 1909.[29]

* * *

If there was a period of comparative calm following George Brown's retirement from his official work, it was the next few years. He told a friend, 'I very seldom go to the office now except to meetings of the Board. I am glad to have less worry and anxiety.'[30] He added in another letter, 'Lizzie helps me when I want her and does a lot of housework. Monica helps everyone I think and is always up to her neck in work for the Auxiliary and the Church. The *Alte Frau* and I just jog along quietly.'[31]

He spent many contented hours in his personal museum of objects and memories, working with his photographic collection, preparing a Samoan Hymn Book and Catechism for the press and writing another book that brought together his years of observations on the geography, languages, art, technology, folklore, religion, customs and culture of the people of the Pacific. This work, *Melanesians and Polynesians: Their Life Histories Described and Compared*, was published in October 1910 in London.[32] That year he travelled to Adelaide for General Conference where he was excited about the ambitious plans of the new leadership for the period 1911–13 with the launch of the Forward Policy for Missions.

Fifty years had passed since Brown arrived in Raglan, New Zealand, to ask young Lydia Wallis to marry him. During one of his long absences from home, Brown wrote recalling his memories of her as the 'bright happy girl' on their honeymoon trek through the wintry bush of New Zealand, and on board the tiny *John Wesley*, sailing for Samoa. Teasingly, he added, 'Though you did think that I was tired of you after three weeks of married life … I only wish I was with you.'[33] Now, after all they had shared over the fifty years, George and Lydia Brown gathered their whole family around them to celebrate their Golden Wedding on 2 August 1910. Brown knew that Lydia's love had not wavered, despite the demands his peripatetic life had placed on her, and that he would always come home to her. The two had learned well the intimate language of their marriage, with its moods and nuances, subtle signs and unspoken

---

28   Mary Elizabeth Brown to her aunt, Mrs Anna Caukwell, 2 September 1909, on board *SS Suevic*.
29   The ship *SS Maori* was wrecked in the storm through which *Suevic* passed. The new liner *SS Waratah* disappeared without trace as *Suevic* left Liverpool.
30   Brown to Johanna Fellmann, 5 July 1910.
31   Ibid., 19 September 1910.
32   George Brown, *Melanesians and Polynesians: Their Life-Histories Described and Compared*, London: Macmillan and Co, 1910.
33   Brown to Lydia Brown, 3 September 1908.

understanding. The quiet loving woman offered the restless passionate man a place to rest, a strength against which he could lean. So often over the years Lydia had been parted from either her husband or her children. Now they were all together, and the bond of love was unbroken.

* * *

If George Brown imagined that he would now invest in a rocking chair and settle to gentle domestic pursuits for his declining years he was mistaken. He had recently been appointed vice-president of the British and Foreign Bible Society and always relished the meetings of the Board of Missions, now held in the Board Room in the newly acquired Methodist property at 139 Castlereagh Street, Sydney. At a meeting of the Board late in 1910 Brown was asked to make a pastoral visit to the Solomon Islands on behalf of General Secretary Danks. Some significant problems had arisen there. Soon after Christmas 1910 he boarded *SS Moresby* and sailed north again for the first time in six years.

It proved to be a bruising task. On his way to the Methodist mission in the Western Solomon Islands, Brown visited the British Commissioner Woodford at his official residence on Tulagi. Woodford told Brown that he had removed an inexperienced young Methodist missionary from the recently established mission on the remote atoll of Ontong Java. Among other accusations, this man was said to have very unwisely struck an object sacred to the local people in their sacred place. Brown was shocked and declared, 'It is a wonder to me that they did not kill him at once.'[34] The Commissioner was angry; he had only just returned from bringing to justice those who had massacred a trader and his family in another part of the Solomon Islands which had led to many revenge killings.[35] In addition there were questions about another member of the mission disobeying mission policy by owning land and running a commercial plantation. As he met and discussed these problems with staff in several locations, Brown became very anxious about the future of the work.

Brown arrived at the head station of Kokenggolo on the Roviana Lagoon on Sunday morning 30 January 1911. He found a welcoming party of one hundred students lined up along the wharf to greet him. Ten years earlier the local people had been fearful and resistant to the idea of receiving missionaries. He was now led into a church filled with people.

> I was simply delighted with the congregation, the singing and the reverential character of the entire service. I was so affected as I considered

---

34   Brown to Danks, begun at Tulagi, Solomon Islands 24 January 1911, concluded at Kokenggolo, New Georgia, Solomon Islands, 2 March 1911, Private Collection.
35   'Bagga Massacre,' *Brisbane Courier Mail*, 5 January 1911; *Australasian Methodist Missionary Review*, 4 March 1911.

the state of these people a few years ago and their present condition and appearance that I could scarcely control my feelings when speaking. Mr and Mrs Goldie have undoubtedly done a splendid service here. They are much beloved by the people and Mr G. has very great influence all over the District.[36]

Even so, all was clearly not well. Over a period of weeks, Brown recorded his observations in a long letter for Benjamin Danks.[37] There were painful interviews with the young missionary who admitted to killing village pigs and 'the act of sacrilege in the heathen temple and you know how serious these are. I felt very much for the young couple but I confess that I would feel more sympathy if I saw some sign of contrition and repentance and a little more concern for the trouble which has been caused.'[38]

'I have had plenty of knocking about here,' Brown told Danks.[39] Brown endured the battering of a number of very rough sea voyages during that month, including a visit with the Commissioner to the atoll of Ontong Java some 240 miles north of Roviana, but found the anger and bitterness of many around him even harder to bear. The Commissioner was irritated with missionaries in general. The young missionary was rebellious at being transferred from the area on the grounds of being 'guilty of excessive zeal'. Brown's attempts to salvage the mission on Ontong Java were met by strong resistance from the local chief who was 'very angry and time after time declared that there should be no more *Lotu* in his land.'[40] It was only with difficulty that he was persuaded to consider receiving a teacher again. John Goldie was outraged at what he believed was a misuse of power by the Board of Missions and Brown himself in the way the case was handled, later suggesting that Brown had colluded with the Commissioner to overturn Goldie's authority.[41] No one was happy. From Brown's perspective, he had done the difficult task he had been sent to do but it had not been a good experience.

When Brown returned to Sydney with his report, he found that the Board of Missions was debating some of the issues raised by the World Missionary Conference held in Edinburgh, Scotland, in June 1910. They were impressed by the news that other major missionary organisations provided three years of training before sending new workers into the field. Would they have avoided some of their recent failures, they asked themselves, if new staff had been better

---

36   Brown to Danks, begun at Tulagi, Solomon Islands 24 January 1911, concluded at Kokenggolo, New Georgia, Solomon Islands, 2 March 1911.

37   Ibid.

38   Ibid.

39   Ibid.

40   Ibid.

41   John F. Goldie, 'The Solomon Islands,' in *A Century in the Pacific*, ed. J. Colwell, Sydney: William H. Heale, 1914, pp. 559–85, pp. 580–81.

prepared? Danks believed that they ought to offer at least one year of training and Brown supported him. It was clear that ill-prepared missionaries were at risk of making serious mistakes out of ignorance and could face grief and disillusionment of mind and spirit in the harsh realities of a missionary life. The Board decided that they must introduce training of future mission staff and began to form a policy.[42]

* * *

A photograph in the mission journal caught Lydia's attention. A familiar shape, a tall cement chimney above a wide open hearth, stood alone tangled in jungle creepers and undergrowth, bereft of its original house. The caption read 'Remains of mission house, Port Hunter, Duke of York Islands.'[43] Years ago, she had stood every day at that hearth stirring a pot of food for her family, watching the smoke rising up through that chimney into the tropical sky. In those days a roof had covered her and her children had been around her skirts as she cooked. Now it was gone and all that was left was a cracked chimney and a cold hearth overwhelmed in creepers. Nearby the new generation of missionaries had erected a memorial plinth on the site of the first little bush church building and gathered to unveil a plaque. The inscription on the stone read: 'Ebenezer. Hitherto hath the Lord helped us. This stone is raised in joyful praise of the Love of God. 1875–1909.' Chairman Heinrich Fellmann spoke of the memories associated with that place and of the time when the people were afraid to travel freely. 'Kinawanua, as the site is called, is one of the hidden corners of the world. No one goes there, there is no native highway, it is buried in the bush. But how sacred are its memories!… Kinawanua had its day—a great day—and now, in keeping with the growing demands of the work, our headquarters are elsewhere.[44]

Within months she learned that both the schooner *George Brown* and the small mission boat *Litia* would no longer be serving the mission; the *George Brown* was to be sold as it was proving too expensive and the *Litia* had been wrecked, beyond repair, on a reef.[45] It seemed that houses and boats had very temporary lives. Yet while property crumbled, and locations changed, important things lived on. Her family was close around her. Guests were always welcome under her roof. The close ties with Pacific islanders were unchanged and from time to time visiting senior ministers and chiefs stayed in her home with their staff in

---

42 'The needs of our newer missions,' Extract from Minutes of Board of Mission, 9 June 1911, in Wesleyan Methodist Missionary Society Correspondence and Papers, vol. 1, ML CY 1365.

43 *Australasian Methodist Missionary Review*, 4 May 1911.

44 Ibid., 4 July 1911.

45 Ibid., 4 October 1911.

the servants' quarters in the back garden.[46] The old buildings were now long gone but the Christian communities that remained were more important than the preservation of houses.

* * *

The work in New Britain had always been very close to George Brown's heart. Nearly forty years earlier he had promoted the region as a New Mission and had invested all his strength and courage in seeing it begun. It came as a shock to read the annual report of the District Synod in New Britain early in 1912. The staff there admitted to deep discouragement and exhaustion as one person after another had retired due to illness and other causes, leaving a handful of men to struggle on. One wrote of a 'nightmare of pressing duties, which after every moment had been filled, is still bound up with the suggestion of duty neglected.'[47] As Neu Pommern was a German colony, the remnant staff argued, with a German bureaucracy, language and officials, it seemed almost impertinence for the work to be controlled from Australia. 'Surely,' they wrote, 'it is the natural thing for a German Church to do the work in a German colony?' and concluded that 'special difficulties lead us to think strongly that it will be well if Australasian Methodism can be relieved of Mission work in New Britain.'[48]

Predictably, Brown was appalled. For years he had had an ambivalent relationship with Germany, valuing close friendships with individual German people while being critical of German policy in the Pacific. He was becoming very uneasy about rumours that the German Reich in Europe was building up its armaments and increasing the peacetime strength of its army. Now, when invited to be part of a committee to form a policy on whether they should invite the German Methodist Episcopal Church to co-operate with the Australians in mission work in New Britain, or hand the work over to them entirely, he had strong views.[49] In his study at home, surrounded by symbols and artefacts of the people of New Britain, Brown defaced his copy of the printed proposal with a fury of exclamation marks, question marks, 'Why?', 'I don't believe this', 'This is another bogey', 'Who can vouch for these wild statements?' and 'There is no evidence for this'. When he had calmed down a little he framed his response.

---

46 Personal letter from Brown's granddaughter Esmay Leader, daughter of Geoffrey and Ada Brown, to her cousin Millicent Bryant, January 1986.

47 W.H. Cox, in the *Australasian Methodist Missionary Review*, 4 March, 4 October 1911.

48 Report from the New Britain Synod of October 1911, published in the *Australasian Methodist Missionary Review* 4 January 1912.

49 Brown, 'Papers for Board in regard Transfer of New Britain: Private and Confidential for Members of Board only,' for Board meeting on 12 June 1912. Wesleyan Methodist Missionary Society, Correspondences and Papers. Members of the Committee with Brown were clergy B. Danks, J.G. Wheen, W. Bromilow, J.E. Carruthers, Sellors, Beale with seven laymen from the Board, with representatives of the New Britain District W.H. Cox (Chairman), H. Fellmann and K. Schmidt.

He did not doubt, he said, the sincerity or integrity of those who had proposed this plan, but he strongly opposed it. In a long, lucid response, he set out his reasons, including the long and courteous relationships between the Australian Methodists and the German Imperial officials, and the very remote control that would result if the work was in the hands of German and, potentially, American Methodists. He concluded, 'I am absolutely certain that it would be disastrous to our missionary interests and work in Australia and in the older Mission Districts and that so far from helping on the cause of Missions in the Bismarck Archipel, it would most effectually hinder if not absolutely prevent the evangelisation of that great group for many years.'[50]

When the Board of Mission met to consider the committee's report it was clear that the possibility of losing their work in Neu Pommern had galvanised them into action. Rather than relinquishing their work in New Britain, they would strengthen it, applying more resources and staff to the region and inviting the German Methodists and their cousins in the Methodist Episcopal Church in the United States to work beside them to pioneer new work in places where there were large populations still 'in a state of heathen darkness.'[51] Brown and his colleagues had confidence that the work they were doing in remote island communities was God's work, despite the voices of criticism that suggested that they were contributing to the decay and collapse of noble and natural societies and were there for unworthy reasons. They could point to transformations. Men on New Ireland recalled the days when they would never have gone into enemy lands unarmed but now travelled in safety far from home.[52] Three Solomon Island chiefs, formerly head-hunters who had lived with fear and sorcery, sent a message with their gratitude for the missionaries who came to 'teach us things that gave us peace and joy.' They wrote that they were happy because 'the *lotu* lives and grows in our midst. Ten years ago we were in very great darkness, but now our eyes have seen the Light and we are all men who belong to Jesus.'[53]

Dismissing the concerns of the Chairman of New Britain District, W.H. Cox, in June 1912, and despite serious correspondence about the possibility with church leaders in Germany and the United States, by April 1913 the Board decided that the transfer of their work in New Britain was 'neither desirable nor practical'.[54] They declared that there must be renewed energy, resources and staff for all their work in the New Britain District, Papua District and Solomon Islands. With the collaboration of their German and American friends they planned to expand into the new areas of West New Britain, New Hanover and

50   Minutes of Methodist Missions Board, Feb 1913–Nov 1917, ML MOM 205 CY3307, 12 June 1912.
51   Wesleyan Methodist Missionary Society Correspondence and Papers.
52   Rev. T. Reddin, in the *Australasian Methodist Missionary Review*, 4 April 1911.
53   Letter from Solomon Island chiefs from Roviana Lagoon area, Gumi, Gemu and Sasabeti 'To Great Missionary Chiefs in Sydney,' in the *Australasian Methodist Missionary Review*, 29 February 1912.
54   Minutes of Methodist Missions Board, Feb 1913–Nov 1917, 23 April 1913.

Bougainville.[55] Being denied the gift of foresight, the Board of Mission began to set out fresh goals. Each of the three Districts was asked to provide their plans for the future. By the middle of 1913, the Solomon Islands had prepared a three year plan, Papua District (formerly British New Guinea) had pictured eleven years into the future with detailed plans for 1913–1917 and New Britain District had produced an ambitious fifteen year plan noting that 'we rejoice at the prospect of a serious attempt being made to adequately work this extensive District within a given time.'[56] The New Britain staff, perhaps to test the mettle of the Board, sent in their request for new workers; nineteen more ministers, five laymen and forty-eight mission sisters![57] If the Board was serious about expansion, then let them prove it.

It was a beautiful vision. They dreamed that the plan would begin to take real substance in 1914.

---

55   Wesleyan Methodist Missionary Society Correspondence and Papers, vol. 1, ML CY 1365.
56   Minutes of New Britain District Meeting, 17 January 1913, in Wesleyan Methodist Missionary Society Correspondence and Papers, vol. 1.
57   Ibid.

21. 'A creed wide enough'

New South Wales, Brisbane, United Kingdom 1913–1914

When Lydia Brown farewelled her husband on his way to General Conference in Brisbane in early winter 1913 she may have hoped that he would return with fewer responsibilities and more time to spend at home. She knew that George loved to be with the grandchildren, in deep conversation with Amy's boys who were now young men, or surrounded by the little ones as he told them stories by the family fireside. His study and museum gave him so much pleasure as he showed a succession of interested guests through its treasures. But Lydia was a realist. His enthusiasm for these grand gatherings was undiminished by his seventy-eight years and she knew that he carried notes in the hope of having opportunities to speak on issues of mission or on anything at all. He had been working with his colleagues in the Board of Missions to prepare a major Development Plan for missions and was eager to be part of the debates about new possibilities.

Any thoughts of a quiet retirement together evaporated a few days later. George Brown sent a message to Lydia from Brisbane with startling news. He would be leaving for London soon after he returned from Brisbane; he had been chosen to represent the Methodist Church in Australasia at the Centenary celebrations of the Methodist Missionary Society around the world, in October 1913. Not only that, but on the first evening of General Conference, in the Albert Street Methodist Church in Brisbane, he had been elected to the role of President General for the next three years! This was the highest honour for any Methodist across Australasia. Later, when she heard the full story, she knew that his election had been by the narrowest of margins. Of the seven nominees, five received almost no votes while Brown and the Reverend J.E. Carruthers received fifty-two and fifty-nine votes respectively. A second vote was taken and this time the old man with the white whiskers found himself with a bare sixty-one votes against fifty-nine for the younger Carruthers. It was hardly a landslide, but after Carruthers had been overwhelmingly elected as Conference Secretary, the two men found themselves side by side on the official platform with the care of the Conference before them.[1] It was said, later, that the election of George Brown to the chair of President General was a 'happy omen' and 'most fitting and timely' because so much of the business of that Conference related to issues of mission.[2] Even so, both Brown and his wife knew well that it could easily have been otherwise and that the burdens and blessings of the role had now been laid on his shoulders whether they liked it or not.

---

1   Minute Book, Wesleyan Methodist Church General Conference, 1890–1913, ML Methodist Church 581, 12 June 1913.
2   *Australasian Methodist Missionary Review*, June 1891–June 1917, 4 July 1913.

August 4, 1913. *THE A.M. MISSIONARY REVIEW.* 5

Rev. GEORGE BROWN, D.D.

President of the General Conference, and Representative to the Missionary
Centenary Celebrations in England, 1913

Figure 26. Rev. Dr. George Brown 1905.

Source: James Colwell, *Illustrated History of Methodism: Australia 1812–1855; New South Wales and Polynesia 1856–1902*, Sydney: William Brooks & Co., 1904.

Many of the debates during that 1913 General Conference were on issues close to Brown's heart. The Board of Missions had prepared a very courageous Development Plan for the period from 1914 to 1917 and the mood of the gathering was so optimistic that it was passed with no voice of dissent. There were plans for wider membership of the Board of Missions, the appointment of three additional Organising Secretaries to work across the country and a large increase in mission staff and resources. Even the challenge to the wider church to increase revenue by 100 per cent over the next five years was not opposed. They were ready to take up a new region for mission in India as well as improving their pre-service preparation and education for mission staff. A new General Secretary, the Reverend John G. Wheen, was appointed to follow Benjamin Danks on his retirement. A warm letter was to be sent to their brethren in the Methodist Episcopal Church in Germany with great appreciation for the excellent men who had been sent, and would be sent in future, to work beside the Australians in the German colonies of Neu Pommern/New Britain and Samoa, 'assuring the German church of the Christian affection and high esteem which the General Conference cherishes towards them and their work.'[3] The sad separation of the Church in Tonga, which had been a cause of pain for over twenty-five years, was still raw but was showing some signs of a possible healing and reunion. Brown was anxious that they be given all possible encouragement by the Methodists in Australia and consented to be a member of yet another committee willing to offer help toward reconciliation. The Conference sent a message to both the Free Church of Tonga and the Wesleyan Church of Tonga, assuring them of prayer for their future reunion, saying that 'should they decide to [be reconciled], the Conference will rejoice with exceeding joy, and will heartily welcome the Ministers, Members and Adherents of both churches to fellowship and brotherhood of the Australian Church.'[4]

From his elevated seat in the President-General's chair, as the Conference finally came close to an end, Brown had a perfect opportunity to tell his church community what he had learned over a lifetime. He may have sometimes regretted that he had been given no formal training in theology but he knew what he believed and he was clear on what drove him to do what he did. He had written detailed notes and spoke from them. He told the gathering, 'I never attempt to apologise for foreign mission work or defend it either on the grounds of expediency, or only on the grounds of successes that have been achieved. We have the divine command, and the test of love is our obedience to it.'[5] He added,

---

3   Minute Book, Wesleyan Methodist Church General Conference, 1890–1913, 12 June 1913.
4   Ibid.
5   Brown, Speech notes, Methodist General Conference, Brisbane, 1913, Wesleyan Methodist Missionary Society Correspondence and Papers, ML CY 1365.

The Fatherhood of God, the brotherhood of all men, the capacity of all men to receive the truths of the gospel and to manifest those truths in their lives and in their characters. Christ himself based his command on the great truth of the divine fatherhood and our common brotherhood. I do not attempt to expound these fundamental truths except to say that in my intercourse with savage peoples I have always found that the declaration that One is our Father, even God, and that we are all members of His family, is the Great Truth which is the surest way to commend the gospel to them. The Fatherhood of God, the redemption of the world by Christ, the presence and work of the Holy Spirit and the fact that we all, black, brown and white are the children of God is a creed wide enough for all of the peoples to whom we go and wide enough for all of us here at home.[6]

He told them that he believed in 'the capacity of all men everywhere to receive the gospel, to assimilate its truths and to manifest in their lives its power to regenerate and change their entire nature and character.'[7] His audience chuckled when he suggested some of the definitions of 'man'—'man is an animal which eats cooked food' or 'an animal which shaves'—but were silent when he said that he liked best John Wesley's definition: 'Man is a creature capable of God.'[8] He had witnessed, he said, 'the compelling power of love,' a love that transformed people and societies. Widows were no longer strangled. Live infants were no longer buried with their dead mothers. Shipwrecked strangers were no longer clubbed and eaten. Men no longer sailed in war canoes to gather the heads of their neighbours. Men could travel and women could work in their gardens in peace and security. Generosity replaced greed and the peacemaker replaced the armed warrior. These were not simply changes forced on unwilling communities by forceful authority but deep changes in thought, attitude and character as men and women became new creatures under the influence of the Christian gospel.

To this point in his address he was on secure ground, material he had spoken many times in the past. But now his notes faltered. At the bottom of the page, after the thoughtful notes on familiar themes, was a scribbled afterthought. He had written 'to do with Australia, the claims of Aborigines'. The Australian Aborigines? In all his years of commitment to the work of mission it seemed that his face had always been turned out to sea, looking toward the islands in the far sunrise. Rarely had he encountered Aboriginal people and though he was seen as an authority on the peoples of the Pacific he knew almost nothing

---

6   Brown, Speech notes, Methodist General Conference, Brisbane, 1913, Wesleyan Methodist Missionary Society Correspondence and Papers.
7   Ibid.
8   Ibid.

about the hidden people of the inland and the far north of the country. It came as a painful jolt as he realised that other people were not blind to the first people of the country. Others were familiar with stories of violence and abuse against Aboriginal people at the hands of those who coveted their country, others saw human need, and others recognised their common humanity. It must have stung him when, near the end of Conference, a plea was made for Christian ministry among the Aboriginal people of the Northern Territory. The grand Development Plan presented by the Board of Mission had not even mentioned such an enterprise, although it was true that the Reverend Samuel B. Fellows, one time missionary in British New Guinea and now a minister in Western Australia, had raised the question at the Annual Meeting of the Board early in the year.[9] But now, at the last minute when the meetings of Conference were almost finished, voices were being raised pointing out that the Methodist Church had no agent anywhere in this work, that 'Her interest in the aborigines [sic] appears to have evaporated … it is her reproach that she has not cast a pitying eye nor stretched a helping hand towards the poor Australian heathen.… Many hearts have been troubled over this neglect over the past few years.'[10]

Words like 'inexcusable neglect' and 'a matter of urgency' were spoken. It was pointed out that an Interdenominational Committee meeting in Victoria was recommending that the churches take up the challenge in the Northern Territory, even suggesting distinct spheres of influence. If such a work were taken up by the churches on the latest modern lines, it was said that the Government was interested in supporting it. To his chagrin, George Brown saw that, unlike his concern for the people of the Pacific islands, he had never had a strong sense of call to offer Christian witness or service to the first people of the land. His back had been turned to them. He could think of excuses, but at that moment any excuse would sound hollow. If indeed he truly believed that all people were the children of God, and that this was a 'creed wide enough' to include everyone, he could no longer ignore the Aboriginal peoples of the land.

Before the members of Conference dispersed to return to their various States, an additional Minute was written into the vast leather-bound Minute Book, following the final statement that they would meet again in Melbourne in May 1917. Under the heading of Supplementary Agenda, it stated that 'the General Conference commence a Methodist Mission among the Aborigines of the Northern Territory,' accepting the sphere proposed by the Interdenominational committee in Victoria and passing responsibility to the Board of Mission to organise and find funds for this new enterprise.[11] Brown was not the only one

---

9   Minutes, Annual Meeting of Methodist Board of Missions, February 1913.

10   Joseph Bowes, 'The Australian Aborigine,' in *A Century in the Pacific*, ed. James Colwell, Sydney: William H. Beale, 1914, pp. 151–74, p. 172.

11   Minute Book, Wesleyan Methodist Church General Conference, 1890–1913, 12 June 1913.

who left the Conference still uncertain quite what this decision would mean in practice. An announcement about the new task in the church journal said, 'Just what this will mean in the way of a call for additional funds and workers, we cannot say at present. But we doubt not that both will be forthcoming when the church has been told what is needed.'[12] It was not long before Brown was invited to join the new Australian Association for the Protection of Native Races, just formed in 1913,[13] to serve as vice-president, but it is unlikely that he was able to give it any time that year. His mind was already preparing for another voyage.

* * *

There were only a few weeks between Brown's return from Brisbane and his departure for London, with Monica as companion. At the July meeting of the Board of Missions Brown's friends recorded their congratulations on his elevation to the role of President General and their hope that 'during the whole term of his Presidency he may be given strength of body and vigour of mind for the onerous duties of that high office.'[14] A brief record was made of the instruction from General Conference: 'A mission to the Australian Aborigines is to be commenced. A definite sphere is suggested. A special appeal is authorised.'[15] It was in the Minutes, but it would be months before there would be any sign of further action.

* * *

The first time George Brown had sailed to London more than sixty years earlier, he had been Geo. Brown, runaway youth from the north; a lad with limited education and a history of unfortunate attempts at employment, hiding from the agents his father had sent to drag him home in disgrace. Now he was to sail for London again and his father would not have recognised him. This time he was the Reverend Dr. George Brown, Fellow of Royal Geographical Society, Corresponding Member of the Zoological Society, farewelled and honoured by the Governor of New South Wales and the Governor-General, the Anglican Primate, the Presbyterian Moderator General, the President of the Congregational Union in Australia and New Zealand, Professors of the University of Sydney and leaders of his own Methodist Church.[16] On the day he sailed, 28 July 1913, he wrote a message for the Methodists across Australia. He urged them to take seriously the demands of the new Development Plan for the expansion of mission work and asked for prayer that

---

12 *Australasian Methodist Missionary Review*, 4 August 1913.

13 'Obituary of George Brown,' *Sydney Morning Herald*, May 1917.

14 Minutes of Methodist Missions Board, Feb 1913–Nov 1917, 15 July 1913, ML MOM 205 CY3307.

15 Ibid.

16 J.E. Carruthers, *Lights in the Southern Sky*, Sydney: Methodist Book Depot, 1924, pp. 65–66.

the whole church may be possessed by a spirit of consecrated generosity and sustained zeal … that perfect harmony may prevail among us …that [the Board of Missions] may be granted wisdom to discern and grace to do the will of God … that people may be prompted to give freely as God may prosper them … that among our young men and women there may be found many with the right spirit and with needed qualifications and gifts to go forth in the all-prevailing Name as ambassadors of Jesus Christ.[17]

It was a triumphant return to the land of his birth. He had walked the streets of London as a young migrant ready to sail to the far side of the earth in 1855 and returned there in 1886 and again in 1908 with stories of regions so obscure to the people of British Methodism that they had trouble finding them on the map. Now, joining the international gathering of Methodists to celebrate the centenary of their missionary enterprise in October 1913, he was the legendary George Brown, pioneer, explorer, storyteller and hero. When he was introduced to the packed audience in the Albert Hall, the whole assembly rose to their feet to applaud and honour 'the veteran from the antipodes.'[18] He was invited to speak at churches across the land, with a demanding program of travel. A writer enthused,

Mr Brown will rank with Livingstone, Moffat, Chalmers and Hannington as a great pioneer missionary and Christian explorer, as an enlightener of dark lands, an opener of closed ports, a herald of civilisation, and a notable promoter of trade and commerce…. [Island inhabitants have been] transformed from naked savages to peaceable and decent folks.[19]

It was sobering to have his name linked with such men—missionaries whose lives had ended violently in Africa and in New Guinea. He too might easily have died violently on a number of occasions but, somehow, he had survived to old age and honour. It pleased him to have the Pacific and its peoples brought before the gaze of the public. Over the years, other regions of Methodist missionary endeavour had been much better known, the vast populations of India and China, the regions of Africa and the islands of the West Indies; even the missionary maps had shown only one side of the planet with perhaps a sliver of coastline to suggest Australia but no sign of the islands across the expanse of the Pacific Ocean. The places and people closest to Brown's heart had been invisible to audiences in Great Britain. Perhaps, however, Brown was not so happy to be seen as chiefly a person who promoted trade and 'civilisation'. Certainly he had a strong sense of being part of a great colonial British Empire,

17 *Australasian Methodist Missionary Review*, 4 August 1913.
18 Brown, Letter, 3 October 1913, in the *Australasian Methodist Missionary Review*, 4 December 1913.
19 'The World's Work,' quoted in the *Australasian Methodist Missionary Review*, 4 December 1913.

and understood the historic role of missionaries in many of the colonies. Yet he would have warmed to one of the major addresses of the Centenary celebrations where a speaker declared that 'tonight all our Imperial and racial enthusiasm is lost in the higher patriotism of the Kingdom of Heaven.'[20]

To the relief of Monica Brown, who had the task of looking after her father's health and comfort, Brown maintained his energy over the months in England, thriving on the attention and stimulation, travelling, meeting church leaders and scientists, family members and politicians. It was a great delight to him to be invited to chair a meeting of the General Committee of the Wesleyan Methodist Missionary Society, and to sit with men at the very heart of the web of Methodist missions spun around the world.[21] Far from the ordinary realities of tropical storm and mosquitoes, sunburn and frustration, isolation and irritation, his admirers wove a cloak of heroics over the shape of his life. Perhaps he had a private chuckle, remembering those men long ago in Auckland who had feared that he was too 'ladylike' to survive the rigours of a missionary life, when he learned that someone wanted to write about him for the *Boys' Own Annual*.[22] As the bleak northern winter began to soften to spring, George Brown and his daughter Monica prepared to sail for home. There was a brief temptation to stay on longer. If he were willing to delay his departure until the annual conferring of degrees at Oxford University, two men from the world of the aristocracy, politics and the sciences were eager to arrange for him to be awarded an honorary doctorate from Oxford.[23] It was a flattering invitation but, although he had always called England 'Home', true home was with Lydia and his family.

It would have been impossible for anyone with a nose for the whiff of political unease and the aroma of approaching conflict to miss the signs in Europe and Great Britain early in 1914. George Brown spent time with men in high places and was aware of a growing anxiety. He and Monica sailed from England for Sydney on 14 March 1914. He would not return.

In January 1914, Lydia stood on the deck of the new mission ketch, just launched in Sydney Harbour. After the *Litia* came to grief on the reef the previous year, Lydia Brown had assumed that her name would now disappear from the islands. The Board thought otherwise, and when a new ketch was commissioned they

---

20 Sir George Smith, President of the Wesleyan Laymen's Missionary Movement, Address given at Albert Hall, London at Centenary Meeting, October 1913, in the *Australasian Methodist Missionary Review*, 4 December 1913.

21 *Australasian Methodist Missionary Review*, 4 April 1914.

22 Letter of request to Brown from the editor of *Boys' Own Annual*, 6 November 1913, Brown, Correspondence, 1908–1916, ML MSS 263/1 CY 3405.

23 Letter from Viscount Bryce to Sir S.J. Way expressing disappointment that Brown was unwilling to delay departure in order to receive honorary degree from Oxford, 4 March 1914, Brown, Correspondence, 1908–1916.

announced that this too would be called the *Litia*,[24] and would serve the islands of New Britain, New Ireland and the Duke of York Islands, sailing in those waters that had once been so familiar to her and her family.[25] Standing with the crowd on deck, Lydia looked around her at the masts and listened to the clatter of ropes in the wind. She had no desire to sail in her. Her days of venturing across endless ocean in very small ships were behind her, and she was thankful. Even so, she prayed for those who would trust themselves to the care of the *Litia*, and those who would look hopefully for her coming with news, supplies and friends to their lonely stations.

News of the Board of Missions came to the Brown household even while her husband was away. Despite the optimism about the expansion of their mission work at General Conference, and the enthusiastic response to their ambitious Development Plan, the Board was struggling. Words were not being matched by practical action. Funds were coming in too slowly to support the existing work, let alone anything new. Pressure of new demands, a large number of retirements and resignations, a cyclone in Fiji, some difficult discipline problems combined with congregations delaying their contributions all had the new General Secretary, John Wheen, very worried indeed. He sent out urgent appeals. The situation was so dire that some sixteen laymen, members of the Board, undertook to give their personal guarantee to the bank for £12,000, but that was only a temporary solution. Negotiations with the Methodist Episcopal Church in Germany were promising, with more men arriving to serve in the New Britain District and the expectation of financial help from Germany, but that would not help them to fulfil their commitment to begin new work in North Australia. Month after month passed by and action for work among the Aboriginal communities was repeatedly postponed.

A cartoon in the monthly *Australasian Methodist Missionary Review* was unintentionally prophetic. It depicted several little vessels setting out across the sea toward billowing black clouds, while a beam from a lighthouse shone to light their way. The caption spoke of mission staff setting off to bring light to dark places with the question: '1914–1918????'[26] An analogy used by Wheen, as he urged Methodist congregations to greater generosity, was also timely. In the streets of Sydney he had recently witnessed a contingent of 18,000 young military trainees marching in all their confidence and pride. Something had blocked the way ahead and the whole mass of men was forced to mark time, going nowhere despite their strength and numbers. Wheen suggested that the

---

24   Minutes of Wesleyan Methodist Missions Board, Feb 1913–Nov 1917, 3 October 1913.
25   *Australasian Methodist Missionary Review*, 4 February 1914.
26   Ibid., 4 July 1913.

Church was blocked and simply marking time.[27] Later, those who saw the young soldiers marching in Sydney streets that day would remember them for other reasons.

New Britain District Synod, Raluana, 1913. *Photo: Anon.*

Figure 27. New Britain District Synod, meeting at Raluana, New Britain in 1913.

Source: The *Australasian Methodist Missionary Review*, June 1914.

George Brown and his daughter returned to Sydney to observe what appeared to be a period of stability and progress. A good working agreement had been reached with the Methodist Episcopal Church in Germany. New young men were arriving from Germany with their brides as well as single women workers.[28] Young Australian couples were also arriving and there was a sense of fresh optimism.[29] Heinrich and Johanna Fellmann had been given permission to move to Sydney in 1913, after fifteen years in the islands, and Heinrich was busily working on a revision of Rickard's translation of the New Testament into the Tolai language.[30] By early 1914 he had moved on to a translation of the Old Testament and had

---

27 Ibid., 4 March 1914.

28 German Methodist staff during 1913–14 included clergy H. Fellmann, H. Wenzel, K. Wenzel, E. Boettcher, K. Schmidt and A. Pratsch and their wives, with single women Sisters Amelia and Annah. Pratsch was due to leave Europe in April 1914.

29 Australian mission staff included clergy W.H. Cox (Chairman), T.B. Lancaster, W. Stocks, J. Margetts and their wives, sisters Kendrick, Ricketts, McKee and McInnes, laymen Broom and Tunnicliff.

30 Minutes of Methodist Missions Board, Feb 1913–Nov 1917, February 1913.

been given an extension of his time in Sydney for this work.[31] A fruit of the great World Missionary Conference in Edinburgh in 1910 was a new zeal and energy in Germany for remote missionary enterprises. Major donations for the work in Neu Pommern could be expected soon from both imperial government and private sources. In the current favourable circumstances, it was reported by a German source that the Methodist Missionary Society in Australia 'will be sure to find the wholehearted support of the German Government and public.'[32]

* * *

Lydia Brown stared at the images in the magazine. Although the photographs were in black and white she could see the colours in her mind and smell the aromas of toasted coconut and frangipani. A wedding party on Easter Monday 1914, caught in the breeze on the deck of the *Litia* bright with bunting, on the way across the channel from the Duke of York Islands to New Britain; friends wait with music and feasting and for Cox to perform the marriage ceremony.[33] Other images showed large groups of young mission staff, Fijian, German and Australian men and women.[34] It was hard to believe that this was the same place where she once had lived. Was this the region of memory where she shed tears of grief, and waited endlessly for her man to come home, and comforted the sick and dying, and cooked dinner for explorers, traders and naval officers, and fed and cleansed the sores of foreign refugees, and walked with her husband through jungle leaves of monstrous dimensions, and talked with cannibals, and buried her children? Her name and his were there still, in ship and college, but the world she remembered had been changed into groomed gardens and ordered coconut and cocoa bean plantations, grand houses, a colonial headquarters complete with police and militia, courts of law and the whole edifice of island government and the intricacies of colonial social life. She was glad that these young people could begin their marriages and their work in a place that seemed safe and tamed. Although she knew she would never go back, she was glad that she had seen it when she did, raw and untamed though it was.

At a meeting of the Board of Missions in July 1914, they honoured and farewelled Sir William Macgregor. Macgregor was leaving Australia after long service as Governor of Queensland and formerly Governor of British New Guinea. George Brown was in the chair and recalled the significance of Macgregor's invitation to the Methodists back in 1890 to begin work in the eastern islands of British New Guinea. Remarkable changes had taken place since that time. Macgregor told them that he had believed the people of Dobu and Normanby Island were among the wildest on the face of the earth and recalled his anxiety for the safety

---

31 *Australasian Methodist Missionary Review*, 4 February 1914.
32 Rev. Karl Schmidt, 'A missionary revival in Germany,' in *Australasian Methodist Missionary Review*, 4 February 1914, pp. 11–12.
33 Wedding of Mr. F. Broom and Miss Cherrie, in *Australasian Methodist Missionary Review*, 4 August 1914.
34 The *Australasian Methodist Missionary Review*, 4 February 1914.

of the pioneer party of Methodists. It was encouraging for Brown and his friends to hear Macgregor's sincere admiration for the work of the Methodist missions, both in Fiji and in British New Guinea. These days they could report some 25,000 people attending worship and fifty-seven local men trained as village pastors in what had been a violent community. Macgregor turned to Brown. He hoped, he said, that they would long have the 'unique experience and the great wisdom of his friend Dr Brown, on whose counsels they could place perfect reliance. No man had gone through the fire in the way Dr Brown had done.'[35] Around the room there were murmurs of 'Hear, hear!'[36]

On 28 June 1914, two weeks before the Board met to bask in praise for the coming of peace to a warlike society, on the far side of the planet an Archduke and his wife had been assassinated—the tinder to set wildfires ablaze across civilised Europe. Ancient tribal groups had already begun to mass their warriors, call on their traditional allies and rattle their weapons. The noise would soon be heard in Australia and the Pacific islands.

At the beginning of August 1914, in New Britain, Australian Methodist W.H. Cox gave a gift to Dr. Hahl, Governor, as he prepared to leave for Germany, in appreciation for 'his friendly and helpful attitude toward the Mission and its work.'[37] It was a copy of the new translation of the New Testament prepared by Heinrich Fellmann, in the Tolai language of New Britain.[38] In Sydney the Board of Missions was delighted to receive a bank draft from Germany for £1,478/15/8, a gift as promised by Bishop Nuelsen of the German Methodist Episcopal Church through the Kaiser's Jubilee Fund.[39]

On 5 August 1914 the news broke. Australia, through her ties with Great Britain was at war with Germany.

---

35 *Sydney Morning Herald*, 17 July 1914; *Australasian Methodist Missionary Review*, 4 August 1914.
36 Ibid.
37 *Australasian Methodist Missionary Review*, 4 September 1914.
38 Ibid.
39 Ibid., 5 October 1914.

22. 'Beloved chief and father'

New South Wales, New Zealand, Fiji, Tonga, Samoa, Queensland
1914–1917

Within days of the news that the Australian Federal Government would mobilise in support of Britain, Lydia wrote to her German friend Johanna Fellmann. Johanna and Heinrich Fellmann were now living in Sydney while Heinrich worked on translation and their older children were living with family members in Germany. Lydia wrote, 'My dear Mrs Fellmann, I cannot tell you how much we all feel for you and Mr Fellmann in the present very trying time and what anxiety you must be feeling for your dear children and friends far away in Germany.' She continued,

> I have been feeling so miserable myself at this sudden breaking out of war and every day the news seems to get worse and worse. We must just go to our Heavenly Father in prayer and trust in Him that He may control and rule all events.... It is very sad indeed to hear of such terrible loss of life and this modern warfare is so very cruel. Monica saw Mr Fellmann this afternoon and she did feel so sorry for him when he seemed so broken-hearted, but may God comfort you both in this sore affliction.... It must be so hard for you when all your friends are in the midst of it all in Germany. How is your dear Mother and your dear boys?... I thought I would like to write you a few lines of sympathy and love ... in which Dr Brown and the girls join.[1]

* * *

George Brown, as President-General of the Methodist Church in Australia, had to consider how to be a Christian leader in a time of national turmoil. He was also very concerned for the combined Australian and German missionary community in New Britain District. News of atrocities in Belgium was filtering through to Australia and young Australian men were already enlisting in high excitement, among them their grandson, twenty-one-year-old teacher Leslie Dinning. His grandfather was proud of his 'fine imperial attitude' as he began his training.

---

1   Lydia Brown to Johanna Fellmann, 7 August 1914, private collection.

Long before the first troops from Australia were anywhere near the scenes of battle in Europe, the war had come suddenly and astonishingly to the Pacific. The Board of Missions was staggered to learn that the first Australian military action of the war had taken place not in distant Europe but in the region they knew as New Britain District. Brown had argued vigorously with W.H. Cox against handing over the District of New Britain/Neu Pommern to the German Church, even though it was a German colony. By September 1914, the Board learned that Neu Pommern had been wrested away from the control of the German colonial authority and was now in hands of an Australian military force. Because there was a superior German wireless installation near Rabaul, as part of a chain providing rapid communication from Berlin to the German fleet in the Pacific, an Australian force was deployed to the area. In a swift action, six Australian ships and two submarines entered Simpson Harbour at Rabaul on 11 September 1914 and, after a brief but violent action, the British flag was hoisted, the Australians had declared a military occupation and, by 21 September the Terms of Capitulation had been signed by German Governor Haber. It was agreed that the German colonial officials would remain at their posts under the military occupation force.[2] In Samoa, the German Governor had surrendered to British naval ships, without violence, by 29 August.[3] The series of detailed maps of some of their missionary regions, recently commissioned by the Board of Missions for distribution to their supporters, were going to be out-of-date before they were even published.[4]

For weeks there was no further news from New Britain. The men of the Board of Missions anxiously tried to imagine what was happening. All the news of war was not only horrifying but unbelievable. George Brown had lived among warring tribes for most of his lifetime; Samoan warriors bearing severed heads, refugees from battle in his own kitchen, the slingshots and axes of angry men of New Britain, the rows of skulls from tribal conflicts in British New Guinea, the elegant enmity of fine war canoes in the Solomon Islands, the Fijian war clubs in his museum. But this was different. As one of their group wrote: 'The dogs of war have been let loose and the great Christian nations of Europe are being deluged with human blood. A few months ago it seemed impossible.'[5] What made it so shocking was that this conflict in Europe was between nations who claimed to be Christian. The Board had watched the growing understanding between British, Australian and German co-workers in New Britain and believed that it was a sign that they saw themselves as brothers and sisters in Christ. Now everything seemed shaken. In rejection of the recent public outcry against all

2   S.S. Mackenzie, *The Australians at Rabaul. The Capture and Administration of the German Possessions in the Southern Pacific*, in *Official History of Australia in the War of 1914–1918*, 12 volumes, vol. x, St. Lucia: University of Queensland Press [1921–1942], 10th edition, 1941, pp. 120–26.
3   *Australasian Methodist Missionary Review*, 5 October 1914.
4   Ibid., 4 December 1914.
5   Ibid., 5 October 1914.

things German, the Board published a wedding photograph of new missionary, the Reverend K.A. Wenzel and his bride Gertrude with a background of palms and the comment that the German staff in New Britain were, 'greatly beloved by their Australian comrades, and whatever changes may come in the future as the result of international complications, we shall always rejoice that German Methodism and Australian Methodism have been associated in this work.'[6]

September 1914 was a month of mixed emotions. George Brown had the honour of opening the grand new Methodist Church on Tryon Road, Lindfield, in peaceful Sydney. They farewelled their grandson Leslie Dinning as he sailed for Europe with the Expeditionary Force and, to their relief, they had news from New Britain. Despite 'a good deal of inconvenience' as a result of the sudden overturning of the German regime, the mission staff was safe and well. They were thankful that 'none of the Missionaries have been called upon to take any active part in the military operations on either side.'[7]

If they thought that the Methodist missionary community could go on with their work undisturbed, they were wrong. Sometime after the event, news of a very disturbing incident reached Brown. The Methodist Chairman W.H. Cox had gone in the *Litia* from the Duke of York Islands to visit the Wenzels on New Ireland. Walking through the German township of Namatanai on his way to the mission, he was seen by a group of disgruntled German residents who were feeling very antagonistic toward missionaries, particularly British missionaries. They had been drinking heavily and brooding over rumours that Cox was a spy. Late that night, fuelled by alcohol and rage, this group approached the mission house. The German missionary, K.A. Wenzel, was lured away from the house on a false errand. Two armed men burst into the house where Cox was drinking tea with Mrs. Wenzel. Cox was dragged outside at pistol point and hauled down the steps from the verandah where three other drunken men were waiting. Gertrude Wenzel, appalled at the actions of her countrymen, demanded to know what they intended to do, and was ordered back into the house. She ran out through the night to search for her husband. By the time the young couple arrived back at their house, the assailants were fleeing, leaving Cox severely bruised after being struck some thirty strokes with a cane. Shaken and distressed, Cox and the Wenzels set out on a nightmare journey through the darkness to try to walk across the island to the safety of the *Litia*, becoming lost on the way. When they finally reached safety, Cox chose to go on immediately to report the assault to Australian Administrator Colonel William Holmes in Rabaul.[8] The matter did not stop there. The entire community, both Australian and German, in the

---

6   Ibid., Neville Threlfall, *Mangroves, Coconuts and Frangipani: The Story of Rabaul*, Rabaul Historical Society, East New Britain Province, Papua New Guinea in collaboration with Neville Threlfall, 2012.

7   Ibid., 4 November 1914. Letters from W.H. Cox, 27 Sept 1914, and K. Schmidt, 22 Sept 1914.

8   Mackenzie, *The Australians at Rabaul*, pp. 120–26; *Australasian Methodist Missionary Review*, 4 December 1914.

area of New Britain was shocked, dismayed that the conduct of a few drunken individuals could bring such discredit on their neighbours. Colonel Holmes sent a detachment of men to arrest the attackers and in due course ordered a 'short, sharp, and exemplary punishment.[9] German male residents were commanded to be present to witness the humiliation of the perpetrators with an extended caning in a public square, but most were given permission to leave after Colonel Holmes made a speech justifying his actions. The German residents were highly offended by this event and experienced colonial administrators withdrew from their roles as advisors to the Australians on local affairs.[10]

* * *

War or no war, George Brown carried the responsibilities of President General and that meant more travel. When invitations came for him to be present at the Methodist Conference in New Zealand in 1915, it gave him an opportunity of travel to some of the regions that had been important to him over the years. This time Lizzie Brown and his son-in-law Percy Slade travelled with him. They left for Auckland, New Zealand on 19 February 1915. Following the Conference, they spent six weeks touring and speaking in churches around the North and South Islands. In Auckland, so far from the sound of gunfire and battle chaos, they first heard confused news of a distant battle. On a rocky hillside in Turkey overlooking the narrow strait called the Dardanelles his grandson Leslie lay wounded but would live. Perhaps it was the first time Brown had heard the name Gallipoli.

Brown must have known that this could be his last chance to visit places and people who had been important to him. At seventy-nine his physical strength was beginning to diminish even though his fiercely independent spirit drove him on. From New Zealand they sailed to Fiji for one day, where he visited the recently relocated Methodist educational complex at Davuilevu.[11] Two days later they reached Tonga where the Reverend Rodger Page and his wife Hannah welcomed them. Twenty years had passed since Brown had last been in Tonga. There were still two separate Churches—the Free Church and the Wesleyan Church—but he wrote, 'I could not, of course, help contrasting the peace and harmony which now prevails in Tonga with the disturbed conditions which existed here some twenty years ago, and I am very glad indeed that I was permitted to witness the great change.'[12]

---

9   Ibid.
10   Threlfall, Neville, *Mangroves, Coconuts and Frangipani: The Story of Rabaul*, Rabaul Historical Society, East New Britain Province, Papua New Guinea in collaboration with Neville Threlfall, 2012, pp.132–33.
11   A. Harold Wood, *Overseas Missions of the Australian Methodist Church, Vol. 11, Fiji*, Melbourne: Aldersgate Press, 1978, pp. 293–96.
12   *Australasian Methodist Missionary Review*, 4 August 1915.

For the first time in twenty years, Brown met with the President of the Free Church, J.B. Watkin. The two old men shared many painful memories of things done and words said that were regrettable. Brown wrote home, 'We both agreed that there had been great mistakes made by both parties, and that I am sure is a good step towards reunion.'[13] When Brown was invited to preach in the central church on Mount Zion to a crowded congregation he was hesitant about his memory of the Tongan language, but confident in his message. He spoke from Romans 10:12 'For there is no difference between Jew and Gentile – the same Lord is Lord of all and richly blesses all who call on him.'[14] After conversations with key Tongan leaders he concluded that a reunion of the Churches could be a possibility in the near future. However it would be another decade before a partial reunion would be effected, and then only with difficulty.[15]

* * *

On the far side of the world men were locked in battles in France and Flanders and in the unforgiving region of Gallipoli. In the Pacific, George Brown travelled on, landing in Samoa on 9 June 1915. As President General, Brown was present for the inauguration of the new Constitution for that District. There was an emotional welcome for 'Misi Palauni'. The Samoan language, so deeply embedded in memory, came back and he amazed newer mission staff with his idiomatic fluency. With the support of Lizzie Brown, on her first visit to Samoa since she left there as a twelve-year-old girl, and Percy Slade, 'the grand old man of the South Seas' set out on a demanding journey around Savai'i and Upolu. They travelled from village to village; night journeys by whale boat, by horse and trap, on foot, carried in a special chair and even twenty kilometres on horseback.[16] He had to admit to being exhausted, sunburned and aching at the end of each day. A violent storm chased them back across the water to Apia. It was understandable if he was weary; during three weeks in Samoa he had travelled at least 500 kilometres, preached fluently in a language he had rarely used in forty years, addressed nearly thirty meetings great and small, met with chiefs and children, been offered generous feasts and shaken hands with endless queues of well-wishers. When the people gathered for a last farewell service the emotion was intense. It was, he wrote, 'the greatest gathering I have ever seen in Samoa.... I have never ceased to love them, and I am very thankful that they still remember with affection their old Missionary.'[17]

---

13   Ibid.
14   Ibid.
15   Wood, *Overseas Missions of the Australian Methodist Church Vol. 1, Tonga and Samoa*, pp. 216–25.
16   Rev. E.J. Neil's account of Brown's visit, in the *Australasian Methodist Missionary Review*, 4 September 1915.
17   *Australasian Methodist Missionary Review*, 4 October 1915.

A witness wrote, 'The memory of our last look upon our beloved father in Israel, as he waved a last adieu, will ever remain.... His courageous work, his great sacrifice, his kindly advice, his paternal love.... Farewell, beloved chief and father, and may God bless thee as thou hast blessed us.'[18] Old men wept as they said goodbye. George Brown sailed from Samoa on 3 July 1915, his own 'eyes dimmed with tears of gratitude and affection.' They all understood that he would never return.[19]

* * *

The protective wall that had sheltered them while they travelled through the islands was ruptured when they arrived back in Sydney in July 1915. The war in Europe, which had seemed so remote from the perspective of a welcome feast in a Samoan village was suddenly very near and very horrifying. Lydia reported anxiously that young men from the congregations at Gordon and Lindfield had enlisted. She and her daughters joined other women every week to pray for their boys and for peace. Johanna Fellmann had a new baby, Liselotte, born in Bondi, Sydney in April 1915, but she and Heinrich were now seen as enemy aliens. Australian men were still on the barren killing cliffs of Gallipoli, trapped in a deadlock that seemed to go on and on, while others fought in the mud of France. The Brown's grandson Leslie was recovering from his wounds. Terrible lists of the dead and wounded appeared in the papers, even though journalists tried to give the impression that the Allies were triumphing. Their church at home was planning to celebrate the centenary of Methodism in Australia, the arrival of the Reverend Samuel Leigh in Sydney in August 1815,[20] and spoke optimistically about plans for new work in North Australia. Yet it seemed hard to be hopeful and feel like celebrating anything while so many men were in grave danger and dying in Europe. In a letter to a friend in England early in the war, Brown had written,

> We can think or speak of nothing but the war these days ... there will, I fear, be a fearful sacrifice of life before the end of the war. The Kaiser will bitterly regret his mad folly, and there will be many alterations to be made to the map of Europe and other maps when peace is established.... We are all intensely loyal here and intend to stand by the dear old Motherland to the very last ditch if necessary.[21]

* * *

18   Ibid., 4 September 1915.
19   Ibid., 4 October 1915.
20   Ibid., 5 July 1915.
21   Brown to minister in UK, 15 September 1914, Correspondence, 1908–1916, ML MSS 263/1 CY 3405.

Not long after his return from Samoa, George Brown began to consider arranging his affairs. Perhaps he realised that his own life was finite. The Librarian at the relatively new Mitchell Library in Sydney invited him to 'carefully consider bequeathing to this Library your manuscripts and books relating to your magnificent labours in the Pacific.'[22] His museum and personal library was crowded with objects that he valued, with shelves and glass cases packed with artefacts, objects suspended from the ceiling, books and documents crammed into every space. New gifts continued to arrive. He knew that sensible decisions would have to be made, even though it was an overwhelming prospect.[23] He was determined that his artefacts should remain as a single collection in his own name, but it was difficult to find a suitable, and willing, recipient. He completed and signed his will shortly before his eightieth birthday.[24]

* * *

It was a strange and subdued Christmas that year of 1915. Around the family dinner table when the extended family gathered at 'Kinawanua' there was the empty space where Leslie Dinning might have sat, and his brother Stanley now announced that he was enlisting.[25] The Australian troops on Gallipoli were silently withdrawn in the week before Christmas, leaving the empty dugouts and their dead; Leslie was on his way to the trenches of France. At the Christmas services at Gordon and Lindfield, young men were missing from their places and women asked anxiously for news. Lydia Brown wanted to gather all her children and grandchildren closely around her but knew that it was not possible. Optimism that had once thought that the war would be over by Christmas was crushed. Two Christmases had passed and there was no end to war in sight.

It was a difficult time to be a church leader. Behind every conversation, every plan, every decision lay the dark shadow of a distant war. The regular ministries of the churches were being distracted from their work. Some seemed to be hiding from the enormity of the war by retreating into their own very small worlds. Men were enlisting to fight and those who had not volunteered in the early months were under increasing pressure to join them. Recruitment drives swept up the willing and the less willing but by the middle of 1916 it was clear that the number of new recruits was falling and failing to keep pace with the frightening lists of war dead. The quota required was 32,000 each month, it was said.[26] Debate raged in the community and the churches about the question

---

22   H. Wright, Librarian at Mitchell Library to Brown, 24 August 1915, Correspondence, 1908–1916.
23   Inventory, Ethnological Collection of the Rev. Dr. George Brown, Uniting Church Archives, North Parramatta.
24   Brown's will, with his intentions for the disposition of his museum collection to Bowes Museum, Barnard Castle, UK, was signed on 17 November 1915.
25   Stanley Dinning (aged 21) enlisted on 8 February 1916 in the 1st Signal Troop.
26   The *Sydney Morning Herald* announced that 31,873 men had enlisted since December 1915, and 86,000 men had already gone to war. See 10 July 1916, 23 September 1916.

of 'Universal Service' which would oblige all able-bodied men to contribute to the national good in one way or another. With his colleague J.R. Carruthers, George Brown supported the principle of universal compulsory service for war purposes. As the year of 1916 went on, news from the front became darker and darker. Not only had thousands of young men left the farms and offices and factories of Australia to fight, but every day newspapers carried news of deaths and unimaginable horrors. In Australian cities and towns divisions deepened. Some believed strongly that every man should be forced to participate in the war effort, whether or not they liked it. Others objected equally strongly to compulsion. People shouted imprecations at each other in public meetings. Political parties, meetings of women, church denominations of different backgrounds, unionists, newspapers of various leanings, all were at odds with each other.

It was a bitter winter. George Brown accepted an invitation to visit Queensland in July, but even the milder climate could not relieve the strain of a world in torment. His daughter Monica travelled with him. He was able to preach in the Albert Street Methodist Church in Brisbane with the Governor in the congregation, attend a civic dinner to meet the Cabinet in Queensland Parliament House and speak at a number of functions, but a bout of influenza slowed him down.[27] To his irritation, for the first time in many years, he was forced to send his apologies for meetings he had been invited to address and cancel an intended further journey to far north Queensland and Cairns; he had to admit unwillingly that he was eighty-years old and ill with the flu.

It was a bitter summer in France. Relentless rain fell on muddy fields and in the unspeakable horrors of fouled and ripped-up earth at Pozieres, shaken by explosions, grey with corruption, Leslie Dinning wrote a letter home; he had survived so far but the dead lay all around him.[28] At the family home of 'Kinawanua' in Gordon, Lydia Brown cared for grandchildren and prayed for those who were far away. With other women she met each week to pray, in the new church at Lindfield. It was said that they prayed 'on behalf of Empire and nation, for statesmen and generals, soldiers and sailors,'[29] but Lydia was less interested in Empire than in the lads she knew well who were on the battlefield, those names that were read aloud and whose messages from the Front were shared. One comfort in the middle of strain was the news that her son Geoffrey was returning to Sydney after seven years away in Chicago and Edinburgh;[30]

---

27   *Sydney Morning Herald*, 4 August 1916.
28   Leslie Dinning, Letter, 8 August 1916, in the *Methodist*, 9 December 1916.
29   *Methodist*, 19 August 1916.
30   Ibid., 14 October 1916.

Geoffrey had been the sole surviving child who had comforted her in New Britain and she longed to see him again. Her fifty-sixth wedding anniversary had passed while her husband was away, as usual.

The gold of the wattles in August brightened the bushland but there was little to lighten the spirits. George Brown arrived home from his journey to Queensland late in August.[31] His family observed that he was moving more slowly and was still unwell with a lingering cold. He was very troubled about the referendum on conscription which the government had called for October. The country was divided. Many Methodists expected to vote YES in favour, and the Methodist President in New South Wales, in calling for a Week of Prayer, urged the people that 'it is right that every human and material agency should be pressed into national service in the present emergency ... even, if necessary, up to the point of compulsory military service.'[32] To Brown, the only possible response to the referendum was to call for compulsory military service. If not enough men were willing to volunteer to support and relieve the men already in the trenches of Europe, then they should be forced to do so. Brown was very disturbed by the lack of response to recruitment and told a friend, 'I would give anything to be in the trenches at the present moment. All my being seems to cry out for a rifle.... I simply cannot understand young men or old in this great empty land standing idly by while others are fighting and working against the common enemy.... But I am too old. I can only look on.'[33]

To their grief, their grandson Leslie lay in a British military hospital seriously wounded, his lungs damaged by a gas attack and his legs paralysed.[34] Boys for whom the women had been praying were dead. Church groups draped their pulpits in purple and white, and hung newly inscribed Honour Rolls with the names of sons and husbands in gold but it did not relieve the pain. As the day of the referendum approached, the voices of dissent became more and more strident. Cartoon and verse, letters to the editor and editorial pen, speeches and processions, all manipulated the emotions and minds of voters, shrieking 'Vote No, or you are condemning someone's son to death' or 'Vote Yes, or you are abandoning our men to their doom'. In his role as President General of the Methodist Church across Australia, Brown believed that he needed to send out a message. But what could he say? Others were making a strong case for the Yes vote, and he personally intended to vote for compulsory military service. He brooded long and prayerfully over his message. In the end, his message appeared in church papers across the land. He wrote, 'I have neither the power nor the wish to give any declaration with regard to the political issues that are

---

31 Ibid., 26 August 1916.
32 Ibid., 2 September 1916.
33 C.Brunsdon Fletcher, 'George Brown and the Pacific', The Royal Australian Historical Society: Journal and Proceedings, Vol. VII 1921.
34 *Methodist*, 30 September, 9 December 1916.

involved.'[35] The Methodist Church was not a political party, he said, and did not authorise anyone to speak on purely political questions. Methodist members 'are citizens and themselves determine their action on all such questions.' He added that the important thing was the

> necessity for the exercise of that charity and forbearance towards those who differ from them which the faith we profess demands from us ... [any action must be] in accordance with the dictates of a conscience enlightened by the Spirit of God, and free from the governance of all lower and selfish motives.... [Voters ought not to adhere slavishly to advice of any political party] from which ever side it may be sought to be exercised ... [but to exercise] a judgement influenced only by the highest considerations and after seeking the guidance of the Great Head of the Church and of the nations whose will it should be our supreme purpose to ascertain and follow.[36]

On the day of the referendum, there was a strange quietness as people approached the polling booths. No one could guess the outcome. The lines of Liberal versus Labor, Protestant versus Catholic, workers versus capitalists were not the only loyalty this time. Although the *Sydney Morning Herald* declared that those who voted 'No' would no doubt be 'trade unions, shirkers and mamma's pets,'[37] other strong emotions were at work. It took several weeks for all the votes to be counted and then it became clear. The nation had voted No.

Brown was angry. He wrote to a relative in England who was now caring for Leslie Dinning, describing local nervousness about rumours of a German raider that might be in the region, putting Australian shipping at risk. In an unguarded moment, he wrote, 'In my opinion it would be a good thing if some ship were to pitch a few shells into Sydney. It would be a good lesson to a lot of those shirkers. Australia is the most rotten country I know.'[38]

The political scene continued to be unstable and Brown was unimpressed with politicians and disgusted with some organisations; according to him one group was 'as bad as they can be' and another had 'gone mad and are expelling all the best men of their party.... Do you wonder that I call the country rotten?'[39] More sober reflection suggested that the key issue for many voters was not unwillingness to support their troops in the war effort, but rebellion against compulsion.[40]

* * *

---

35   Ibid., 14 October 1916.
36   Ibid., 14 October 1916.
37   *Sydney Morning Herald*, 28 October 1916.
38   Brown to Will Slack in UK, 27 December 1916, Private collection.
39   Ibid.
40   *Sydney Morning Herald*, 13 November 1916.

George Brown was finding it more and more difficult to keep his busy schedule of engagements. To his frustration, he often needed a supporting arm or his walking stick, although he continued to attend meetings. At a meeting of the Board of Missions it was reported that there was fierce fighting between tribal groups in the Choiseul area of the Solomon Islands.[41] It was hard to be disapproving while the tribes of so-called civilised nations were locked in extreme conflict; the rationale for a renewed regime of headhunting and head-splitting in honour of new war canoes was defended—'The white man fights, why not the black?'[42] By late in 1916 he was forced to miss some significant events because of illness but took great pleasure in participating in the laying of foundation stones for Wesley College on the campus of the University of Sydney on 2 December, days before his eighty-first birthday.[43] He had been promoting the establishment of a Methodist University College in association with Sydney University for some years.

* * *

Just before Christmas, George Brown was guest and speaker at Newington College Speech Day. Perhaps the small, frail white haired old man did not look much like the hero and adventurer the boys had been led to expect. He began to speak and soon the hall full of schoolboys was responding to his warmth and loving personality. He hoped to live long enough to see the opening of Wesley College and victory in the war in Europe, he told them. As he looked out at those young faces, some of them old enough to be among the next wave of recruits in a deadly war, it seemed to him that this was not the time for tales of adventure in the Pacific. There was a word far more urgent to be spoken. If he had done anything worthwhile with his life, he told them, it was because as a young man, not much older than some of them, he had given his heart to God and accepted the Lord Jesus Christ as his Saviour. Personal religion, he said, was not holding to a creed, or observing a religious form but communion with a living person, the living Christ. Many years earlier he had written a quote from John G. Whittier in the autograph book of a friend, 'Nor name, nor form, nor ritual word / But simply following Thee.'[44] This was still his belief. As he carefully stepped down from the platform, he was not to know that this was his final public address.[45]

* * *

---

41 *Australasian Methodist Missionary Review*, 4 October 1916.
42 Ibid., 15 March 1917.
43 *Methodist*, 9 December 1916.
44 Brown's entry in the Autograph Book of Johanna Fellmann, January 1897.
45 *Methodist*, 23 December, 30 December 1916, 14 April 1917.

The referendum on compulsory military service had made it plain that Australian men were not willing to be compelled to enlist. As news from the war front continued to be unrelentingly grim, the question now was: could men be persuaded to enlist? Church leaders were encouraged to add their voices to the pleas for recruits. With the national leaders of the Anglican, Presbyterian and Congregational Churches, George Brown, as President General of the Methodist Church of Australasia, added his signature to a document titled 'Recruiting: Appeal to Australian Manhood'. They appealed to 'all citizens for a yet fuller response to the call of duty and patriotism.'

> We understand better than we did that we are fighting for our hearths and homes, the honour of our women, the lives of our children, and the future of our race.... We appeal for the preservation of national unity at all costs.... We urge that at least during the war there be an end of all industrial cleavage, which is an even greater menace to unity, and therefore, to victory.... Let us prove that even if we have been divided on questions of policy we are not divided on the necessity for Australia maintaining her five divisions at full strength.[46]

When it was suggested by some that the Methodist General Conference, due to be held in May 1917, should be cancelled or at least postponed, he agreed with the writer who declared that a key church council 'which decides that it can serve no useful end by meeting in critical times such as these, forfeits its right to exist.'[47]

It was becoming more and more difficult to do the things he wished. It delighted him to be asked to baptise the infant son of missionaries from Tonga, the Reverend and Mrs. Rodger Page, at Gordon Methodist church; in a dark world and as he experienced the limitations of old age, this new life was a sign of hope.[48] In February 1917 he took the chair at the opening session at the Annual Meeting of the Methodist Missionary Society of Australasia.[49] As reports were read he listened to the familiar names—Samoa, Tonga, Fiji, New Britain, New Guinea/Papua, the Solomon Islands, with the new work in India and North Australia[50]—and he could see the faces, and even hear the voices in his heart. This had been his life. But by the time he reached home, exhausted by the

---

46   John Charles Sydney (Primate of Australia and Tasmania), Ronald G. Macintyre (Moderator-General of the Presbyterian Church of Australia), George Brown (President-General of the Methodist Church of Australasia), W.J.L. Closs (Chairman of the Congregational Union of Australia), 'Recruiting: Appeal to Australian Manhood,' in the *Methodist*, 6 January 1917.

47   *Methodist*, 6 January 1917.

48   Baptismal certificate of Rodger Page Jr., born 2 May 1916, son of Rev. Rodger and Hannah Page, baptised by George Brown at Gordon Methodist Church 19 January 1917.

49   *Methodist*, 17 February 1917. The Annual General Meeting of the Board was held from 7–10 February 1917.

50   *Australasian Methodist Missionary Review*, 4 December 1915, 4 January 1916.

day and the suburban train journey, he knew that he was deluding himself to think he could travel hundreds of miles to Melbourne in May. He would have to content himself with sending a message to the General Conference as he passed the mantle of the President General to another man.

Day by day, the world of George Brown became narrower. Lydia and their daughters realised that he was failing. He had addressed his last crowd, chaired his final meeting and preached his last sermon. Visitors came to see him at home. One brought a copy of a newly published book in which his name was mentioned in glowing terms as 'one of the great empire-builders in the Pacific,' 'a fine type of the strong clear-headed, wide-minded missionary,' and from his old friend Sir William Macgregor, comparing Brown to other church men who had impressed him: 'You would have had no difficulty in a Life of Dr George Brown, a man that has either no weakness, no defect, or is the most cunning man I have ever met in concealing it ... Dr Brown is the most limpid, the most pellucid man of my acquaintance.'[51]

The world continued to shrink around him. The women of his family cared for him, family members and other visitors came and went. A visitor was moved when he witnessed Monica offering to read to her father as he lay, unable to hold a conversation. He asked her to read the Bible and whispered 'Luke chapter 15'.[52] Resting with eyes closed, he listened to the ancient story told by Christ, of the runaway boy who left home to seek adventure and experience, who, in the end, despite his wanderings, his blunders and stupid choices, is welcomed home at last into the embrace of the Father.

Easter in early April was a sombre time. In Europe, Australian troops were bracing for the terrible carnage that would soon be wreaked at Bullecourt, France. In Russia, violent revolution had just overthrown the established social order and on Good Friday, 6 April 1917, the United States of America announced that they were joining the war on the side of the Allies. In Sydney, German residents were being interned under the War Precautions Act and workers were making employers nervous with industrial unrest.

Late in the evening of Easter Saturday 7 April 1917, the family of George Brown gathered around his bed. Each breath was difficult. Soon one breath would be the final one. They could only wait and pray. His sons and daughters were there, and Lydia. Perhaps Lydia wondered at this scene. A man full of years, with his family lovingly around him, was gently breathing his way to death. As a friend would write, it was 'a peaceful slipping of the anchor and a quiet gliding out

---

51   Viscount Bryce, 'Preface,' to C. Brunsdon Fletcher, *The New Pacific: British Policy and German Aims*, London: Macmillan and Co, 1917, pp. xiv–xv.
52   Rev. Dr. J.E. Carruthers, 'Tribute,' in the *Methodist*, 14 April 1917.

into the open sea.'[53] It so easily could have been otherwise. Lydia had waited fearfully for him to come home so many times over the years. He could have died in shipwrecks in the Atlantic or the Pacific oceans, from a Samoan war club, a New Britain spear or a Solomon Island axe or gun. He had gone into danger, often unwisely and against advice. Did he deserve to have such a peaceful end? She could only be thankful for the many years when he had always come home to her at last.

George Brown died on 7 April 1917 in his family home in Gordon, Sydney. The next day was Easter Day.

Lydia Brown sat quietly through the speeches, eulogies, prayers and tributes that seemed to be endless. It was hard to look at the casket and she found herself staring at the crown of flowers on it for their 'beloved President' from the General Conference. Men who had worked beside her man, men who had revered him as their beloved elder, men who respected him as scientist, political writer and missionary, so many had something to say. It seemed natural that only the men should speak, but the women and children had loved him too. She leaned on her children, Lizzie and Monica, Claudia and her family, Fred and Geoffrey and their families, and all the cousins and nieces and nephews who gathered. Those closest had been together for a private service in the family home before they moved to a crowded church at Gordon and finally to the graveside at Gore Hill Cemetery where a vast crowd gathered.[54] Her man was described as 'a many-sided man', 'a man of many voyages', 'ever wide in his sympathies, wide in his purposes', 'a well-spent life', 'a man of unique gifts', 'the greatest of modern missionaries'. One theme recurred in every speech. Brown had loved people. It did not matter whether it was a child or a young woman, a peer or a politician, cannibal or clergy, scientist or sorcerer, he met each one as a human being, a child of God, and loved them, showing in his own life, as one friend said, 'in his own original way, something of the manifold, the variegated, the many-coloured grace of God.'[55] A speaker recalled an evening by the family fireside when Brown had declared, 'The longer I live the more I am convinced that the mightiest power in the world is the power of love.'[56]

In Lydia's old autograph book, carried with her over the years since she was a young girl in New Zealand, was the inscription written by George when he came to ask her to marry him. It had seemed an odd message at the time, full

---

53 *Methodist*, 14 April 1917.

54 In the lengthy accounts of the funeral, fifty-eight Methodist ministers are listed by name plus thirteen leaders from other Protestant Churches. One of the few missing was the Reverend Heinrich Fellmann, who was interned as a German national. See the *Methodist*, 14 April 1917.

55 Funeral reports and obituaries for Brown appeared in *Sydney Morning Herald*, 9 April, 17 April 1917; *Methodist* 14 April 1917; Minutes of Board of Methodist Missionary Society 13 April 1917; Memorial Service, 18 April 1917; *Teesdale Mercury* [UK]16 May 1917, NLA JAFp BIO 66.

56 *Methodist*, 14 April 1917.

of images of sowing and harvest, and of 'weary days of toil' ahead, an unlikely statement from a bridegroom to his beloved. But then he wrote of 'the promise-keeping God' and asked, 'Shall we doubt His power and love? Oh, no.... Though the day may be full of toil and sorrow ... yet the day will come when they who have gone forth weeping bearing precious seed shall doubtless come again with rejoicing bringing their sheaves with them.'

Tears, toil and sorrow, yes, and rejoicing, too. Their arms were filled with harvest.

Epilogue

George Brown had hoped to live long enough to see the opening of Wesley College at the University of Sydney and the end of the War. He saw neither. The business of his beloved Methodist Church went on without him. Another man was installed as next President General at General Conference but Brown was not there.[1] The war in Europe staggered on, through ever deeper carnage, for another seventeen months. Memorial services for Brown were held in Sydney, Barnard Castle and in the islands of the Pacific as people honoured their old friend. Glowing obituaries appeared in journals, listing his achievements.[2] Before the last of the funeral flowers had withered, Monica had collapsed with exhaustion after months of sharing the care of her father. Lydia, sad and tired, continued to care for her grandchildren with the help of Lizzie. Once more, her notepaper was rimmed with a border of black.

As the months of war ground on, the Methodist people, along with the whole society of Australia, struggled to understand the meaning of the horror. They asked, Why does God not stop the war? Who is to blame? A second referendum was called in 1917 and again the result was 'No' to conscription. Political power changed hands. Antagonism against Germany and German citizens resident in Australia became sharper as the months went by but the women of the Brown family retained their friendship with their German missionary colleagues. Lydia Brown wrote lovingly to Johanna Fellmann, feeling with her the pain of being parted from her older children in distant Germany as war raged around them.[3] The war came to an end at last on 11 November 1918. That day, in Sydney, the Brown women were distressed to read in their morning paper that the German Chancellor was warning Germans living outside the Fatherland that they would be 'surrounded by hatred and malicious rejoicing'. That evening, writing to Johanna Fellmann on behalf of Lydia and Lizzie, Monica Brown wrote,

I want to assure you dear Mrs Fellmann that this is not the case, our hearts go out to you and always have done during these past four years.... While we rejoice today, it is not with a malicious hatred.... Accept our love for you which has never changed.[4]

It would be February 1920 before the Methodist mission office finally was able to secure permission for the repatriation of the Fellmann family to their original home in Germany.[5] In August 1920, on the ship *Miltiade*, the family sailed at

---

1 The new President General was the Rev. J.E. Carruthers, a former colleague of Brown.
2 *Sydney Morning Herald*, 9 April 1917; *Methodist*, 14 April 1917.
3 Lydia Brown to Johanna Fellmann, 6 March 1918. In private collection of Nancy Joyce.
4 Monica Brown to Johanna Fellmann, 11 November 1918. In private collection of Nancy Joyce.
5 *Australasian Methodist Missionary Review*, June 1891–June 1917, 4 February 1920.

last for home via London, after twenty-three years of missionary service. The connection with the Brown family was not broken, however, and George and Lydia Brown's great-granddaughter Nancy Joyce in Sydney continues a family tradition of friendship with the grandson of Heinrich and Johanna Fellmann, Dr. Ulrich Fellmann in Aachen, Germany to the present day.

* * *

Soon after Brown's death, discussions began about creating a fitting memorial. The women of the Women's Auxiliary to Foreign Missions offered a plan which they believed would have pleased Brown. They would raise funds to establish a George Brown Memorial Home in Sydney, a place where women could be prepared for missionary service. At first there was some hesitation by the Board who acknowledged the need but thought that the 'time is inopportune'.[6] The time was right in one respect; for the first time in the history of the Board of Missions, four women had been elected to the Board, including Monica Brown.[7] Within weeks a group had been formed of men and women to work towards the establishment of a training Home.[8] The women worked actively against the grim backdrop of war and its aftermath and by September 1920 the new George Brown Memorial Home was ready for its first residents.[9] Over the next decades, this missionary training establishment moved from its original location at The Avenue, Waverley to 5 Rogers Avenue, Haberfield, trained both men and women and changed its name several times. The legacy for the training of Christian leaders continued in new incarnations and the name of 'George Brown' has been retained on property at the Centre for Ministry of the Uniting Church in Australia at North Parramatta since 1988.

* * *

The home at 'Kinawanua' in Gordon, after the death of George Brown, continued to be a haven for family members and others in need. The women of the family gave shelter to a nephew, Leslie Dinning, returning from the war a paraplegic, and another niece, Hazel Dinning, joining her sister Amy Eadith after the death of their father. Other nieces and nephews came and stayed for extended periods with their aunts. Lydia Brown was becoming increasingly frail. She and her older sister Elizabeth Watkin (formerly Fletcher) were now respected old ladies in their eighties. Most of their siblings had died and they were among the last of those who remembered childhood and youth in the little mission house on

---

6   *Methodist*, 16 February 1918, ML MOM 278-279.

7   The first women members were Miss Monica Brown, Mrs. W.J. Eggleston, Mrs. C.T. Newman and Mrs. J.R. Uren. They first attended the annual meeting of the Board in February 1918.

8   *Methodist*, 23 February 1918. Women on the panel were Monica Brown, Mrs. Blow (Treasurer) and Mrs. Heighway (Secretary).

9   *Methodist*, 12 October 1918, 4 September 1920.

the rise above the Whaingaroa River in North Island, New Zealand, or the two young ministers, each determined to be a missionary in the Pacific, who came seeking their brides.

* * *

Lydia Brown died on 7 August 1923. Toward the end, it was said, 'gradually and peacefully, she faded out of life,' cared for by her daughters. Perhaps she remembered, a few days before the end, that it would have been the sixty-third anniversary of the day in 1860 when she and George Brown pledged their lives to each other. An obituary for Lydia Brown said that 'her name ... is as an ointment poured forth,' generous, fragrant and healing.[10] Her daughters lived to old age after years of service to family and church. Monica Brown died on 7 January 1950 and Mary Elizabeth Brown died on 22 July 1952; in her later years her fine mind was clouded with dementia.

* * *

In his later years, George Brown had tried to arrange the safe keeping of his collection of artefacts and photographs. In his will, after planning his legacy to his own family and a bequest for the Methodist Foreign Missionary Society, he directed that his collection should go either to the new Bowes Museum in his birthplace of Barnard Castle, England, or to the Mitchell Library in Sydney. If neither establishment wanted it, then he bequeathed it to the New South Wales Methodist Conference. He insisted that the collection must remain as a whole.[11] Someone, perhaps Lizzie Brown, typed a long inventory with 683 items listed, many in multiples or bundles of ten.[12] When the Bowes Museum finally agreed to buy the collection, after complex negotiations, the vast accumulation of the years was packed and shipped across the world, far from the Pacific Islands where the pieces had been made and used. Over the years, as connection with Brown faded and interest in the objects of remote outposts of Empire was lost, much of the collection was relegated to storage. In 1953 the collection was sold to the University of Newcastle on Tyne for their new department of anthropology, passing in 1974 to the care of the Hancock Museum at that university. In the 1980s, to the dismay of many, the Hancock Museum decided to sell the collection to the National Museum of Ethnology in Osaka, Japan, which has a high reputation for excellence. The collection was now recognised as being very valuable, and there was fierce debate over the proposed sale; some declared that it should be retained in the United Kingdom or repatriated to

---

10   'Memoriam', *Methodist*, 1 September 1923.
11   A copy of Brown's will is held in the Archives of Uniting Church Synod of NSW/ACT.
12   'Ethnological Collection of the Late Rev. Dr. G. Brown,' Archives of Uniting Church Synod of NSW/ACT.

Australia and the museums of newly independent Pacific nations.[13] Despite this outcry, the collection was sold to the National Museum of Ethnology in 1985, complete apart from four particularly valuable pieces which were bought by the British Museum. The Museum in Osaka presented a major exhibition of the George Brown ('Jōji Buraun') collection in 1999 and continues academic study and publications related to the collection.[14] As for the photographs of Pacific people and events taken by Brown, the Australian Museum in Sydney was able to purchase the negatives in 1930. In 2002 a selection of photographs taken on his 1898 visit to Samoa was exhibited at the National Museum, Apia, Samoa,[15] and later at the Uniting Church Centre for Ministry, Sydney, which has a significant community of Pacific Island students. In 2010, enlargements of a selection of Brown's photographs 1880–1905, on loan from Australian Museum Archives, were included in the *Body Pacifica* exhibition at Casula Powerhouse, Sydney.

* * *

George Brown and his life had already taken on a legendary status before his death in 1917. As the years went on, his name was associated with the beginnings of missionary work in Samoa, the New Guinea Islands region and the Papuan Islands region of what was to become Papua New Guinea, and the Solomon Islands. Institutions were given his name, including High Schools and training centres for Christian leaders. In 1925, fifty years after he first arrived in the Duke of York Islands, Jubilee celebrations were held in that region with guests from Australia present to witness the re-enactment of Brown's first arrival. Some old men could still remember that time. There was great dancing and feasting, with schoolchildren on display and students from the George Brown College among the dancers, as the festivities moved from place to place around the district.[16] The *Litia* was in harbour at the time. By the time the centenary of the arrival of Brown and his party was celebrated in 1975, the tradition of marking 15 August as George Brown Day was well established and would become an accepted public holiday. By 1975, the fragile early beginnings of Christian ministry in the islands had grown into an independent Church, the United Church of Papua New Guinea, inaugurated in 1968, and some 15,000 villagers and guests gathered in Rabaul for a combined service of thanksgiving for the changes over one hundred years.[17] One visitor was heard to mutter that he was completely

13   Jonathan Benthall, 'The George Brown collection,' in *Anthropology Today*, vol. 2, no. 4 (August 1986): 1–2.

14   For a longer description of the issues surrounding the Brown collection, see Helen Bethea Gardner, *Gathering for God: George Brown in Oceania*, Dunedin: Otago University Press, 2006, pp. 150–54.

15   Jude Philp, 'The Reverend Dr George Brown in Samoa,' in *Muse*, magazine of the Australian Museum, February–April 2003.

16   Miss Jessie March, 1925 photograph album of Jubilee festivities in New Britain. Uniting Church Assembly Archives, Centre for Ministry, North Parramatta.

17   Joy Udy, 'The impact of one hundred years,' in the *Methodist*, 18 October 1975.

'Browned-off' after multiple re-enactments of Brown's arrival. 'George Brown Day' is celebrated in Papua New Guinea in regions where Brown's influence once had an impact, often combined with major choir competitions and the obligatory re-enactment. In recent years, a descendent of Brown, who found the connection with his forebear something of an embarrassment, was irritated to arrive in Port Moresby by ship with equipment related to his work; it could not be unloaded, he was told, because they had arrived on a public holiday for George Brown Day. The name of Brown is also respected in Samoa. When great-grandson, Julian C. Brown, arrived in Samoa on a visit in 1978, he went to the Methodist Church offices in Apia to seek some information from church records about his forebear. He was surprised to see a painting of George Brown, copied from the portrait in his autobiography, hanging in the office, and when he explained his quest he was greeted with great excitement and welcomed into the home of the Samoan Church Secretary. He was told of Brown's initiatives in training leaders, in pioneer work and in peacemaking, and was shown the George Brown Junior High School. 'It was clear that George Brown has had an immense impact on Samoa,' he wrote.[18]

* * *

Not everyone has shared reverence toward the figure of George Brown. While some have written in admiring terms, others have been scathing.[19] A journalist writing so-called 'historical features' asked whether he was 'Dedicated Parson or Ratbag Imperialist?' and, in sketching the controversy surrounding his work, hinted that he only posed as a missionary; 'In reality he was an agent of British imperialism, happy to flaunt his authority over the islanders simply to sate his vanity.' He suggested that following the murders in 1878 'horrified Wesleyan authorities hastily transferred Brown to an entirely different job as mission visitor.'[20] Historians include missionary Brown in their studies of the Pacific with varying views of his contribution. Theological students living in George Brown House in the 1990s found some of Brown's colourful tales quite bizarre and were known to declaim heroic passages from his autobiography in silly voices. Brown would probably have joined in their laughter. He is likely to have cared more for the opinion of Pacific Island people who had known him, men like Ione who called him 'a true Father and a man of love' and Kuliniasi who said 'It is not easy for us dark people to forget Dr. Brown. This chief was like one anointed, he carried fragrance wherever he went.'[21]

* * *

18   Julian C. Brown, personal letter to family, 8 May 1978. In private collection of Nancy Joyce.
19   Admirers include C. Brunsdon Fletcher, *The Black Knight of the Pacific*, Sydney: Australasian Publishing Co, 1944; J.E. Carruthers, *Lights in the Southern Sky*, Sydney: Methodist Book Depot, 1924; R.J. Lacey, 'George Brown,' in *Encyclopaedia of Papua and New Guinea*, ed. Peter Ryan, Melbourne University Press in association with the University of Papua and New Guinea, 1972, pp.124–26.
20   *Daily Mirror*, 8 Nov 1968; an article in a similar vein appeared in the *Daily Mirror* on 11 April 1989.
21   Quoted in the Journal of Rev. Roy E.S. Taylor, 2 November 1919, manuscript loaned by Rev. Don Affleck.

Much has changed since Brown's time. Regions in the Pacific that he saw in the early years of contact are now independent nations. Leadership in the churches of the Pacific nations is in the hands of the indigenous people, a dream Brown cherished from his first encouragement of new converts to begin to share their faith. The Methodist 'mission' in the islands of New Guinea and Papua has become the United Church of Papua New Guinea. The Methodist Church in Australasia has become part of Uniting Church in Australia, inaugurated in 1977; Brown participated in the early and unsuccessful attempts to achieve this. The two Churches that developed from the early work of the London Missionary Society and the Wesleyan Methodist Missionary Society continue to work independently in Samoa. The two Churches that were divided in Tonga in the 1880s remain divided. In the Duke of York Islands rising sea levels continue to erode the shore line below the hilltop where once the Brown family lived at Kinawanua and the little cemetery has gone.

* * *

On 15 August 2007, on the anniversary of the day that George Brown and his Fijian and Samoan companions arrived in their region in 1875, a crowd of thousands gathered in East New Britain. Dignitaries from the Fijian High Commission and a delegation of clergy from Fiji had been invited to come to receive a ceremonial apology from the people of East New Britain for the actions of their ancestors. Memories of the murder and cannibalism of the bodies of four Fijian missionaries in 1878 had been kept alive through the generations, as had stories of the violent retribution that followed. Now, Ratu Isoa Tikoca, Fiji's High Commissioner in Papua New Guinea, accepted the apologies. Four great torches were lit to honour the four Fijians and Ratu Isoa said, 'We are deeply touched and wish you the greatest joy of forgiveness as we finally end this record disagreement.'[22]

If George Brown had been there that day he would have been profoundly thankful. It was yet another evidence of the many-coloured grace of God whom he had served for so long.

---

22   *Fiji Times*, 16 August 2007.

Bibliography

Primary Sources

Mitchell Library, State Library of NSW

Brown, George, Correspondence and Papers, 1911–13, ML A1686-18 CY 1365.

Brown, George, Correspondence and Papers, vol. 7, Miscellaneous, ML A1686-24.

Brown, George, Correspondence, 1908–1916, ML MSS 263/1 CY 3405.

Brown, George, Journal, 1860–71, ML A1686-8-9 CY 225.

Brown, George, Journal, 1872–75, ML 1686-25.

Brown, George, Journal, 1874–1876, ML A 1686-10-12 CY 2759.

Brown, George, Journal, 1877–Dec 1879, ML A1686-13, 14, 15 CY 2762.

Brown, George, Journal, 1888, ML A1686-16-17.

Brown, George, Letter Book, 1871–76, ML A1686-2 CY 2767.

Brown, George, Letter Book, 1876–1880, ML A1686-3 CY 2772.

Brown, George, Letter Book, ML A1686-1.

Brown, George, Letter Books, 1880, ML A1686-18.

Brown, George, Letter Books, 1886–1887, ML A1686-4 CY 2810.

Brown, George, Letter Books, 1888–1889, ML A1686-5 CY 2810.

Brown, George, Letter Books, 1888–1890, ML A1686-6 CY 2799.

Brown, George, Letter Books, 1902–1909, ML A1686-7 CY 2810.

Brown, George, Letters, 1862–78, ML MOM 102.

Brown, George, Manuscript of autobiography, ML A 4096-97.

Brown, George, Wesleyan Methodist Missionary Society Correspondence and Papers, 1890–1895, ML A1686 CY 1365.

Dyson, Martin, Papers, Journal, 1858–1865, ML A 2579 CY 269.

Dyson, Martin, Papers, Life History, ML A 2580 CY Reel 270.

Minute Book of Wesleyan Methodist Conference, New South Wales, 1892–94, ML 287.1/7.

Minute Book, Wesleyan Methodist Church General Conference, 1890–1913, ML Methodist Church 581.

Minute Book, Wesleyan Methodist General Conference Minutes, May 1881, ML Methodist Church 580.

Minutes of Australasian Wesleyan Methodist Conference of NSW and Queensland: 1891, ML 287.1/7 CY 1365.

Minutes of Board of Methodist Missionary Society of Australasia, 13 April 1917.

Minutes of General Missions Committee of Australasian Conference of Wesleyan Methodist Church, 1865–1898, ML MOM 1-4 CY 354.

Minutes of New South Wales and Queensland Conference of Australasian Wesleyan Methodist Church, 1880–1888, ML 287.1/7 CY 1365.

Minutes of New South Wales and Queensland Conference of Wesleyan Methodist Church, February 1874.

Minutes of New South Wales Wesleyan Methodist Conference, 1896, ML 287.1/7 CY 1365.

Minutes of New South Wales Wesleyan Methodist Conference, 1894, ML 287.1/7 CY 1365.

Minutes of Wesleyan Methodist Mission, Samoa District, 2 October 1873.

Minutes of Wesleyan Methodist Missions Board, 1865–1898, ML MOM 1-4 CY 354.

Minutes of Wesleyan Methodist Missions Board, 1906–1909, ML MOM 3 CY 354.

Minutes of Wesleyan Methodist Missions Board, Feb 1913–Nov 1917, ML MOM 205 CY 3307.

Minutes of Wesleyan Methodist Missions Board, Jan 1910–Jan 1913, ML MOM 204 CY 3306.

Minutes of Wesleyan Methodist Missions Board, May 1898–July 1906, MOM 203 CY 3305.

Official report of investigation initiated by Commodore Crawford Wilson and carried out by Captain Purvis of *Danae*, 21 September 1879, ML A1686-18 CY 1365.

The 64th Report of Wesleyan Methodist Missionary Society, London 1878, in *Wesleyan Missionary Notices relating to the Missions under the Direction of the Australasian Wesleyan Methodist Conference*, London, November 1878.

Watsford, James J., Journal of a trip to New Britain, 1878–79, ML MOM 127.

Wesleyan Methodist Missionary Society Correspondence and Papers, vol. 1, ML CY 1365.

Wesleyan Missionary Notices relating to the Missions under the Direction of the Australasian Wesleyan Methodist Conference.

National Library of Australia

Annual Report of Australasian Methodist Missionary Society for 1897–98, NLA 266.7 MET.

Australasian Wesleyan Methodist General Conference Report, 1888, NLA N 287.09961 BRO.

Brown, Australasian Wesleyan Methodist General Conference, *Report by the Rev. George Brown, Special Commissioner of the Australasian Wesleyan Methodist General Conference to Tonga*. Reports written December 1888 and 26 April 1889 and includes correspondence for the period between Shirley W. Baker and Brown. Printed Sydney 1890 NLA N 287.09961 BRO.

Brown, G. and B. Danks, *A Buk Na Wetiri U Ra Lotu ma ra Buk na Niluluk*, Emerald Hill: Donaldson & Hartley, 1883, Rare Book Collection, NLA SR 499.1204321 B 877.

Brown, George, 'The life history of a savage: notes of a recent journey to New Guinea and New Britain,' *Australasian Association for the Advancement of Science*, January 1898, NLA JAFp BIBLIO F7495.

Brown, George, *A Journey Along the Coasts of New Ireland and Neighbouring Islands*, Proceedings of the Royal Geographical Society and Monthly Record of Geography, April 1881.

Brown, George, Letters from Levuka, Fiji, 1875, 'Communications respecting the Wesleyan new mission to New Britain etc.,' NLA JAFp BIBLIO F7493a.

Brown, George, *Na buk na wawera ma a kum kelekele, Lesson Book with Hymns, Prayers and Catechism in Duke of York Language,* Sydney 1879, NLA JAF 499.36 BRO 1879.

Brown, Rev. Dr. G., 'For Members of Conference Only. A Personal Statement, 1905,' NLA Ferg/6162.

Brown, Rev. George, *Communications Respecting the Wesleyan New Mission to New Britain etc.,* Leaflet published Sydney, 20 July 1875, NLA JAFp BIBLIO F7493a.

Macgregor, Sir William, Address given at London Missionary Society Centenary Meeting, Free Church Assembly Room, Edinburgh, 11 March 1895, MS NLA mfm G 23005.

Macgregor, Sir William, Diary, 14 November 1890–19 June 1891, MS NLA mfm G 23005.

Vagabond 1843–1896, 'South Sea massacres by the author of "The Vagabond Papers",' Sydney: The *Australian'* Office, 1881, NLA N996 V126.

'Wesleyan College and Seminary,' in the *New-Zealander,* Auckland, New Zealand December 1852, NLA, JAF Drawer, Petherick Reading Room.

'Winter Excursion' invitation from Australasian Methodist Missionary Society, signed by Brown, for tour in 1899, NLA JAFp BIBLIO F6291a.

Archives of Assembly of Uniting Church, and Synod of NSW and ACT, Centre for Ministry, North Parramatta, NSW

Honorary Doctoral Certificate for George Brown from McGill University, Ottawa.

Inventory: 'Ethnological Collection of the Late Rev. Dr G. Brown,' with copy of Brown's will.

Missionary Notices Wesleyan Methodist Missionary Society, Sixth Series Vol. III, London 1888.

'Organ of the Willoughby and Gordon Methodist Church,' in the *Messenger,* 1 February 1907.

Photograph album with images of celebrations in New Britain in 1925 to mark fifty years since arrival of Brown. Gift of Miss Jessie March.

The Wesleyan Missionary Notices Vol. XXII, 1878–1880, Fifth Series vol. 1, 1878, London 1878.

Australian Museum Archives

George Brown photographic collection, AMS 318.

Archives of Methodist Church, New Zealand

Wallis, Rev. James, Letters to Mission Secretaries, 1809–1895, Wesleyan Methodist Missionary Society, London, written between 15 December 1834 and 10 May 1854. Typescript. Original held at Auckland Institute and Museum, MS # 320, 'Letters and Papers concerning Rev. James Wallis.'

Wallis, Rev. James, Narrative, written for grandson Rev. T.J. Wallis in period 1880–1890, original manuscript in Trinity Theological Library, Auckland; typescript in Methodist Connexional Office, Christchurch, New Zealand.

Newspapers and Journals

Australasian Methodist Missionary Review, June 1891–June 1917.

Brisbane Courier.

Wesley's South Seas Heritage: South Pacific Regional Conference, World Methodist Historical Society.

Christian Advocate.

Daily Telegraph.

Melbourne Age.

Methodist, March 1892–September 1923

New Zealand Methodist.

Spectator.

Sydney Mail.

Sydney Morning Herald, August–September 1860; 26 January 1869; 23 September 1878; 21 June 1880; 4 December 1883; 30 January 1890; 4 February, 6 February, 7 February 1890; 14 February 1891.

Town and Country Journal.

Weekly Advocate, 21 September 1878; 14 December 1878; 26 July 1879; 27 May 1879; 20 Dec 1879; 26 February 1881; 12 March 1881; 15 March 1881 4 June 1881; 8 August, 18 September 1882; 2 February 1884; 4 February, 11 February, 12 May, 19 May, 26 May 1888; 21 December 1889; 18 January, 29 March,19 April, 17 May, 24 May , 9 August, 8 November, 29 November, 6 December 1890; 3 January 10 January , 7 February, 21 February, 28 February, 7 March, 14 March 25 April, 10 May, 23 May 1891 NLA mfm NX 392.

Wesley Historical Society of New Zealand, *Proceedings of the Wesley Historical Society (New Zealand)*, no. 55, Auckland: The Society, 1990.

Documents in Private Possession

Autograph Book, kept by Johanna Fellmann, 1896–1950. Held by Dr Ulrich Fellmann, Aachen, Germany.

Autograph Book, kept by Lydia Brown; entries from 1853–1880. Held by great-granddaughter Miss Nancy Joyce, Artarmon, Sydney.

Bible presented to Brown and signed by thirty young men from the Young Men's Christian Association, Auckland 1860; held in Historical Museum, Mangungu, New Zealand.

Birthday Book belonging to Monica Brown, with record of births, deaths and marriages of extended family and friends from 1830s until 1940s. Held by Miss Nancy Joyce.

Buddle, Thomas, letter to Wesleyan Methodist Missionary Society, London, 9 Oct 1851.

Catalogue for Exhibition of George Brown Collection, Museum of Ethnology, Osaka, Japan, 1999. In Japanese.

Family Tree: Wallis family.

Fletcher, Rev. Joseph, to Rev. Dr. Beecham, letter from Wesleyan College and Seminary, Auckland, NZ, 27 Dec. 1850.

Photograph album of Fellmann family and friends. In possession of Dr Ulrich Fellmann.

Photograph albums of the extended Brown family. In possession of Miss Nancy Joyce.

Series of personal letters between Johanna Fellmann and George, Lydia, Mary Elizabeth and Monica Brown, 1896–1918. Held by Miss Nancy Joyce.

Watson, Harry, Barnard Castle, County Durham, UK, letter to George Carter in Auckland, 20 March 1986.

Wesleyan College and Seminary, Auckland, Annual Report, 1851.

Wesleyan College and Seminary, Auckland, Cash Book, 1849–1856.

Secondary Sources

Allardice, R.W., *The Methodist Story in Samoa 1828–1984*, Apia, Western Samoa: Methodist Conference of Samoa, 1984.

Anderhandt, Jacob, *Eduard Hernsheim, die Südsee und viel Geld,* Biography, Münster: MV-Wissenschaft, 2012.

Austin, John, *Missionary Enterprise and Home Service: A Story of Mission Life in Samoa and Circuit Work in New South Wales* (illustrated), Sydney: J.A. Packer, 1922.

Badger, Geoffrey, *The Explorers of the Pacific*, Sydney: Kangaroo Press, 1996.

Bavin, Cyril, 'The Indian in Fiji,' in *A Century in the Pacific*, ed. James Colwell, Sydney: William H. Beale, 1914, pp. 175–98.

Bennett, Judith, *Wealth of the Solomons: A History of a Pacific Archipelago, 1800–1978*, Honolulu: University of Hawai'i Press, 1987.

Bennett, William E., 'Fiji,' in *A Century in the Pacific*, ed. James Colwell, Sydney: William H. Beale, 1914, pp. 439–506.

Benthall, Jonathan, 'The George Brown collection,' in *Anthropology Today*, vol. 2, no. 4 (August 1986): 1–2.

Bowes, Joseph, 'The Australian Aborigine,' in *A Century in the Pacific*, ed. James Colwell, Sydney: William H. Beale, 1914, pp. 151–74.

Brereton, Brigid, *Law, Justice and Empire: the Colonial Career of John Gorrie. 1829–1892*, Kingston, Jamaica: University of the West Indies, 1997.

Brown, George, *A Brief Account of Methodist Missions in Australasia, Polynesia and Melanesia, their Past History, Present Conditions and Future Possibilities*, Sydney: Methodist Missionary Society of Australasia, 1904.

—— *George Brown: Pioneer-Missionary and Explorer: An Autobiography*, London: Hodder and Stoughton, 1908.

—— *Melanesians and Polynesians: Their Life-Histories Described and Compared*, London: Macmillan and Co, 1910.

Bryce, Viscount, 'Preface,' to C. Brunsdon Fletcher, *The New Pacific: British Policy and German Aims*, London: Macmillan and Co, 1917, pp. xiv–xv.

Burton, John Wear, *A Hundred Years in Fiji*, London: Epworth, 1936.

Cameron, James, *Centenary History of the Presbyterian Church in New South Wales*, vol. 1, Sydney: Angus & Robertson, 1905.

Campbell, I.C., *Worlds Apart: A History of the Pacific Islands*, Christchurch: Canterbury University Press, 2003.

Carruthers, J.E., *Lights in the Southern Sky*, Sydney: Methodist Book Depot, 1924.

Carter, George, 'An introduction to the South Pacific activity of Wesleyan Methodism,' in *Wesley's South Seas Heritage: South Pacific Regional Conference, World Methodist Historical Society*, Auckland: Wesley Historical Society (NZ), 1987, pp. 17–27.

Chapman, J.K., *The Career of Arthur Hamilton Gordon: First Lord Stanmore 1829–1912*, Toronto: University of Toronto Press, 1964.

Chaseling, Wilbur, *I Met my Hero: George Brown's Story*, Sydney: Light of the Pacific Series, 1959.

Clark, Manning, *Manning Clark's History of Australia*, abridged by Michael Cathcart, Melbourne: Melbourne University Press, 1993.

Clarke, Patricia (ed.), *Steps to Federation: Lectures marking the Centenary of Federation*, Melbourne: Australian Scholarly Publishing, 2001.

Colwell, James (ed.), *A Century in the Pacific*, Sydney: William H. Beale, 1914.

Colwell, James, *Illustrated History of Methodism: Australia 1812–1855; New South Wales and Polynesia 1856–1902*, Sydney: William Brooks & Co., 1904.

Danks, Benjamin, *In Wild New Britain: The Story of Benjamin Danks, Pioneer Missionary*, from his diary, ed. Wallace Deane, Sydney: Angus & Robertson, 1933.

—— *New Britain Mission: A Brief History*, Sydney: Australasian Wesleyan Missionary Society, Epworth Press, 1901.

Davies, Rupert E., *Methodism*, Middlesex: Penguin Books Ltd, 1963.

Denoon, Donald and Philippa Mein-Smith, with Marvic Wyndam, *A History of Australia, New Zealand and the Pacific*, Oxford: Blackwell Publishers, 2000.

Dyson, Martin, *My Story of Samoan Methodism, or a Brief History of the Wesleyan Methodist Mission in Samoa*, Melbourne: Fergusson and Moore, 1875.

Evans, Raymond, Clive Moore, Kay Saunders, and Brian Jamison, *1901 Our Future's Past: Documenting Australia's Federation*, Sydney: Macmillan, 1997.

Fellmann, Ulrich (ed.), *Von Schwaben in den Bismarckarchipel: Tagebücher der Missionarsfrau Johanna Fellmann aus Deutsch-Neuguinea 1896–1903*, Wiesbaden: Harrassowitz, 2009.

Fellmann, Ulrich, 'Missionarsfrau Johanna Fellmann geb. Class und die wesleyanischen Methodisten,' *EmK – Geschichte*, Quellen, Studien, Mitteilungen, vol. 25 (2004): 5–11.

Fletcher, C. Brunsdon, *The Black Knight of the Pacific*, Sydney: Australasian Publishing Co. Pty. Ltd., 1944.

—— 'George Brown and the Pacific,' *Royal Australian Historical Society Journal and Proceedings*, vol. 7, pt 1 (1921): 1–54.

—— *The New Pacific: British Policy and German Aims*, London: Macmillan and Co, 1917.

Gardner, Helen Bethea, *Gathering for God: George Brown in Oceania*, Dunedin: Otago University Press, 2006.

Garrett, John, *A Way in the Sea: aspects of Pacific Christian history with reference to Australia*, Melbourne: Spectrum Publications, 1980.

——*To Live Among the Stars: Christian Origins in Oceania*, Geneva: World Council of Churches Publication, 1982.

Gash, Noel and June Whittaker, *A Pictorial History of New Guinea*, Milton, Queensland: Jacaranda, 1975.

Goldie, John F., 'The Solomon Islands,' in *A Century in the Pacific*, ed. J. Colwell, Sydney: William H. Heale, 1914, pp. 559–85.

Grainger, Gareth, 'The Fakaongo exiles from Tonga to Fiji 1887–1890,' in *Tonga and the Tongans: Heritage and Identity*, ed. Elizabeth Wood-Ellem, Melbourne: Tonga Research Association, 2007, pp. 161–77.

Grattan, C. Hartley, *The South West Pacific to 1900: A Modern History*, Ann Arbor: University of Michigan Press, 1963.

Gutch, John, *Martyr of the Islands: the Life and Death of John Coleridge Patteson*, Auckland, Sydney and London, Hodder and Stoughton, 1971.

Hames, E.W., *Out of the Common Way: The European Church in the Colonial Era 1840–1913*, Auckland: Wesley Historical Society of New Zealand, 1972.

—— *Walter Lawry and the Wesleyan Mission in the South Seas*, Auckland: Wesley Historical Society, 1967.

Harrigan, Rosemary, *They Were Expeditioners: The Chronicle of Northern Italian Farmers – Pioneer Settlers of New Italy with Documentation of the Marquis de Rays' Four Expeditions to New Ireland Between 1879 and 1881*, Werribee, Victoria: Rosemary Harrigan, 2006.

Hilliard, David, *God's Gentlemen: A History of the Melanesian Mission 1849–1942*, St. Lucia: University of Queensland Press, 1978.

Ishimori, Shuzo, *Cultural Heritage of the South Pacific: The George Brown Collection at the National Museum of Ethnology*, Osaka, Japan 1999. English translation of catalogue for 1999 exhibition of Brown Collection.

Jolly, Roslyn (ed.), *The Cruise of the* Janet Nichol *among the South Sea Islands; A Diary of Mrs Robert Louis Stevenson*, Sydney: University of New South Wales Press, 2004.

Joyce, R.B., *Sir William Macgregor*, Melbourne: Oxford University Press, 1971.

Lacey, R.J., 'George Brown,' in *Encyclopaedia of Papua and New Guinea*, ed. Peter Ryan, Melbourne University Press in association with the University of Papua and New Guinea, 1972, pp.124–26.

Lovett, Richard, *James Chalmers: His Autobiography and Letters*, London: Religious Tract Society, 1914.

Macintyre, Stuart, 'Corowa and the voice of the people,' in *Steps to Federation: Lectures Marking the Centenary of Federation*, ed. Patricia Clarke, Melbourne: Australian Scholarly Publishing, 2001, pp. 39–53.

Mackenzie, S.S., *The Australians at Rabaul. The Capture and Administration of the German Possessions in the Southern Pacific*, in *Official History of Australia in the War of 1914–1918*, 12 volumes, vol. x, St. Lucia: University of Queensland Press [1921–1942], 10th edition, 1941.

Methodist Church Great Britain, *Book of Offices Being the Orders of Service Authorized for Use in the Methodist Church*, London: Methodist Publishing House, 1936.

Moulton, J. Egan, *Moulton of Tonga*, London: Epworth Press, 1921.

Murray, A.W., *Forty Years' Mission Work in Polynesia and New Guinea, from 1835 to 1875 Forty Years in Polynesia*, London: James Nisbet & Co, 1876.

—— *Missions in Western Polynesia: Being Historical Sketches of these Missions, from their Commencement in 1839 to the Present Time*, London: John Snow, 1863.

Neider, Charles (ed.), *The Complete Short Stories of Robert Louis Stevenson with a Selection of the Best Short Novels*, New York: Da Capo Press, 1998.

Nettleton, Joseph, *The Foreign Field of the Wesleyan Methodist Church Vol. IV 1907–08*, London: Wesleyan Methodist Mission House, 1908.

Neumann, Klaus, *Not the Way it Really Was: Constructing the Tolai Past*, Honolulu: University of Hawai'i, 1992.

Niau, J.H., *Phantom Paradise: The Story of the Expedition of the Marquis de Rays*, Sydney: Angus & Robertson, 1936.

Nobbs, Raymond, *St Barnabas and the Melanesian Mission Norfolk Island*, Sydney: Macquarie University Australian History Resources Centre, 1990.

Northcott, Cecil, *Glorious Company: One Hundred and Fifty Years Life and Work of the London Missionary Society 1795–1945*, London: The Livingstone Press, 1945.

Philp, Jude, 'The Reverend Dr George Brown in Samoa,' in *Muse,* Magazine of the Australian Museum, Feb–April 2003, pp. 6–7.

Powell, Wilfred, *Wanderings in a Wild Country: Or Three Years Amongst the Cannibals of New Britain*, London: Sampson Low, Marston, Searle, and Rivington, 1883.

Reeson, Margaret, *A Singular Woman*, Adelaide: Open Book Publishers, 1999.

Robson, R.W., *Queen Emma: The Samoan-American Girl who Founded an Empire in 19th Century New Guinea*, Sydney: Pacific Publications, 1965.

Rogers, Edgar, *A Pioneer of New Guinea: The Story of Albert Alexander Maclaren*, London: Society for the Propagation of the Gospel in Foreign Parts, 1920.

Rutherford, Noel, *Shirley Baker and the King of Tonga*, Melbourne: Melbourne University Press, 1971.

Scarr, Deryck, *Fragments of Empire: A History of the Western Pacific High Commission 1877–1914*, Canberra: ANU Press, 1967.

—— *Viceroy of the Pacific: The Majesty of Colour, A Life of Sir John Bates Thurston*, Canberra: the Australian National University Press, 1980.

Sidal, Morven, *Hannah Dudley: Hamari Maa, Honoured Mother, Educator and Missioner to the Indentured Indians of Fiji 1864–1913*, Suva: Pacific Theological College, 1997.

Sinclair, Ruta, Sione Latukefu *et al.*, *Polynesian Missions in Melanesia from Samoa, Cook Islands and Tonga to Papua New Guinea and New Caledonia*, Fiji: University of the South Pacific, 1982

Spate, O.H.K., *Paradise Found and Lost*, Canberra: ANU Press, 1988.

Stacy, Geoffrey, *A Cloud of Witnesses: At Tryon Road Uniting Church 1896–1996*, Sydney: Lindfield Tryon Road Uniting Church Centenary Committee, 1996.

Stevenson, Fanny and Robert Louis, *Our Samoan Adventure*, London: Weidenfeld & Nicholson, 1956.

Swainson, William, *Auckland, the Capital of New Zealand, and the Country Adjacent: Including some Account of the Discovery of Gold in New Zealand*, London and Auckland: Smith, Elder and Co., 1853.

Synge, Frances M., *Albert Maclaren, Pioneer Missionary in New Guinea: A Memoir*, Westminster, England: Society for the Propagation of the Gospel in Foreign Parts, 1908.

Taliai, Siupeli, 'Ko e Kau Fakaongo,' in *Tonga and the Tongans: Heritage and Identity*, ed. E. Wood-Ellem, Melbourne: Tonga Research Association, 2007, pp. 147–60.

Thompson, Basil, *The Diversions of a Prime Minister*, Edinburgh and London: William Blackwood, 1894.

Thornley, Andrew, *Exodus of the I Taukei: The Wesleyan Church in Fiji: 1848–74*, Suva: Institute of Pacific Studies, 2002.

Threlfall, Neville, *Mangroves, Coconuts and Frangipani: The Story of Rabaul*, Rabaul Historical Society, East New Britain Province, Papua New Guinea in collaboration with Neville Threlfall, 2012.

Tippett, Alan R., *People Movements in Southern Polynesia: A Study in Church Growth*, Chicago: Moody Press, 1971.

—— *Solomon Islands Christianity: A Study in Growth and Obstruction*, London: Lutterworth, 1967.

Vennell, C.W. and Susan Williams, *Raglan County: Hills and Sea 1876–1976*, Auckland: Wilson & Horton, 1976.

Waterhouse, J.B. (ed.), *The Secession and Persecution in Tonga*, Sydney: Wesleyan Book Depot 1886.

Wesleyan Methodist Missionary Society, 'Review of George Brown D.D., *Pioneer Missionary and Explorer: An Autobiography*,' in *The Foreign Field of the Wesleyan Methodist Church*, no. 56, vol. 5 (April 1909).

Whittaker, J.L, N.G. Gash, J.F. Hookey and J.R. Lacey (eds), *Documents and Readings in Papua New Guinea History (Pre-History to 1889)*, Milton, Queensland: Jacaranda Press, 1979.

Wood, A. Harold, *Overseas Missions of the Australian Methodist Church Vol. 1, Tonga and Samoa*, Melbourne: Aldersgate Press, 1975.

—— *Overseas Missions of the Australian Methodist Church, Vol. 11, Fiji*, Melbourne: Aldersgate Press, 1978.

—— *Overseas Missions of the Australian Methodist Church, Vol. III, Fiji-Indian and Rotuma*, Melbourne: Aldersgate Press, 1978.

Wood-Ellem, Elizabeth (ed.), *Tonga and the Tongans: Heritage and Identity*, Melbourne: Tonga Research Association, 2007.

Wright, Don and Eric G. Clancy, *The Methodists: A History of Methodism in New South Wales*, Sydney: Allen & Unwin, 1993.

Young, Robert, *The Southern World: Journal of a Deputation from the Wesleyan Conference to Australia and Polynesia, Including Notices of a Visit to the Goldfields*, London: Mason, 1854.

Zelenietz, Martin, 'The end of headhunting in New Georgia,' in *The Pacification of Melanesia*, ed. Margaret Rodman and Matthew Cooper, ASAO Monograph 7, Ann Arbor: University of Michigan Press, 1979, pp. 91–108.